HOMEMADE MONEY

The Definitive Guide to Success in a Homebased Business

THIRD EDITION

BARBARA BRABEC

BETTERWAY PUBLICATIONS, INC.

WHITE HALL, VIRGINIA

Published by Betterway Publications, Inc.
P.O. Box 219
Crozet, VA 22932

Typography by East Coast Typography, Inc.

Library of Congress Cataloging-in-Publication Data

Brabec, Barbara.
  Homemade money.

  Includes index.
  1. Home-based businesses.   1. Title.
HD62.7.B68   1989   658'.041   88-34957
ISBN 1-55870-110-9

Printed in the United States of America
0987654321

Dedicated to the Memory of
William J. Schaumburg

Unlike his children, my father did not have the benefit of a good education. Yet he was smart enough to teach himself what he needed to know to make a living, first as a farmer and, later, as an auto mechanic and repairman who never met anything mechanical he couldn't figure out.

With little more than talent, determination, and a belief in himself, he built his own home and garage business in a small farming community in Illinois, where he lived until he died in 1982.

As children, my two sisters and I did not realize that our father, by example, was quietly instilling in each of us his work ethic and entrepreneurial spirit, but as three self-employed women, we certainly know it now.

This book is for him.

Acknowledgments

I am especially indebted to the following professionals who made special contributions to this book by checking my manuscript for accuracy of facts and information: Julian Block (taxes and tax law); Bernard Kamoroff (accounting); Mary Helen Sears (copyright law, patents, and trademarks); Edward F. Hughes (labor law); Don H. Alexander (banking); and Mary Kaufmann (insurance). Their time and talent, so generously contributed, has benefited all of us.

I also wish to thank the attorneys at The Center on National Labor Policy for letting me use some of their research material on state and federal laws relating to cottage industries. Kate Kelly's contribution of sample press releases from her book also is appreciated.

Special thanks, too, to Jerry Buchanan, Jean Dubois, and Donald Moore for giving me permission to reprint published articles. Their viewpoints and opinions have added special balance and perspective to topics discussed in this book.

Finally, a nod of gratitude to my husband, Harry (last on the list, as usual), for his patience in "sitting out" this book and for taking so much of the regular work load off my back while I was writing it. He didn't see much of me during this period, and I owe him one.

All of the information in this book is presented to assist homebased businesspersons; those already in business, those planning to start, and those with hopes and dreams — but less certain plans. Much of the material offered is in such "professional service" categories as legal, tax, and accounting. While the information provided has been researched and prepared with great care and is accurate as this edition goes to press, it is not the business of either the author or Betterway Publications, Inc. to render such professional services. Readers are asked to exercise normal good judgment in determining when the services of a lawyer or other professional would be appropriate to their needs.

Table of Contents

Introduction: An Overview of the Home Business Industry

MILLIONS OF AMERICANS are generating income from an incredible variety of homebased activities. I call it "homemade money," and this book tells you how to get in on the action.

In the few years since *Homemade Money* was published, the home-business boom that was only then beginning has now grown to surprising proportions. In 1982, the U.S. Chamber of Commerce released information stating that ten million individuals who had filed a Schedule C form with their annual income tax returns had listed home addresses for their businesses. It was also pointed out at that time that the number of self-employed people had increased 18 percent in the last five years.

In 1984, an AT&T survey showed that 13 percent of all U.S. households were home to a business, and more than half these businesses were full-time operations providing the bulk of the household income.

More recently, Electronic Services Unlimited, a New York research and consulting firm, estimated that 18 million or more self-employed individuals will be working at home by the mid-1990s.

Numbers aside, what it boils down to is that homebased businesses are no longer a fad — they're an economic trend, and one that will continue to grow as the nation's economy shifts from an industrial base to one of information and services.

This change in our economy is automatically opening up millions of opportunities for individuals to earn money from home, either as homebased employees, or self-employed individuals. For example, the Electronic Services survey mentioned earlier estimated that more than seven million jobs — many of them computer-related — have the potential to be transferred to the home or to satellite offices located near employee's homes. Such industry is now being called "the homework industry," or "the electronic cottage," the latter phrase being coined by Alvin Toffler in his book, *The Third Wave*, (Bantam).

Although computers are going to be important, if not vital, to the success of all business in the future, this book is not as concerned with the homework industry or the electronic cottage as it is with the entrepreneurial spirit in America that is prompting so many individuals to become self-employed, homebased business owners.

What kind of people are most likely to start a homebased business

It is extremely difficult for anyone to get a handle on exactly how many people now work at home, but the following quotes from several authoritative sources give a good, overall picture of the situation.

*****

According to an AT&T survey, 41 percent of residential households that are home to a business have incomes of $30,000 or more. It's not surprising, then, that a recent Yankelovich, Skelly and White poll showed that earning a living at home is the secret dream of fully a third of American workers.

— Reader's Digest,
January, 1986
(From the article "How to Start a Business In Your Own Home," by Samuel A. Schreiner, Jr.)

An "invisible workforce" is changing the face of American Business. While invisible, these workers are making their mark. They are generating $20 to $60 billion a year — in their homes. Not too long ago, it was something of an embarrassment to admit you worked out of your home. But times are changing.

— Choices, *Spring, 1986*
(from the article, "Home-Based Entrepreneurs: The Invisible Workforce," by Maria Anton

today? We might begin with the millions of people who are disenchanted with job opportunities available to them or are unemployed. Consider millions more, now retired or quickly approaching retirement, who need additional income to supplement Social Security benefits. Add millions of other Americans who are satisfactorily employed, but no less in need of additional income for a variety of reasons. The sum total is a staggering number of men and women who are currently, sometimes desperately, seeking an answer to both present and future financial needs.

Obviously, then, many people view extra money earned at home as the solution to current job problems or their best guarantee for a comfortable old age. But countless others, like my husband and me, desire more than just extra income. We also want control of our lives. We prefer to be independent and totally self-supporting, answering to no one but ourselves. A full-time business at home makes this possible.

Almost anyone can make a little extra money at home these days, but it takes a certain degree of skill, experience, and knowledge to actually turn a money-making venture into a profitable home business. Through the years my work has put me in touch with thousands of people who are engaged in a variety of homebased, money-making activities. Two things always come to mind when I think of these people collectively. One, many of them do not consider themselves to be "in business," and two, those who do often lack business expertise.

Furthermore, many of these money-making activities/businesses are underground operations as far as the Internal Revenue Service is concerned. While some people may think they are pulling a fast one on the IRS, they are more likely cheating only themselves. That's because there are numerous personal and financial advantages in bringing a home business to the surface, and this book explains them to you, along with a lot of other things you will be surprised to learn.

Home-business novices who might have failed a few years ago have a much greater chance for success today because of the many helpful books and periodicals which have recently appeared on the scene. The resource chapter of this book describes them; all you have to do is read them to gain a thorough education in the operation and management of any kind of small business.

Most beginners, of course, do not know about these resources, nor are they aware that a great deal of free information and assistance is available to them from various organizations and government agencies. Some people with already-established businesses are equally in the dark about their opportunities because they are not networking with others who share their interests and concerns.

A "network," as you probably know, is a system of supportive people who are interested in one another and willing to help each other succeed. Your involvement in even one established home-business network could make the difference between success or failure in your particular endeavor. An involvement in several, of course, could double, triple, or quadruple your chances for success.

Home-business owners and dreamers alike need a lifeline with others who share their interests, ambitions, and dreams, but most of all they need a continuous supply of up-to-date information and idea-simulators, of which this book is only one. Its companion newsletter, *National Home Business Report,* is another. Together, these publications have enabled me to build a strong support system for homebased business owners nationwide. When you have finished this book, I invite you to contact me so you, too, may become a part of it. (See Resource Chapter for more information.)

Meanwhile, this book offers immediate answers to thousands of questions on how to start, operate, expand, and STAY in business. In addition, it directs you to hundreds of little-known sources of information that will help you answer the more complex questions that are bound to arise as your business enters advanced stages of growth.

Behind the Scenes

Years ago, when I first began to gather information of all kinds and tuck it into the hundreds of file folders that now populate my office, I had no idea why I was doing all this fanatical reading, clipping, and filing. Instinct alone told me that information was power, and the more I read, the more I realized this to be true. A few years later, after my crafts hobby had become a business which eventually led my husband and me into self-publishing, everything became clear. I then realized my potential as a writer and saw that, through writing, I could share all the information I was able to gather. That's precisely what I've been doing since 1971, and what I plan to keep doing as long as my fingers can prance around on a keyboard.

Incidentally, unlike some authors of home-business how-to guides, I work full time at home and I actually have done, or am doing, the things I discuss in this book. Furthermore, I've made many of the mistakes I'm now warning you about, stepped into some potholes you now can easily avoid, and learned most of what I know the hard way, through trial-and-error experience. Although this may still be the best way to learn, it is also the most expensive in terms of time and money. Many people cannot afford trial-and-error experience for this reason and, frankly, there's no need for you to learn everything the hard way because so many people are willing to share the benefit of their experience with you.

Successful people know that knowledge is the golden key to success in any endeavor. Samuel Johnson, a famous English poet and critic who lived in the 1700s, summed it up beautifully when he said: "Knowledge is of two kinds: we know a subject ourselves, or we know where we can find information upon it." I don't pretend to know everything there is to know about the topic of home business, but through the years I have learned what is really important: how to find the specific information I might need at any given time. You can do the same.

If you already operate a business, *Homemade Money* will show you how to expand it and realize a greater profit from your endeavor.

If you are a home-business dreamer who's still uncertain about what you can do to make money at home, this book will get you started and keep you going. And if you've tried and failed in the past to make extra money at home, now is a good time to try again. The only real failures in life are those who fail to try again.

Without question, the experience of trying new things, and learning from your mistakes over a period of years, will ultimately bring its own special reward, so be encouraged to follow your dream, whatever it may be. Don't be surprised, though, if you eventually end up in a business far different from the one you originally started. Often, as people find the right matchup of product and market, their business plans change considerably. Be realistic, too, about the

"According to Martin Lefkowitz of the United States Chamber of Commerce economics department, 15 million businesses in the United States file IRS reports under Schedule C (sole proprietor). 'Only 5 million of those businesses list an address away from home,' he said. 'The other 10 million list home addresses. Many of those businesses are operated by women.'"

— *Syndicated newspaper article, "The Cottage Industry: Rural Explosion," by Vivian N. Doering, December, 1982*

"Women business owners have been succeeding in new businesses at twice the rate of men. The Labor Department predicts that within the next 10–15 years, about 40–50% of the American work force will be working at home. Contributing to this trend are: inflation, higher gasoline costs, and the burgeoning computer industry. Women with homebased businesses already have a head start."

— *National Alliance of Home-based Businesswomen,* Alliance Newsletter, *November, 1981*

Notes

*Measurement and Evaluation
of the Populations of
Family-Owned and
Home-Based Businesses*

In 1985, the SBA initiated a ten-month study to determine the best approaches for counting, describing, and measuring the economic contributions of family-owned and home-based businesses. The following comments are from the preliminary Executive Summary of this report issued in mid-1982.*

"A home-based business is an enterprise producing goods or services that is operated in or from the home. Business owners represent only one of several categories of home-based workers. Employees also may work in or from their homes full time, part time, intermittently, or overtime. Some moonlighting employees operate home-based businesses. Individual "contractors" are not easily categorized. The Department of Labor applies strict criteria to define an individual as either an employee or as an independent business operator. These workers themselves may define their activities as a home-based business.

"The numbers of home workers are growing, but we do not know how rapidly. Because the different surveys of this population do not use the same definitions of home-based work we do not know precisely even their current numbers."

*The complete report (some 200 pages long) will eventually be for sale to the general public through the Department of Commerce, Technical Information Services division, Springfield, VA.

amount of profit to be derived from your home business in the early years because so much will depend on the amount of time and money you invest in it.

Interestingly, many small business owners have told me that making lots of money is not nearly as important to them as making *enough* money for their particular needs. I agree. To me, the most important thing is that I am doing exactly what I want to be doing, secure in the knowledge that I'm spending my life in the most satisfying and profitable way possible. Too few people today are able to make such a statement, so I feel especially fortunate to be sitting here now, revising this book for you. My wish is that the information in it will enable you to share the same enjoyment, satisfaction, and sense of pride I feel each morning as I get up to go to work . . . in the comfort and privacy of my home.

Barbara

P.S. There's only one way to read this book: with marking pen in hand. Try a yellow "highlighter" pen and underline or otherwise mark all the information that's important to you. When you have finished the book, go back to the beginning and follow up on every mark you've made. The more marks, the more opportunities.

Notice

Throughout the text, you will find references to certain resources, such as books, periodicals, government booklets, organizations, etc. Addresses are not given in the text, but you will find complete information about each resource in the Resource Section at the end of the book — with the exception of a few books and periodicals which have gone out of print recently. They may still be available in libraries, however.

Assessing Your Situation

1.

If you already have started a home business, you might have a tendency to skip this chapter, but that would be a mistake because it offers insight you may not have had when you began. It also alerts you to some problem areas you may have overlooked until now.

Are You a Good Home Business Candidate

Success in a home business begins with a clear understanding of yourself, your capabilities *and* your limitations. You must know your strengths so you can build on them, your weaknesses so you can shore them up.

Find out if you're a good home-business candidate by taking the following "test." There are no right or wrong answers, of course; I just want you to do a little thinking about your strong and weak points. After you have answered the questions, ask your spouse or a close friend also to answer them with you in mind. If there is disagreement, it could be that you either are trying to fool yourself, or you never have let other people see the real you.

> *"The idea stage for any business begins when you stop dreaming about being on your own someday and start taking definite steps to do it."*
>
> — *from* The Two-Boss Business *by Elyse & Mike Sommer*

Yes	No	
☐	☐	I'm not afraid to make decisions, even though they may be wrong.
☐	☐	I can take criticism and rejection.
☐	☐	I enjoy taking charge of things and seeing them through to the end.
☐	☐	I am an organized worker.
☐	☐	I'm an independent, self-confident person.
☐	☐	I get along well with most people.
☐	☐	I like to work, and I'm willing to work hard for something I want, even if financial rewards are slow in coming.

Partners

Although they live 165 miles apart, Anne Grice and Joye Burkhardt are partners in a home business called Anjo Etc. They publish needlecraft books, produce kits for mail order, and market a limited line of lucite accessories.

"Our telephone bills are interesting to say the least," says Anne, "but our opposite backgrounds and interests compliment each other. Joye is an art and English major with an advertising background; I am a business major. Joye has trouble with invoices and checkbooks, and I can't draw. She doesn't like to stitch and I don't like to sell. Together we are able to do what we might not have been able to do alone."

The partnership agreement Anne and Joye have signed states that their partnership shall be dissolved if:

(1) one partner demands it;

(2) one partner files a voluntary petition in bankruptcy; or,

(3) both partners unanimously agree to dissolve.

Notes

☐ ☐ I am willing to do a lot of self-studying, research, and planning to make my home-business dream a reality.

As you probably have guessed by now, the more "yes" answers you have, the more likely a home-business candidate you are. Having a couple of "no's" doesn't mean you have to give up your business dream, but it could be a sign of trouble to come.

For instance, the person who is afraid to make decisions will certainly encounter difficulty the first time a major business decision has to be made. The person who cannot take criticism and rejection may crumble the first time a customer says "no" to a sales pitch. Anyone who is reluctant to take charge, or unwilling to accept responsibility, should not subject himself to the stress of managing a home business. On the other hand, all of these problems might easily be overcome if one were to join forces with a partner who did have these desired business qualities.

If you answered "no" to the questions about being organized, having confidence, or getting along well with others, this is an indication that you would benefit from some self-help books on these topics. With time and effort, anyone can learn the secrets of organization, develop a greater degree of self-confidence, and improve working relationships with other people.

I do hope you answered "yes" to the last two questions because a home business definitely requires concentrated effort, time, and energy, to say nothing of patience, perseverance, *and* planning. From experience, I can assure you that your home business, whatever its kind or nature, will take twice the amount of time and energy of any salaried job you may have held in the past; and, unless you are extremely lucky, it will also take longer than you think to make a profit from your endeavor. Therefore, be patient in your financial success expectations. Allow at least two years, and as many as five, depending on your type of business, the time, energy, and money you give it, the skills and experience you bring to it, and so on.

Above all, remember that a successful home business requires planning, in detail and on paper. "People don't plan to fail," goes an old saying, "they fail to plan." Trying to build a business without any kind of plan is like riding an exercise bike: You do a lot of pedaling, but you don't get anywhere.

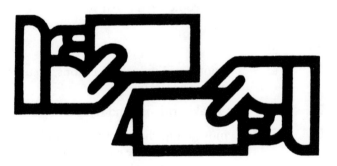

Why Most Businesses Fail

Few people would try to build a house without a blueprint and some skill as a builder. However, year after year, thousands of people with little or no real business sense try to build a business without any kind of plan. Often, new business owners — particularly home-business owners — begin as dreamers, believing that their good ideas and willingness to work hard will get them through. Unfortunately, that is not enough, as the following statistics[1] prove:

> 27% of all small businesses fail in 3 years or less.
> 55% of all small businesses fail in 5 years or less.
> 82% of all small businesses fail in 10 years or less.

About 95% of all small business failures are attributable to poor management, confirms the Small Business Administration, and these figures seem to hold true year after year. Don't let these statistics frighten you away from your own business. Do let them serve as a constant reminder that certain business and management skills are essential to success in any money-making endeavor. If you do not possess them, and feel you cannot acquire them, at least have the good sense to work with someone who does have a "head for business," such as a spouse or friend who can be your business partner.

Also use outside business services when you need them, such as bookkeepers, accountants, advertising agencies, publicists, or business consultants. Such professionals can often make or save you far more than they cost, and the added peace of mind they bring to a small business is priceless.

"Do what you do best and hire out the rest," is excellent business advice, but also keep this in mind: "Trust least the advice of those who have the most to gain if you take their advice."

Many people who think they do not possess the necessary talent and skill to start and operate a successful business generally are surprised to discover their true abilities and potential for success once they get going. Thus, what you may be doing best a year or two from now compared to the things you now do best, will no doubt amaze you. Once you have started your business, I wager you'll soon be saying, "I can't believe I'm actually doing this. I had no idea I was capable of such things."

To help you identify your many talents and skills, I've included a special worksheet at the end of this chapter. I hope you will take the time to complete it. Actually, it will be a nice ego trip for you because it encourages you to acknowledge a variety of skills and know-how you probably take for granted. I suggest you mark this page so you can come back to it easily as you continue to read the book. Then, each time you are reminded of something else you know or do well, go back and add it to your list. By the time you have finished, I guarantee you'll be impressed, particularly if you're a homemaker who has thought of herself for years primarily as a wife and mother.

This book is not for women only, of course, but it is a fact that more women than men are apt to start homebased businesses. Since the very job of homemaking tends to release a woman's creative abilities, it is not surprising that so many home businesses are closely allied to such homemaking arts as cooking, sewing, child care,

---

A Special Message For Women

"Observers have noted that the ability to focus on a task in both its large and small dimensions, despite distractions and limited resources, is characteristic of women's role in the home and is also needed for entrepreneurial success. The displaced homemaker, who is frequently turning to entrepreneurship, is finding that experience gained nurturing a family is useful in nurturing a business. In addition, many observers comment that women entrepreneurs show a greater willingness than male entrepreneurs to admit ignorance, to seek help, and to do their homework. Many entrepreneurial women need only business training and equal opportunity to be successful."

— from the 1980 Annual Report to the President Interagency Committee on Women's Business Enterprise

Notes

---

[1] from Dun & Bradstreet's *Business Failure Record.*

Notes

needlecrafts, handcrafts, music, art, gardening, interior decorating, and pet care. Often out of need, boredom, or accidental discovery, the idea for a home business just sneaks up on a woman and before she knows it, she's making money.

Why People Avoid "Business"

The homemaker who suddenly starts to make extra money at home seldom feels like a businesswoman, and she may never feel as though she's "in business," even though she may continue to make money at home for several years.

This reluctance to look upon one's money-making activity as a business is common among women in general, and particularly prevalent among the thousands of men and women who sell art, crafts, and other handmade items at fairs and flea markets throughout the country each year. Yes, money is being made from such homebased enterprises, but little *profit* is being realized by the majority of these sellers. That's because so many of them are part-time hobby sellers who lack business expertise and an understanding of the crafts or giftware marketplace. Unfortunately, their failure to look upon their endeavor as a business makes profit almost impossible to attain.

Why are so many people so hesitant to approach their homebased, money-making activity as a business? I think the answer is fear. The very word, "business," seems to scare some people half to death, particularly women who never have held outside jobs. And a certain number of men and women alike are apt to shun the idea of a business by saying, "Who, me? Nah, I just want to make a little extra money," or "pin money," as some people call it. In reality, some of these people are not ambitious enough to build a real business. Others are afraid they would fail if they tried, and still others are afraid of success.

Fear of Success

Why do people fear success, of all things? *Because it signals change.* For example, if a home business were suddenly to "take off," it might necessitate, among other things, out-of-town business trips to find buyers or participate in trade shows, the hiring of employees or sales representatives, and a large investment of time and money. Women working at home are especially fearful of success when it involves such things, and with good reason. They have certain responsibilities, and they know that if a home business were to become too successful, the whole family lifestyle would have to change. Since many husbands are reluctant to accept change in any form, this is not a concern to regard lightly.

Many women have told me that it would have been impossible to build their home businesses without the full cooperation and support of their husbands. I heartily agree. If a man is unsupportive and is going to use the home business as an excuse to criticize the way his wife does housework, she's going to experience stress with a capital S and not every woman can handle it. In a case like this, I would suggest that the home business idea be dropped *unless* the woman feels compelled to follow her dream, is confident of her abilities, and reasonably sure she can handle whatever comes.

Some women of my acquaintance have had to ask themselves this disturbing question: "If my business succeeds, will my marriage survive?" On the positive side, however, my correspondence with many women business owners leads me to believe that many men are easily swayed from one side to the other as soon as a home business begins to show signs of success. In fact, I don't believe there is anything more impressive to the average man than a pile of cash that suddenly appears in his lap from "the little woman's hobby." Often, that first surge of business income is all that's required to make a fellow realize the financial potential of his wife's home-business dream.

Now, lest I offend any of my male readers, let me remind everyone that where marriages and home businesses are concerned, one has to consider the "generation gap." Older, longer-married couples will probably have more problems in this area than younger or more enlightened couples who have an entirely different viewpoint about "wifely responsibilities."

If you're a woman who falls into the first category, consider this advice from Joan Anderson, author of *The Best of Both Worlds — A Guide to Homebased Careers:*

"A wise beginner captures her husband's support in a variety of subtle ways. After initially explaining her plans, she keeps the job low-key (avoiding long drawn-out discussions about her plans to run IBM eventually), does her work inconspicuously, and adjusts household schedules by degrees, rather than dramatically. Eventually, her spouse discovers that nothing drastic has occurred, mutually-shared values have remained intact, the budget crunch is easing, and best of all, his wife is a more fulfilled and interesting partner. When a husband reaches this point (and it may take some time), he often becomes her most supportive ally, filled with pride at her accomplishments and ready to tell the world about them."[2]

My own contact with women working at home confirms this advice, and I'm happy to report that it is not at all unusual these days to hear about men who are planning to quit salaried jobs so they can work full time at home on businesses their wives started a few years earlier. This is particularly true in the crafts field and, as home businesses of all kinds come to be recognized as a vital economic force in America, we're going to be seeing more and more couples striving for The Great American Dream — a full-time, self-supporting business of their own. If such couples are wise, they will work together from the very beginning, each assuming a certain responsibility for the business as well as for the home and family.

What's Holding You Back?

People can come up with all kinds of excuses for not doing something about their home-business idea. You will find a list of excuses — and my responses to them — on another page in this chapter. The most common excuse, besides fear, is the worry that one will not have enough time or money to do the job right. Yet, many people with full-time jobs and growing families have managed to find the time to start a business at home, and just as many have started on the proverbial shoestring.

As I see it, there is no "right amount" of money required for

[2]from The Best of Both Worlds. © by Joan Wester Anderson. Used by permission of Betterway Publications, Inc.

a home business except that *you do need enough for your needs.* Those needs can be determined by preparing a written business plan, which you will soon learn how to do.

As for time, sometimes the lack-of-time excuse is merely a cover-up for one's fear of the unknown. Regardless of your situation, I urge you never to let lack of time stop you from trying to achieve the things that are important to you. My own experience leads me to believe that we only find time for special things by simply beginning. Then, mysteriously, the needed time materializes in direct reversal of Parkinson's Law (i.e., that work expands to fill the time available). In this case, it is time that expands to make room for all the things we want to do.

Taking a Chance on Yourself

If you have a strong desire to be self-employed, but are being held back because of a full-time job, you may have considered quitting and "going for it." While I would not recommend this to everyone, sometimes it is the best solution. Sometimes a person really does have a profitable idea, the necessary skills, the right experience, the right market, and enough money to take the risk, plus the necessary confidence and determination to make a home business a success. In that case, it may be "now or never." In my case, it was also, "put your money where your mouth is."

After I wrote *Creative Cash* I began to receive a lot of mail from readers who had interesting questions and useful information to share. When, in January, 1981, I started a newsletter to communicate with these people, I began with the simple notion that this would be "a little sideline business," in addition to my full-time job (at that time, I was general manager of a small book publishing company). It wasn't long before I realized I could not do justice to both tasks at once. Something else began to bother me, too. Here I was, sitting high and dry with the security of a good-paying job, telling other people they ought to start their own home business. It occurred to me that I ought to heed my own advice. Besides, how much credibility would I have if I didn't practice what I preached?

So, in June of that year, I took courage in hand and quit my job. It was a simple quote in *Reader's Digest* that moved me to action:

> "Progress always involves risks. You can't steal second and keep your foot on first." — Frederick B. Wilcox

What this said to me was that it is sometimes necessary to take personal and financial risks to get what you want. I took the risk and it paid off. It might for you, too. But, please . . . *don't quit your full-time job to start a full-time home business unless you're absolutely sure you understand the risk involved.* Stealing second is only part of the game. The question is, can you make it to home plate before your money runs out?

This book presents a clear picture of the home-business industry and your opportunities in it, but you'll still have to do a lot of reading, self-study, market research, and careful planning to acquire all the information and insight you will need to succeed as a full-time, home-based entrepreneur. To be on the safe side, never risk

---

"After many discussions about the opportunity we both saw ahead of us, we decided to risk it all. The chance to run our own business was too much to pass up. I quit my job.

"We have had high points and low points through this time (expansion of the business). There have been good decisions, bad decisions, and no decisions; late nights, early mornings, long weekends, no vacations, and the like. Is it worth it? We think so. We took a chance on ourselves and changed our lives. We've gained control of our todays and tomorrows."

— *Roger Lehman, from an article in* The Crafts Report. *Roger's wife, Barbara, launched Luv-Kins, a raffia doll business, in 1976. In 1981, Roger left his position as a corporate sales manager in paper products to work full time on the business. The Lehmans live in Duxbury, Massachusetts.*

Notes

more than you can afford to lose, be it time, money, confidence, or your reputation.

Overcoming the Fear of Failure

If fear is the main thing holding you back from starting even a parttime business at home, ask yourself what is the worst thing that could happen if you tried? Failure? Of course. But failure can be a beneficial experience because it teaches you what NOT to do the next time around. Therefore, don't be afraid of it. As one of my newsletter readers told me, "Some things I've failed at have left me with more time for better things."

I certainly have had my own share of failures. In fact, my first, fulltime home business was profitable only in terms of experience, knowledge, and friendships gained (not a bad bargain at that). But there never was any financial profit, so when the business ended, I felt like a failure. But only for a short while. Then I began to realize the important lessons failure had taught me. In looking back, I now see that failure in one area is often a necessary step to success in another.

In his book, *How to Get Whatever You Want*, M. R. Kopmeyer says, "If you do not fail some of the time, you are attempting too little — and will accomplish nothing worthwhile." He adds that ". . . tender, timid people who are afraid of failure actually assure their own failure by being afraid to really try to succeed, and thus in seeking to avoid failure, they miss unlimited opportunities which lead directly to success."[3]

Mr. Kopmeyer also points out that failure is the principal research method used in all scientific, medical, and industrial research. It is ". . . simply the means of finding out what will not work so that it can be eliminated in the search for what *will* work," he explains. "Failure does not take something out of you; failure builds a lot of necessary character and personality qualities into you. You are not weaker because you fail; you are tougher, stronger, more determined — and much wiser!"

Since the very act of beginning involves the unknown, most of us have a tendency to shy away from it. Yet we cannot make gains either as individuals or home-business owners if we do not constantly explore unknown territory and test our new ideas and theories.

"Knowledge is the antidote to fear," said Ralph Waldo Emerson, and the more you learn about business and the marketplace, the more courage you'll have to get started and keep growing as a home-business owner. Or, as Benjamin Franklin put it, "An investment in knowledge pays the best dividends."

If you have a business idea in mind at this time, but are being held back for one reason or another, don't be discouraged. Instead, use this time to sharpen old skills, acquire new ones, and gain an education in business basics. Remember that starting a home business right now may not be nearly as important in the long run as being able to do it well when the time is right.

Each new thing learned will broaden your economic base, each new skill acquired and sharpened will increase your income potential.

America is not the only country concerned with self-employment, as the following quotation from The Entrepreneur *magazine in England indicates. Here is one of the best arguments for a home business you'll ever hear:*

"We believe that a man or a woman, in or out of work, should be carrying on a home-based activity which is productive of both pleasure and profit; we believe that every woman who decides that family responsibilities of one kind or another should keep her at home should be developing a home-based means of adding to the family income — that she, too, should be producing a proportion of the total home profit. We believe that even the children should be drawn into this essential profit-producing process, for they are a part of this world and the sooner they're introduced to its realities the better.

"What we're saying, therefore, is that those who're gifted with the wit, vision, ability, and stamina to be self-employed should become self-employed, and those not so gifted — and most people are not — should nevertheless regard their home not simply as a place in which to live, relax, rear a family, or stew in front of the 'telly,' but as a place where work is undertaken in return for the well-being of their souls . . . and money. We're talking about SURVIVAL, and the whole family should be involved."

— Donald Moore from The Entrepreneur, *1983, Cumbria, England*

3© 1972 by M. R. Kopmeyer. Used by permission of The Success Foundation, Inc.

Notes

Everything you do to develop your skills and business expertise is like depositing money in a special savings account. Invest in yourself. You'll never find a more worthy investment.

Excuses, Excuses

People have a lot of reasons for not doing something about their dreams and ambitions. Here are some of the more common excuses, and my rebuttal to them. Check the ones you have been using lately. (If none apply to you — my congratulations!)

☐ **But my job leaves me with no time for my home business idea.**

You need to change your attitude about time. Everyone has the same number of hours to spend each day. As someone once said, "Some people count time; others make time count." Once you get involved in something you really want to do, time has a mysterious way of materializing. Many people automatically "find time" by not doing certain things they used to do — things which no longer seem important after the business is begun. After all, what's more important: being able to say you have just shipped a big order or completed a profitable job, or that you have the best-looking lawn or cleanest house in town?

☐ **But I have no money to start or expand a business.**

Many home businesses can be started with a small amount of cash, and there are ways to generate capital even when one has no collateral for a bank loan. (See the A-to-Z business section.)

☐ **But there's no room in my home to set up an office or workroom.**

I know people who run home businesses in house trailers. You have to let your home know who's boss. Don't let it dictate the way you live in it. Make room for what you want to do by changing the way you live. Turn the dining room table into a temporary work table by covering a board with fabric and laying it on top. (At day's end, store the board against the wall, turning it into a decorative accessory.) Claim any drawers you can find, and lay siege to at least one closet. I once turned a small pantry into an efficient office by laying a board across the middle (for a desk) and adding shelves from ceiling to floor. Consider the use of a room divider to turn one large room into two; and take a serious look at the back porch, the garage, the basement. You have space somewhere. The trick is in learning to use it efficiently. Books and magazines will give you ideas.

☐ **But my family won't support my efforts.**

You may be surprised by the support you'll receive once you have started and shown your family how serious you are about what you are doing.

☐ **But I'm always being interrupted in anything I do at home.**

And you'll continue to be interrupted until you "lay the law down.'' Tell family and friends that you must work, and you cannot be disturbed at certain times of the day. Establish a work schedule for yourself — even if it's only two hours a day - and stick to it.

☐ **But I'm too old to start a business.**

You're only as old as you feel, and no one is too old to make money at home. It takes only a good money-making idea and the ambition to see it through. Talk to older people you know who are working; for example, those you see exhibiting their wares at craft fairs and flea markets. Some of their ambition is bound to rub off on you.

☐ **But I'm handicapped!**

Many people are handicapped in one way or another, mentally or physically. If you do have a physical handicap, gain the courage you need by reading books and magazines written especially for handicapped people. (Ask your library for a list of them.) Also discuss your ideas and dreams with friends and professionals who might be able to help you.

☐ **But I don't have a good education.**

In a home business, a formal education is not nearly as important as the education you can give yourself. If you can read, and are willing to study, you can learn what you need to know. Increase your education by taking special courses and attending workshops and seminars related to your interests. Join appropriate organizations ad network with others who share your dreams.

☐ **But I'm scared because I don't know anything about business.**

The education you give yourself will dispel many of your fears. This book is a good beginning. Think of it as a college course in home-business basics. The more you learn, the less frightened you will be.

Special author's note:

As you're beginning to realize, this is not a casual book you can read and absorb in an evening or two. Instead, it is a manual with worksheets, checklists, and blank spaces that invite your own notes, thoughts, reminders. If the book you are now reading is one you have borrowed from the library or a friend, I urge you to obtain a copy for yourself as soon as possible.

If a nearby bookstore does not have *Homemade Money* on the shelf, you can easily order a copy by mail from me or the publisher. (See Resource chapter.)

The Cowards Never Started

In many ways, home business entrepreneurs are like the pilgrims who came to America on the Mayflower. Some have the courage of their convictions, others don't:

"It was alright to talk about it. They made plans. They had a moment's vision, a fleeting dream. But in the end, some lack in their moral fiber, some gnawing, nibbling fear held them back. They never started . . . they stayed where they were. They dropped back. They failed somehow to release within themselves that power which lies in every individual, and is released only when he starts forward in a straight line for the object about which he has dreamed. The man who never starts, never feels that sense of power."

— from The Cowards Never Started *by Ray Dickinson © 1933 by Franklin Publishing Co., Inc.*

Assignment: List below your special skills, talents, work experience, and practical know-how.

Include education, hobbies, abilities, volunteer activities, job experience, favorite home activities, extracurricular or social activities, etc. For example: Do you have good communication skills? Do you enjoy using the telephone . . . meeting people . . . speaking in public? Do you have writing ability . . . a flair for design or decorating . . . skill as a cook . . . a fundraiser . . . a tour guide? Can you type . . . operate business machines . . . use computers? Do you have a "green thumb"? Are you good with children . . . animals, older adults? Do you sew . . . do stitchery . . . make handcrafts? Do you have teaching experience . . . accounting or bookkeeping skills . . . legal training . . . managerial ability? Any experience in sales? Are you an organizational wizard . . . a "take charge" person . . . a creative thinker . . . a problem solver? Are you especially knowledgeable about one thing in particular? Is your background unique? Are you a Jack or Jill of all trades? What do you do that others might like to do?

You've got the idea, I'm sure. And you probably have more skills and talents than you realized.

Special Skills/Talents	Work Experience	Practical Know-How

For help in identifying your many skills, see the book, *Discover What You're Best At*. It includes a series of aptitude tests, which will reveal your strengths and weaknesses.

Which Home Business for You?

2.

YOU ARE SEVERAL STEPS AHEAD of many readers at this point, if you're already in business or at least know what you want to do. But don't skip this chapter . . . it's guaranteed to spark new ideas you haven't considered, as well as alert you to some "home-business opportunities" that are illegal or simply unprofitable.

"I wish I could discover or devise a magic formula for combining all my talents and interests into one tremendously successful package," someone once said to me. That's the trick, all right, and I believe that each of us can create some magic in our lives through a combination of concentrated self-study, patience, determination, and perseverance.

"Perseverance," said Longfellow, "is a key element of success. If you only knock long enough at the gate, you are sure to wake up somebody." Right now, I'm the one who's knocking on your gate, trying to wake you up to the many home-business possibilities awaiting you. The problem, of course, is that there are *so many* possibilities. For instance, a study by one home-business organization in 1978 defined over 200 homebased occupations among their membership alone — just one indication of the wide variety of money-making activities both men and women can pursue at home. To really boggle your mind, visit the library and check out several of the general home-business guides listed in this book's resource chapter.

Although I appreciate these books and their writers, I do have one complaint about them. Many devote at least half their content to an enthusiastic but very haphazard listing of dozens, even hundreds, of home business ideas. "Decorate cakes!", "Restore antiques!", "Sell your crafts!", or "Start a typing service!" are but a few examples. One that really made me chuckle reads: "Be a rowboat maker. Make a mold and manufacture fiberglass rowboats."

Sure sounds easy, doesn't it? Unfortunately, only the right person, in the right place, with the right kind of experience, know-how, and marketing expertise — to say nothing of sufficient business capital — could succeed in a rowboat-building business. That's why I decided to speak about home business opportunities in a more general and practical way. Instead of giving you a list of 500 specific business ideas (most of which would be either impractical or unprofitable for you), I have simply given you two charts, each with a host of basic ideas. I leave it to you to pick and choose or mix and match these product and service-business ideas in your own unique way.

"There is no new thing under the sun," according to the Bible,

> *"As a general rule, those who thrive on working from home are self-starters who like the line of work they are in and enjoy working independently. They're goal-directed achievers and are comfortable with minimal structure, capable of setting up and following their own schedules and deadlines."*
>
> *— from* Working At Home *by Paul and Sarah Edwards (Jeremy P. Tarcher, Inc.)*

*The Power of Your
Subconscious Mind*

*One's subconscious mind has the
ability to accept as real any impression that reaches it, whether negative or positive, constructive or
destructive, reliable or unreliable.
That's why it's so important to
condition one's mind to seek circumstances and things that are
desired, while protecting it from
undesirable influences and suggestions.*

*"Believe that you will succeed,"
said Dale Carnegie, a man who has
helped millions to greater achievement. "Believe firmly, and you will
then do what is necessary to bring
success about."*

Notes

but every product or service in the world can be changed, improved, presented or sold in a new way, or simply offered to a different audience. And that's what makes business so exciting, and your opportunities so many and varied.

Two Basic Kinds of Business

In spite of the hundreds of individual things you might think of that could bring in extra income, there are just two kinds of businesses after all: those which are *product-oriented*, and those which are *service-oriented*. Taking things two at a time, let's analyze the two kinds of businesses just mentioned.

Product-oriented businesses fall into two categories, as indicated on the chart that follows: (1) Products which are self-created, or man-ufactured; and (2) products which are made by others and either pur-chased for resale or sold for others on a direct-sales or drop-ship basis.

Service-oriented businesses also fall into two main categories: (1) Services performed *at* home (work generally performed at home after sale of service); and (2) services performed *from* home (some or all work performed away from home after sale of service). These "at home" and "from home" services are sold to two primary markets, as indicated on the second chart in this chapter: (1) Individuals at home, and (2) people in the business community (including business professionals, companies, shops, stores, organizations, and institutions). Sure, there's bound to be some overlapping because some services can be sold to both markets, but I believe the profit potential of any service business can best be analyzed by viewing it from this marketing standpoint: *Simply ask yourself which market you are most qualified to serve and best able to reach.* The same logic can be applied to product businesses, too.

As you study the information on the two charts, try to relate what you see there to the self-profile you recorded on your skills/talents/experience worksheet in chapter one. (If you haven't done this yet, it would be a good idea to stop now and complete this mind-stimulating exercise. I think you'll find it well worth the effort. Ideas can literally flow from the point of a pen once it's put to paper.)

At this point, your main goal should be to get your brain vibrating with ideas, on both a conscious and subconscious level. Your mind is like a giant computer, one whose software few of you have begun to learn how to use. The more "input" you give it, the more you'll get back. Throughout your entire life, your subconscious mind has been gathering all kinds of information, impressions, and ideas, storing them for possible future use. You know a lot more than you think you know. Now is the time to retrieve this data for your financial profit.

If you already know what you want and have established certain goals for yourself, you have taken an important first step to success. Just hang on to the mental picture you have of your idea and begin to develop it. Be sure to call on your subconscious mind for help, because it will never fail to obey any clear and emphatic order you give it. Success experts will tell you that if you can clearly see something in your mind, and you strongly believe in it, it can be achieved. (Read *The Magic of Believing*. It's one of the most inspiring books I've read.)

If things are not yet beginning to fall into place in your mind, don't be too concerned. All home business beginners have to go through the process of matching their capabilities to the needs of the

Notes

marketplace. It does take time, so be patient. You may have to operate your business for a year or more just to know if you're going in the right direction or not. In fact, actual experience may be the *only* way to determine this. Remember what I said in the introduction: "Often, as people find the right matchup of product and market, their business plans change considerably."

Product-Oriented Businesses

Self-Created (or Manufactured) Products	Products Made by Others (Manufacturers or Publishers)	
Made for sale at retail, wholesale, or on consignment. Involves inventory.	Purchased wholesale & resold (at retail or wholesale). Involves inventory.	Generally purchased for re-sale only on direct-sales or drop-ship basis. May or may not involve inventory.

PRODUCT EXAMPLES

Books/Directories	Kits (craft, hobby)	Advertising specialties	Brushes and household supplies
Crafts*	Patterns & designs	Antiques & collectibles	Cookware
Fine art & prints	Periodicals	Books and booklets	Cosmetics
Food products	Reports & Informa-	Calendars & posters	Craft & hobby kits
Furniture	tion sheets or book-	Craft supplies & materials/kits	Diet/Health products
Greeting cards/notes	lets	Crafts and needlework	Encyclopedias
Herbs, plants	Rubber stamps	(finished products)	Giftware
Household items	Tools, equipment	Flea Market goods	Greeting cards
		Housewares	Household equipment
		Imported gifts and novelties	How-to books
		Jewelry	Jewelry
		Office supplies	Perfume
		Perfume	Vacuum cleaners
		Stationery & note cards	

*The "crafts" category is so broad as to be almost indescribable. Basically, it includes anything made of wood, metal, clay, glass, fiber, fabric, and all materials in between, and covers such specific items as gifts, decorative accessories, miniatures, toys, dolls, novelties, jewelry, clothing, sewing, weaving, needlework, and so on.

HOW AND WHERE SALES ARE GENERALLY MADE
(Detailed information appears in chapters six and seven)

Retail Sales	Wholesale Sales
• *Direct selling* to consumers on a face-to-face basis — at fairs, shows, bazaars, flea markets, home parties, person-to-person sales and in-home demonstrations. • *Indirect selling* to targeted consumer markets — through direct mail promotions, special distribution programs, and media advertising.	• *Indirect selling* to consumers — through retail shops and stores, mail-order dealers or distributors and other wholesalers, by means of sales calls, trade shows, sales representatives, direct-mail promotions, special distribution programs, and trade advertising.

Consignment Sales

Neither fish nor fowl, consignment selling is simply an alternative marketing method for people who can't sell at wholesale.

Note: The resource chapter lists many special-interest how-to books to help you start and operate the specific product-oriented businesses listed above.

Service-Oriented Businesses
Generally sold locally, in person; some also sold and performed by mail.
The listings below are merely *examples* — no attempt has been made to list every possible service one might sell.

"At Home" Services

Sold to Individuals	Sold to Business Community
Beautician	Accountant
Calligrapher	Ad Consultant or Agency
Child Care Specialist	Agent (literary, sales, booking entertainment, insurance
Class Instructor (cooking, sewing, crafts, etc.)	Artist/Craftsman (architectural commissions, interior design)
Consultation (career, weddings, fashion, business, art, beauty, diet, etc.)	Artist/Designer (of brochures, catalogs, books, printed materials, signs)
Custom Designer (crafts, gifts)	Bookkeeper
Dressmaker or Tailor	Calligrapher (diplomas, scrolls, certificates, etc.)
Food Specialist (party food preparation, special diets, menu planning, party cakes)	Clipping service
Hairdresser (cutting, shampoos)	Computer Programmer
Inventor	Counselor (investments, social services)
Mechanic (engine repair, oil changes, brake service, etc.)	Financial Advisor/Planner
Pet Care Specialist (kennel, grooming, training)	Organizational Expert
Private Teacher (music, special education, drama)	Printing Consultant or Broker
Repairs/Restoration Specialist (art, antiques, furniture)	Publicist
Tax Preparer	Researcher
Taxidermist	Secretary/Typist (legal, academic, business)
Telephone Salesperson	Tax Preparer
Therapist	Typesetter
Writer (family memoirs)	Writer (copywriting, press releases, resumés, newsletters, ghost writer)

"From Home" Services

Sold to Individuals	Sold to Business Community
Appliance Repairman	Coordinator (Special events, projects)
Auctioneer	Courier/Messenger (bonded)
Babysitter	Efficiency/Organizational Expert
Caterer	Entertainer (supper clubs, organizations, private groups)
Craft Demonstrator (trade shows)	General Contractor
Chauffeur	Human Resource Development Consultant
Chimney Sweep	Instructor (sports, drama, dance)
Escort (children, the elderly)	Janitor (offices)
Hairdresser or Barber (house calls, shut-ins, hospital patients)	Photographer (specialized — medical, horticultural, etc.)
Home Handyman	Plant or Floral Service (flowers/plants delivered and maintained)
Insurance Agent	Producer (cultural events, shows, plays)
Interior Decorator/Designer	Public Speaker (seminars, workshops, keynote addresses)
Landscape/Gardener	Sales Representative/Agent
Maid or Butler	Stenographer/Secretary (have pen, will travel)
Model	Tour Guide (museums, parks, sightseeing buses)
Mover (furniture, equipment)	Translator
Party Engineer (singer, instrumentalist, magician, puppeteer)	
Party Planner/Coordinator	
Personal Shopper (gifts, goods)	
Photographer (people, events, possessions for insurance)	
Private Teacher/Tutor (math, music, horseback riding, swimming — at client's home)	
Sitter (house, pets, people)	
Snow Removal Service	
Studio Instructor (dance, exercise, music, etc.)	
Tradesman (plumber, carpenter, painter, etc.)	

Note: The resource chapter lists many special-interest how-to books to help you start and operate the specific service-oriented businesses listed above.

A few words about FRANCHISES . . . from the U.S. Department of Labor

Starting fresh with a new business certainly permits you the most freedom, since you are not restricted by what has gone before and are not regulated by someone else's rules. On the other hand, there are distinct advantages to buying an established franchise.

Here, the purchaser or franchisee receives the right to operate a business under the leadership of a well-known distributor or manufacturer. In return for a fee and royalty payments, the franchisee has immediate access to a proven product, a consumer image, publicity, and goodwill. In many instances, the franchisor provides the goods — whether they be automobiles or fried chicken — as well as the training and techniques for conducting the operation. If the franchise is a sound one, the likelihood of success in one's own business is increased.

There are, however, disadvantages to franchises: you have to conform to the chain's standards, sell only their product at their price, share in the problems of the distributor though they may be none of your doing, perhaps find that centralized management is unresponsive to your needs, and, of course, shave the profits.

If you are considering buying a franchise, you should visit other franchises, the Better Business Bureau, and the Chamber of Commerce to investigate the company's reputation and track record. Before you sign any contract you should consult your lawyer, since your agreement will regulate such key items as exclusivity, inventory, royalty rates, purchase requirements, and investment obligations.

The great attraction of entering business through a franchise is that all the planning comes prepackaged for the franchisee, often at a far lower price than if he or she were to start fresh. This avoids the problem of raising large sums of money — the most difficult part of establishing a business.

— from *More Than A Dream: Raising The Money*

* * * * * * * *

Author's note: Although most product-oriented franchises cannot be operated as a home business, there are many service businesses available on a franchise basis, including tax, accounting, and collection services, businesses that involve cleaning, lawn care, entertainment, furniture repair and so on. The minimum investment for a franchised service business seems to be about $5,000.

For more information, see the books on franchising listed in the resource chapter.

Notes

Multi-Level Marketing Plans

It has been about two years since multi-level marketing (MLM) plans began to sprout up like spring dandelions around the manure pile. The green pastures of American small business have turned into a sea of yellow blossoms — if you can call dandelions blossoms. Not a day goes by that my mail box is not filled with brand new MLM offers. The major goal of each operator seems to be the proselytizing of downliners from one plan to his own company ladder. In religious terms, the word *proselyte* means to convert from one belief to another. It means the same here.

While a multi-level marketing plan can be a very legitimate way of conducting a sales force, if the emphasis is primarily on selling products, too many of these Johnny-come-latelies are only out to make a fast buck for the originators. To fool potential investors and participants, these pyramid promoters often take on a product or line that has no established market value — such as new miracle products or exotic cures. This makes it difficult to tell whether there is a real consumer market for them. The recruitment program, more than the sales story, is what brings in the dollars. Each new participant is blinded by the pyramid story and promises of great wealth without working. It's the same old basic "all you have to do is recruit 5 people, each of whom will . . ." and so it goes to the fifth level when supposedly you will not have to sell any products yourself, but simply see to it that your "down-liners" are motivated to sell.

In almost every instance, the promotional material for these plans will point to Amway, Shaklee, or Mary Kay Cosmetics to prove how effective MLM can be. What they fail to point out is that these multi-million dollar corporations also had their problems and growing pains, but were able to restructure themselves at huge cost, whenever legislators stepped in and passed more stringent laws concerning MLM.

But my main concern with new multi-level marketing organizations is simply this: if they really do come up with an original product that really does what is promised for it, even though it is fully patented — you can be certain that a large corporation will soon be producing a product featuring the same benefits, at lower prices, and available in your supermarket. You can take that to the bank! And when that happens, where does it leave all those eager salespeople you have recruited? Behind the eight-ball, of course. It is still "the greatest fool theory." If you can live with that on your conscience, more power to you. I can't.

— Editorial by Jerry Buchanan, editor and publisher of *TOWERS Club, USA Newsletter*, June, 1983
© 1983 by Jerry Buchanan, Reprinted by permission.

* * * * * *

Author's note: Readers who wish to explore multi-level marketing opportunities will find additional information in the resource chapter.

A Small Mail Order Business

If you think of a small mail-order business as an interesting sideline, you may be thinking of a new way to lose your shirt. The mail-order business is overcrowded and highly competitive in spite of the fact that it is far and away the most expensive method of doing business. In addition, the mail-order world has to fight basic mistrust: John Q. Public is absolutely convinced that mail-order companies are right up there with used-car dealers when it comes to honesty and reliability.

And as if that wasn't enough, mail-order businesses also have to fight the fact that there are thousands of people who will spend all day shopping in a mall, but haven't got the energy to sit down and fill out an order form. I know for a positive fact that the average American home has neither envelopes nor stamps in it, and that if George Gallup were to go around asking, he probably would discover that 70% of American householders haven't filled out an order form since Miss McDonald showed them how to do it in Consumer English 101!

Then why is anyone in the mail-order business?

Why? *Because it's fun!* Because you can do it right there in your own home, at your own pace, on your own schedule. If you like to sleep late in the morning and work all night, who's to say you can't? You're your own boss. If you're like me, habitually wandering out to the mailbox in the middle of the morning and feeling depressed the rest of the day if it's empty, you will find mail-order a permanent cure.

You'll have friends all over the world, friends who stick in a note about their families, their work, their experiences with your products every time they order from you. And don't forget they stick a check in there, too. The money's part of the fun. If you are in the mail-order business, you're sharing your life, your home, your skills and talents, with a vast host of people, and they'll share with you in return, especially if you let yourself shine through your advertising.

Mail-order requires special skills in combination: in addition to management, you need to be able to express yourself in writing, to type, to file, to put budgets and sales campaigns together, to fill out tax forms. And you'll need the simple mailroom tricks of efficient folding, stuffing, and sorting.

Mail-order business is *not* a sideline. It is not a recommended court of last resort when you can't find markets elsewhere. It is time-consuming, demanding, expensive. It requires willingness to work long hours, to take big risks, assume great responsibilities. It demands managerial skills: the ability to organize dozens of details so they all mesh at once; the ability to live at least six months in the future; the ability to "read" the market and exploit it.

Unless you enjoy business for itself, unless it feeds your ego in a special way, unless you have the particular skills required — that is unless you're *good* at business — you will be better off finding other outlets for your work.

— Excerpt from the article, "Mail-Order Merchandising" in *CraftsWoman* magazine, August, 1982. By Jean Dubois, Director of LaPlata Press. © by Jean Dubois. Reprinted by permission.

Author's note: See the resource chapter for several excellent books on how to start and operate a mail-order business.

Notes

Time and Money Factors

Lack of time and money are, without doubt, the two most troublesome problems of any home business owner, new or established, and these two factors will play an important role in one's choice of a business.

If you currently hold a full-time job, you have a lack-of-time problem that leaves you with but two choices for extra income: a part-time business, or "moonlighting." Although more women than men start home businesses, more men than women are apt to moonlight. According to a study by the Bureau of Labor Statistics, as reported in the July 10, 1983 issue of *The Chicago Tribune* " . . . about 4.8 million people work two or more jobs, and more are joining the moonlighters all the time." Predominant among moonlighters are professional and technical workers, teachers, and police and fire fighters.

If extra income is your primary goal, moonlighting does serve the purpose, but if you desire to become more self-sufficient, then a part-time home business is the preferred choice. A moonlighting job could end just as suddenly as your primary job, and then where would you be? Consider that a home business, no matter how small, is a good form of unemployment insurance if the worst should suddenly happen. I'm reminded of a letter I received from one of my newsletter readers: "On March 3rd," Tom wrote, "I walked into my place of work at 8 a.m. and out at 9:30 with no job. Fortunately, I wasn't without a means of support, thanks to my home framing business, which kept me going until I found a new job."

Some people feel they have to take a moonlighting job because they simply have no money to invest in a home business. But remember that service businesses are often started with little more than the service itself and some word-of-mouth advertising. One satisfied customer with a few friends can really get the ball rolling. Some service businesses which could be started with little or no capital are custom dressmaking, teaching, telephone sales, appliance repairman, party planner, and so on. The service chart in this chapter should give you other ideas.

Many product-oriented businesses also can be launched with a minimum of money, particularly those which fall under what I call "the arts and crafts umbrella." A small investment in raw materials can result in a sizable array of finished goods which might be taken to a local crafts fair or shop, and the resulting profits could be used to buy material to create even more products. Also, the products of many manufacturing companies are available to homebased entrepreneurs who are interested in party-plan selling, open-house presentations, or multi-level sales opportunities. Examples of such companies are Tupperware, Avon, Mary Kay Cosmetics, and a host of others who produce food, health, or skin-care products, as well as housewares, jewelry, and so on.

And don't forget mail order, the Great American dream and the one, nearly-perfect, part-time home business. The beauty of a mail-order business is that one can easily control its size and dollar volume simply by increasing or decreasing the number of ads or mailings which bring in business. And yes, it really is possible to start small and make it big in mail-order, in spite of what "mail-order experts" may say to the contrary. I've been involved with creative, ambitious people too long to pay much attention to skeptics who say you have to have several thousand dollars to start a mail-order business. Maybe you do . . . if you plan to buy merchandise from other people. But if you create your own products or publications, you can start a mail-order business on the proverbial shoestring, with as little as one product and an inexpensive classified ad.

My book, *Creative Cash,* includes two inspiring mail-order success stories which prove my point. Love-Built Toys of California, and Platypus of New York, both began with one product (patterns for hobbyists) and a classified ad. These two businesses have grown steadily through the years and are now grossing annual incomes of six figures or more. Similar success stories abound in the crafts industry today, but we need not limit ourselves to this field.

Jerry Buchanan, publisher of the *TOWERS Club Newsletter,* could give you dozens of other examples, I'm sure. Jerry is in "the information business." Through the years he has helped thousands of people get started in writing, self-publishing, and mail-order. In fact, his own business began with a 700-word report on how to eliminate moles and gophers from the garden. It cost less than $25 to print, and $33.60 to advertise in a local farm journal. To date, says Jerry, that report has generated some $33,000 in sales and it's still selling. See what I mean about starting on a shoestring?

Of course, a mail-order business grows in direct proportion to the time, money, and talent invested in it, and you certainly need a good product to begin with. As Jerry reminds us, "To be a success in business, be daring, be first, be different."

Zoning Restrictions and State and Federal Laws

I hate to say this . . . but you may come up with the world's greatest idea for a profitable home business only to discover that it is restricted by zoning ordinances or state or federal laws. Since this topic is discussed at length in the A-to-Z business section, I'll remind you only to keep this thought in mind as you make your plans.

I can almost feel some of you shuddering at this point, especially those of you who are already in business. Some people violate a law out of ignorance, but others do it deliberately, perhaps because they feel a law is unfair. It well may be unfair – even unconstitutional in the eyes of many people — but the fact remains that ignorance of the law is no excuse, and anyone who deliberately *or* unknowingly breaks the law must also be prepared to pay the consequences. This might mean the complete stoppage of a business, a stiff fine, back taxes (plus interest), or even a jail sentence. In some cases it could mean an expensive lawsuit instigated by your state or federal government.

A primary goal of this book is to help you understand what you can and cannot do legally as a home business owner, as well as to make you realize the personal and tax advantages of operating your home business in an up-front manner. At a recent workshop, after I had talked for three hours about all the technicalities and legalities of operating a home business, a small voice in the back asked, "Is it really worth all this effort?" I said I didn't know if it was worth it to her, but it was worth it to me. Only you can decide the answer to that question. Just remember that every big job is intimidating at first, even to a professional. The secret is to

Notes

make a plan of the big job, then break it into a lot of little jobs. The task then becomes not only less frightening, but easier to do. As someone once said, "The only way to eat an elephant is one bite at a time."

"Great" Business Ideas That Aren't So Hot

Have you ever read about a money-making opportunity that sounded too good to be true? *It probably was.* Beware! There are some real con artists out there today who literally are lying in wait for would-be entrepreneurs. Most of the "golden opportunities" they offer are illegal, financially risky, or just plain unprofitable. You probably are too smart to fall for most of the slick "business opportunity" advertisements that promise easy money for little work and no skill or experience, but you may not be aware of all the work-at-home schemes and mail-order ripoffs I am about to describe. I wonder, too, if you realize there are certain things you cannot do as a business because of postal code regulations or copyright laws. Read on.

Envelope Stuffing/Circular Mailing/Aprons and Baby Booties. According to a Law Enforcement Report issued by the Chief Postal Inspector, the most common of the work-at-home frauds involve stuffing envelopes at home, and/or mailing circulars. "Others may be for making a product, such as baby booties, aprons, or Christmas wreaths," this report warns, "with promotions aimed usually at the elderly, the disabled, the unemployed, and spouses trying to supplement family incomes."

The promoters of such schemes may guarantee your complete satisfaction and a full refund of your money, but they simply won't deliver. They may offer to buy all the products you make, but they won't, and their reason will probably be that your work "does not meet their standards." It never will, because they have no intention of ever buying anything from anyone. They are interested only in *selling* something.

"The Postal Inspection Service knows of NO work-at-home promotion that ever produces income as alleged," emphasizes the above report. "A homework scheme promoter will . . . take your money and give you little or nothing in return except heartbreak and grief."

The Council of Better Business Bureaus, Inc. confirms this fact in their pamphlet, "Tips on Work-at-Home Schemes." They add that most of the ads are "simply lures by the advertisers to sell information on how to set up your own business or conduct the same scheme as the advertiser's."

False Representation of Products Sold by Mail. Many companies have been put out of business because they have engaged in a scheme or device for obtaining money or property through the mails by means of "false representation," a phrase that packs a powerful punch. For instance, one case in the aforementioned Law Enforcement Report indicates that one man was put out of business because he was selling herbs and herbal formulas through a catalog called, "Herbs and Spices for Home Use."

Now this in itself would have been okay; but this seller maintained that the advertised products had certain "curative powers" which "dissolved malignant tumors," among other things. To say that certain herbs are *believed by some* to have curative powers is one thing; *to claim that they will cure anything* is selling by means of false representation.

Chain Letters and Pyramid Schemes. Although chain letters and pyramid schemes are illegal, we all continue to receive them in our daily mail. Some people think they are getting around the illegality of chain letters by saying they are offering a "mass merchandising mail order program," or simply a hobby or recipe exchange. But since some states have laws against pyramid schemes of any kind — even when no money is changing hands — a no-money recipe or hobby chain letter may be as illegal in your state as one that asks you to send money.

Be smart. Whenever you receive chain letters of any kind, either pass them along to your Postmaster, or throw them away.

Mail-Order Schemes and Promotions. There is a certain kind of mail-order promoter of whom you especially should be aware; that's the one who offers you the chance to build a profitable mail-order business using the promoter's ads, catalogs, and products. Mail-order how-to booklets are a common product promoted in this way. *Although these business promotions are NOT illegal, they often are unprofitable.* What promoters neglect to tell interested prospects is that, although they supply the ad copy to sell such products, the dealer must place and pay for all the ads. The promoter may supply the mail-order catalogs, but dealers must pay for the postage to mail them, and also buy their own mailing lists. What mail-order beginners do not realize is that they may receive as little as a 1% or 2% order response from any mailing — which is between 10–20 orders for every 1,000 pieces mailed. And that's if the list is *good;* if it's bad, it's entirely possible to get only one or two orders, or *none.*

Unless you are an experienced book seller with a good customer mailing list, it generally is unprofitable to sell books published by other people. So take a tip from me and stay out of the mail-order field unless you are selling at least some of your own products and publications, and have a good understanding of the mail-order business as a whole.

As the Council of Better Business Bureaus cautions, and which I can affirm, "Building a solid, profitable mail-order business is a demanding, full-time task. Few inexperienced individuals can learn enough about the business before their capital or patience runs out." (See the resource chapter to order the Council's free pamphlets on work-at-home schemes and mail-order profit mirages.)

Other Business Opportunity Frauds. In their free brochure, "Promises, Check 'em Out!", the Direct Selling Education Foundation warns of advertisements and promotions relating to the sale of vending machines, video games, and other rack product opportunities, adding that promises of great locations, easy servicing, and competitive pricing should be carefully verified. They point out that sellers of certain business opportunities are required by the Federal Trade Commission to provide certain information about their company to all potential purchasers. This information, with guidelines on how to obtain it, is found in the above-mentioned brochure.

Thanks to an increased awareness program by the postal service, more and more consumers are notifying the Inspection Service of

Notes

suspicious advertising, and several thousand phony work-at-home operations have been put out of business as a result. Ask your Postmaster for a free brochure on this topic, and for information on how to report questionable work-at-home promotions you may become aware of in the future.

In summary, remember that any business opportunity that sounds "too good to be true" probably is. But if you still are interested in it, check it out — *carefully*. For help available to you locally, contact the nearest Better Business Bureau or the Chamber of Commerce. An attorney also can provide information, as can the attorney general's office or the Federal Trade Commission.

You and the Copyright Law

Some people start businesses based on the intellectual property of others, property which is protected by the copyright law. The average person does not understand the copyright law and thus often breaks it unknowingly, sometimes only to his or her embarrassment, other times at some cost on the wrong end of a legal case. As a businessperson, you cannot afford to be ignorant of this federal law.

Since whole books have been written on this very complex subject, I will include here only the most important information about copyright: what it is, how to claim and hold onto your copyrights, how to stop infringers from using your copyrighted works for their profit, and how to avoid legal problems with other copyright holders.

By learning what you can do as a copyright holder, you will also learn what you can't do in regard to the copyrights of others. Following are answers to questions I've been asked most often in the past, along with a whole list of business ideas that would violate the copyright law.

Since I am not a copyright attorney, the following information does not constitute legal advice, but merely represents my studied opinion of what I believe the law to be. As an added precaution, however, I asked attorney Mary Helen Sears of Washington, D.C. to read the following material, plus that in the A-to-Z business section which pertains to copyrights, patents, and trademarks. Mary Helen has been in private law practice since 1961, and is a principal in Irons & Sears, specializing in patents, copyrights, trademarks, unfair competition, and related matters. You have her assurance that my information on these topics is correct. (Any suggestions she made were incorporated into my material.)

The copyright law was enacted in 1790 and most recently amended in January, 1978. It is designed to protect the rights of creators of intellectual property in seven broad categories of work:

(1) literary works
(2) musical works, and accompanying words
(3) dramatic works, and accompanying music
(4) pantomimes and choreographic works
(5) pictorial, graphic, and sculptural works
(6) motion pictures and other audiovisual works
(7) sound recordings.

To avoid violating the copyright law, you must learn to recognize and respect all work that is protected by it. A properly copyrighted work of any kind will bear a notice containing these three essential elements:

(1) the word "copyright" or its abbreviation, "copr.", or the copyright symbol, ©

(2) the year of first publication of the work (when it was first shown or sold to the public)

(3) the name of the copyright owner. Sometimes the words, "All Rights Reserved" will also appear, which means that copyright protection has been extended to include all of the Western Hemisphere.

EXAMPLE: Copyright © 1984 by Barbara Brabec. All Rights Reserved.

While the copyright law is very generous to authors, one can lose the copyright by not putting a copyright notice thereon, and the notice must be properly noted, as shown above. *Any other wording is unacceptable.*

Copyright protection for works created after January 1, 1978 lasts for the life of the author or creator plus fifty years after his death. If the work is created anonymously, pseudonymously, or done for hire, copyright protection lasts 75 years from year of first publication, or 100 years from creation, whichever occurs first. For works created before 1978, there are different terms which a copyright lawyer can give you.

If you make or manufacture items of any kind (including one-of-a-kind works), and these items contain original designs or images you wish to protect, be sure to include the proper copyright notice on each item offered for sale. This will notify the public that you own the copyright, and warn them against using your work for their own profit. The copyright notice can be affixed in a number of ways, including handwriting, printing, stamping, burning, etching, sewing, etc. The important thing is that it be placed on the article where it can be seen easily.

What you and some of your buyers may not realize is that the sale of an object you have made does not give the buyer any automatic right to reuse the design or image on that object. *Your copyright can be conveyed to another person only in writing, or by other transfers that occur by operation of law.* For example, if you're an artist who sells a painting, the buyer will own the physical piece of art, but you will still own the image of that artwork, and only you have the right to copy it. Only you can legally make prints for sale, or postcards, or calendars, or greeting cards, or anything else with that image on it. Of course you may, if you wish, transfer this reprint right — *this right to copy* — to someone else in the form of a license. Commercial objects such as those with Mickey Mouse on them, for instance, plus all the other commercial designs so familiar to us all, have been made only by permission from the original creator, or copyright holder. Anyone who uses such designs without permission, and without paying mightily for the privilege, is asking for legal trouble. (Yes, I know that people all over the country sell Snoopy designs and Raggedy Ann dolls, etc., but many of these people are violating the law and inviting legal trouble.)

It's important to realize that, under the current law, copyright protection exists from the moment a work is created. (Note: Before 1978, the copyright did not necessarily arise automatically.) To illustrate: If you give a speech, you own your words the moment they fall from your lips, and you're the only one who has the right

Notes

to put those words into written form, or on a cassette tape, for purpose of profit.

Everything you draw or write on paper, even a letter to your mother, is your property the moment it appears on paper, and no one else has the right to use or sell it without your permission. That is one reason why you need not be concerned about sending articles or book manuscripts to magazine editors and book publishers without registering the copyright first. In addition to the fact that editors and publishers usually are ethical people who do not steal from writers, it is understood that you are the owner of that material, *until such time as you decide to sell or convey its copyright to someone else.*

If you write a book, the book publisher will register the copyright in your name when the book is printed and offered to the public. As the copyright owner, you will receive a royalty on each book sold. Your book contract temporarily conveys to the publisher the right to profit from your work, too, in the form of a book. But unless you agree to it in your book contract, the publisher could not put your words on a recording, or sell them to anyone else, such as a magazine. (Such rights are generally included in a book contract, with the author receiving half the amount the publisher receives from such extra sales of the work.) If and when your book is no longer offered for sale by the publisher, and goes out of print, the copyright will usually revert back to you, according to the terms of your book contract — a legal document that a lawyer should read and approve, by the way.

In working with magazine editors, it's a slightly different story. At the time you offer your work for publication — and this might be an article, a poem, a design, pattern, or how-to instructions for some project — you must consider whether you are going to sell only "first rights" or "all rights" to that publisher. If you elect the latter, which some beginners have to do just to get published, *you automatically lose ownership of the copyright to your material.* Selling "all rights" means you have conveyed your copyright to the publisher, and you cannot use that material again without the publisher's written permission.

Selling "first rights," on the other hand, means that you have given the magazine permission to print your article once, for a specified sum of money, after which time you alone have the right to resell that article to someone else, reprint it in a publication of your own, include it in a book you are writing, incorporate it into kit instructions, and so on.

Something a bit different is selling designs and ideas to manufacturers. You're getting into a tricky area here, and you would be wise to consult an attorney before you show your design or idea to a manufacturer, and again before you sign any kind of agreement with a manufacturer or company, either for an outright sale, or a royalty on the merchandise to be sold. *At the very least, never show a manufacturer your designs until you've registered your copyright on them.* If you are trying to sell an idea, ask for an agreement or waiver that will protect your rights.

And now let me explain the real "trick" to the whole copyright business. You can place a formal copyright notice on anything you create and thereby announce your claim to copyright . . . *but you do not have to register it in The Copyright Office and pay the $10 registration fee.*

On the other hand, if you do *not* file this official claim, you can't sue anyone who copies, or "infringes" upon, your copyright.

Thus, in each copyright situation, you have to decide how important your work is to you in terms of dollars and cents, and ask yourself (1) whether you value it enough to apply for a $10 copyright registration on it and, (2) whether you would be willing to pay court costs to defend your copyright, should someone steal it from you. If you never intend to go to court to protect your designs, there's little use in registering them officially.

But since it costs you nothing to add the copyright notice to your work, you would be foolish not to do this. In essence, the notice wards off a lot of people who might have copied your work if no notice had appeared at all. There will always be people who will use copyrighted works, either innocently or deliberately, and if you become aware of an infringement of one of your copyrights, you can send a cease-and-desist letter to the infringer even if you have not registered the copyright. You just cannot sue them at this point. Because infringers have no way of knowing whether you have registered the copyright or not, they will probably stop using your work to avoid any legal problems. Naturally, it helps if your cease-and-desist letter is written with authority on impressive stationery, and it will carry even more weight if a lawyer writes it for you. In addition, you *can* file the registration after you discover the infringer.

Note: Although it is not necessary to apply for copyright registration when you use a copyright notice, there *is* a mandatory deposit requirement (no charge) for all works published with a notice of copyright. Two copies of the work must be deposited with the Library of Congress. Get the details on Circular R7d from the Copyright Office.

Moneymaking Ideas That Violate the Copyright Law

The only copyrighted material you can safely use for your own profit, without written permission from the copyright holder, is material currently in the "public domain," which means material on which the copyright has expired *or has not been claimed.* (Some people believe that anything published before 1910 is automatically in the public domain. Not true. Copyright duration before the 1978 act varied greatly and many copyrights were renewable.)

As I understand the law, it can be risky to use any material that appears to be in the public domain, simply because someone else may have obtained rights by putting it into new form, and claimed a copyright on that new form. Dover Publications, for instance, has reorganized and reformulated many books that were once in the public domain and obtained copyrights for their own new forms. Thus, in all cases, if you plan to use previously-published and copyrighted material for your own profit, you would be wise to obtain a legal opinion from an attorney who specializes in copyright law.

Some people have started businesses selling handmade products they make, but have not designed, often taking the designs for such products from popular how-to magazines or books. This is not a wise idea, however. You'll recall what I said about designers who sell only "first rights" to a magazine. Even though their design or project may be published in a how-to magazine, they may still retain the exclusive right to sell finished products or kits made from that

Notes

design. Unfortunately, magazines and designers do not always warn the public in such cases. So, if you plan to sell a considerable quantity of any product you have not designed yourself, you first should obtain permission in writing from the original creator. (You need not be concerned if you only plan to make a couple of things for a church bazaar; it's "going commercial" with someone else's designs that is the problem here.) You always can write to the creator in care of the publisher who issued the book or magazine containing the design.

This kind of copyright violation, sometimes called "pattern piracy," is a matter of growing concern today as an increasing number of craft and hobby consumers unknowingly break copyright laws and thus affect the profits of craftspeople, designers, writers, publishers, and manufacturers. As a result, a growing number of creators are considering lawsuits today. Make sure you don't become "another case for the books."

Now let me give you several specific "copyright no-no's." Pattern piracy and other copyright law violations occur *whenever the copying of something in any way affects the profits or labors of the original author or creator and/or results in profit to the user.* To avoid problems:

1. Do not make for sale any reproductions of such copyrighted characters as Snoopy, Raggedy Ann & Andy, the Sesame Street Gang, or the Walt Disney characters unless you have written permission from the copyright holders to do so. (Commercial patterns or kits of such characters — which have been offered to buyers by licensed manufacturers — can, of course, be made for personal use or gifts. And, unless a magazine, book, or pattern specifically warns against reproduction for profit, the innocent person who makes the handmade item for sale will not be held liable in a court of law.)

2. Do not photocopy — for sale or trade — any pattern, article, or other printed material from any book, magazine, newsletter, etc. which bears a copyright notice. (Such use denies the creator the profit from a copy which might have been sold.)

3. Do not photocopy any part of any copyrighted publication — particularly books and manuals — for use as a teaching aid unless you plan to use it only once, or are teaching a charity group without charge.

4. Do not reprint and offer for sale any previously published material still protected by the copyright law (not in public domain), even though such material may no longer be available from the original publisher. That publisher, or the creator, still owns the copyright to that material, whether he wants to do anything with it or not.

5. Do not duplicate records, cassettes or tape recordings, videotaped television shows, etc. for sale or trade. Sound recordings and audiovisual works are fully protected by copyright laws, as are computer programs.

6. Do not copy and republish recipes from books or magazines exactly as they have appeared. A group of previously published recipes *can* be republished in new form, however, provided you make changes, such as: (1) the recipe's title, (2) the order in which ingredients are used, or the amounts of ingredients used, and (3) the way the instructions are written on how to put the recipe together.

7. Do not use poems or poetry written by other people without their written permission. Novice self-publishers often use the work of well-known poets in their newsletters, magazines, booklets, or

on greeting cards or calendars, etc. But the use of an entire poem is a flagrant violation of the copyright law because it represents the use of a whole work of an individual creator who is receiving no financial benefit from such usage. Giving credit to the creator is not enough. The use of one or two lines of a poem, or a paragraph or two from a book or other publication may be considered "fair use," according to the copyright law, but some publishers are now asking that even such limited usage be cleared with them beforehand.

8. Do not copy, for purposes of resale either as a design or a finished product, the designs on handcrafted products or commercial gift items because all commercial manufacturers and many professional craft designers/sellers protect their work by copyrights or design patents.

Finally, in spite of what you may have heard, it is not all right merely to "change one thing," or use a different color or material. Merely changing the way a design is used does not alter the fact that it is a copy. A work does not have to be identical to the original to be a copy, but only has to repeat a "substantial part" of it, according to The Copyright Office. Unless you can legally define the words, "substantial part," it would be wise to avoid altering commercial patterns for sale as original designs, or selling any handmade object that has been designed by another person.

However, it *is* possible to get your own copyright in a "derivative work." You may need the copyright owner's license and have to pay a royalty, but if it's a new twist on the old and well received, you may still make money — and your own copyright will block those who want to exploit your special new twist.

As you can see, the copyright law is complex indeed. In the end, my best advice may be: *to be safe, be original.*

P.S. See the A-to-Z business section of this book for guidelines on how to register a copyright and find some resources on this subject.

Building a Pathway to Profit

WHEN THEY WORK AT HOME, the British call it "fiddling." Here in America a lot of people earning money at home probably feel as though they're just fiddling, too. But if that's the way you feel about your business or your ideas for one, you might as well close this book now because this is *not* a hobby-business guide. I'm going to tell you how to bring in the dollars from a business at home — *a real* business. It may be small, and you may have little time to devote to it, but there's no reason for it to remain profitless. Even small, part-time businesses can generate a fair amount of capital and profit if they are properly managed and promoted.

A lot of people work long hours at homebased activities that generate very little income, let alone profit. Some of these people simply don't know what to do to make more money; others know, yet are reluctant to do anything about it for a variety of reasons.

I remember an article I read about a woman whose business is baking bread on Saturdays. By working twelve hours that day, she can turn out as many as 60 loaves of bread which she sells locally for 70¢ a loaf. At that rate, she's grossing only $42 for a very long day's work — or $3.50 an hour — but she says she's happy doing it. Still, I bet she would be a lot happier if she were grossing $350/week instead of the $35 she says she now averages after expenses. (And do you think she counts as expenses the gas or electricity she uses to run her oven, or her car expenses in delivering the product? I doubt it.)

If this woman had the desire to expand her business instead of just making a few dollars on the side, she probably could do it. However, like thousands of other homebased workers, she seemingly has her mind set on staying small, for reasons we can only guess. She probably will continue to do what she has been doing all along — no more, no less — and she may never raise her prices, even though she admits they're too low. Probably she fears the bread would not sell at a higher price, and then she wouldn't have even the $35 per week. This kind of logic prevails among hobby-business owners.

When I hear about people like this, I want to shake them to make them realize that their possibilities are so much greater! I can identify with hard-working individuals like this, but I can't encourage others to follow in their footsteps, as so many authors have done in their make-money-at-home books. Perhaps I'm too ambitious for my own good, and perhaps I do push people a bit too hard

> *"A head for business — that's not something inherited, or something shared by only the talented few, it's something you can acquire, and it's essential."*
>
> *— Colette Wolff, author, designer, owner of Platypus Publications*

Notes

when I am speaking or writing about running a home business or striving for self-sufficiency. But I also know, from my daily mail, that my insistent prodding has helped many people understand the all-work, no-profit home business traps they have set for themselves — and it has helped many escape from those traps.

It is a trap to think small. If you think small, you probably will stay small. I believe that if we dare to think big, we have at least a chance of making it big, financially speaking. That's why I am urging you to E-X-P-A-N-D your thinking. S-T-R-E-T-C-H your capabilities, and R-E-A-C-H farther than you ever have reached before. *Please understand that you know more than you think you know, and you can do more than you now believe possible.*

Developing a Mindset for Business and Financial Success

Success in a home business begins with the right attitude: *a money-oriented mindset for success.* You have to want money to make it, and you must desire success to attain it. Without a professional, businesslike attitude about what you're doing, you are destined to remain a small-time, hobby business forever. If that's what you want, okay. If you are satisfied with that, I won't try to lead or propel you into anything else. Secretly, however, I really think you want more than hobby-business income. Believe me, you can get it if you are willing to work for it.

Since success experts remind us that we can't achieve any goal until that goal is clearly pictured in the mind, it's important for you to define "success" before you reach for it. Some people equate success only in terms of dollars, saying, "I want to create/make/invent something I can sell for thousands of dollars in mail-order catalogs/exclusive shops/chain stores." This kind of goal, neither realistic nor clear cut, is unachievable. If you set such goals, you will become quite discouraged when you don't reach them. Remember this rhyme: *To be achievable, a goal must be believable and conceivable.*

In the beginning, home business owners need a series of small gains and achievements to keep them going. It is important to set realistic dollar goals for yourself. For instance, a first year's goal might be: "I'm not going to lose more than $1,000 this year." (A paper loss, we hope.) Just think how great you'll feel if you lose only $500 the first year. If you have met or bettered your first year objective, raise your goal the second year to break even, or perhaps make a small profit.

Remember that it often takes two years just to work out the kinks in a home business — to refine and improve products or services, test new theories, set up efficient office systems and procedures, locate necessary suppliers, and establish basic marketing channels. By the third year, things are beginning to fall into place, and a true profit might be realized for the first time. (I say "true profit" because it's not fair to you or your business to say that you have made a profit if you've worked all year without a salary, as most home business owners do for two or three years. The employees and all other expenses get paid first, then the owner.)

It's not businesslike, either, to ignore the overhead costs of your business that fall into the area of "home expenses" — like the rent or mortgage payment, electric or gas bill, and telephone. Whether these costs increase as a result of your business is not really the point. What you need to consider is this: If you build your business on a no-overhead principle, what will happen if you become successful to the point where you must move to outside quarters? In all probability you will not have set your prices high enough to cover the now-unavoidable overhead costs, and you will have to do some fancy figuring to get out of this trap without losing your customers or clients, who by now will be accustomed to your low prices.

"Profit" is another good word for you to define as you develop your mindset for success. It is not always synonymous with cash, of course. New businesses can lose money for several years in a row and still be extremely profitable to their owners. For instance, a profitable year might mean valuable business contacts, acquired knowledge and experience, a new understanding of your strengths and weaknesses, or the discovery of a new marketing channel that will pay off big the next year. It can also mean that you have made money, but you put it into an IRA or Keogh Plan, or simply reinvested every dime into the business, perhaps in the form of equipment, larger inventories, new employees, a computer, and so on.

A sideline venture that has failed also can be profitable if it points the way to a better idea that will work, or if it reveals something important in your character that encourages you to go forth in a new direction. Again, failure has its redeeming qualities; you always will learn something from it.

To be Legal or Not — That is the Question

It's not surprising that so many home business owners ask, "Why be legal?" All they need to do is look about in any direction to see friends and relatives with "little things going on the side." Such thoughts are only reinforced by widely publicized reports of IRS estimates that self-employed individuals fail to report a substantial part of their earnings. But if the IRS is aware of this, you can bet they are in hot pursuit of a lot of these same tax dodgers.

For instance, a recent law change requires direct-sales companies, such as Avon and Amway, to supply the IRS with the names of salespeople who buy more than $5,000 worth of products per year. This kind of information will help them decide whose returns get selected for audit.

Are you one of those folks who operate an underground business or think of your income as "money under the table?" If so, let me remind you that this is just another trap you are setting for yourself. No business can grow if it remains hidden; it needs visibility to survive and prosper.

But why should you be legal, especially when so many others are obviously "getting away with it?" Even if you think the chances are pretty good you will not be "caught," I think it boils down to whether you want to be an honest — or dishonest — individual. Do you prefer the feelings of pride and accomplishment that are the rewards for honest actions, or shall you live instead with Fear and Guilt, companions to dishonesty? As ordinary people, we have enough feelings of guilt in our everyday lives without having to worry about the fact that we're cheating on our taxes and could

On Getting Ideas

"To get a sound, profitable idea, we have to learn to look past the end of our nose. We have to obliterate our preconceptions and prejudices. Look around. Observe what is successful. Then, start brainstorming. Ask yourself a thousand questions and try to answer them. Ideas do not hide from us. They are everywhere we go, in everything we do. They are not beyond reach. But some of us are mentally blind."

*— John Sheehan
former newsletter publisher*

Notes

Notes

get caught, publicly embarrassed – and punished — at any moment. I recall one woman who told me she finally was going to "go legal" simply because she was beginning to wake up in the middle of the night in a cold sweat, convinced the IRS would soon be knocking on her door. Surely no amount of taxes saved could be worth this kind of anxiety.

"Taxes are the price we pay for a government that guarantees us the freedom to earn enough money to pay our taxes," someone once said, and it is this same government that has recently given the homebased worker a number of special tax advantages. What too few people realize is that self-employed people qualify for many breaks that substantially lower their taxes. You see, once you are "in business," and not just "fiddling around," you'll find you are entitled to a great many tax deductions that just naturally offset a sizable portion of your annual gross income. In fact, in the early years of a business, it is quite likely that you will end up with a business loss, at least on paper, which can be used to offset income from salaries and other sources, and thus cut taxes.

If you are fortunate enough to end up with a profit after only a year or two, you legally can avoid taxes on a considerable sum of this money by starting a Keogh Plan or by opening an Individual Retirement Account (IRA), or both. In addition to the deductions for contributions to a Keogh or IRA, you also avoid taxes on the interest or other income earned while the funds accumulate in your account. Those earnings remain tax sheltered until you start to draw them out. Usually, that is not until retirement, at which time one generally is in a lower tax bracket.

Once you begin business operations, it will not seem at all unusual to the IRS that you need to buy office equipment, a computer, or a new car to advance your business. Lo and behold, a large percentage of such costs can immediately be offset against receipts, or written off (depreciated) over a specified number of years.

Naturally, when your business occupies a portion of your home, and that space is used regularly and exclusively for business, you become entitled to deduct a comparable percentage of your rent (or depreciation on the home you own), plus a host of other home-related costs, such as utilities, telephone, repairs, and maintenance. (See the A-to-Z business section for complete details on all of this, plus a checklist of specific expenses and business deductions you can take against a home business that is being operated for profit. Add them up. You'll be amazed.)

Finally, another often-overlooked break is that it may be possible for you to employ your children, which can result in sizable tax savings. As Julian Block, a former IRS agent and author of *Guide For Year-Round Tax Savings,* explains: "Putting your youngster on your payroll can be a savvy way to take care of his or her allowance at the expense of the Internal Revenue Service. Significant tax savings can result merely by moving the money from one family pocket to another."

Note that you are not liable for social security taxes on wages paid to a son or daughter under the age of 21. Moreover, as of 1989, a child can earn up to $4,490 without paying taxes. Do check with an accountant on this point, however, as this relates only to "earned income." If a child also has "unearned income" on top of this maximum dollar amount, there may be tax complications.

Of course, certain records must be kept, and your children must actually work for your business. Adds Julian, "The IRS scrutinizes deductions for wages paid to your own family members, so it is important to treat your child the same as any other employee and keep the usual records showing amounts paid and hours worked."

In conclusion, with all these delicious and perfectly legal tax deductions to which a legitimate home business owner is entitled, who but a fool (and a dishonest fool at that) would continue to hide his or her income and give them up?

Besides, if you're trying to prove your credit worthiness — possibly to get a business loan — you will want your gross income (and net profit) to be as high as possible.

Projecting a Professional Image

A professional image does not just happen. It has to be created by you, then carefully maintained throughout the life of your business. It involves everything from your business name and logo, to good-looking printed and promotional materials, to efficient communications and services.

One problem many homebased workers have is getting family or friends to accept the fact that they truly are in business and not just playing around with a hobby. If this is your problem, you need a strategy to combat this hobbyist image, and it must begin with your own attitude about yourself and your business. The way you conduct your business influences the way people think of you.

Begin by setting up some ground rules. If your neighbors are used to dropping by for coffee and conversation, tell them how much you're going to miss this contact with them, but ask them to kindly respect your business hours in the future. Emphasize that you are not just "messing around," but have started a business, and you need undisturbed periods of time in which to work. Tell them what you are doing and ask them to help you by spreading the word to prospective customers or clients. In the future, arrange to visit friends in the evening, or perhaps on the weekend. (Most home business owners tell me, however, that this is one of the first luxuries to fall by the wayside. There will not be much time for socializing once you start a business at home.)

If you plan to see customers or clients in your home, be sure that it is neatly maintained at all times, and greet people like the well-groomed professional they expect to see. Don't apologize for working at home, but instead stress this benefit: *You can provide a quality product or service at a more reasonable price because you are a homebased business.*

If you have young children, keep them away from the phone. The last thing you want is a child yelling into the ear of a prospective client, "It's for you, mommie!" The one I especially dislike is the precocious youngster who answers the phone and then insists on knowing your life history before he'll go fetch mom or dad; or the child who picks up the phone, then leaves it off the hook without calling the person you want. If your children could ruin the business *illusion* you are trying to create, a separate business phone or answering machine should be considered.

Note that I said "illusion" in the preceding sentence. Half of all big business is one big bluff, and you might as well play the game, too. It's important to maintain the illusion of business — and success — even at the worst times when your home is a disaster area, your business is terrible, and you feel like throwing in the towel. When dealing with business contacts in person or on the phone,

"In general, I would say the single most important concept for homebased business owners to clarify before they start out revolves around their commitment level and comfortability about working at home. If you feel confident about your competence in your chosen field and are determined to make the business go, then all the difficulties — for some, the stigma — of working from home dissipate. If there is a niggling doubt that you are somehow less professional or competent because you are homebased, then you should entertain and not gloss over that doubt. It is central to your success or failure.

"As a homebased businessperson, you have to project the utmost in confidence and professionalism, and that comes from within — not from the external trappings. You won't have the luxury of promoting yourself with the corporate or established name of a business preceding you. You won't have the benefit of others' public relations working for you. You won't even have a fancy place of business with secretaries or a parking lot. YOU are it! If you don't believe in yourself and what you are doing — 100% — no one else will. If you do, it doesn't matter if you are working out of a cave. If you have done your market research, you have it made."

— Ciya Stuart, Marketing & Small Business Consultant, Boxford, Massachusetts

Notes

always speak in confident tones, even when you are unsure about something. People like to deal with confident, successful people because it makes them feel more important. And since nothing sells like success itself, even the illusion of success may be enough to convince a prospective buyer that your product or service merits consideration.

Selecting a Business Name

Your business needs a name, and that name should tell customers or clients something about you, your product, publication, or service. You may wish to use your own name, especially if you are known and respected in your community or a particular field of endeavor. Your name on a business service, such as "Brown's Catering" or "Thomas Smith Photography" will automatically conjure a certain image in the minds of those who know you. I'll never forget the advice a businessman gave me years ago. "Don't sell your products," he told me, "sell your good name. Once people know and accept you, they'll also accept your products or services." Keep this in mind, especially if you're trying to promote a business locally. Consider joining your Chamber of Commerce and any professional business groups in your area to make your name better known in your community. Also register with the Better Business Bureau.

Some people are able to cleverly tie their last name into a phrase that makes people want to know about their businesses. Two examples from my files include: *Highley Decorative,* by Linda Highley, Arnold, Missouri, and *The Powers That Be . . .* by Trish, Tom and Chris Powers of Sylvania, Ohio.

Pat Cody of Ft. Worth, Texas has gone a step further by incorporating her last name into the middle of her business name and using excellent graphics to illustrate it:

calico•dysigns

By the way, Pat says that she was not required to register her business name because it includes her last name. "The typeface is readily available at quick-print shops," she says, "so nice graphics can be had with minimum investment. And the name is general enough to cover all my business activities: design sales to magazines, wearable and fiber art consignment sales, and books."

Instead of using their own names, some people merely use initials, such as "The T & T Company." While this may have meaning for the owners and even look great in a business logo, it will mean nothing to customers, and it won't give them a clue as to what the business is about. Some people pick clever names because they think they will be remembered, and often they are. But it's wise to avoid names like "Kathy's Klever Kreations," or "Sam's Sawin's," if you are trying to buy supplies and materials from wholesalers. Many will not sell to hobby businesses, and names like these are a dead giveaway. (Having a business letterhead and sales tax number may make no difference.)

Julie Felzien's business name, *The Mad Tatter,* is an example of how to tie a name to a literary work that tends to make people

These letterheads, courtesy of several home business owners in the author's network, illustrate a variety of ways to design business stationery. Note that designs fall into five basic categories:

1. Artwork straight across the top, with address information incorporated into the overall design. (Ex: Sarah Zaleski)
2. Right- or left-hand motifs. (Ex: Platypus and Barbara Boatright)
3. Artwork centered at top with address; additional information at bottom of letterhead (centered) — such as area of specialization. (Ex: Novelnook Originals)
4. All-around artwork, incorporating a kind of "box" design. (Ex: Aames-Allen, Design Source.)
5. Overall design motif that illustrates one's special art or craft abilities. (Ex: Calligraphy letterhead)

Remember that letterheads do not have to be printed on white paper with black ink. The addition of color, either in the ink or the stock, may not cost as much extra as you think. In the examples shown here, Sarah Zaleski has printed green on ivory; Aames-Allen, green on gray; Design Source, black on ivory; Novelnook Originals, green and brown on white; Barbara Boatright, brown on buff; the others, black on white.

Notes

think they've heard of you before. And look what some folks in Texas have done with their name, which I noticed in a business periodical: *The Greatest Little Storehouse in Texas.* Brings an immediate smile, and a desire to go there, doesn't it?

You probably realize that you cannot use the words, "Limited," "Ltd.," or "Inc." unless you are an incorporated business. But I tip my hat to the people who named their business *Textiles, Ink.* This name not only is appropriate, but it sounds like an incorporated business without being one.

Two things you might avoid in a business name are long names and words that are difficult to pronounce or remember. And consider *not* using the word, "enterprises." So many beginners now use this word as part of their business name that it has become synonymous with amateur or homebased operations.

In summary, your business name should not be selected in haste because your financial future could depend on it. Try to pick a name that won't tie you down, should you decide to branch out into other areas. And if you already have named your business and now realize you made a poor choice, change it. The cost of the printed materials you may have to throw out will be insignificant when compared to the probable increase in business a more appropriate name will generate. Times change, and we must change, too, or be left behind. Robert Compton, a Vermont potter, illustrates my point.

When he first began to sell, he operated as "The Mad River Potter," a folksy name that suited the times. As his work improved, however, and his prices increased, he realized the need for a more professional-sounding name, one that would offer customers more psychological security. By changing his name to Robert Compton Ltd., he enhanced his professional image, which enabled him to raise prices, which increased profits.[1]

For information on how to register and protect your business name and logo, see the A-to-Z business section.

Designing Promotional Materials

One way to make your business look successful, even when it's not, is to have classy printed materials — a well-designed business card, a good letterhead and matching envelopes printed on quality stock, and a brochure. It's nice, but not necessary, to have your card match your letterhead. Talk to a graphic artist about your need for a business logo and letterhead design. You probably will save money by working with a homebased worker like yourself, and a bartering of services may work here. If there are no artists locally, seek people who can work with you by mail, connecting with them through business newsletters like mine, or through memberships in organizations which publish a directory of members.

Be prepared to spend some money on these important promotional materials, but don't go overboard. It is not necessary to spend $300 to get good stationery designed and printed. Shop around, and be sure to get more than one quote from both artists and printers. Elsewhere in this chapter you will find examples of some outstanding business cards and letterheads contributed by people in my home business network. Don't copy them, but do use them for inspiration in designing your own original card.

---

[1]from an article in *The Crafts Report.*

These business cards from the author's collection illustrate a variety of product- and service-oriented businesses. Interesting effects have been achieved through the use of different colors of card stock and ink. For example, the "Soft Hearted" and "In Stitches" cards use red ink for accent. The "Critter Craft" card is printed in blue ink on a lighter blue card stock. "Judy's Originals" is brown on brown, and the "Fiber Fantasies" card is brown on buff with the business name not printed (as was necessary to illustrate card) but embossed to give an impressive raised-letter effectt.

THE *Aspen* SHOPPE

Doris A. Linville
1815 Somersworth Dr.
South Bend,
Indiana 46614
(219) 291-9161

PINE RIDGE VINEYARD
AND CLOCK WORKS
7218 W. DUPONT ROAD
FORT WAYNE, IN 46818

(219) 489-5123   GLEN BAKER

The *Talent* Company

(701) 838-8085

BOX 3145, MINOT, N.D. 58702

a communication network serving home businesses

PAT EGGEN

FAST PROFESSIONAL SERVICE FOR EVERY TYPING NEED

Carla L. Culp
TYPING SERVICE

PHONE: (618) 656-5665   EDWARDSVILLE, ILLINOIS 62025

P.O. Box 118
Nehalem, OR 97131
(503) 368-5730

Toe Toe The Clown
Enterprises

Promotions   · Face ·   Conventions
Stage Shows   Painting   Parties
Schools   Special Events

The Calligraphic Studio

ROBERT J. MYERS
IOWA FALLS, IOWA 50126
HAND LETTERING, DRAWINGS AND PAINTINGS (ESTIMATES)

HOME   ART INSTRUCTOR AT
515-648-3915   ELLSWORTH COLLEGE 648-4611

Rex Allan
301 37th Street N.E.
Cedar Rapids, Iowa

Ph: (319) 366-7400

Satisfaction Guaranteed or double your soot back!

SonShine
CHIMNEY
SWEEPS

(516) 223-4829

ISLAND CRAFT
& BUSINESS CONSULTANTS
ADVERTISING • MAIL ORDER • PUBLIC RELATIONS
Publisher of:
"THE L.I. ARTS, CRAFTS, &
COLLECTIBLES DIRECTORY"

EXECUTIVE OFFICE:
798 Vivian Court
Baldwin Harbor
New York 11510

PROFESSOR JACK K. MANDEL
Marketing Consultant

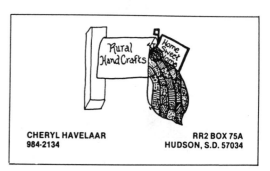

As your business grows, you will need a number of other printed materials to add to your professional image and, of course, to sell your products or services. You probably will need inexpensive flyers from time to time, a good brochure or catalog, price lists, order forms, and so on. Since few small businesses have much of a budget for printing, they often learn to create their own camera-ready art, thus saving a great deal of money. This is not as difficult as it sounds.

To begin, visit an art store and take a look at the wide selection of transfer lettering they offer, plus the charting and drafting tapes commonly used by newspapers to create borders and other design effects. (These materials are also available to you by mail; you will find some catalogs listed in the resource section of this book. In particular, order the free catalog from Dover Publications, because it contains a series of clip-art books and copyright-free designs you can use in any way you wish.) Most people learn to do paste-up work for a printer simply by beginning, and with the tips offered elsewhere in this chapter, you should have little difficulty. Try to find a cooperative printer who will take a little time to explain some of the finer points to you. He should be glad to do this in return for your steady business.

An important part of the job of preparing printed promotional materials involves copywriting, which is more difficult to master than paste-up work. The best-looking flyer, brochure, or catalog won't bring in business or pull orders if the copy itself does not motivate people to buy. Therefore, pay particular attention to the copywriting tips I have included in the advertising chapter. Also do some studying on your own. Most mail-order guides contain special chapters on how to write effective copy; several are listed in the resource chapter.

This sample graphic art aids sheet illustrates the technique used to cut out and transfer type to artwork. Other companies offer sheets of letters, numbers, and art which may be transferred simply by rubbing. Check local art supply shops for more information.

How to Prepare "Camera-Ready Copy" for Printers

• For best results, always use black ink and white paper for your artwork or copy, regardless of the color your work will be when printed. You can use certain colors, however, like light blue and yellow, which appear as white to the camera's eye. (Buy a "non-repro blue" pen from the art supply store to mark printing instructions on your artwork.) You can use the color red in your artwork, but the camera will see it as black. (The use of red and black together, then, would appear as one black blob to the camera's eye.)

• India ink is not required for artwork. Excellent results can be achieved with a variety of non-messy art pens available in art supply stores.

• In preparing artwork, you can paste one sheet of paper onto another, making several layers, if need be, and the edges of these papers will disappear into the background so long as they are white and not thick enough to case a shadow when light is shined on it. (Shadows create a black line on the printed material.)

• Save money on typesetting by using transfer lettering sheets to create headlines, and use an electric typewriter with a carbon ribbon to prepare written material. (If you have your typed material reduced to 85% of its original size, you will find it looks quite similar to typeset material. Ask your printer how to do this with the use of a reduction/enlargement scale, also available in art supply stores.)

Standard Printer's Folds

1. Single fold

2. Accordion fold

3. Standard letter fold

4. Double parallel fold

5. French fold

6. Gate fold

These illustrations will give you ideas on how to create simple brochures or mail pieces which can be printed on paper of any kind, or card stock (useful if you need a reply postcard incorporated into the piece). Do a little experimenting with blank sheets of paper of various sizes to create a brochure that's just right for your needs.

Note that some of the specialty printers listed in the resource chapter provide similar pieces for use as package inserts. Many include envelopes which are attached in the order form/business reply position of the mail piece.

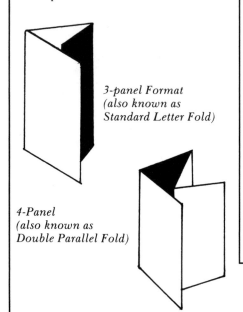

*3-panel Format
(also known as
Standard Letter Fold)*

*4-Panel
(also known as
Double Parallel Fold)*

You will save money on your printing by learning how to reduce artwork because, often through reduction of certain material, you can print on one page what might otherwise have required two.

• When using a second color in your printing, always place the color to eliminate extra runs through the press. (Ask your printer to tell you how the printing masters are stripped together, and what size sheet he'll be using. Often this determines how you can use color most economically.)

• The final print job will be only as good as your artwork, or "copy," so remove all smudges, excesses of glue or wax (which attract dirt), and cover up unwanted lines with a white-out solution available at office supply stores. Remember that anything your eyes can see, the camera's eye also will see, only better.

• Artwork or copy is photographed to make either a quick-print paper master, or a long-running metal plate. Quick-print masters are fine for short-run jobs like flyers and promotional pieces, and may yield up to 3,000 good copies or more. However, if your artwork has a lot of solid black design or heavy line art, you'll find that quick-printed materials look a bit gray. The sharpest impressions, of course, are obtained with metal plates, which yield thousands of copies. Ask your printer what he charges to make such a plate, and decide if this cost (usually under $10) is justified for each job. (If you plan to reprint a certain job, a plate justifies its cost.) Note that work involving a second color always requires metal plates, one for each color.

• Always have another person proof your camera copy for typo errors and misspelled words before you go to press. There are few things more embarrassing, or upsetting, than finding an error after 5,000 copies have been printed.

• In creating printed materials, experiment with different folds. Illustrated here are six of the most popular folds available from printers. They will suggest ideas on how to design the most effective

Suggested stock: paper or card stock, 6⅛" to 8½" wide × 11" long

BUSINESS REPLY SIDE	BACK COVER	FRONT COVER
PAGE 5	PAGE 6	PAGE 1

Side 1 of artwork

ILLUSTRATIONS AND COPY AREA		ORDER FORM
PAGE 2	PAGE 3	PAGE 4

Side 2 of artwork

Suggested stock: paper or card stock, 6⅛" to 8½" wide × 14" long

BUSINESS REPLY SIDE	ILLUSTRATION AND COPY AREA	BACK COVER	FRONT COVER
PAGE 7	PAGE 6	PAGE 8	PAGE 1

ILLUSTRATIONS AND COPY AREA			ORDER FORM
PAGE 2	PAGE 3	PAGE 4	PAGE 5

brochure for your business. A word of caution: Always check the weight of a sample piece before printing to make sure it can be mailed at the rate you desire (brochures under one ounce, for instance). Also make sure the size of your mail piece is standard, according to U.S. Postal regulation, else you may incur penalty charges on each piece mailed.

Planning for Success

4.

BUSINESS PLANNING NEVER STOPS. It is something we must do at the beginning, in the middle, and even at the end of a business. In every business, there is a need for a variety of plans, including time plans (short-, medium-, and long-range planning), creative, routine, and problem-solving plans, marketing plans, and comprehensive business plans.

Business experts generally stress the importance of a business plan in connection with getting a loan. Experience has shown, however, that small, homebased businesses seldom qualify for bank loans, at least in the first few years of existence. Generally they are financed with money from personal savings or family loans. So if you're not planning to apply for a loan, and you are the only person who will ever see your business plan, why should you prepare one?

Peace of mind is one answer. "The benefit of a business plan is security in knowing what you need to do, how much it's all going to cost, and where you can go wrong," says Colette Wolff. Adds Carol Adleman, another mail-order business owner, "Many hours were spent organizing my three-year business plan, and, as a result, I have an easy-to-follow plan of action. In retrospect, this work was probably of most value to me as the planner and I were writing it. It affirmed my commitment to my business — and it certainly impressed the loan officer at the bank."[1]

> *"The first management job is planning, a combination of realistic calculations and crystal ball gazing. It is an exercise in arithmetic and imagination, in separating the possible from the impossible."*
>
> *— from "More Than a Dream — Running Your Own Business," a Department of Labor booklet*

Developing a Business Plan

A business plan need not follow any set pattern, nor be any set length, but it is important to get as much information on paper as possible. For instance, a business plan might cover thirty pages and contain several elements, including (not necessarily in this order):

- Business history — how, why, and when it came into being.
- Business summary — a description of your business goals, products, and services, including unique features or customer benefits.
- Management information — who's behind the business, his/her experience, background, qualifications.
- Manufacturing plan (if you are a manufacturer or creator of goods) — description of required equipment and facilities;

---

[1]from the article, "What a Business Plan Entails," in *Sharing Barbara's Mail.*

Notes

how and where raw materials will be obtained, their estimated cost; how/where you will store/inventory them; labor and overhead costs involved in the manufacturing process.

- Market research findings — your market, your customers, your competition.
- Marketing plan — how you are going to reach and sell to your market (distribution), and the anticipated cost of your marketing effort.
- Production plan — how the work will get done; by whom, and at what cost.
- Financial plan — your expected sales and expense figures for one year, cash flow figures for a year, and a balance sheet showing what the business has, what it owes, and the investment of the owner.

If you do not plan to apply for a loan, why should you bother with a written description of the first three elements in the above business plan outline? You'll know the answer to this the first time you have an opportunity for publicity. These are the points of most interest to many interviewers, reporters, and editors who may give your business publicity in a feature article. Thinking them through in the beginning will not only make you feel good about yourself, but will actually give you ideas on how and where to get publicity once your business is rolling. Press releases are often "hooked" on "news pegs" like these, as you'll learn in the publicity chapter of this book.

If you're a manufacturer, you will need to incorporate a manufacturing plan into your overall business plan. (Be sure to order the free booklet, "Business Plan for Small Manufacturers," available from the SBA. It contains special worksheets to help you figure all your costs and sales projections.)

By the way, many of you who make things may not consider yourselves "manufacturers," but in truth you are. Check the dictionary. Anyone who makes anything — by hand or by machinery — is a manufacturer, so when this word is used in later places in the book, remember that it applies to you even if you make only one-of-a-kind, handcrafted wares.

An important consideration in a small (one-person) manufacturing company — and one not covered in the above-mentioned booklet — is who eventually will make the goods when demand for a product increases beyond the owner's ability to produce it. At this point, many business owners turn to independent contractors for assistance, forming small cottage industries that involve a number of homeworkers in one's community. Before you decide on the direction your growing company will take, however, be sure you are well versed in all the legal and tax aspects of using independent contractors vs. employees. I have spelled them out for you in the A-to-Z business section, but you would be wise to consult an attorney for an opinion on how this information might apply to you, your business, and your future plans for growth and expansion.

Market Research

Before you can successfully start any business, you need to define the market for your particular product or service by employing *market research*. Basically, market research identifies, describes, and categorizes the current and future market for a particular product or service. This research is concerned with the customer, the competition, the product, and outside forces (like the economy) which might affect one's business. It is interesting detective work and an essential marketing tactic.

To take the mystery out of marketing, look for clues on who your customers or clients might be, where they are located, and how you might reach them with publicity, advertising, or sales calls. It's not enough to know that a market exists for what you offer. *What is important is that you know — in advance — exactly how you're going to connect with it, promote to it, and sell to it.* Too many sellers make the mistake of offering a product or service that pleases them, rather than one that people may want to buy. This is backwards thinking. You will find it is a lot easier to fill an existing need than it is to create your own market.

What is the difference between selling something people *need*, as opposed to that which they may only *want?* Here's how a family income development report, issued by Michigan State University, answered this:

> "Most items produced by home industries . . . represent *wants* (discretionary purchases) on the part of the final consumer, not *needs* or necessities. The closer an item is to a necessity, and the farther the market extends beyond the local community, the greater the potential for success of the business."

Nearby are twenty-five market research questions to which you will need to develop answers. As you read them, remember that good marketing begins with market research. It's wise to put answers to these questions on paper. In chapters six through nine, you will find the information you need to complete your marketing plan.

The Many Hats of Business

If you are like most home business owners, you'll end up doing all the work for awhile, so you may chuckle a bit when you get to the production plan. Still, it's important for you to figure out, in advance, exactly how you are going to get everything done in the time available to you. Stop and think about all the "business hats" you may have to wear for awhile, and be realistic about your ability to do all the work that may be involved. Following is a list of the many different people you may have to be at one time or another:

- **General Manager.** You may have the worrisome job, of course, because you're the decision-maker and risk taker. You also get to make all the business plans.
- **Marketing Manager.** You get the job of figuring out who customers might be, where they are, and how you can sell to them.
- **Advertising Manager.** You work closely with the marketing manager to decide when and where to place ads, and what type to place.
- **Promotion Copywriter.** You get to write the copy that goes into the company's sales brochures, flyers, and catalogs, as well as the press releases.
- **Graphic Artist and Printer Liaison.** Naturally, you must work very closely with both copywriters to achieve the right blend of copy and art on all printer materials, and you get the fun

> *"Market Research can't guarantee your business's success, but it'll help you design, package, and promote your service or product in a way that minimizes your risks and maximizes your potential to turn a profit."*
>
> — *from* Extra Cash For Women *(Writer's Digest Books)* © *1982 by Susan Gillenwater and Virginia Dennis. Reprinted by permission of Writer's Digest Books.*

Notes

Notes

25 Market Research Questions

- What, exactly, am I trying to sell? (If you can't define your product or service in 50 words or less, you will have a hard time trying to publicize or advertise it.)
- Why do I think my product or service will sell?
- Is my product or service something people *want,* or *need?* What are its benefits to buyers?
- If it's something people do not need, why might they want to buy it anyway? (As a gift? For leisure time enjoyment? Business convenience? To save time, money, aggravation? To beautify the home, enrich one's life, or satisfy a nostalgic desire?)
- Who is my ideal customer or client? (Male? Female? Young, middle-aged, older? A white-collar worker? Blue-collar workers? Corporate executive? Homebased businesspeople? Professional or technical worker, homemaker, consumer . . . who, *exactly?*)
- Where do my clients or customers live or work? (In the community, my county, my state, a specific geographic region, or nationwide? World-wide, maybe?)[2]
- How can I connect with these people? What trade or consumer periodicals, organizations, trade shows, directories, or mailing lists are available? What established networks exist for my clients or customers?
- What kind of competition will/do I have . . . locally, regionally, nationally?
- Is my product or service available elsewhere in stores, or by mail? At retail or wholesale prices? Can I compete pricewise?
- Is my product or service newer, better, different from that of my competition? Does it offer higher quality? Longer life? More speed or efficiency? (The very fact that competition exists proves a demand, or at least a need, for what you offer. In the end, your competition may become your marketing strength, provided you work with it and not against it. More about this later.)
- How does my competition publicize and sell? Will the same techniques work for me?
- If there is no competition, why? (Maybe the need for your product or service is being satisfied in some other way, or maybe it simply is not a profitable idea to begin with.)
- Is there currently a strong demand for my product or service? Why? Is it related to the economy? Is demand likely to increase, or decrease, with a change in the economy? Is the current demand a fad, or one that should endure for a long time? If a fad, can I move quickly to capitalize on it before it dies?
- Is the market for my product or service likely to expand slowly, quickly, or not at all? Is my product or service closely tied to some other, similar product or service for which the market could expand — or collapse — very quickly?
- Is my entry into the marketplace more dependent on price than on quality? If so, can I successfully compete in this type of market, given my access to raw materials or supplies, and my ability to purchase them?

---

[2]Sophisticated marketers use demographics available from government sources (such as the Census Bureau), and statistical information compiled by trade associations, publications, and private research firms. Small businesses rarely need to go to such lengths to learn about their market.

- job of pasting everything together for the printer, as well as following through to the completion of each job.
- **Production Manager.** You get to make the work schedules and determine the quality control standards of your product line.
- **Production Worker** (maybe the whole line). You must complete the work on schedule while meeting the above-mentioned quality control standards.
- **Mail List Supervisor.** You're the one who sets up and maintains the company's 3 × 5 card decks or other list addressing systems, adding and deleting names, making address corrections, etc. (Lucky you if you have a computer for this job.)
- **Bulk Mail Expert.** And you get the aggravating job of figuring out the post office requirements for third class bulk mailings.
- **Order Fulfillment Clerk.** You get to process orders and type the necessary order forms and shipping labels.
- **Shipping & Receiving Clerk.** Lucky you! You get to unwrap all incoming packages (office supplies, raw materials, etc.) and also pack for shipment all outgoing orders, plus take a physical inventory at the end of the year for tax purposes.
- **Secretary and Customer Relations Service.** At last, a job that's fun! You get to compose and type the business letters, handle customer complaints, and send away for everything needed by management (such as the resource materials listed in this book).
- **File Clerk.** And you get the job of figuring out what to do with the mountain of paperwork everyone else in the company is generating every day.
- **Bookkeeper.** You get to keep inventory records, and post all the figures to the company's journals and ledgers — after you have set them up, of course.
- **Accountant.** You get to record the company's income, pay the bills, write checks, balance the checkbook, fill out government forms for tax deposits or payments, handle paperwork related to employees, and organize and file all receipts for tax purposes, preparing income statements, profit and loss statements, and possibly doing the annual income tax forms as well.

Whew! That is some list, isn't it? And we haven't yet added family and home responsibilities. Since there is a limit to what any person can do alone, it's wise to acknowledge your limits and plan early to find outside help. Include all possibilities for assistance, and think of creative ways you might pay for it, including bartering of services or products with business acquaintances, sales commission plans for people who might help you market your product or service, and family bribes, if necessary.

You may be thinking that it's impossible for any one person to do all the individual jobs I've just listed; yet, that's exactly what you have to do if you are a sole proprietor with no money to hire outside help. Now do you understand why so many new businesses fail? Too many people start with no idea of all the individual jobs that must be done, let alone the special skills or experience some of them require. As you now see, there are a lot of individual and important jobs to be done, even in the smallest business, and your job now is to decide which ones you are capable of doing — or learning — and which ones you'll have to hire out.

Except for the preparation of tax forms (which I hate and never intend to do), I have learned to do every job on this list. Although I do not have a college education, I've been working and studying all my life. I have always believed I could do exactly what I wanted

---

Get Your Family Involved In Your Business

"Enlisting help from your family can be a real, learning/sharing experience for the whole family," says Darlene Brooks, owner of a homebased drapery company. *"Sometimes we look so hard for help elsewhere, and then find it's right under our nose at home.*

"The trick in getting this help is to turn resentment energy into something positive. Also, keep priorities in mind. Creative people do have a tendency to get so engrossed in their endeavors that it may sometimes appear they don't care about anything else."

— *from* Sharing Barbara's Mail

Notes

> ### Barbara's Business Motto
>
> *Hope for the best, but prepare for the worst . . . and always leave yourself an escape route.*
>
> *Figure out the worst that could happen, then plan how to get out of trouble if it does. That knowledge alone will give you tremendous courage to try new ideas.*

Notes

to do, and so far I've attained every goal I've set for myself. You can do the same.

Remember that there's a how-to book for everything you can imagine, and your self-education can easily be reinforced with free information and assistance from the Small Business Administration and SCORE volunteers, as well as with seminars and workshops or outside consultants. True, it may take the next five years for you to learn what you need to know, but if self-sufficiency is your ultimate goal, what's five years in the scheme of things? Keep reminding yourself of what I emphasized in the beginning of this book: *Each new thing learned broadens your economic base, and each new skill increases your income potential.* Go for it!

Your Financial Plan

This brings me to the eighth element of a good business plan: a financial plan. If you're like me, you hate the idea of having to prepare a written financial plan, but it can be critical to the success of your endeavor, whether financing is being sought or not. You simply must know, in advance, how much everything is going to cost, and where you are going to get the money you need. So many businesses start in a whirlwind of activity only to falter a few months down the line because there is not enough money to keep going.

If you're already in business, it's not difficult to estimate the next year's sales and expenses. But how do you do this if you are just starting? It takes a lot of assumptions, to be sure. For example, when I prepared the financial plan for my newsletter, I "assumed" I could get 5,000 subscribers in short order because I had a large in-house mail list and easy access to my market. I "assumed" I would generate a certain amount of publicity, make a certain number of direct mailings, and place a certain number of ads. All my sales and marketing assumptions, of course, were based on having at least $5,000 capital to work with. My business plan looked terrific on paper, but I could not get the loan I needed for quick growth because I lacked sufficient collateral at that time. So I went home and reworked my plan based on my limited capital.

You are the only one who reasonably can project sales for the first year, and this projection can only be based on what you believe to be the salability of your product or service, and your ability to market it. Much depends, of course, on the time you're going to give your business. If you are a manufacturer, you probably can determine an estimated number of units that might be produced in a year, based on how long it takes to make one, and the number of hours you plan to devote to production each week. By setting a suggested retail price for each unit, you can estimate the revenue that would be generated if certain quantities were sold to certain markets at certain discounts.

If you offer a service, figure out the price you're going to receive for it and estimate the number of customers or clients you could reasonably expect to get as a result of your planned marketing efforts.

If you have difficulty thinking of all the expenses you might possibly incur in the first year, take a look at the checklist of tax deductions and other business expenses in the A-to-Z business section, and use it to prepare an estimated expenses worksheet.

No plan is etched in stone, of course, and all plans have to be changed regularly, based on the records of past experience.

Planning thus becomes more realistic, and easier, the longer you are in business.

"Wise planners take a somewhat conservative view of what is realistic when estimating what can be accomplished with any given level of staff and other resources," notes the Department of Labor in its booklet, *"More Than A Dream."* "It is a disastrous mistake to assume that everything will go according to an ideal utilization of these resources, with no allowance for breakdowns of machinery, delayed deliveries, sickness, and other disturbances of the perfect plan. You must build in a a generous contingency factor in any plan — slippage is part of the human condition."

Slippage? You bet. The most important thing I have learned in my several years as a homebased worker is that nothing is as simple as it seems, everything takes longer than expected, and unexpected happenings are always forcing me to change my well-laid plans. As all home-based workers know, there is so much more to running a business at home than just taking care of the business details involved in it. In addition to business, *there is life,* with its infinite variety of large and small crises — family problems, accidents, illness, death, divorce, fires, flooded basements, and what have you. Experience thus has taught me to build a "disaster element" into all my plans. Given the unpredictability of life in general, and home businesses in particular, it's wise to ask yourself what is the worst possible thing that could happen to your plans. (Remember Murphy's Law.) Once the worst thing has been imagined, you generally can plan around it — or "build in a generous contingency factor," as the Department of Labor suggests. Quick decisions, on the other hand, can be disastrous.

I recall a newspaper publisher who set her subscriber rates according to her print costs. She was working with the least-expensive printer in town and when he went bankrupt, she found that she could not afford the higher rates of other printers. After publishing only a few issues, she was forced out of business. *No matter what your business, always have an option in reserve. Never leave yourself without an escape route.*

Planning a Marketing Strategy

Like Alice in Wonderland, many business beginners lack a sense of direction:

> Alice asks the cat: *"Can you tell me, please, which way I should walk from here?"*
> The cat replies, *"That depends on which way you want to go."*

So it is in marketing. Once you have determined your most likely market, you need a plan — some kind of roadmap - to get your products from here to there. To begin with, don't let the word "marketing" intimidate you. It is just a cumulative word that describes a company's total promotion, advertising, and sales activities. There is a difference between sales and marketing, and you should know it since you probably will have to do both jobs for awhile.

A *salesperson* is concerned with what products he or she has to offer, and which of their features can be emphasized to make the sale. The *person in marketing,* on the other hand, needs to concern himself with what customers want, how many different kinds of customers there are (called his "universe"), and how they first can

Notes

be located, and then convinced of the benefits of the company's products.

"The marketer must know what he wants the customer to perceive," says Herman R. Holtz in his book, *The Secrets of Practical Marketing for Small Business.* "All marketing must then be directed toward creating that image and making it a credible one. Your perception of your business is not worth two cents unless it agrees with the customer's perception. Or perhaps we ought to turn that around and point out that you must somehow create a customer perception that fits the perception you have."[3]

So what you need to concentrate on is not your product or service, per se, but its benefits to users. More important to customers than the quality of your product or the swiftness of your service is how well it's going to satisfy their needs or desires. Or, as one writer said in a marketing article, "People buy drills because they want holes."

In an article in *Publishers Weekly,* Leonard Felder explained how marketing concepts have changed in recent years. In the old days, he pointed out, all you had to do was build a better mousetrap, then go out and sell it. Now, he says, "Any old mousetrap can catch mice. But consumers want a silent unseen trap that leaves no mess and won't hurt domestic animals; they want, in other words, not only relief from mice, but also safety, cleanliness, convenience, and peace of mind." In short, Felder explains, " . . . the goal of selling mousetraps has now been replaced by the goal of marketing a service to customers who need safe, clean, and convenient protection from mice." If you are going to bring in the dollars from a business today, you need to apply this kind of thinking to every product or service you sell.

Sophisticated marketers talk in terms of "positioning" their product, but you don't have to be sophisticated to understand and use this concept, which is illustrated in the following examples:

- When the J. C. Penney Company decided to quit selling appliances, automotive parts, lawn and garden supplies, paint, fabric, and certain hardware items, they announced they would spend one billion dollars in the next five years to reposition 450 of their largest stores as apparel and home furnishing stores.
- The traditional cedar chest (often called the "hope" chest) was falling out of favor with young brides a few years back. So the Lane Company began to call its products "love chests," and positioned itself as "the company that makes furniture for lovers."
- A candymaker who began with a mailing to 75 friends on his Christmas card list is now generating candy sales of more than a million dollars a year. Positioning in the marketplace was his key to success. Instead of selling candy in food and gourmet shops, where it would be expensive in relation to other items being sold, he sells it in fine gift shops, where it is inexpensive when compared to other items being sold. (In addition, it usually is the only edible in the shop.)

What you call a product can have a lot to do with how well it's going to sell, and sometimes a marketing problem is not with the product itself, but with its market. It is just as easy to sell the right thing to the wrong market as it is to sell the wrong thing

---

[3]© 1982 by Herman R. Holtz. Used by permission from Prentice-Hall, Inc.

to the right market. Through market research and careful planning, however, one can anticipate problems like this and figure out solutions.

Remember that no product can be all things to all people, and if you do not deliberately position your product — or your business — you may find that it has been positioned by circumstances you do not control, and not always to your advantage.

One way to position products is to give them a special name or identity. If you are an artist, for instance, ask yourself whether you're selling "fine art," "art prints," "Early American Primitives," or "folk paintings." The market most likely to buy from you can then be determined.

Sometimes a motto can help position a business, such as "A communications network for homebased businesses," or "Gifts for the Young at Heart." Slogans that capture the essence of a business can be particularly effective when they point to an unfilled niche in the market or emphasize things that are lacking in a competitor's product, as in "the only soap that floats."

Speaking of competitors, let me stress here that one of the smartest marketing moves you can make is to work with your competitors, not against them. Donald Moore, a publisher in England, says it best: "Your competitor as an enemy will give you nothing but competition; as a friend, he will give you information you can obtain in no other way. Everyone running a business should be keen to meet as many men and women in the same field of endeavour as can possibly be managed."

As a leader in the home business industry, I have worked very closely with my competitors for years and, in fact, credit much of my success to their support of my work. A trend I see developing, particularly in the crafts industry, is that many small mail-order sellers and publishers are banding together with their competition to sell a variety of products and publications through cooperative display ads, direct mailings, and marketing cooperatives.

For example, Colleen Bergman wanted to launch a magazine for doll lovers. She knew she could not afford to do it alone, so she invited a number of her competitors in the doll world to work with her to create *The Cloth Doll,* a "cooperative magazine," and an entirely new idea in publishing. Although Colleen and her husband own the magazine, advertisers who work with them can advertise at low rates, and they are also invited to write promotional feature articles about their businesses. Unlike most magazine editors, Colleen does not have to pay for such articles, advertisers get additional publicity, and everyone's business grows as a result. Because advertisers worked as hard as the Bergmans to promote the magazine, its circulation quickly rose to 5,000 after only a few issues — remarkable growth for a magazine which started on a shoestring budget.

Colleen also got the bright idea of creating a full-page cooperative ad to be run in *Crafts,* the country's most popular how-to magazine. By signing a specially-negotiated, 12-month advertising contract, Colleen was able to obtain ad space at more economical rates. Each ad included several individual ads artistically arranged on the page to make it look like one major promotion. (See illustration.) Advertisers were billed by Colleen according to the space occupied by their ads. Although *Crafts* magazine no longer offers this type of cooperative ad arrangement, this is an idea that might work for other groups of sellers or advertisers, in other magazines. The key

---

Marketing Tip

If you have a particularly tough marketing problem, or just need some help with your market research, contact a local college or university business school. Sometimes the students of a marketing class — under the direction of a professor and possibly in cooperation with the Small Business Administration — can provide marketing research assistance that would otherwise cost thousands of dollars. Marketing assistance is also available to you at no charge through SBA offices around the country.

Notes

is to first find and organize a willing group of "competitors" with small advertising budgets, then approach selected magazines and try to negotiate a deal. Ad rates are not written in blood. Money is the bottom line and most advertising managers will "talk turkey" with a good advertising prospect.

Example of one of the full-page cooperative ads placed by The Cloth Doll *magazine (shown in reduced size). Although this type of ad is uncommon (and no longer accepted by* Crafts *magazine where it was originally placed), it illustrates a concept that might work in certain periodicals, especially those published by individuals. Their ad policies are apt to be less rigid than those of major consumer magazines.*

Notes

Here are additional things to consider as you plan your marketing strategy:

- What can you do to stand out in the crowd? Is there a niche your competition has failed to fill? Can you, perhaps, become a specialist in an area where there are many generalists? Specialization is an important marketing key today.
- What is your competition's marketing strategy? How are they advertising and promoting themselves? What consumer benefits do they stress? What can you offer, say, or do that they can't? How might you work with your competition to strengthen the overall market for your product or service?
- Is your competition overlooking a segment of the market you can reach easily? Larger companies often ignore smaller markets because they are not worth their time and trouble, but such markets may be perfect for the small, homebased business owner. This is particularly true in the mail order field.

- What is your target audience? You can't sell to everyone, so don't try. Determine the most profitable market and concentrate on reaching it first. Then branch out to other markets as time and money allow.
- What are you really trying to accomplish with your advertising and promotion? Do you want to strengthen your professional image locally or nationally? Do you want orders with cash up front, sales leads, or are you building a mailing list so you can sell by direct mail?
- Are you always going to be the main salesperson in your business? Do you plan eventually to exhibit at trade shows or use sales representatives to crack specific wholesale markets? If so, plan your strategy with this goal in mind.

"A sound marketing plan," says one marketing expert, "is a prophecy of coming events. It contains the specific steps designed to make the prophecy come true." Like a business plan, a marketing plan will always be changing, based on sales results and the results of any special tests you may run. Marketing is something you must do throughout the entire life of your business, so don't think you can rest on your laurels once you have come up with a good marketing plan. It may work beautifully – for awhile. But you cannot expect to stay ahead of your competition unless you constantly test new markets, new marketing methods, and new advertising and promotional ideas. Nothing stays the same, least of all business, so be aware of changes taking place which may affect your business. The best way to do this, of course, is to subscribe to a variety of periodicals related to your field, and join professional organizations so you can meet and network with your competition and customers.

In time, you may find it necessary to change your prices, your product or business name, your packaging, designs or colors, your marketing outlets, the function of your product or service, even the entire image or personality of your business. You will know when it's time to make changes, too, because your sales will level off or begin to drop for no apparent reason. By doing a little planning before the worst happens, you'll be prepared to take off in a new and more profitable direction very quickly.

For more information on this topic, see the free SBA aid, "Planning and Goal Setting for Small Business."

Time Management

Time management, like money management, requires an awareness of how much one has to spend. Although it takes time to plan how to spend time, such planning generally saves more time than it takes. That's because disorganization wastes time. Organization saves it.

The first principle of time management is to do one thing at a time, and finish it before starting another. That's fine if you happen to be talking about task consolidation, but all the successful businesspeople I know say their time-management secret is to do *two* things at once. Certainly that's my secret. Take this book, for instance. It has been a start-and-stop job from its very beginning. Write a while; stop and do mail for a day. Write a while; then go out of town for a week of workshops. Write a while; then stop to get out a newsletter, write a column, handle important correspondence. At any given moment in the daily life of my diversified home business, I am apt to be juggling a dozen different jobs at once.

The time which we have at our disposal every day is elastic. The passions that we feel expand it, those that we inspire contract it; and habit fills up what remains.

— *from* Within a Budding Grove

Notes

Ideally, it would be terrific to have to think about only one of them at a time, but so often one thing is dependent upon another, and what you do in one area automatically requires some kind of counter-action in another area of the business. (Anyone who has a business knows exactly what I'm talking about. The rest of you will learn soon enough.)

Doing two things at once may sound difficult, but each of us does it all the time. For instance, I always work on the next day's meals as I am fixing the evening meal. I always work at something in the kitchen if a friend calls me, and at my desk, during a business conversation (if the phone call is a chatty one requiring little concentration). In fact, this is about the only time my desk ever gets dusted or organized. I never fold laundry during the day, but during the evening, while watching the news; and when I do watch TV, I have reading material nearby for commercials. I pay bills in the morning while waiting for my husband to come to the table, put last night's dishes away while the eggs are boiling, carry out the garbage when I walk the dog, throw in laundry on my coffee break, and on and on.

As homebased workers, each of us can easily find ourselves in the position of rushing to complete a job or meet a deadline while also preparing to entertain guests for the weekend. In airports or in a doctor's office, we may wait, but we may also be doing business reading or planning. The more time we need for our business, the more creative we become in our attempts to save it by doing two things at once.

"We all have 24 hours a day," says Dottie Walters, a popular author, speaker, and owner of a million-dollar advertising firm. "Most people waste much time. Do all the things in one direction together," she advises. Dottie is one of the busiest and most productive people I know, and if anyone knows about task consolidation, she does. She also practices the advice given by Kipling, who said, "Fill every unforgiving minute with 60 seconds worth of distance run."

To do this, you have to look at everything you do — production, paperwork, mail handling, etc. — with an eye to grouping certain jobs which require similar physical movements, tools, supplies, or a particular mindset. You lose time each time you have to change mental gears or physical position, so any time you can do a large block of work that takes a certain kind of mental concentration or physical movement, you will save time.

If you make a product, you will find that you'll greatly increase output if you do the same step on perhaps two dozen items at a time, then move on to the second step and do that on those same items, etc. For example, imagine that you're making a sawed-out, hand-painted toy. First you would transfer the pattern to the wood for 24 items, then cut out (saw) 24 items, then sand them, and so on. If your painted design involved six colors of paint, you'd add the first color to 24 items, then the second color, and so on. *Every unnecessary movement you can eliminate will save time and speed production.*

Production techniques like this can be applied to every part of our daily and business lives, resulting in the saving of many precious minutes each day that can be put to better use. Start thinking now about things you can do to give yourself the extra hours you are going to need for your business.

Many people waste time in handling paperwork and mail, so here are a few tips on how to be the most productive in this area. If you are putting out a batch of mail that involves say, a letter, a two-page, stapled report, and possibly other insertions as well, you'll waste a lot of time if you do each "package" as one unit. Instead, collate all the two-page reports laying them crossways in a pile to separate each unit. Then go back and *staple* all the reports; then go back and *fold* all the reports. Next, fold all the letters. Then, lay all folded materials and other insertions in stacks in the order in which they are to go in the envelopes, and collate the individual packets, laying them crossways in stacks to keep units separate from one another. Finally, insert those packets into envelopes.

Take about ten business-size envelopes and "ruffle" them out to the right so you can see about ⅛″ of the flap end of each envelope, a movement you might make if you were going to count them easily. Now, holding these envelopes in your left hand (reverse everything if you're left-handed), use your right hand to pick up a packet of material to be inserted into the envelope. Now, with the little finger of your right hand, flick the flap of the envelope open and, as the hand starts the downward swing, insert the packet of material into the envelope (all the while holding the other envelopes in position beneath). Drop the stuffed envelope off to the right with envelope flap still in the up position — and still holding the rest of the envelopes in your left hand in their original position — and repeat the process until you have all envelopes stuffed. Then stack the stuffed envelopes in their original envelope box or similar container, flaps up. This takes a bit of practice, but if you ever have to mail several hundred pieces (or thousands, as we have done so many times), you'll find that this little trick will save you countless hours.

Sealing the envelopes can be done in quantity, as follows: lay the stuffed envelopes, flaps up, one on top of the other, until only the glue area of each envelope's edge is showing. Now hold the flaps down flat with the fingers of one hand while taking a wet pastry brush or sponge in the other, and lightly coat the entire glue surface of all envelopes in a couple of quick movements. Now — quickly, before the glue starts to dry – turn down the flap of the first envelope on the pile and with the left hand flick it away from the rest of the stack, then press down the flap of the next envelope, flick it away, and so on until all envelopes are sealed. Then pick up all packets and give them an extra press to insure a good seal. You can work with more than ten envelopes at a time once you get the hang of it. I can assure you that this is one of the greatest time-savers you ever will discover in the handling of mail in quantity.

Many people waste time in handling their daily mail, doing a little bit every day just to "get it out of the way." This can be a real time-waster, especially if your mail-handling job involves numerous operations, as ours does. For instance, we have inquiries for catalogs, we have orders for a variety of products, plus subscriptions, renewals, "special handling mail," and so on. Each step of our mail-handling operation requires a different type of handling, and we have found that we can save at least one whole morning a week by doing mail only two or three days a week, instead of piecemeal, five days a week. All book orders are handled at once, then all inquiries, then all subscriptions, etc. The idea behind this is simple: Whenever you can do twenty or thirty things at a time, versus five or six, you'll save time because you are incorporating production-line techniques into your work schedule. (Your customers will never notice this short delay in handling orders; in fact, ours frequently compliment us on our speedy service.)

People who have learned to control time, instead of letting time control them, are generally organized, self-disciplined workers.

Tips on Time
How to find it, save it, use it more efficiently

- *Try keeping a time sheet for awhile so you can see exactly what percentage of your time is being spent on personal and business endeavors; then seek ways to cluster your various jobs to save time.*

- *Organize your home and your work space. You waste time every time you look for something that isn't where it ought to be. In getting organized, don't ask where to put something; ask how you plan to use it. This will suggest where to put it. If you don't need it, throw it away.*

- *Learn to do two things at a time, and develop production techniques in all your routine jobs.*

- *Time represents money to any businessperson, so don't give it away by selling your products or services too cheaply. And be selective in giving time and advice to others who would "pick your brain" once you have become successful in a given area of endeavor.*

- *Don't let family and friends steal your time, either. Be firm about having some private time for yourself, and set specific times for family activities or visits with friends.*

- *Establish a regular working schedule. Start work at the same time each day. Learn to leave business behind at the end of your working day, so you can enjoy a personal life, too.*

- *Change your attitude about time. Plan ahead. Make lists. Study to improve skills and speed work processes. Move faster, sleep less. In short, use the time you do have in the most productive way possible . . . and quit wasting time talking about your lack of time.*

Notes

"Keeping track of time on a daily basis is a form of self-discipline," says Ambrose J. Rouble, a certified public accountant who works with many small business owners. "If you work 10–12 hours a day and don't seem to accomplish anything, try to record how you spend your days. Then analyze the information."

Keeping track of your time is good advice even if you feel you are accomplishing a lot. You can't begin to save time if you don't know how you're spending (wasting) it, and a written record will clearly show this. (It's the same principle as noting everything you eat when you are on a diet, to see where all those extra calories and pounds are coming from.)

A record of how you spend your time will help you to get organized, and this could be essential to your success in business. "You cannot afford not to be organized to the utmost," says Ciya Stuart, a homebased business consultant who often writes and lectures on time management. "Being based at home makes it doubly hard to keep personal and business calls, letters, papers, files, inventory, and belongings separate and organized. Without a clearly thought out system of space allocation and time allocation, it is insidiously easy to find that you are always working, or never working, or working all the time and feeling that you are never working. Clear parameters are essential to your business productivity and mental health."

Being organized is not the same as being neat, by the way. Years ago, one of my favorite bosses, then co-owner of a direct mail advertising firm in Chicago, had a desk I couldn't believe. It was always loaded with foot-high stacks of one kind of paper or another, and I longed to organize it. But on my first day in the office, Bob warned me sharply, "Don't ever touch a thing on my desk. It may look a mess, but I know where everything is." And he did. Often when I would ask him for a certain file, he'd run his fingers down a stack of material and, to my astonishment, pull out exactly what I needed.

Now I think I know why Bob worked this way. Out of sight, out of mind. I worry about things I can't see, and if I file something that requires any kind of later action, I forget about it because I have too many things on my mind all the time. So the best way for me to remember what has to be done is to actually see the work stacked somewhere, begging my attention. Thus, my desk is always surrounded by groups of manila file folders, metal sorting trays, boxes, and so on. It doesn't look beautiful, but I know where everything is, and it saves me a lot of filing time besides.

Time management experts always advise, "make lists," and busy, organized people do tend to be list-makers. As a list-maker myself, I know this saves not only time, but mental anguish. Often, without a list, you may feel there is so much to do you can't possibly handle all of it. Yet, when a list is made, it seems less impossible. It's a good idea to start each day with a list of things you want to accomplish — small daily goals — but since you seldom will get everything done on the day you have planned, be sure to put the most important things at the top of the list.

In setting priorities on the things to be done, note that the 80/20 rule will apply. In mail order, this rule relates to the fact that 20% of one's customers generally account for 80% of one's business. In an office, it means that 20% of the people do 80% of the work, and, in matters of time, it means that 20% of what you do will probably yield 80% of the results. So be sure you identify — and place uppermost on your list — the 20% of the work that's the most important to your business or personal life. In addition to being time-efficient, lists of things to be done are great spirit-lifters. The very act of scratching off each task as it is completed gives one the sense of accomplishing yet another small goal. It's little things like this that keep us going when the pressures of business tend to pull us down.

If, after all your planning, you still feel there are not enough hours in a day, consider this thought. There are 24 hours in a day, and even if we must work 8 hours at a job, and sleep still another 8 hours, that still leaves 8 hours a day for other things — *or* one-third of our lives. While some people may choose to spend this time allotment on such things as television, reading, sports, family activities, etc., others invest it by starting a home business. And when even more time is needed, some people simply decide to sleep less.

In his book, *Sleep Less, Live More,* Everett Mattlin points out that it never has been proven that our bodies require eight hours of sleep to regenerate cells and rebuild energy. As one who has suffered from insomnia for years, due mainly to an over-stimulated mind, I know for a fact that I can perform as well on four hours' sleep as most people can on eight or nine. In fact, only last night I lay awake until 5:30 a.m., having made the mistake of starting a mind-stimulating book at 10 p.m. But I didn't let my insomnia worry me. Instead, I used this quiet time to make plans, jotted notes on the pad I always keep at my bedside, and actually solved a problem that had been bothering me for weeks. When I got out of bed at 8:30 to start the day, I told myself that I felt fine, and sure enough I did, after a good breakfast and an hour or so of moving about. In the end, it is the mind, not the body, that rules here.

Thus, if you can find no time at all in your busy life, simply manufacture a couple hours a day by sleeping two hours less each night. The Mattlin book explains how to do this (and emphasizes the importance of gaining these two extra hours gradually, over an extended period of time).

Oh, yes. The book that kept me awake all night was by a new writer friend, Dennis E. Hensley, who says he never sleeps more than six hours a night, and is at his most productive from 10 p.m. to 2 a.m., the time when he does most of his writing. Despite all the demands upon his time, he has found time to become a professional writer. In the space of only 15 years, he's written several books and more than 1,500 articles, and is active as a lecturer, teacher, publicist, businessman, church deacon, husband, and father.

Says Dennis, "That's probably why today I don't have a lot of sympathy for people who tell me, 'I always wanted to be a writer, but with all my other responsibilities there just wasn't any time to write.' " His response to such remarks is usually, "How badly did you *want* to be a writer?" One does not have to aspire to this profession to get the point Dennis is making: *If you really want to do something, you'll find time to do it.* And as Dennis also reminds us, time *is* running out for all of us. "Death is life's only example of fair play: everyone is guaranteed one death and no one is overlooked. The years leading up to that final moment should be as active and as dignified as we choose for them to be."[4]

---

[4]from *Staying Ahead of Time,* by Dennis E. Hensley. © 1981–1982, The Research & Review Service of America. Used by permission.

An A-to-Z "Crash Course" In Business Basics

THIS HANDY BOOK-WITHIN-A-BOOK will enable you to find answers to questions or business problems quickly, as they arise.

Information is presented by topic, in alphabetical order (see table of contents on page 77). You can check the index when you need specific information on a particular topic.

Notes

THE INFORMATION IN THIS BOOK — and the following section in particular — does not constitute legal advice. Presented, however, is reliable information, along with the author's opinions and viewpoints as a homebased business owner. For your added assurance, the following individuals, each a specialist in his or her own field, have read the material related to their field, and verified it for accuracy of facts and information presented at the time of this edition's printing. Any changes they may have suggested were incorporated into the text.

- Julian Block, author of *Julian Block's Guide to Year-Round Tax Savings,* is a former IRS agent and nationally-known authority on tax-saving methods. He covers taxes for Prentice-Hall Information Services in Paramus, NJ, and practices law in Larchmont, New York.

- Bernard Kamoroff, CPA, is the author of *Small-Time Operator* and owner of Bell Springs Publishing in Laytonville, CA. He lectures occasionally at the University of California.

- Mary Helen Sears has been in private law practice in Washington, DC since 1961. A principal in Irons & Sears, her practice is mainly devoted to patents, copyrights, trademarks, and related matters.

- Edward F. Hughes, a specialist in labor law, is staff attorney at The Center on National Labor Policy, Inc. in North Springfield, Virginia.

- Don H. Alexander, author of *How to Borrow Money From A Bank,* is in commercial lending at a Seattle bank, and owner of DHA & Associates, a family-operated publishing company.

- Mary S. Kaufmann, CLU, is the owner of MSK Insurance Consultants, an independent insurance agency in Ft. Collins, Colorado. The agency specializes in life, health, and business insurance. Mary has been teaching classes on insurance and financial planning for the past four years.

Once again . . . a reminder that all books and other resources mentioned in the text are fully detailed in the resource chapter of this book, which includes how-to-order information.

Author's Cautionary Note

This section of *Homemade Money* includes important information on many legal and technical topics, including taxes and accounting. I have been advised that it might be better for a book of this nature to omit all discussion of taxes, in particular, simply because tax laws change so often and so quickly. Yet to do so would be lax, in my opinion, because a general understanding of this area is critical to the financial success of any business, and homebased businesses in particular. If I did not at least acquaint my readers with these topics, some of them might never take the necessary steps to learn more about them.

Although my experts (named on the preceding page) have read and approved material related to their respective fields, it should be stressed that they did so with the understanding that some information could be incorrect or out of date by the time this edition of *Homemade Money* is printed. State and federal laws discussed in this book could change at any time.

As I see it, however, this in no way detracts from the value of the information you are about to receive because (1) it serves to familiarize you with important areas of concern to homebased business owners, and (2) it gives you enough information to enable you to ask the right questions when you meet with your own tax adviser, accountant, or other professional. I do ask, however, that you read and accept all the technical and legal information in this chapter with the proverbial grain of salt, and remember to double-check it with your own professional adviser before making an important business decision based on this information.

Table of Contents
A-to-Z Business Basics

Accountant (Also see "Bookkeeper.")

Contrary to the usual advice given to all new businesspeople, an accountant is not needed at the beginning of a business *if* the business is small and one is capable of setting up the necessary record-keeping system to operate it. But everyone needs an accountant, or at least a highly qualified tax preparer, when tax time rolls around. Be sure to look for someone who is thoroughly familiar with the many special deductions to which a home-business owner is entitled. Not every accountant is comfortable in this area.

Many business novices hire accountants when they actually need bookkeepers. Although accountants know how to do bookkeeping, they are not bookkeepers. Their primary function is to analyze your books and prepare tax returns based on the figures in them. In the process, however, they often perform other important jobs as well. In truth, a good accountant can be something of a management consultant for you, helping you to understand your total financial picture and make wise decisions in all areas of your business.

For instance, an accountant will give you advice on whether or not to purchase equipment, hire employees vs. independent contractors, take on a partner, or incorporate your business. If you need a business loan, an accountant can prepare the necessary financial reports in a way that will show your business in the most favorable light. He or she can also help you plan strategic financial moves that will save or defer taxes each year, and represent you should the IRS audit your return. And when you do reach the point of hiring employees, even if it's just your spouse or children, an accountant will take the hassle out of all those aggravating government tax forms and quarterly reports and perhaps save you tax dollars.

Pick an accountant the way you would select a doctor or lawyer; ask around. Get recommendations from other business owners like yourself, as well as from your banker or lawyer if you have one. Like doctors, no two accountants are the same, and some know more than others about certain fields like home business. Before you finally pick an accountant, ask whether you can come in for a short, no-charge discussion of how he or she can help you in your business. Don't hesitate to ask the accountant to furnish the names of clients who are in financial brackets and occupations similar to yours. Also ask about the firm's fee structure, because there are several ways to bill for services.

C.P.A. (Certified Public Accountant). Not all accountants are certified. A CPA is licensed by the state after having passed an exam given by the American Institute of Certified Public Accountants on completion of four years of college and one to two years on-the-job training. In view of this extra education, CPAs charge more than non-certified accountants and are more likely to specialize in larger businesses. Although you may prefer to use a CPA, the average small home business does not require one. More important than the title is the fact that the accountant you pick should have knowledge of your particular occupation or type of business, and be willing to work with you.

Tax Preparers. Tax preparers generally work only with the figures a taxpayer gives them. As a rule, they are not trained to handle the more complicated tax reports of homebusiness owners. Unless you are knowledgeable about every business deduction to which you're entitled, and can prepare all the necessary figures for

Notes

your annual tax return, you'll be wise to use an accountant, not a tax preparer. (You'll probably save more money in taxes than you'll spend for the accountant's fee, which is tax deductible, just the same as your payment for this book.)

Attorneys/Lawyers

How to Get Along Without Them for Awhile. Contrary to popular belief, you may not need a lawyer to start a simple home business. Many small businesses have never used a lawyer, and never intend to. Of course, if you need someone to hold your hand through the start-up process, a lawyer will be happy to do it, while giving you a lot of fast answers to your questions. But with a book like this, you're getting the same thing for a lot less money.

Don't forget that additional support is available to you from other sources, such as your local Chamber of Commerce, City Hall, and the library, as well as from SBA offices and SCORE volunteers who offer free business consultations. (See Small Business Administration in the resource chapter.)

As your business grows, and various legal questions come to mind, you'll often be able to answer them yourself through a study of books and periodicals like those described in this book's resource chapter. Your library has others.

Lawyers: When you really need them. There are certain times when you should hire a lawyer, even if you're strapped for funds, because the alternative might cost far more than your legal fees.

To cite an obvious example, if you lack a good layman's understanding of the kind of legal language normally found in contracts, it could be an expensive mistake to sign one without the advice of legal counsel. Of particular concern should be long-term agreements, such as partnerships, cooperatives, exclusive dealer or distributor agreements, licensing or franchise arrangements, and royalty contracts. And *never* purchase property or buy a business without the guidance of a lawyer who will make sure you're not placing yourself in an uncomfortable legal or tax situation. (Of course, your accountant or CPA can also advise you on tax matters. Not all lawyers are tax experts, just as all tax lawyers are not authorities on contract law.)

Do you need a lawyer to incorporate your business? Legally, no; for peace of mind, yes. Books in the library may give you the how-to-steps to set up your own corporation, but the time you spend trying to figure everything out will take valuable time away from your business. If you can afford to incorporate, you ought to be able to afford an attorney to take care of the matter for you.

At times, your business may require the help of an attorney who specializes in a particular field, such as taxes, patents, copyrights or trademarks. But before you hire such expensive experts, do a little studying of available self-help guides because one book could save you a small fortune in legal fees. *Remember that time is money in a lawyer's office,* and you'll save a lot of both if you go prepared. Try to gain a complete understanding of your situation or problem, be able to clearly explain it to your lawyer, and know which questions to ask.

Note: You do *not* need a copyright lawyer, or any lawyer for that matter, to get a copyright. Some business novices have paid attorneys $100 to do something they can easily do themselves for just $10: fill out a copyright application form. For more information, see "Copyrights" elsewhere in this section.

Lawyers: How to "shop" for one. As with accountants, one "shops" for a lawyer by asking for recommendations from friends or business acquaintances, including one's accountant or banker. If you have neither, ask for a recommendation from any other business professional you know, and whose advice you trust, including your doctor, dentist, or minister. What you should be looking for is a good, low-cost attorney with some experience in business law. When you think you've found one, be sure to ask about his fee structure before you go in for a visit. In fact, ask if a free, initial consultation is offered.

When you find an affordable attorney you like — and one you'd like to consult with more often — discuss a retainer arrangement. On this basis, you could get a lot more advice for your money. For instance, in a newspaper article written by a lawyer,[1] I found these guidelines: A $100 retainer, paid in advance, might entitle a person to two, 15-minute calls per month; two 30-minute in-person consultations per year, and the preparation of one short legal document each year. The same article emphasized that a good, low-cost lawyer would accept this kind of deal, and if the offer was rejected, it simply meant that you weren't dealing with a low-cost lawyer.

For more information, see H.A.L.T., a non-profit organization which offers a free manual, "Shopping For A Lawyer" as part of its membership benefits.

Automobile, Business Use of

All business-related travel is tax-deductible. *Document this information with a diary.* Note the odometer reading at the beginning and end of each year, and log each business-related trip you make, including visits to the bank, post office, printer, office supply store, sales calls, delivery trips, travel to speaking engagements or workshops, trips to the newspaper to place an ad, appointments with clients, and so on. Your mileage-log book should include an explanation of where you've gone on each trip plus a notation of the odometer reading before and afterwards. If you make a lot of trips to the same place, such as the post office or printer's, you could get a mileage reading on the first round-trip and simply multiply that figure times the number of trips made each year. (But keep a record of each trip.)

One way to deduct business-related car expenses is to use a mileage allowance. For the tax year 1988, the allowance is 24¢ per mile up to 15,000 miles per year and 60,000 miles per car. Beyond these limits, the per-mile deduction is only 11 cents per mile. But you likely will find that your car deduction will be much larger if you calculate on a different and legally acceptable method: basis of total operating costs. In this case, you'd add up all expenses for the year, including gas, oil, supplies, repairs, maintenance, parking and tolls, towing, washing, tires, garage expenses, license tags, inspection fees, taxes, insurance, depreciation, even Motor Club memberships. Then take the total miles driven for business and divide that figure by total miles driven for the year to get a percentage of business use. Multiply your total car costs by this percentage figure

---

[1]From *The Goodfellow Review*, "Do Crafts Artists Need Legal Advice?" by Bill Rowen, an attorney practicing in Oakland, California.

Notes

to get your business-related, tax-deductible automobile expenses for the year. (Check this point with an accountant to make sure you're getting the highest deduction allowed by law.)

Bad Checks, How to Avoid Them (Also see "Collection Techniques.")

If you have a mail order business and you receive a check that looks suspicious, remember that you have thirty days' time in which to ship the order without violating FTC rulings. Thus, you may wish to deposit the check, wait a couple of weeks (if a check is going to bounce, you'll know it by then), and then ship the order. (Some mail order businesses follow this procedure as a matter of general practice, viewing all personal checks as "suspicious.")

If the check is large, and you're doubtful about it for any reason, you can also call the bank that issued the check and ask if there are sufficient funds in the account to cover it. (Get the bank's phone number by dialing the bank's area code and 555-1212, which is Long Distance Information.)

In taking checks from buyers at consumer fairs or shows, always ask to see identification and check it. Look at the pictures on driver's licenses, jot down license numbers on checks, and make sure each check has an address and telephone number on it. You might also ask to see a credit card and jot down the number and card name.

What else might merit your attention? We do not like checks with signatures we can't decipher, nor those without a printed address or sequence number, although such checks are common and certainly legal. (Note: Experts say that checks with sequence numbers below 300 are more likely to bounce than those with higher numbers.)

For all our caution with checks, several years' experience as a mail-order bookseller has proven that the checks which make us suspicious are almost never bad. In fact, a study of one year's records revealed that, of 2,695 checks deposited, only eight were bad, and two of them were for amounts of 50¢ and $1.00, believe it or not. All but five checks cleared the bank when they were redeposited.

Bartering

If you trade services or products for personal use, the IRS code requires that the value of that trade be declared as taxable income. This is a tricky area. Best to check with a qualified tax adviser.

Better Business Bureau

You can give your business added credibility by registering it with your local Better Business Bureau. As long as you have a license for your business, they will be happy to register your company. All that's involved is the completion of a simple questionnaire, to which you may wish to attach copies of customer testimonials, your promotional literature, and any favorable publicity you've received. Then, if people should inquire about you, the BBB can say, "Yes, they're registered; we've had no complaints about them." A good reference, indeed.

Note: Registration does *not* entitle you to use the name of the BBB in your advertising copy.

Bonded Service

Bonding is a form of insurance you buy to give your customers peace of mind — assurance that you are trustworthy and reliable, and that they're fully protected against loss. Some services can be sold more easily if they're bonded, such as "house-sitting" or vacation services where one would have access into someone's home during their absence. Another example would be a delivery service that normally handles valuable documents or expensive objects — jewelry, art, etc., or possibly a photographer who is taking pictures for insurance purposes.

Bonding companies are listed in the Yellow Pages. Call one of them for more information about bonding procedures and costs.

Bookkeeper (Also see "Recordkeeping.")

Someone once said that " . . . the difference between an accountant and a bookkeeper is a sizable figure." The primary job of a bookkeeper is to post all business transactions to a company's journals and ledgers. Some small business owners consult with bookkeepers for help in setting up their books while others hire them to do all their bookkeeping. However, Bernard Kamoroff, a CPA and author of *Small Time Operator,* says that all business owners should keep their own books for at least a year, just to learn how to read and use the books once they've been posted.

Most small home businesses use single-entry bookkeeping systems which keep paperwork, figurework, and headaches to a minimum while still providing all the information one needs to properly manage a business and prepare tax returns. The above-mentioned book takes the mystery out of bookkeeping and accounting and clearly shows you how to set up and maintain your own books, including all the ledgers and worksheets you'll need for a year.

You may also want to investigate commercial bookkeeping systems such as the *Dome Simplified Monthly,* available in office supply stores.

Business Cards (Also see "Telephone, Use of Personal Phone for Business.")

Don't skimp on this important promotional tool. An originally-designed card can speak volumes about you and the quality of your business, product, or service. Its cost is always justified. The kind and color of card stock you select, the ink, the art work — all these things convey to your customer or client an image of you and your business. Make sure you convey the image you want them to have.

Standard-sized cards are most likely to be saved in regular business card files, but oversized cards may have their place, particularly when they serve a functional purpose. Some people use oversized cards so they can print a map on the back to direct customers to their out-of-the-way business; others suggest that their card can double as a bookmark. Folded cards may also be appropriate, and impressive, especially if you want to include more than the usual amount of information about you or your business. In fact, this kind of card can become a mini-brochure.

In preparing the information for your card, remember to include your name as well as the business name, plus a line that describes your business specialty, your products, or your service. Some people use their motto. I'm reminded of the line on a chimneysweep's card:

"Satisfaction guaranteed or double your soot back!" If you list your telephone number, don't forget to include the area code. Also add the zip code to your address. Not everyone who ends up with your card will live in your area.

Business Checking Account

Do *not* use your personal checking account to conduct the transactions of your business. A separate, business checking account is essential for accurate recordkeeping and *substantiation of business deductions for tax purposes.*

You can save money if you select your business bank with care because each financial institution has a different way of charging for services. Call several banks in your area and prepare a worksheet that answers the following questions, then fictionalize a typical month's banking activity. You'll be amazed by the wide variation in monthly bank charges.

- Is there a charge for *each deposit made?*
- Is there a charge for *each check deposited?* (Some banks make a charge for each deposit, while others charge for each out-of-state check deposited — very costly for mail order businesses.)
- Is there a charge for *each check written,* or are checks purchased in quantity for a flat fee?
- Is there a charge for *bounced checks?* (Some banks charge $10.00 per check.)
- Is *interest* paid on the checking account balance?

Another consideration, especially if you're dealing with a savings and loan institution that offers checking accounts, is whether the S&L will provide a line of credit or a business loan, should you need it. (The S&L that has our business account offers neither service.) If you plan to offer your customers a bank card charge service, also find out if the bank or S&L offers this service. Not all do.

A few check-writing tips: If your checking account pays interest, hang on to your money as long as possible. Bills paid later in the week take longer to clear because of the weekend.

Never type checks using a self-correcting typewriter ribbon because this kind of ink can be lifted off the paper. In the wrong hands, a check could be written for a larger amount.

When writing the dollar amount of a check, always place figures close to the printed dollar sign on the check to make it impossible for anyone to add another figure between your figure and the dollar sign.

EXAMPLE:　$9.85 _____　$　9.85 _____

　　　　　　　(Correct)　　　　(Dangerous)

When spelling out the dollar amount on the second line of a check, take the same kind of precaution, filling the total space on the line. EXAMPLE:

Nine and 85/100******************* Dollars

Business Deductions Checklist for Home Business Owners

NOTE: The tax laws are constantly changing, so be sure to verify annually
the following deductible items with an accountant or other tax authority.

How many of the following deductions have you been overlooking? (These are in addition to the deductible expenses on the other checklist elsewhere in this section, and the deductions normally allowed on your personal income tax report.)

☐ Accounting or Bookkeeping services
☐ Advertising expenses
☐ Bad debts/Bounced checks
☐ Books related to business
☐ Briefcase or samples case
☐ Business development expenses[1]
☐ Business gifts
☐ Christmas cards for business associates
☐ Cleaning services (office, business, uniforms, equipment)
☐ Commissions (sales reps, agents, other sellers)
☐ Consulting fees
☐ Conventions & trade show expense
☐ Delivery charges
☐ Donations (charitable or business-related)
☐ Dues to professional organizations
☐ Educational expense (business seminars, workshops, classes, handbooks, manuals)
☐ Entertainment, business-related (must be carefully documented)[2]
☐ Equipment lease costs
☐ Equipment purchases (may be depreciated or expensed)
☐ Freight and shipping charges
☐ Insurance premiums (product liability, special riders on homeowner's policy, computer insurance, etc.)
☐ Interest on business loans or charge cards, late tax payments, etc.
☐ IRA or Keogh account deposits[3]
☐ Labor costs (independent contractors)

☐ Legal and professional fees
☐ Licenses and permits
☐ Mail list development & maintenance
☐ Maintenance contracts on office equipment, and other repairs
☐ Membership fees in business-related organizations
☐ Office furnishings (depreciated)
☐ Office supplies
☐ Postage
☐ Product displays
☐ Professional services (artists, designers, copywriters, etc.)
☐ Refunds to customers
☐ Research and development (R&D) expense
☐ Safe Deposit Box (if it holds documents related to production of income)
☐ Sales Commissions
☐ Stationery and printing
☐ Subscriptions to business periodicals
☐ Supplies and materials
☐ Tax preparer's fee
☐ Tools of your trade
☐ Travel expenses connected with business (meals and lodging for overnight stays, plus airfare, train, bus, taxi, auto expense, tips, and tolls)[4]
☐ Uniforms or special costumes used only in trade or profession
☐ Union dues (related to home-based business or profession)
☐ Wages to employees, including those paid to spouse or children

Footnotes:

[1] Note that *start-up expenses* are deductible only when one is already in business; major expenditures should be deferred until that point.

[2] Deductions for entertainment are a touchy area, and one that has been affected by recent tax law changes. Ask an accountant for help in taking such deductions from now on. (They could trigger an audit.)

[3] Under the Tax Reform Act of 1986, deductions for IRAs are now limited to those who do not participate in the pension plan of their employer.

[4] Under the Tax Reform Act of 1986, the deduction for business-related meals and travel expenses is limited to 80%.

Notes

Business Deductions

Tax evasion can lead to a stay in the slammer; tax *avoidance*, however, is the right of every American taxpayer. If you operate a business at home, a wide variety of expenses become deductible, provided you can show that they are *ordinary, necessary, and somehow connected with the operation and potential profit of your business.* See the nearby chart for a master checklist of business deductions available to home business owners. (An additional chart appears near the listing, "Business Use of One's Home." It shows home-related, tax-deductible expenses many people overlook.)

Business Expenses, Other

The homebased business owner is entitled to many special deductions at tax time, as the two tax checklists in this section show. However, not everything one spends in connection with a business can be "expended," or deducted, at the time the money is spent. Some purchases must be depreciated over a specified number of years. Others, like inventory purchases (anything bought for resale) are expensed only when actually sold. (Example: You buy $1,000 worth of inventory but sell only $700 in the year of purchase; you deduct $700 of inventory costs and carry the remaining $300 worth of inventory to the next year's tax report.)

As a general rule, you are not entitled to a deduction for legal and accounting advice you obtain *before* you start a business. This is considered an organizational expense. Therefore, it would certainly be tax-advantageous if you were to establish your own business before you hired any legal or accounting advice that might be needed in the early days of your business.

Also not deductible are security deposits of any kind, as you'll eventually get this money back.

Business Loans

Bank Loans: Few individuals are able to get a bank loan at the start of their home business, either because they lack start-up investment capital or the kind of collateral the bank requires, or they're simply reluctant to pledge to the bank what collateral they do have, usually savings accounts, equity in a home, or cash surrender value of an insurance policy. In the end, many people decide that it's easier to borrow from their own savings account, or perhaps a relative. Others simply figure out how to raise their own venture capital through a variety of entrepreneurial activities.

"Collateral" is an asset that can back up a loan. Generally it means property, stocks, bonds, savings accounts, life insurance, and current business assets — any or all of which may be held or assumed to insure repayment of a loan. In addition to collateral, banks also consider the overall health of one's home business — how much money it's generating, or can be expected to generate — and one's ability to repay the loan. An individual's character, credit history, and net worth are also of great importance.

A banker told me that it's also important for a borrower to know the kinds of loans a bank normally offers. For instance, there are banks who specialize in making loans to people who are into art or oil, as opposed to those who might invest in a chicken farm or a race horse; still others give "conventional" loans only. In short, each bank has to feel comfortable in its ability to sell the kinds of things they accept as collateral on a loan. If they're not into art, oil, chickens, or horses as an investment, they wouldn't know what to do with this kind of collateral if they had it. But every banker knows what to do with stocks, bonds, and other securities, thus their preference for them as collateral. Bankers also like to deal with people who have accounts in their bank.

If you ever expect to get a bank loan, you have to know how to speak the language of bankers and write a proper loan proposal. For clear, easy-to-understand information on both points, read *How to Borrow Money From a Bank,* by Don H. Alexander, a commercial lending officer at a Pacific Northwest bank. And for additional, free information, obtain the SBA management aid, "The ABC's of Borrowing."

Note: One kind of collateral that might get you a short-term business loan is a sizable purchase order. It would demonstrate your ability to repay the loan (the one you need to buy the materials so you can fill the order). Of course, the bank may be concerned about your account's ability to pay you, so the bigger the buyer's name, the better your chances for a loan.

Line of Credit. Talk to your banker about the possibility of obtaining a "line of credit" instead of a loan. There are both secured and unsecured lines of credit. If your total net worth is, say, between $50,000 and $100,000, I'm told you might be able to get a $5,000–$10,000 line of credit against which you can borrow whenever you need it. A line of credit normally has an expiration date of a year, and it may be renewed, providing you have had a profitable year. Although payable on demand, few banks would call in this kind of loan unless they were unduly concerned about a lender's ability to repay it.

Although collateral is needed for a line of credit, as with a bank loan, the requirements may not be as steep, particularly if you have an excellent credit rating and an account with the bank that's in good standing. Having an already-established business with a steady cash flow would also help your situation immeasurably.

By establishing a line of credit before you actually need the money, you'll have added peace of mind that you'll be able to handle unexpected business expenses in low cash-flow months, take advantage of special sales on supplies or equipment, or make other, major business purchases earlier than you might otherwise have been able to do.

Bank Charge Card Loans. In unskilled hands, charge cards are a dangerous thing. Used properly, however, they can be an effective business tool. In addition to helping one build a good credit rating, charge card receipts provide an excellent tax record of business transactions.

A special feature of a bank charge card is that it gives you access to emergency cash at any time, especially useful when traveling. Simply present your card to any bank and receive an immediate cash advance (determined by your account's balance and credit limit).

Many small business owners also use charge cards to obtain short-term loans to cover business expenses. Although interest rates are high, it seems a small price to pay if one has a great and immediate need for a certain sum of cash. If each spouse were to have two major bank charge cards with high credit limits, one might

Notes

have access to as much as $10,000 overnight — a comforting thought, indeed.

Life Insurance Loans. Don't overlook this possibility for business capital. If you have an insurance policy with cash value, you may be able to borrow on it at rates as low as 5%. (Some smart investors borrow on life insurance policies even when they don't need the money simply to reinvest the loan money in higher interest-bearing investments, such as government securities or money-market funds.)

Government Loans. State and federal governments have an assortment of programs to assist economic development through financing new business, says the Department of Labor. But it took an individual writer to pull all this information together in a form that the average small business person could understand. In his book, *2001 Sources of Financing for Small Business*, Herman Holtz has done an incredible job of digging up all the hard-to-find information on this topic — everything from programs offered by state and federal governments to money available through grants, foundations, banks, and venture capitalists. Regrettably, the publisher has allowed this book to go out of print. You may be able to obtain a copy through your library, however.

Note: The Department of Labor points out that the processing of applications for government loans or loan guarantees is a lengthy procedure taking many months. Thus it may be better to consider government assistance as an additional or secondary source of financing once the business is underway, rather than a source for startup funding.

SBA Loans. At the federal level, the Small Business Administration currently makes loans to certain new/young businesses on a guaranteed basis — but only if local banks will not provide a loan. Furthermore, before the SBA can process any loan, it needs the signature of the local zoning officer to verify that the business is operating legally — a fact that would automatically eliminate many homebased business owners for consideration.

More information will be found in the SBA booklets, "Your Business and the SBA," and "Business Loans From the SBA." To further assist loan applicants, SBA sponsors management training programs and offers private counseling sessions with SCORE volunteers.

Business Name (Also see "Trademarks.")

After you've picked your business name, but *before* you order stationery and cards, you should check with the county clerk to make sure no one else is using the name you've selected. You're on safe ground if your own name is part of your business name. If both your first and last names are used, you won't have to register an assumed name with the county. Some states require registration if only the last name is used, however.

A "fictitious name statement" (see next page) must be filed with the county if you use an assumed name such as "Sally's Catering Service," or "Country Classics." Your assumed, business, or trade name should be registered with the state, too, to prevent its use by any corporate entity. Of course, your name must be free of conflict from corporate names already registered. (If it isn't, you'll be notified.)

To protect your name and business logo on a national level, see the listing on trademarks elsewhere in this section.

d/b/a: This is simply an abbreviation for "doing business as." Banks often use this abbreviation in their records to connect a depositor to his or her fictitious name, as in "Jack Robinson, d/b/a Antiques Galore."

Fictitious Name Statement. If you're doing business under any name that is not your own, you are required (in most states) to file a fictitious name statement with the county clerk and publish a specially-worded notice in the legal section of a local newspaper of general circulation. The purpose of such registration and notice is to give the public information about your identity. A fictitious name has to be connected to the name of a person who can be held responsible for the actions of a business.

Many small businesses do not bother to register their names, but if you're investing time and money into the development of a business, you'll be smart to protect your business name. I once heard about an unscrupulous entrepreneur who went through county records checking on whether certain local businesses had registered their names. He then filed fictitious name statements for all the unregistered businesses, approached each business one by one, and told them they either had to stop doing business under that name (because he now owned it), or pay him a stiff fee to buy it back. Since registration of your name is a simple and inexpensive matter, take care of it today, even if you've been in business for some time. The form you have to complete doesn't ask for the date your business was started, so no one will be the wiser about your delay in registering. *Find out, too, when you have to renew this registration.* The county won't notify you about this, and you wouldn't want to lose the name over such a technicality.

Business Use of One's Home (See nearby checklist of tax-deductible expenses.)

To take a tax deduction for using a part of your home in business, that part must be used *exclusively* and *regularly* as:

(1) The principal place of business for any trade or business in which you engage, or

(2) A place to meet or deal with your clients or customers in the normal course of your trade or business, or

(3) A structure that is not attached to your house or residence and that is used in connection with your trade or business. (Examples: garage, studio, barn.)

To deduct expenses for your home, you must be able to show the part of your home that you use for business (take photographs), and also show that you use this part exclusively and regularly in the normal course of your business.

To figure the part of your home used for business, figure the total square footage of your home, then the square footage used in your business. This will give you a percentage figure you can use to apply to all the expenses related to the maintenance of your home. Another acceptable way of figuring the percentage is to count the rooms of your home — provided they are all about the same size — and divide the number of rooms used for business by the number of rooms in the home.

1988 Update on
Business Use of Home

The Tax Reform Act of 1986 limits the deduction for business use of a home.

Before 1987, the amount that could be deducted for these expenses was limited to the gross income from the business use of the home.

Beginning in 1987, the deduction is limited to the gross income from that business use minus the sum of:

1) The business percentage of the mortgage interest, real estate taxes, and casualty losses, and

2) The business expenses other than those related to the business use of a home.

Therefore, the deduction is limited to a modified net income from the business use of a home — the net income of the business without including the home expenses (other than the business percentage of mortgage interest, real estate taxes, and casualty losses). Thus, deductions for the business use of a home will not create a business loss or increase a net loss from a business.

Deductions in excess of the limit may be carried forward to later years, subject to the income limits in those years.

— from IRS Pub. 921
(Aug. 1987)

Notes

EXAMPLES:

2,500 square feet in home, with 500 sq. ft. used for business = 20%

10 rooms in home, with 2 used for business = $^2/_{10}$, or $^1/_5$, or 20%

To determine applicable home deductions, then, you would add your total costs for gas, electricity, insurance, repairs, etc. (see checklist) and take the percentage figure that applies to your business or, in this case, 20% of each amount.

Although this is the basic principle on which home deductions are calculated, there are some exceptions plus a number of special guidelines for each type of expense. You can obtain exact information about each from the IRS publication #587, "Business Use of Your Home," or from an accountant.

Canadian Orders

If you do business with Canadians, always ask for payment in U.S. dollars to avoid rate-of-exchange problems and high fees that banks charge to handle Canadian checks. Also note that postage costs are higher when you deal with Canadian accounts or customers simply because all mail must be sent in envelopes — no self-mailers, like newsletters, catalogs, brochures, etc. This usually adds an extra ounce to the package. Bulk mail, of course, is not acceptable at all.

Chamber of Commerce

Membership in the Chamber of Commerce is an indication that you're a stable part of the business community. It provides an opportunity for networking with other businesspeople in your area, and enables you to contribute to the development of your community as a whole.

New members may tend to ask "What will the Chamber do for me?" when, in fact, they should be asking, "What can I do to help the Chamber help the community?" Depending on the size of your community, dues may vary from as little as $25 per year to almost $300. Call your Chamber of Commerce for more information. This kind of increased visibility for your business could be helpful to its growth.

Collection Techniques (Bounced Checks and Unpaid Invoices)

If a check bounces because of "insufficient funds," it may be that the account was temporarily overdrawn. If the check is a small one, you may wish to redeposit it without notifying the individual who wrote it. Usually, it will clear. A check can only be redeposited once, however, so if it's for a large amount, you may want to telephone the person who wrote it to make sure there will be sufficient funds to cover it the second time around.

If the check bounces again, send a letter notifying the recipient that you intend to put the matter into the hands of an attorney if payment has not been received within the time you specify. (You may not have an attorney, but the recipient of your letter won't know this. A well-typed letter on good stationery will add considerable strength to your demand for payment.)

Hang onto the bad check as proof of the customer's indebtedness to you. If you believe there has been intent to defraud, and the check

Checklist of
Home-Related Tax-Deductible Expenses
for Home Business Owners

Note: Stay aware of changes in tax laws which could affect the following deductions at any time.
(For general information on how to calculate the following tax deductions, see nearby
listing, "Business Use of One's Home.")

Direct Expenses: Those which benefit only the business part of your home. You may deduct all costs of direct expenses, which include:

☐ Decorating or remodeling costs/expenses: painting or repairs made to the specific area or room used exclusively for business; or repairs done to change an ordinary room into a place of business, such as rewiring, plumbing changes, walls or flooring, etc.

☐ Certain room furnishings. Larger purchases, such as office furniture and equipment, must be depreciated, as a general rule. Inexpensive items, like an office bulletin board, for example, could be deducted under office supplies and materials.

Indirect Expenses: Those which benefit both the business and personal parts of your home. Only the business part is deductible as a business expense.

☐ rent (on percentage of home used for business).

☐ mortgage interest (percentage related to use of home for business. Balance of interest is deductible on the personal portion of your tax return).

☐ insurance premiums on home.

☐ depreciation of home (not the land, however; see note below).

☐ utilities (gas, electric, oil).

☐ services (trash removal, snow removal, yard maintenance). The latter two may be questionable unless clients or customers normally visit your home.

☐ home repairs, plus related labor and suppliers (furnace, roof, etc.)

Other Expenses:

☐ *Personal Computer.* If you use your personal computer for business at least 50% of the time — and have documented this usage with the required (by IRS) diary or time log, you may depreciate the business percentage of the computer's cost, and also take deductions for related supplies and materials.

☐ *Telephone.* Fully deductible are all business-related long distance telephone calls and all extra charges for business extensions or services, such as call forwarding, call holding, etc. However, beginning with the 1989 tax year, homebased business owners may not deduct a percentage of the basic monthly charge for the first phone line coming into the home. (See also "Telephone" in this section.)

☐ *Family Automobile.* See "Automobile, Business Use of," earlier in this section. All business-related mileage — or actual operating expenses related to business use — is deductible.

☐ *Child Care Expenses.* If you are self-employed, and you pay someone to care for your child, or an invalid parent or spouse, so you can work, a portion of the cost may be deductible.

☐ *Medical Expenses.* After 1986 and before 1990, self-employed taxpayers may deduct, as an adjustment to income on Form 1040, 25% of the amount paid for medical insurance. (Deduction cannot exceed net earnings from self-employment.)

Note: Ask your accountant to explain the tax problem that can occur if you take a deduction for depreciation of your home, and then sell it at a considerable profit. Taxes may be due on the same percentage of profit that you used to figure the deduction. However, an IRS ruling states that if you cease to qualify for the home office deduction in the year you sell your home, (i.e., stop your business) the entire gain can be treated as a "rollover," if you buy and occupy a new residence within 24 months after you've sold the old one.

Notes

is for a substantial amount, you may wish to send a copy of the returned check, along with notes about your efforts to collect the money, to the District Attorney's office, or perhaps simply to your local Police Department. It *is* a crime to deliberately write a bad check.

Another option for collecting on a bounced check is to take it to your bank and ask them to try to collect for you. There may be a small fee for this. Normally, the bank sends the bounced check back to the originating bank with instructions to pay you as soon as funds have been deposited to the account. However, if a deposit isn't made during this holding period — usually a month — you're out of luck.

Note: If you use the accrual method to report income, you are entitled to a deduction for bad debts (bounced checks and other uncollectible accounts) because they were previously counted as reportable income. If you use the cash method, however, you cannot deduct an uncollectible account because the payment was not previously counted as reportable income. For more information, obtain the free SBA management aid, "Outwitting Bad-Check Passers."

Collection Agencies. Can't collect an invoice? You might try a collection agency. You may not get your money, but at least you'll get some satisfaction that a deadbeat is being legally hassled by a bill collector.

The better credit agencies will belong to the American Collector's Association, which has 2800 collection agency members at present. They will try to collect accounts locally, but when you need to collect from someone out of state, they simply pass along your account to a member collection agency in the appropriate state. All member agencies trade accounts this way, and make regular 90-day reports back to the originating agency. If and when collection is eventually made, the agency would normally take 40% of a local account, and 50% if the collection was made by a member agency. Since half is better than none, a collection agency is at least an alternative bill collection technique you may wish to try at some point in your business.

Also see Dun & Bradstreet's special collection service, described in the resource chapter.

Small Claims Court. If someone owes you an amount under $750 (this amount will vary from state to state), you can sue them in Small Claims Court for a modest filing fee. I've been told by people who've done this that "it's cheap, quite direct, and painless." Although you may win a small claims court judgment, note that you're still the one who has to collect. (As I understand it, papers are given to the constable or other authority in the account's area, and he collects the cash for you. At this point, a debtor's assets can be seized by the court if that's what it takes to get you the money.)

Consumer Safety Laws (Also see "Insurance, Product Liability.")

All levels of the government are concerned about consumer protection and, as a consumer yourself, you're no doubt pleased by this concern. But as a businessperson, you must look at consumer safety in a different light. Three areas of special concern to homebased manufacturers are:

- **Toys and other goods for children.** *The Consumer Product Safety Act of 1972* created The Consumer Products Safety Commission, which establishes and enforces mandatory safety standards for consumer products sold in the U.S. One of their most active regulatory programs has been in the area of products designed for children. If you make toys of any kind, avoid problems by making sure your toys are (1) too large to be swallowed; (2) not apt to break easily or leave jagged edges; (3) free of sharp edges or points; (4) not put together with easily exposed pins, wires, or nails; and (5) nontoxic, nonflammable, and nonpoisonous. (The latter requirement explains why most craftsmen/toy manufacturers do not paint or varnish wooden toys.)

- **Textiles.** (Garments, quilts, stuffed toys, knitting, rugs, yarn, piece goods, etc.) Manufacturers — and that includes individual craftspeople — involved with textiles and wearing apparel must affix two different labels to their products.

  The Bureau of Consumer Protection, in connection with its *Textile Fiber Products Identification Act,* requires a label or hang tag that shows: (1) the name of the manufacturer or person marketing the textile fiber product, and (2) the generic names and percentages of all fibers in the product in amounts of 5 percent or more, listed in order by predominance by weight. Examples: "100% combed cotton," and "50% cotton, 50% polyester." If the item contains wool, it falls under the *Wool Products Labeling Act of 1939,* and thus requires additional identification.

  In connection with its *Fabric Care Labeling Rule,* The Federal Trade Commission requires a permanently affixed "care label" on all textile wearing apparel and household furnishings. Such labels must give care and maintenance instructions for the item, such as "Wash in warm water; use cool iron." Manufacturer can design and make their own labels or use standard ones available from a variety of sources, a few of which are listed in the resource chapter.

  In addition to labels, the textiles manufacturer must also be concerned with the flammability of fabrics and fibers used in the production of wearing apparel and home furnishings. Handwoven, hand-dyed items, as well as fabrics of all kinds, must conform to the standard of *The Flammable Fabrics Act,* which is policed by the Consumer Products Safety Commission.

  For more information, obtain all the free brochures available from the above-named agencies.

- **Items with Concealed Stuffing.** *The Bedding and Upholstered Furniture Law* is a very aggravating, frustrating state law that affects everyone who manufactures items with concealed stuffings, including dolls, quilts, pillows, soft picture frames, and so on. The law not only requires yet another label to be permanently affixed to each item, *but a $100 license for each state in which goods are sold.*

  The frustrating thing about this law is that it makes no distinction between the manufacturer of pillows and mattresses and the craftsperson who sells a few dolls in the local craft shop. Especially aggravating to some people is the fact that this law is being arbitrarily enforced. In one state, makers of such items, and the shops who sell them are "getting away with it," while those in another state are having their merchandise removed from shop shelves and show exhibits. (Some unhappy people in the latter group have been known to seek revenge by turning in other people who haven't yet been caught.)

  For more information, contact your state's Department of Health

---

New Labeling Rules for Wool and Textile Items

New Federal Trade Commission regulations covering the labeling of wool and textile products went into effect on May 17th (1985). The new regulations were promulgated to be consistent with amendments to the federal Wool Products Labeling Act and the Textile Fiber Products Identification Act.

The most important new requirement is that the labels of all wool or textile products clearly indicate when imported ingredients are used, even if the product is made in the United States. Thus the label for a scarf sewn in the United States from imported silk must indicate that fact with wording such as "Sewn in the USA from imported products" or some variation of such a legend. Items which originate entirely in the United States need only state "Made in USA" or "Crafted in USA" or some similarly clear terminology.

The new regulations also require such terms to be used when describing wool or textile products in mail order catalogs and promotional materials that are directed to the ultimate consumer. Other requirements cover the location of the label in the garment, and the labeling of packaged products.

The complete rules, and comments made to the FTC by the public during the rulemaking process, were published in the Federal Register on April 17, 1985 (pages 15100 to 15107) and are available on request from the nearest regional office of the Federal Trade Commission, or from the FTC in Washington, DC 20580.

— Reprinted by permission from The Crafts Report.

Notes

and try to connect with "the bedding official." (In some states, you may have to call or write State Tagging Law Enforcement Officials, usually listed under bedding, milk or food, product safety, health, home furnishing, sanitation or Department of Health & Environment.)

Ask the "bedding official" for samples of the required tag and a source where labels can be bought. If you find the minimum quantities too high, write to some of the label supply companies listed in this book's resource chapter; some have good prices on design-your-own labels. Or, if you need only a few labels, visit a large fabric store and see if they will give you the extra labels that normally come with the bolts of fabric they buy.

One enterprising garment manufacturer of my acquaintance solved her label-making problem by buying a $35 silk screen set. She prints her own labels on ribbons and has the flexibility of using different colors of ribbon to match differently-colored garments and pillows.

Note that you may also be able to buy pillows with labels already affixed.

Contracts

A written contract is a lot easier to prove in court than a verbal one, but verbal contracts are just as legal and binding — unless it is for the sale of goods over a certain amount. (This amount varies from state to state, but in many states it is $500.)

Any written agreement, dated and signed by the parties involved, can serve as a legal document, and legal language is not required. Complicated agreements, however, should at least be approved by a lawyer, and certain contracts and agreements should NEVER be signed without advice of counsel, as mentioned earlier. (For more information, see the book, *Business Agreements: A Complete Guide to Oral and Written Contracts.*)

Copyrights (Also see "Patents," and "Trademarks.")

Since copyright has already been discussed in considerable detail in chapter two, we need only be concerned here with how to obtain and file a copyright registration application. There are several different copyright forms, and you must use the proper form to register each specific copyright. The forms most likely to be of interest are:

Form SE: Used to register a copyright for a serial, which includes periodicals, newspapers, magazines, bulletins, newsletters, annuals, journals, and proceedings of societies.

Form TX: Used to apply for copyright registration for other non-dramatic literary works, including books, directories, and other work written in words, such as the how-to instructions for a crafts project.

Form VA: Used to apply for a copyright registration for a work of the visual arts, which applies to pictorial, graphic, or sculptural works, including fine, graphic and applied, photographs, charts, technical drawings, diagrams, and models.

Other forms include **Form PA** for a work of the performing arts, **Form SR** for a sound recording, and so on. Application forms may be ordered by mail or by phone from the Copyright Office. The completed application form must be returned to the Copyright

HOW TO FILL OUT FORM TX
Specific Instructions for Spaces 1-4

**APPLICATION
FOR
COPYRIGHT
REGISTRATION**
for a
Nondramatic Literary Work

FORM TX

UNITED STATES COPYRIGHT OFFICE
LIBRARY OF CONGRESS
WASHINGTON, D.C. 20559

page of Form TX,
ation, and refer to

being registered is a contribution to a periodical
ons for "Publication as a Contribution."

les: Complete this space if there are any addi-
which someone searching for the registration
r which a document pertaining to the work

tion: If the work being registered has been
periodical, serial, or collection, give the title of
eaded "Title of this Work." Then, in the line
ution," give information about the larger work

HOW TO

• F

• Sec

• Th

• Fou

WHEN TO USE FORM TX: Fo
to use for copyright registration c
whether published or unpublished.

WHAT IS ʌ **"NONDRAMATIC**
gory of "nondramatic literary works"
dramatic works and certain kinds of
all types of works written in words (o
A few of the many examples of "no
tion, nonfiction, poetry, periodicals
tories, catalogs, advertising copy, and

DEPOSIT TO ACCOMPANY /
copyright registration must be accom
entire work for which registration is
general deposit requirements as set f

Unpublished work: Deposit
ord).

Published work: Deposit two
of the best edition.

Work first published outsid
complete copy (or phonorecord) of t

Contribution to a collectiv
(or phonorecord) of the best edition
These general deposit requirements
further information about copyright

FORM TX

UNITED STATES COPYRIGHT OFFICE

REGISTRATION NUMBER

TX   TXU

EFFECTIVE DATE OF REGISTRATION

....
Month   Day   Year

DO NOT WRITE ABOVE THIS LINE. IF YOU NEED MORE SPACE, USE CONTINUATION SHEET

①
Title

TITLE OF THIS WORK:

If a periodical or serial give: Vol. . . . . . . No. . . . . . . Issue Date . . . .

PREVIOUS OR ALTERNATIVE TITLES:

PUBLICATION AS A CONTRIBUTION: (If this work was published as a contribution to a periodical, serial, or collection, give information about the collective work in which the contribution appeared.)

Title of Collective Work . . . . Vol. . . . . No. . . . . . Date . . . . Pages. . . . .

②
Author(s)

IMPORTANT: Under the law, the "author" of a "work made for hire" is generally the employer, not the employee (see instructions). If any part of this work was "made for hire" check "Yes" in the space provided, give the employer (or other person for whom the work was prepared) as "Author" of that part, and leave the space for dates blank.

1

NAME OF AUTHOR:

Was this author's contribution to the work a "work made for hire"? Yes. . . . . . No. . . . . . .

AUTHOR'S NATIONALITY OR DOMICILE:
Citizen of . . . . or { Domiciled in . . . .
(Name of Country)   (Name of Country)

AUTHOR OF: (Briefly describe nature of this author's contribution)

DATES OF BIRTH AND DEATH:
Born . . . . Died . . . .
(Year)   (Year)

WAS THIS AUTHOR'S CONTRIBUTION TO THE WORK:
Anonymous? Yes. . . . . No. . . . . .
Pseudonymous? Yes . . . . . No. . . . . .
If the answer to either of these questions is "Yes, see detailed instructions attached.

2

NAME OF AUTHOR:

Was this author's contribution to the work a "work made for hire"? Yes. . . . . . No. . . . . . .

AUTHOR'S NATIONALITY OR DOMICILE:
Citizen of . . . . or { Domiciled in . . . .
(Name of Country)   (Name of Country)

AUTHOR OF: (Briefly describe nature of this author's contribution)

DATES OF BIRTH AND DEATH:
Born . . . . Died . . . .
(Year)   (Year)

WAS THIS AUTHOR'S CONTRIBUTION TO THE WORK:
Anonymous? Yes. . . . . No. . . . . .
Pseudonymous? Yes . . . . . No. . . . . .
If the answer to either of these questions is "Yes, see detailed instructions attached.

3

NAME OF AUTHOR:

Was this author's contribution to the work a "work made for hire"? Yes. . . . . . No. . . . . . .

AUTHOR'S NATIONALITY OR DOMICILE:
Citizen of . . . . or { Domiciled in . . . .
(Name of Country)   (Name of Country)

AUTHOR OF: (Briefly describe nature of this author's contribution)

DATES OF BIRTH AND DEATH:
Born . . . . Died . . . .
(Year)   (Year)

WAS THIS AUTHOR'S CONTRIBUTION TO THE WORK:
Anonymous? Yes. . . . . No. . . . . .
Pseudonymous? Yes . . . . . No. . . . . .
If the answer to either of these questions is "Yes, see detailed instructions attached.

③
**Creation
and
Publication**

YEAR IN WHICH CREATION OF THIS WORK WAS COMPLETED:

Year. . . . .
(This information must be given in all cases.)

DATE AND NATION OF FIRST PUBLICATION:

Date. . . . .
(Month)   (Day)   (Year)
Nation . . . .
(Name of Country)
(Complete this block ONLY if this work has been published.)

④
Claimant(s)

NAME(S) AND ADDRESS(ES) OF COPYRIGHT CLAIMANT(S):

TRANSFER: (If the copyright claimant(s) named here in space 4 are different from the author(s) named in space 2, give a brief statement of how the claimant(s) obtained ownership of the copyright.)

• Complete all applicable spaces (numbers 5-11) on the reverse side of this page
• Follow detailed instructions attached
• Sign the form at line 10

DO NOT WRITE HERE
Page 1 of . . . . pages

Illustration of a copyright form. The clear instructions provided with each type of form make it easy to complete. (Note: It takes the Copyright Office 6–8 weeks or more to process an application and return the registered copy. Be patient.)

BIRMINGHAM (AL) NEWS, February 24, 1983: "Abuse of Labor Law."

This is not a sweatshop situation, where a greedy employer is taking advantage of a hapless group of immigrants. The working agreement is between consenting adults made without force or pressure, and is in the best tradition of the free market.

How then is it incumbent on the U.S. government to step in and order them to dissolve the arrangement?

MILWAUKEE JOURNAL, March 24, 1983: "Eyes on Wisconsin," by Deb Hillard.

Now, it's Wisconsin's turn at bat, and the eyes of women around the country are watching. On its way to federal court in Milwaukee is a group of women determined to rid your state of the effects of a 40-year-old Labor Department "Cottage Industry" law. That law, passed in 1942, pretended to "protect" women from being exploited by low-paying consumers. The law makes it illegal for women to make money at home by embroidering, knitting, making women's clothing, jewelry, and other accessories. Besides "protecting" women, the law makes it illegal for industrious home workers to pose a threat to organized labor.

Office with the required $10 fee plus two copies of the "best edition" of the work.

Naturally, the Copyright Office has a list of criteria that determine exactly what the "best edition" is in each case. In printed matter, for example, it would mean a hard-cover book instead of the paperback edition; for other graphic matter, the best edition would be the one in color, instead of black-and-white. In the case of three-dimensional works, photographs or accurate drawings may be accepted in lieu of actual copies.

Some additional points concerning copyrights:

1. You cannot copyright names, titles, and short phrases, but brand names, trade names, slogans, and phrases may be entitled to protection under the provisions of the Trademark Laws.

2. Inventions cannot be copyrighted, but may be patented. (The *drawing* or written description of an invention, however, could be copyrighted.)

3. Ideas are not copyrightable, nor is the procedure for doing, making, or building something. However, the expression of such ideas, fixed in tangible form (in a book or product insert, for instance) can be copyrighted.

To help you understand the difference between copyrights, trademarks, and patents, remember this:

The *artwork* on a can of cola can be *copyrighted*. The *name — and the way it is expressed on that can —* can be *trademarked*. The *formula* for the cola itself can be *patented*.

Please note that the Copyright Office is prohibited from giving legal advice or opinions about your rights in connection with cases of alleged copyright infringement, "or the sufficiency, extent, or scope of compliance with the copyright law." Thus, if you have a copyright problem, consult a copyright attorney.

For more information, see the free publications available from the Copyright Office, plus the books on copyright which are listed in the resource chapter. One, in particular, is excellent: *Making It Legal* has an extensive section on copyrights, patents, and trademarks, and it will be of particular interest to craftmakers, visual artists, and writers.

Cottage Industries (Also see "Employees," "Independent Contractors," and "State Laws Restricting Homework.")

Reference: Department of Labor law concerning Employment of Homeworkers in Certain Industries (Title 29, Part 530 of the Code of Federal Regulations).

Some people call any kind of home business a "cottage industry," but in actuality, a cottage industry is one that is based on a central marketing and management operation, with production of craftwork at home — usually in the homes of people other than that of marketing and management. For example, you might start a small manufacturing company, then hire other individuals in your community to do the actual labor involved in the production process, allowing them to perform this work in their own homes for a per-piece price.

For years, people have hired such labor on an independent contractor basis, instead of an employee basis, primarily for two reasons: (1) to avoid all the tax and paperwork problems associated with the hiring of employees, and (2) because the homework restrictions only cover employees, and not independent contractors.

ARKANSAS DEMOCRAT, February 25, 1983: "Thou shalt not work!"

Two years ago, women knitters from Vermont marched on the Department of Labor and won exemption of their specialty from the ban — against extreme labor opposition. On this page yesterday, *Democrat* columnist Donald Lambro quoted one of the laborite opponents as saying incredulously. "That's anti-social. You want every worker to be free to work at home at whatever they desire to do, under whatever conditions they desire to work!"

Exactly!

It's hard to believe that the right doesn't already exist. Section 14b of Taft-Hartley doesn't confer it outright. An individual doesn't have it unless his state enacts a law declaring that nobody has to join a union to get work in an organized shop. But the regulatory ban on home handiwork is far worse. Where Section 14b confers only a conditional right to work, the Labor Department ban denies the right totally in six different crafts — foreclosing the livelihoods of countless women, on grounds that buyers are certain to exploit them.

THE JEFFERSONIA (Towson, MD), March 3, 1983: "The Investigator's Notebook," by Jack Edward Rytten

The reason that the union brass so vehemently opposed the homeworkers is because homeworkers don't pay union dues. Steve Antosh, executive director of The Center on National Labor Policy concurs with this report. "Instead of keeping American jobs afloat, union heads and their friends the bureaucracy operate like kamikaze pilots. They shoot down American jobs which later resurface overseas."

Big Labor wants no part of individual initiative or self-reliance. It would make too many inroads into their dynasty of Entrenched Greed. Their vassals in the bureaucracy support union despotism, for it is from this source that their election campaign expenses flow. If Big Labor is the working man's Santa Claus, this reporter prefers Ebenezer Scrooge.

THE WASHINGTON POST, April 8, 1983: "Homework in Maryland."

The Garment workers' union has been pushing a bill through the Maryland state legislature that would prohibit industrial garment manufacturers from employing people who work in their homes. The union is concerned about allegations that contractors have been exploiting homeworkers by paying them rates for their completed work that, when equipment rentals and other costs are taken into account, are far below legal minimums and compete unfairly with factory manufacturers. Housewives in western Maryland, where unemployment is very high, protest that the new law will deprive their families of their only source of income.

ENTERPRISE NEWS SERVICE, Washington, DC, 1983: Editorial, "Union Knit-Picking."

A long, hard battle is guaranteed. On the one hand are the unionists fighting tooth and nail to keep the homeworkers' doors locked. On the other is the Center on National Labor Policy contending that people should be free to work at home making anything they wish — whether it's handkerchiefs, mittens, embroidery, or whatever.

Until the homeworkers win their right to work once and for all, better tell Grandma to keep her embroidery secret.

Comments from the Media on "The Homework Law"

THE PHOENIX GAZETTE, February 16, 1983: Editorial, "Homework helps adults, too."

Union officials continue to oppose the change — homeworkers do not pay union dues — by conjuring up images of abused workers laboring in sweatshops. That is not the case. Far from worsening conditions, legalizing cottage industries would provide homeworkers protection under fair labor laws.

The Reagan administration certainly should support changes that would promote employment while at the same time helping families to be economically independent. Labor market analysts predict that by 1990, an estimated 15 million jobs could be done in the home. It's time the Labor Department caught up to the present and prepared for the future.

Background Information on Restricted Home Industries

In 1943, union officials convinced the federal government to forbid homework in seven industries (noted in text at right). In 1981, women knitters in Vermont united to protest the restriction on their industry and eventually won exemption, against extreme opposition. This case resulted in nationwide publicity (see comments beginning on page 96), and brought attention to the remaining six restricted industries.

After more pressure from union officials, the knitwear restriction was reinstated in early December, 1983, but lifted again the following November. Currently, manufacturers may hire people to work in their homes in the knitted outerwear industry, provided they obtain a U.S. Labor Department Certificate and comply with all requirements of the federal Fair Labor Standards Act.

In March, 1988, new rules were proposed by the Labor Department to lift the regulatory ban on the remaining six industries. However, it was announced in November that restrictions would be lifted only on five industries. This rule change does not *lift the ban against home manufacture of women's apparel — the industry thought to cover the largest number of workers. This news came as a terrible blow to homebased manufacturers of women's garments, who now cannot legally expand their operatons by hiring homeworkers to sew for them.*

— Author's note, November, 1988

If you're going to use independent contractors, you have to be able to establish that they are, indeed, independent contractors and not employees. (See the list of guidelines in the "Independent Contractors" listing in this section.)

And if you're working in one of the restricted industries, WATCH OUT! The above-mentioned labor law has caused a groundswell of opposition from the media and leaders in the home business movement because it affects the constitutional rights of certain individuals who want to earn a living by working at home in these specific industries: *knitwear, embroidery, gloves and mittens, handkerchiefs, buttons and buckles, jewelry, and women's apparel.* See left for current status of this problem; see following page for information about a Bill before Congress which may eventually resolve this problem.

Important: The Department of Labor is *not* concerned with sole proprietors working in these industries who make (manufacture) their own goods for sale, but only with the outside homeworkers they may hire when they decide to expand their businesses. Although your lawyer and accountant may tell you that you can hire "independent contractors" at this point, instead of "employees," *do not listen to them because they're only half right, as the law now stands.*

They're right as far as the Internal Revenue Service is concerned, but the IRS and the Department of Labor are in direct opposition on this matter. *The Department of Labor maintains that all workers who perform work in the seven restricted industries are, in fact, "employees," no matter what they or the people they work for may call themselves.*

Thus, when you seek legal advice on any matter relating to the formation or operation of a cottage industry that will employ homeworkers in the above-mentioned industries, be sure to *hire a lawyer who specializes in labor laws.* Any other lawyer is apt to be less informed on this very touchy topic, and may actually get you into a lot of legal trouble with the Department of Labor, who can, and will, demand the payment of thousands of dollars in back wages and taxes which were not withheld from employee's paychecks.

See page 103 for general guidelines on using independent contractors in industries other than those above, and read *National Home Business Report* for continuing information on this topic.

Credit

If you do not have a personal credit history, this should be an immediate goal. If you're a married woman with a home business, be sure to open your business checking account in your name only. If you add your husband's name, it becomes a joint account with credit history going automatically to his file.

Apply for a bank charge card whether you need it or not, and use this card to charge as many business expenses as possible. You'll incur no interest charges if you pay the bill before the due date. Meanwhile, you're building a credit history in your name. The more you use the card, the higher the credit limit can be set, and the more useful the card in obtaining emergency cash.

Credit/Trade References

Always ask for them when you're opening an account for one of your customers. Get two trade references (other businesses your customer deals with on credit) plus the name of a bank. Also make sure you

99TH CONGRESS
1ST SESSION

S. 665

To amend the Fair Labor Standards Act of 1938 to facilitate industrial homework, including sewing, knitting, and craftmaking, and for other purposes.

IN THE SENATE OF THE UNITED STATES

MARCH 14 (legislative day, FEBRUARY 18), 1985

Mr. HATCH (for himself, Mr. WALLOP, Mr. NICKLES, Mr. ARMSTRONG, Mr. COHEN, Mr. DENTON, Mr. EAST, Mr. KASTEN, and Mr. McCLURE) introduced the following bill; which was read twice and referred to the Committee on Labor and Human Resources

---

A BILL

To amend the Fair Labor Standards Act of 1938 to facilitate industrial homework, including sewing, knitting, and craftmaking, and for other purposes.

1 *Be it enacted by the Senate and House of Representa-*
2 *tives of the United States of America in Congress assembled,*
3 That section 11(d) of the Fair Labor Standards Act of 1938
4 is amended—

5   (1) by striking out the word "The" and inserting
6   in lieu thereof "(1) Subject to the provisions of para-
7   graph (2), the"; and

8   (2) by adding at the end thereof the following new
9   paragraph:

2

1 "(2) Nothing in paragraph (1) of this subsection shall be
2 construed to prohibit an individual from engaging in industri-
3 al homework (including sewing, knitting, jewelry or craft-
4 making) or performing any service in or about the individual's
5 place of residence as an employee of any employer covered
6 by the provisions of this Act if the employer pays the mini-
7 mum wage rate prescribed by this Act and complies with the
8 maximum hours provision of this Act.".

Excerpt from a Statement of Sen. Orrin Hatch, Utah*

In keeping with our traditional national spirit of creativity and resourcefulness, American women have . . . transformed their home-making or other marketable skills into profit-making enterprises. Working out of their own homes, they have been able to use their own personal skills, to keep their own flexible schedules, and earn a much-needed income.

Unfortunately, these women are now confronting an additional obstacle: their own government. Under the Fair Labor Standards Act, the Department of Labor is required to regulate, restrict, or prohibit industrial homework by employees of an employer subject to the Act. In 6 of every 7 instances, those prohibited from working are women with family responsibilities.

Basically, any person who wants to work at home and who does not qualify for the statutory exceptions must be an independent contractor. He or she must be involved in all aspects of the business. In practice, however, many homeworkers have neither the time nor experience to conduct market analyses or cost comparisons. They prefer to work with a distributor who can tell them which products are selling and provide other marketing decisions. Unfortunately, this kind of relationship is considered by the Labor Department and the courts to be that of an employer-employee and under the Fair Labor Standards Act, any work flowing from this relationship done at home would be prohibited.

The bill (see left) before this distinguished subcommittee will correct this problem by amending the Fair Labor Standards Act to permit industrial homework.

In sum, the bill preserves the intent of the Fair Labor Standards Act — preventing unfair worker exploitation — and, at the same time, restores a homeworker's right to choose his or her kind and place of employment.

*Before the Labor Subcommittee Hearing on Amendment of the Fair Labor Standards Act of 1938.

---

*1988 Update on
"Expensing" Business Property*

It may be tax-beneficial to completely "write off" certain business property that would normally be depreciated, particularly in years of high income. Check with an accountant to be sure.

For property placed in service after 1986, the maximum cost that may be expensed was increased from $5,000 to $10,000 under the Tax Reform Act of 1986.

Notes

have the owner's name and telephone number in file. Some accounts go uncollected simply because the owner can't be tracked down.

Naturally, you'll be asked to provide similar references whenever you open supplier accounts.

Depreciation

Business assets, such as equipment, office furnishings, and other major purchases connected with your business are expensed through depreciation. Recent tax changes have greatly complicated the way depreciation is claimed. You may need professional advice on this topic.

Depreciation must be taken in the year in which it is sustained. You cannot deduct in any one year the allowable depreciation that you failed to take in a prior year.

If you begin your business using certain equipment previously purchased with personal funds, you may be able to take a business depreciation on such items. Talk to an accountant about this. For instance, you might already have an office in your home, with an expensive typewriter, computer, file cabinets, and so on.

For more information on all of the above, obtain the IRS publications on depreciation and the election to deduct part of the cost of certain depreciable property in the year of purchase.

Employees (Also see "Independent Contractors" and Labor Laws.")

As an employer of *non-family employees,* you must comply with certain labor laws discussed elsewhere. As an employer of your own family members, however, your concern will largely be one of taxes and corresponding paperwork.

First, it must be emphasized that the IRS may *carefully* scrutinize the tax aspects of transactions involving family employees. Therefore, make sure they are performing "meaningful work," and that you keep careful records of the hours they are employed and the manner in which you've calculated wages.

What are the tax advantages of hiring family members? Prior to 1988, wages paid to one's spouse were exempt from unemployment and Social Security (FICA) taxes. Sole proprietors no longer enjoy this tax deduction, however, except as it pertains to wages paid to one's children.

Check with an accountant about the amount you can pay a child employee without having to pay taxes. This amount would be a deduction for your business which would lower taxes on your business profits.

When you pay your spouse to work for your business, you may take this as a business deduction, which lowers the amount of Social Security taxes paid on Schedule C business profits. However, your spouse must pay Social Security taxes on his or her earnings (and state and federal income tax must also be withheld from such income), so there is no real tax advantage here. One simply needs to decide in whose Social Security account deposits would be most advantageous.

Note: It may be possible to also hire your spouse as an independent contractor, useful if you only need help for major jobs a few times a year. In this case, you would issue a 1099 form at year's end, and your spouse would report his or her income on a Schedule

SCHEDULE C
(Form 1040)

Department of the Treasury
Internal Revenue Service (0)

Profit or (Loss) From Business or Profession
(Sole Proprietorship)
Partnerships, Joint Ventures, etc., Must File Form 1065.

▶ **Attach to Form 1040, Form 1041, or Form 1041S.** ▶ **See Instructions for Schedule C (Form 1040).**

OMB No. 1545-0074

19**87**

Attachment
Sequence No. **09**

Name of proprietor	Social security number (SSN)

A Principal business or profession, including product or service (see Instructions)

B Principal business code
(from Part IV) ▶

C Business name and address ▶ ....

D Employer ID number (Not SSN)

E Method(s) used to value closing inventory:
　(1) ☐ Cost　　(2) ☐ Lower of cost or market　　(3) ☐ Other (attach explanation)

F Accounting method:　(1) ☐ Cash　　(2) ☐ Accrual　　(3) ☐ Other (specify) ▶ ....

		Yes	No
G	Was there any change in determining quantities, costs, or valuations between opening and closing inventory? (If "Yes," attach explanation.)		
H	Are you deducting expenses for an office in your home?		
I	Did you file **Form 941** for this business for any quarter in 1987?		
J	Did you "materially participate" in the operation of this business during 1987? (If "No," see Instructions for limitations on losses.)		
K	Was this business in operation at the end of 1987?		
L	How many months was this business in operation during 1987? ....▶		

M If this schedule includes a loss, credit, deduction, income, or other tax benefit relating to a tax shelter required to be registered, check here. . ▶ ☐
If you check this box, you **MUST** attach **Form 8271**.

Part I　Income

1a Gross receipts or sales	**1a**	
b Less: Returns and allowances	**1b**	
c Subtract line 1b from line 1a and enter the balance here . . .	**1c**	
2 Cost of goods sold and/or operations (from Part III, line 8) . .	**2**	
3 Subtract line 2 from line 1c and enter the **gross profit** here . . .	**3**	
4 Other income (including windfall profit tax credit or refund received in 1987). . . .	**4**	
5 Add lines 3 and 4. This is the **gross income** . . . . ▶	**5**	

Part II　Deductions

6 Advertising		**23** Repairs		
7 Bad debts from sales or services (see Instructions.)		**24** Supplies (not included in Part III) . .		
8 Bank service charges		**25** Taxes	/////	/////
9 Car and truck expenses		**26** Travel, meals, and entertainment:	/////	/////
10 Commissions		**a** Travel	/////	/////
11 Depletion		**b** Total meals and entertainment .		/////
12 Depreciation and section 179 deduction from Form 4562 (not included in Part III)		**c** Enter 20% of line 26b subject to limitations (see Instructions) .	/////	/////
13 Dues and publications		**d** Subtract line 26c from 26b . . .		
14 Employee benefit programs		**27** Utilities and telephone		
15 Freight (not included in Part III) . . .		**28a** Wages . . .		/////
16 Insurance	/////	**b** Jobs credit . . .		
17 Interest:		**c** Subtract line 28b from 28a		
a Mortgage (paid to financial institutions)		**29** Other expenses (list type and amount):		
b Other		....		
18 Laundry and cleaning		....		
19 Legal and professional services . . .		....		
20 Office expense		....		
21 Pension and profit-sharing plans . . .				
22 Rent on business property				

30 Add amounts in columns for lines 6 through 29. These are the **total deductions** . . . . . . ▶ | **30** |

31 **Net profit or (loss).** Subtract line 30 from line 5. If a profit, enter here and on Form 1040, line 13, and on Schedule SE, line 2 (or line 5 of Form 1041 or Form 1041S). If a loss, you **MUST** go on to line 32 . . . . . | **31** |

32 If you have a loss, you **MUST** answer this question: "Do you have amounts for which you are not at risk in this business?" (See Instructions.) ☐ Yes ☐ No
If "Yes," you **MUST** attach **Form 6198.** If "No," enter the loss on Form 1040, line 13, and on Schedule SE, line 2 (or line 5 of Form 1041 or Form 1041S).

For Paperwork Reduction Act Notice, see Form 1040 Instructions.　　　　　　　　　　　　Schedule C (Form 1040) 1987

Notes

C Report, which is one of the easier tax forms to understand and complete. (See sample nearby.) Schedule C income, of course, *is* subject to self-employment taxes.

You definitely need the help of an accountant when you hire an employee, even one in your own family, because there are a number of aggravating tax forms to be completed and filed. Included are: (1) an SS-4 form to get your Employer Identification Number; (2) a form 940, which will exempt you from paying unemployment taxes on wages paid to family members; (3) a W-4 tax registration application for withholding tax, similar to the form you must complete when you file for a tax identification number to collect sales tax; (4) an Employer's Quarterly Federal Tax Return (Form 941), which indicates wages paid to family employees, and taxes withheld — your accountant will give you a handy chart for this; and, at year's end, (5) W-2 forms stating income paid to each employee for the year, plus (6) a W-3 Transmittal form to accompany the W-2 forms you must send to the appropriate Social Security Administration office and your State's Department of Revenue.

I know, I know. All this sounds awful. I felt the same way about it, which is why I turned the chore over to an accountant who told me which forms to send when and where. Once I got past the initial paperwork, it wasn't bad at all. Certainly the tax advantages at year's end are worth it all.

Employer's Identification Number (EIN)

This federal taxpayer number is required by the government at the point when one becomes an employer. Partnerships, corporations, and non-profit organizations also need an EIN number. Sole proprietors without employees may also obtain and use an EIN number instead of their Social Security number on all business forms that ask for a "taxpayer identification number." This number is obtained by filing IRS Form SS-4, available wherever tax forms are found.

Environmental Protection

There are several restrictions on the taking and use of protected wildlife and plants. If your business in any way involves such things — particularly feathers, bones, claws, or ivory — obtain additional information from the U.S. Fish and Wildlife Service, Department of the Interior.

Federal Trade Commission (FTC)

In addition to the laws pertaining to consumer safety and the labeling of certain products (as discussed earlier in the section, "Consumer Safety Laws"), the FTC is especially concerned with truth in advertising and the mail order industry. See chapter eight for FTC guidelines on advertising and information about the 30-day mail order rule.

Hobby Income

Is yours a "business" or a "hobby?" Do not confuse a hobby with a trade or business. The IRS says that you are in business if you (1) are sincerely trying to make a profit, (2) are making regular business transactions, and (3) have made a profit at least three years out of five.[2]

If you do not meet IRS criteria, your "business" will be ruled a "hobby" and any loss you deducted will be disallowed. (You can show a loss on a business, but not on a hobby.)

If you decide you only want to work at home as a hobby, you are still required to report your hobby receipts on Schedule C of Form 1040, and list all the expenses you incurred to earn this income. If you end up with a profit, you'll have to pay taxes on it. If you end up with a loss, however, you are not entitled to a deduction.

Independent Contractors

This is a very troublesome term right now, in view of several current court cases which are debating whether certain people are "employees" or "independent contractors." The problem is simply that no one has yet legally defined this term, not the IRS or the Department of Labor, two government agencies who do not always see eye-to-eye on this topic. So, until these words are defined in a court of law, doubt is apt to remain.

Ordinarily, the hiring of independent contractors presents no problems for the small business owner. Often it's just a matter of one business buying the products or services of another business. The problem comes when you, as a business owner, hire an individual to "work for you" in some capacity when that individual, in truth, is *not* a self-employed businessperson. To quote IRS: "If an employer-employee relationship exists, it does not matter what it is called." In short, an employee *is* an employee if the IRS (or the Department of Labor) says so. In general, an "employee" is one who "follows the usual path of an employee" and is dependent on the business which he serves.

The Supreme Court has offered certain guidelines which are considered "significant" in the determination of whether a person is an employee or independent contractor. They include:

1. The extent to which the services in question are an integral part of the employer's business. (The more integral they are to the employer's business, the more it will tend to show an employee-employer relationship.)

2. The permanency of the relationship. (The more permanent the relationship, the more it tends to show an employee-employer relationship.)

3. The amount of the alleged contractor's investment in facilities and equipment. (The more substantial the investment[2], the more it will evidence an independent contractor relationship.)

4. The nature and degree of control by the principal. (The more control exercised by the principal over the person, the more it will evidence an employee-employer relationship.)

5. The alleged contractor's opportunities for profit and loss. (The more opportunity he has to make a profit, or sustain a loss, the more it will evidence an independent contractor relationship.)

6. The amount of initiative, judgment, or foresight in open market competition with others required for the success of the claimed

---

[2]There have been exceptions to rule number 3. In the end, the most important factors are the amount of time you devote to your activity, plus the way you present yourself to the public as being engaged in the sale of products or services; also the way you keep records of your business.

Notes

independent enterprise. (The more initiative, judgment, and foresight that is required, the more it will show an independent contractor relationship.)

For more information, see the Department of Labor Booklet, "Employment Relationship Under the Fair Labor Standards Act." The IRS also offers a mouthful-of-a-form that may be helpful (or possibly more confusing): "Information for Use in Determining Whether a Worker is an Employee for Purposes of Federal Employment Taxes and Income Tax Withholding." (Form SS-8, available at local tax offices, or by mail from IRS).

Obviously, the small business owner prefers to use independent contractors whenever possible because it cuts paperwork in half and eliminates tax withholding. If you hire independent contractors, all you have to do at year's end is complete a 1099 form (Statement for Recipients of Non-Employee Compensation) for each individual to whom you have paid $600 or more. One copy goes to the IRS and the other to the contractor.

Insurance

Half of us are probably "insurance poor," and the other half so under-insured that we're worried to death about what will happen if "the worst" happens. Some of us have both problems.

It's easy to be insurance poor these days in view of the high cost of all kinds of insurance, particularly medical and health policies. As a self-employed individual, one secret to cutting insurance costs is to belong to an organization that offers group plans. (Under "Insurance Programs" in the chapter four Resources you'll find information about a few of the plans I've investigated to date. When you write to the various business and professional organizations I've also listed, ask especially about any insurance plans they may offer members.)

Meanwhile, here is other insurance information I've gathered to date. Some of it is likely to propel you to the telephone for a consultation with an insurance agent.

• **Homeowner's or Renter's Insurance Policies:** It's important to tell your insurance agent that you run a business at home because your regular homeowner's or renter's policy will *not* cover business equipment, supplies, or inventory nor, in all probability, any losses due to fires that may be caused by such things. Note that "goods for sale" are considered business property which *must* be separately insured, either with an individual policy or a special rider.

One such rider is a *Business Pursuits Endorsement*. This can cover liability for people in your home for business purposes as well as materials and products you are storing. If you are storing over $3,000 of inventory, you should probably obtain a separate fire, vandalism, and theft policy.

Computers present a problem, too, if they're used in conjunction with a home business. Most homeowners' policies will not cover computers in this capacity, and even if the computer and software is protected against fire or theft, that still leaves you with possible risks related to damage caused by water, high humidity, or power surges. The latter can cause extensive damage to circuits, although a voltage surge suppressor can prevent this.

If you sell art or handcrafts, normally taking them to fairs or shows, you might want to investigate special policies designed to protect such property both at home, in your studio, or in transit to and from exhibitions and shows. (See the policies offered by Artists Equity Association and the American Crafts Council.)

P.S. Do you know that, for very little extra each year, you can obtain *replacement-value insurance* on all your possessions? With a regular homeowner's/renter's policy, what you get in the event of loss is figured on the current value *after depreciation*. This often brings dollar amounts down to little or nothing. A replacement-value policy, on the other hand, will pay you whatever it costs to replace any item that's been damaged or destroyed, regardless of its age at time of loss.

No insurance policy will be worth much, however, if you can't prove what you owned prior to total destruction by fire or other disaster. Thus, you should make a photographic record of all your possessions and keep it, along with all documentation possible as to the value of each item in a safe place — not your home. You might put the photos and back-up material in a safe deposit box and, for added protection, place the negatives somewhere else. (Even safe-deposit boxes have been destroyed in some instances.) If you have special collections of any kind, (antiques, diamonds, silver, furs, guns or cameras, artwork, etc.) be sure to have them appraised and insured by a separate rider.

• **Liability Insurance.** Each of us can be held liable for a lot of things, and when you have a business at home you need to be doubly careful. *Personal liability insurance* protects you against claims made by people who have suffered bodily injury while on your premises, while *product liability insurance* protects you against lawsuits by consumers who have been injured while using your product.

Regarding personal liability insurance, ask your insurance agent if you're covered in these cases: A deliveryman (maybe the UPS driver) slips on the ice on your steps while delivering a business package, breaks his back and can never work again. Big lawsuit! Or a customer or client suffers bodily injury while in your home on business and sues for hospitalization costs and loss of job income. *Why* these people are on your property will determine the coverage your insurance policy provides. Read the fine print and talk to your insurance agent.

Inquire about an "umbrella policy" that will take over where your present coverage stops. You might be able to buy a million dollars' worth of liability insurance for as little as $100 per year. The same kind of umbrella policy is available on your automobile policy as well. Here, the difference in premium costs for one million vs. five million dollars' of insurance may be ridiculously small. (Insurance agents never quote prices on such high coverage unless they're pressed on the matter. So *ask*.)

• **Product liability insurance** is equally important to many business owners, but more expensive, and sometimes critical to the sale of merchandise. A garment maker of my acquaintance had to cancel a large order because the store she was doing business with insisted that she have product liability insurance on her products — gifts for babies and children, a very touchy area. National mail-order catalog houses often insist on product liability insurance, too.

When this book was first written, it was not terribly difficult for product makers to obtain affordable insurance policies. The picture has since changed dramatically. The sharp increase in the number of liability claims, coupled with steadily rising insurance premium costs, has put all of us in the midst of an unprecedented liability crisis. Some insurance premiums have risen by as much

Notes

as 1000 percent or more, while some insurance companies have reduced coverage for businesses or withdrawn it altogether.

Parks are closing across the country because insurance is no longer affordable, doctors and other professionals are ceasing practice rather than pay exorbitant insurance premiums . . . and many small business owners are being faced with a hard decision: Should they continue to operate without liability insurance, or cease operation?

Historically, few craft manufacturers have carried product liability insurance because most handcrafted/handmade items are considered relatively safe. But ceramic pots have been known to break and spill hot contents on the owner's lap, doll's eyes have been swallowed by children, and stained glass windows have shattered in the process of being hung. According to the book, *Making It Legal*, the legal rule of product liability is: *"Defective product plus injury arising from customary or foreseen use equals maker or seller pays."*

Thus, try to guard against customer injury of any kind, set high quality control standards, "idiot-proof" your products, and try to design away any potential harm. If the latter isn't possible, at least warn the public of possible harm by including instructions on the proper use of your products to avoid that harm.

In hopes that this liability situation will improve in time, I'm including some of the information that appeared in the first edition of this book. It will at least serve as a guideline when searching for protection against today's litigious consumers.

Look first for a nearby agency that sells business or commercial insurance, including well-known companies like American Family, Allstate, and State Farm. One insurance agent told me that product liability insurance rates vary greatly from state to state, depending on your annual gross sales (or anticipated sales), the number of products you sell, and the possible risks associated with each of them. An insurance company will look closely at what your products are made of and consider possible side effects you'd never imagine. If your income is low and your product line small, you may be able to buy an affordable policy. In your desire to save insurance premium money, however, don't overlook the fact that you do need high limits of coverage. It's also wise to have a policy written so that limits apply on a "per claim" basis instead of a "per occurrence." For example, a flaw in the manufacturing process which causes hundreds of defective products is a "single occurrence" to the court, and a "per occurrence" limit in a policy might not cover the several "per claim" lawsuits that could result.

Some small business owners incorporate their businesses merely to obtain legal protection for personal assets in the event of a lawsuit. While incorporation does afford a certain degree of protection, it is not the complete answer. As attorney Leonard D. BuBoff pointed out in an article for *The Crafts Report* (June 1986): " . . . individuals who are actually responsible for wrongful acts will remain liable for those acts. The corporation will protect your personal assets from being exposed only when your employees or agents are responsible for the business' liability."

If you're concerned about your liability situation, you would be wise to consult an attorney, who could present "a worst scenario" and possibly offer a solution to your problem. Meanwhile, for more general information, order the booklets from The Consumer Products Safety Commission, as noted in the resource chapter. In particular, order "Consumer Product Safety," a free booklet available from the Department of Commerce.

- **Disability Insurance (Or Income Replacement Insurance):** If you are the major breadwinner in your family, what would happen if you could not work for a month, three months, a year . . . or ever again? Investigate the cost of a policy that would give you at least some income during this period.

- **Business Interruption Insurance:** Another "for instance": Your home is destroyed by a fire or a tornado, and your business stops until you can piece it together again. Business interruption insurance could make a big difference, and it may not be as expensive as you think. Talk to an insurance agent about it. Investigate group plans offered by professional organizations.

- **Worker's Compensation Insurance:** If you hire employees, your state may require that you carry worker's compensation for them. The amount you pay will vary depending on the number of employees you have and the kind of work they do for you. Contact your state capitol to connect with the office that administers this program. This can also be purchased through your insurance agent if you prefer to have all your coverages through one agency.

- **Partnership Insurance:** If you are in partnership with someone, it is necessary to establish a Buy-Sell Agreement, funded by life insurance. By law, at the death of a partner, your business is dissolved and can no longer operate until it is either liquidated or reorganized. The agreement, prepared by an attorney, establishes the price the survivor will pay for his share of the business, and that the heirs will sell for, and the insurance provides the money to complete the transfer.

For more information, see free SBA aids, "Insurance Checklist for Small Business" and "Business Life Insurance."

IRAs (Individual Retirement Accounts) (See also "Keogh Plans.")

Every self-employed individual should have an IRA because it's an excellent tax shelter and a great way to build a retirement nest egg. Wage earners are entitled to put up to $2,000 of earnings into an IRA. (Self-employed individuals may also contribute to a Keogh Plan.) This money will eventually be taxed, of course, but you will presumably be in a lower tax bracket when you retire. Withdrawals from an IRA may begin at age 59½ or be delayed up to age 70½. There is a 10% penalty for a withdrawal before age 59½ and taxes would be due on such funds at that time. (You may draw on an IRA without penalty if you become disabled before age 59½, and in the event of death, IRA funds are paid to one's beneficiary.)

Under the Tax Reform Act of 1986, *deductions* for IRAs are now limited to those who do not participate in the pension plan of their employer. In addition to contributing to one's own IRA, a current entrepreneurial tax strategy is to hire one's spouse to perform work for the business, pay that spouse at least $2,000 per year, and take this amount as a business deduction. Meanwhile, the spouse places this $2,000 into an IRA, legally avoiding taxes on it until retirement age.

You have until the due date (not including filing extensions) of your tax return each year to establish or contribute to an IRA. Once you open an account, you can contribute varying amounts each year, or make no contribution at all. And if your first IRA ends up paying lower interest rates than new ones that come to your

Notes

attention later, you can stop paying into the first one and open one or more additional accounts as desired. All will continue to earn interest for you until you decide to withdraw funds. At retirement, you can elect to withdraw all the funds at once (and pay taxes accordingly), or withdraw money in installments as needed. For more information, talk to a banker, accountant, lawyer, or investment counselor.

Keogh Plan

Self-employed individuals may establish Keogh plans for purposes of sheltering larger amounts of their earnings each year than is possible with an IRA. There are many similarities between IRAs and Keogh plans, such as withdrawal requirements and penalties, but each has advantages and disadvantages. The main difference with a Keogh is that a self-employed individual may shelter far more than $2,000.

If you have employees, you may have to include them in your plan, too. Talk to your banker, accountant, or lawyer about the advisability of a Keogh Plan for your business.

Labor Laws

The Department of Labor administers several laws which affect the operations of American businesses both large and small. *The sole proprietor, however, need not be concerned with any of them (save minimum-wage laws) until non-family members are hired as employees.* At that point, the following laws apply to one's business:

• **The Fair Labor Standards Act of 1938, as Amended.** This law establishes minimum wages, overtime pay, recordkeeping, and child labor standards for employees individually engaged in or producing goods for interstate commerce, and for all employees employed in certain enterprises described in the act, unless a specific exemption applies. Employers are required to meet the standards established under the Act, regardless of the number of their employees and whether they work full or part-time. A complete copy of this act, and additional information about the hiring of employees, can be obtained from your nearest Wage & Hour Division of the Department of Labor. (See "U.S. Government" in your telephone book.)

• **Occupational Safety and Health Act (OSHA) of 1970.** This statute is concerned with safe and healthful conditions in the workplace, and it covers all employers engaged in business affecting interstate commerce and who have one or more employees. Employers must comply with standards and with applicable recordkeeping and reporting requirements specified in regulations issued by OSHA. Some states operating under OSHA-approved state plans conduct their own occupational safety and health programs. The law provides that a small business may request loans through the Small Business Administration when it can show that substantial economic injury is likely to result from a requirement to comply with standards issued by either Federal programs or by approved state programs. In all states, business men and women may request the services of consultants who advise employers about compliance with OSHA, but who are not inspectors and do not issue citations for non-compliance. Priority for consultation is given to small business employers. OSHA training and educational materials and services may be obtained from 91 local agency area offices of the U.S. Department of Labor.

• **Social Security Act of 1935, as Amended.** This act is concerned with employment insurance laws, and each state requires employers who come under its employment insurance law to pay taxes based on their payroll. For more information, contact your local Employment Security or Job Service Office, or talk to an accountant.

• **Other laws administered by the U.S. Department of Labor.** You need not be concerned with these laws unless you are involved in situations that concern (1) garnishment of employee's wages; (2) hiring of disadvantaged workers; (3) federal service contracts using laborers and mechanics; (4) federal contracts for work on public buildings or public works; (5) employee pension and welfare benefit plans; (6) government contracts, and other special situations.

Legal Forms of Business

On the following page, you'll find a chart which compares the advantages and disadvantages of the three basic forms a business can take: sole proprietorship, partnership, and corporation.

Most small businesses are sole proprietorships simply because this is the easiest kind of business to start, operate, and end. A disadvantage of this form of business is that the owner is fully liable for all business debts and actions, meaning that personal assets are not protected from lawsuits.

Many small businesses elect to form a partnership so the work load and responsibility for the management of the business can be shared. It's important to have a contract in any kind of business partnership and advice from legal counsel. Be cautious about entering into a partnership with a close friend because many friendships have been destroyed in the name of business.

A corporation is the most complicated form a business can take. While it offers special advantages, such as protection for one's personal assets in the event of a lawsuit, it involves a lot of paperwork, plus legal and accounting services.

A corporation is a legal entity unto itself, and it does not die with the retirement or death of its officers. Investments may be transferred from one party to another without affecting the operation of the company. Although some small businesses incorporate themselves at the beginning to protect their personal assets from the possibility of a lawsuit, it might, at times, be less expensive and just as safe to simply buy liability insurance. Other times, however, a homebased business needs to be incorporated because it involves individuals from two or three families, and this is the best way to protect everyone's interests.

Some experts have said that incorporation does not justify its additional costs unless one's business profits have reached five figures and exceed personal income needs. However, only you and your lawyer or accountant can determine what's best for your particular business and personal tax situation. It is entirely possible, and quite legal, for you to incorporate without the services of a lawyer, but this is not something a business novice should attempt. One lawyer pointed out to me that it will cost more to unincorporate yourself than to incorporate, so you don't want to make the wrong decision. This is just one more reason to seek professional advice.

Legal Forms of Business

	Pluses	*Minuses*
Sole Proprietorship	1. Controlled by owner 2. All profits to owner 3. Little regulation 4. Easy to start 5. Earnings personally taxed	1. Liability unlimited 2. Limited resources 3. No continuity at retirement or death
General Partnership	1. Joint ownership and responsibility 2. Access to more money and skills 3. Earnings personally taxed 4. Limited regulation and easy to start	1. Conflict of authority 2. Liability unlimited 3. Profits divided 4. No continuity at retirement or death
Limited Partnership	1. General partner(s) run the business 2. Limited (silent) partners have no liability beyond invested money 3. Profits divided as per partnership agreement 4. Earnings personally taxed	1. Limited partners have no say in business 2. General partners have unlimited liability 3. More regulations to start than general partnership
Corporation	1. Limited liability 2. Ownership interest is transferrable 3. Legal entity and continuous life 4. Status in raising funds	1. Regulated by states 2. Costly to form 3. Limited to chartered activities 4. Corporate income tax plus tax on personal salary and/or dividends
Subchapter S Corporations	1. Receives all advantages of a corporation 2. Electing corporation taxed as sole proprietorship	1. Highly regulated both by state and IRS 2. Restricted to certain kinds of business and limited number of stockholders

The above information is reprinted from the U.S. Department of Labor booklet, "More Than a Dream: Raising the Money."

Notes

Subchapter S Corporation: This is a corporate structure for new or low-income businesses. Unlike the usual type of corporation, profits or losses of a Subchapter S are reported on a shareholder's Form 1040, as in a partnership.

For more information, see the free SBA management aids, "Selecting the Legal Structure for your Firm," and "Incorporating a Small Business."

Licenses and Permits (Also see "Zoning.")

Although many, *many* home business owners have never bothered to get a local (municipal or county) license or permit — and probably never intend to — most businesses apparently need one if they are to operate completely within the law. No one goes around checking to see who has licenses and who doesn't, however, which probably accounts for the lack of attention people generally pay to this detail.

In general, food-related businesses will always be subject to special restrictions and inspections by local and state health departments. The Fire Department may have to give some kind of permit or official okay if you work with flammable or dangerous materials. If your business causes the release of any materials into the air or water, you'll need approval from the local environmental protection agency. Door-to-door sellers probably need some kind of peddler's license. A day-care center would have to conform to certain local and state regulations. If you work with animals or agricultural products, check the Department of Agriculture; if you work with the handicapped or elderly, contact the social services department of your local or state government. Even a small mail-order business probably needs a permit of some kind to comply with local zoning ordinances.

Certain professional people and tradesmen, such as accountants, auto mechanics, photographers, cosmetologists, TV repairmen, and others, will need occupational licenses issued by the state. Such licenses, designed to protect consumers, are issued by the state agency that administers consumer affairs. Contact your state capitol to connect with this particular agency to see if you need an occupational license of any kind.

Whether you get a license or permit for your business may depend on zoning regulations in your area. In some parts of the country, all home businesses are outlawed. (See discussion of zoning at the end of this section.)

Generally, a business license or permit will cost from $10 — $100, depending on your business. If you operate without one, you run the risk of discovery, at which point you could be fined and your business could be brought to an abrupt halt. Thus, it's a good idea to find out how solid the ground is under any unlicensed business you may already be operating. Take a trip to the city or county clerk's office under the guise of " . . . just wondering about starting a business . . ." and get the facts. You may find it a simple and inexpensive matter to legally establish your business, and then you won't have to worry about it any more. If you're truly concerned by what you learn on this "research trip," ask a lawyer for advice on what to do next.

For more information, see *Business Kits for Starting and Existing Business*. Eventually, a book will be issued for each state, containing all the specific information a businessperson needs for that state.

Notes

Licensing

If you want to use a famous copyrighted design or character, such as Snoopy, you must be licensed by the copyright holder before you can reproduce this image on any product or even use its name. Some people who have become "personalities" also license others to use their name or face on some product or service.

Such licensing arrangements are expensive and usually involve royalty payments based on sales. You may never have any intention of obtaining such a license, but if you ever find yourself in a position to license others to reproduce a design you've created, you'll want to know about The National Stationery Show in New York. Apparently a lot of "licensing connections" are made here. (See "Trade Shows" in resource chapter.)

Occupational and Health Hazards

"100 million Americans may be using dangerous materials without knowing it," says The Center For Occupational Hazards, a national clearinghouse for information on this topic. If you have an undiagnosed illness, it could be related to your improper use of certain materials related to your work. Particularly harmful when not properly used are paints, paint thinners, plastics, photo chemicals, dyes, lead, asbestos, and dozens of other materials or substances. See the resource chapter for more information on The Center for Occupational Hazards, and how to educate yourself to the hazards in your workplace. Note that the Center offers a list of physicians across the country who are qualified to diagnose work-related illnesses which often go undetected by regular physicians.

In addition to occupational hazards related to your health, there may be hazards relating to your safety as well, particularly if strangers ordinarily come to your door in the normal course of business. Take these sensible steps to insure your personal safety:

- If you don't know your customer, don't advertise the fact that you are alone in the house. There is much you can do to create the impression someone else is at home.
- Never tell anyone except trusted neighbors and your mailman that you're going to be out of town. Casually-dropped information like this can easily be overheard by the wrong person, making you a prime burglary candidate.
- Don't tell people on the phone that you'll be "gone until 4:30" for the same reason.
- A course in self-defense might make you feel safer. So would a guard dog.

Patents

A patent is a "grant issued by the United States Government giving an inventor the right to exclude all others from making, using, or selling his invention within the United States, its territories and possessions," according to a booklet issued by the Patent Office. A patent lasts for 17 years from its issue date and may be granted to anyone who invents or discovers a new and useful process, or any new and useful improvement thereof. All this sounds simple enough but, in truth, patents are a very complicated, and very expensive, way of protecting "intellectual property."

Theoretically, patents are a good way to protect your good ideas and original inventions. But in the *NBC Magazine* television show first aired in December, 1980 and rerun in July, 1981, the moderator said — and I quote: "The patent office is still run as if this were the horse and buggy age, and many patents aren't worth the paper they're printed on."

One expert called the patent system a "cruel hoax," pointing out that many patents have been granted only to be later invalidated. One reason is because patents are still being filed the way they were a hundred years ago, stuffed in cubby holes or heaped in overflowing file boxes on the floor. Nothing is on computer, of course.

Sure, you can "search the files" to see if a patent already exists on your idea, but as many as 20% of the files can be missing at any given time, so you can never be really sure if a similar patent exists or not.

And "similar" is the key word here. First, you cannot patent anything that would be obvious to anyone skilled in the process or field; second, if your patent is contested by a company with clout, it will be child's play for them to prove that your patent resembles some item already patented, and this will automatically void any patent you may hold.

Since a patent gotten with the help of a patent attorney can cost as much as $5,000, you might be better off selling your idea to a manufacturer for a flat fee up front, or on a royalty basis if you can get it. But attorney Mary Helen Sears stresses, "It is dangerous to submit a patentable item to a manufacturer before filing a patent application unless the manufacturer, *in advance* of hearing the invention, commits itself that *you* are the owner. Don't do this without competent legal help or you will lose *all*."

If you decide to manufacture the product yourself, the best thing you can do is get it on the market fast to beat the crowd, because a good idea *will* be stolen the moment you display it at a trade show. "Also," adds Ms. Sears, "if you do decide to manufacture, that is the time the patent usually *is* worth the investment and effort involved — in part because it deters others from suing you on *their* patents, and in part because it *does* deter some copiers as well."

One lawyer on the above-mentioned program said that a patent itself only gives you the right to file an action in court, and it isn't valid until you go to court and prove it. "You can't stop an infringer." he added. "And if you do go to court, you'll lose."

So why waste your time and money on a patent?

Design Patents. Design Patents are primarily for manufacturers who want to protect new and ornamental designs on two- and three-dimensional objects. This might include anything from the design of a garment to the motif on a belt buckle, to the shape of a coffee mug. Fabric designers are often protected this way, also. Like copyrights, design patents are hard to police and just as expensive to defend in court. Unless you're a commercial manufacturer, they're probably not for you. To qualify, a design must be new or novel, original, ornamental, and inventive in character. These patents can be obtained for different terms of years, depending on the fee paid.

For more information, obtain the booklet, "General Information Concerning Patents," available from the Superintendent of Documents, and the free SBA publications, "Introduction to Patents" and "New Product Development." Also see the book, *Making It Legal.*

Postal Service

As a businessperson, you must acquaint yourself with the way the

Notes

postal service operates. Learn about the various types of mail in addition to first class mail, including third class bulk, first class pre-sort, and express mail. Learn about certified and registered mail, too, and postage-paid reply envelopes. Make sure you know what sizes of printed materials are acceptable for mailing before you design and print them. (I'm reminded of one mailer whose catalog was too wide to fit the stamping machine, which required an extra 9¢ postage on each of the 1,000 catalogs being mailed. Odd sizes present problems, so check them beforehand.) Your postmaster will give you a number of free booklets which explain all of the above.

Some people wonder whether they should use a post office box number as their business address. Although the post office will deliver business mail to your home address, a post office box number is the best way to keep a low profile in the community, and also deter drop-in customers. It may also be a solution to zoning problems. For example, a mail order seller in New York who uses her home address for her business had to obtain a "special use permit" to operate. On the other hand, a homebased publisher in California was advised by the license bureau to obtain a post office box number for his address because "the post office is in a commercial zone," and that eliminated the need for any "special-use permit." Check this out, because it may work in your area, too.

Moving presents a problem for many mail-order businesses because mail is normally forwarded for one year only, after which time it is stamped "Moved, not forwardable," and returned to sender. Since ads and publicity in books and magazines often pull for several years, this is a great way to lose orders and prospective customers. The answer I've found is *not* to enter a change-of-address card, but instead retain the post office box as long as sufficient mail is received to warrant its cost, and hire someone locally to pick up and forward the mail. This person can rubber-stamp all first class mail with your new address (i.e., "Please forward to . . .") and drop it into the nearest mail box. The post office will forward this kind of mail indefinitely at no extra cost. Other classes of mail, however, must be repackaged (fourth class mail) and forwarded at regular postage costs.

At the point when you wish to discontinue the use of the box and hiring of an individual to forward your mail, *then* enter a change-of-address card, at which point the post office will continue to forward your mail for yet another year. Note, however, that to receive magazines and third-class mail, you'll have to guarantee forwarding postage on them.

In the past, fourth class packages which contained first class mail had to be so identified, and extra postage affixed to the package to cover that mail. Now, however, first class mail can ride free of extra cost in fourth class packages, and no mention of its inclusion in the package need be made.

Printers

There are printers . . . and there are *printers*. When you find the latter, you've found a helpful companion for your business.

A good printer will take the time to help you with your printing problems and will answer your questions because the more you know, the easier his job will be. Also, the better your camera-ready artwork, the better the finished job, and the happier you'll be.

If you live in a rural area with no printer anywhere for miles around, or if you're just not satisfied with your present printer, you might want to check the listings in the *Directory of Book, Catalog, and Magazine Printers*. (See Resource Chapter.) You will be able to find several printers who can easily work with you by mail.

When it comes to a decision between price and quality, only you can decide what's essential for your business. But remember that your customer will often judge you, your product, and your service on the quality of your printed materials. The best printing job isn't always necessary for promotional flyers, price lists, and certain other printed material like inner-office forms and order blanks. But your brochure or catalog — the piece that really carries your business — *that* should look not just good, but great. So should your stationery, business cards, and the catalog sheets for wholesale buyers. You don't apologize for your products or your service; neither should you have to apologize for the printed materials which describe them.

Sometimes you need a specialty printer instead of an offset printer like the "quick-print" shops you hear about. Some printers specialize in printing only envelopes, or package inserts, or business forms and stationery, and often these specialty printers will give you the best job for your money. Several have been listed in the resource chapter.

It's always a good idea to get quotes from more than one printer, and samples of their work, too. In requesting a quote for any printed job, put your specifications in writing, and ask for quotes on different stocks and weights of paper. Sometimes paper alone can double or triple the cost of a job, and sometimes it also throws the weight of your printed piece into a different postage bracket. Colored stock will normally add 15–20% to the cost of any print job as compared to using white paper. Each color of ink used in addition to black adds to your cost, too, because the press has to be "washed" after each color is used.

Ask for quotes on different quantities, too, such as 500, 1,000 and 2,500 for small press runs, and 5,000, 7,500 and 10,000 for larger runs. What too few beginners realize is that it's the first 500 copies that cost the most, due to the printer's expenses in preparing negatives and plates and setting up the presses. Past these basic quantities, the primary expense will be paper and press time only, which is nominal in comparison to other costs mentioned.

Elsewhere I've discussed "quick printing" vs. "metal plates," so let me only say here that if you've paid for the latter, the corresponding negatives belong to you. The printer will be happy to store them for possible future use, but be certain he understands whether you want them back or not, should he have a certain limit on the length of time such materials are retained for customers.

Always put your printing instructions in writing, one copy for you, one for the printer. All kinds of things can go wrong in a print shop, and if the error is the printer's, you'll want to be able to show it with your written instructions. Good printers will always do a job over at no charge if they've made the mistake. For everyone's protection, especially yours, ask to see a "blue line" before final plates are made for a long press-run job. Better to find typo errors and other problems at this point than to end up with 5,000 catalogs that have something wrong with them. (And this kind of thing has happened to all of us in business at one time or another.)

Notes

Finally, if you've prepared the copy, ordered the type, and done the paste-up work, get someone else to proof the camera-ready art. It's almost impossible for the creator of such work to spot the errors in it because the mind only sees what it knows is supposed to be there, whether it's there or not.

Recordkeeping

"Records are at the heart of controlling your business' destiny," says a Department of Labor booklet, and all businesses must deal with a variety of them. Among others, there are company and accounting records, correspondence, papers relating to sales and purchases, shipping and freight, insurance and personnel.

Most small business owners want to know the kind of records they must keep for tax purposes, and how long they have to keep them. The IRS prescribes no specific accounting records, documents, or systems. They do, however, require that you maintain permanent books of account or records which can be used to identify your business income expenses and deductions. These records must be accurate and kept so that they are available for inspection by IRS officers should the need arise. Since the burden of proof lies with the taxpayer, make sure your records reflect ALL income and expenses.

For a sole proprietorship, a simple system consisting of a check book, a cash receipts journal, a cash disbursements journal, and a petty cash fund is quite sufficient. How long should you keep records? The IRS can bring assessment or collection proceedings for a given taxable year for up to three years after a return is due or filed, so keep all records relating to income and expenses for at least this long, in case of an audit. Some accountants advise that you keep such records for at least *six* years. Certain business documents, of course, should be kept throughout the life of a business.

An important first consideration in setting up your recordkeeping system is whether you will operate on a cash basis or accrual basis.

Cash Method: Used by some small business. All income is taxable in the year it's received, and expenses are generally deductible when paid, with some important exceptions an accountant can explain.

Accrual Method: Tax must be paid on earned income, whether it has been collected or not; expenses may be deducted when they have been incurred, whether they have been paid or not.

"Hybrid System": A mix of the above types of accounting systems. For example, a small business might use the accrual system for inventory purchases and the cash method to record all income and expenses. An accountant will help you decide which method is best for you. (Some businesses are required by law to use the accrual accounting method.)

As important as the records of your business is the way in which you *protect* them once they're established. I've heard many sad stories about a businessperson's loss of irreplaceable records and other papers — everything from damage caused by pipes that burst in the winter to flooded basements where such items are stored, to total destruction by fires or tornados. Until you imagine the results of such a loss, you cannot begin to take steps to protect against it. Ask yourself which of your business documents, mailing lists, correspondence,

---

1988 Tax Update on Cash Method of Accounting

For tax years beginning after 1986, the cash method of accounting may not be used by:

1) Corporations (other than S Corporations) and
2) Partnerships having a corporation (other than an S Corporation) as a partner.

artwork, printed materials, etc. are absolutely vital to the continuation of your business, then take steps to protect this material accordingly. Some of it can be duplicated and stored in fireproof drawers or safe deposit boxes. Other things can at least be centrally located in your home or office so you could grab them on a moment's notice as we did one year when a tornado was sighted a couple of miles from our home.

Since printed materials are an important part of any business, it's a good idea to get in the habit of setting aside a couple of "master copies" of everything you have printed. Even if the original art is lost, at least you'll have an image to work from and all your valuable copywriting won't have been lost.

For more information on how to set up records and do your own bookkeeping, obtain the free publications available from IRS, the SBA, and the Department of Labor. Also see the books, *Small-Time Operator* and *Basic Accounting for the Small Business.*

Sales Tax

Resale tax numbers are required by sellers in most states.

Anyone who sells a product (goods) in a state that collects sales tax must obtain a tax number from the state, even if they do not sell directly to the ultimate user. This resale number may be called different things in different states, but the idea is the same everywhere. You collect sales tax on sales *to the final user* in your state, then send this money to the state with the appropriate form. Small businesses may be able to file annual reports; others will have to file quarterly or monthly, depending on total sales and amount of taxes normally collected.

When you apply for your tax number, your state will send you information and instructions on how much tax to collect, when to file, and so on.

Some people think their tax number entitles them to avoid sales tax on business-related purchases; not so. *This number applies only to merchandise purchased for resale.* The suppliers you deal with will want your number for their files, and whenever you sell to a dealer, be sure to get his number for yours. This documents to the state why you haven't collected tax on a sale. (If you sell wholesale to dealers who do not have a tax number, you have to charge them sales tax on their purchase.)

Another misconception about a sales tax number is that it automatically entitles one to buy goods at wholesale prices. This is not true. Each manufacturer and wholesaler has his own terms and conditions of sale. In addition to establishing certain minimum quantities, these suppliers may also have strict policies against selling to anyone who is not a retailer (owner of a shop or store). This problem is discussed in the pricing chapter.

Social Security Taxes

When the profit on your Schedule C tax report reaches $400 or more, you must file a Self-Employment Form along with your regular income tax form and pay into your personal Social Security account. It is distressing to report that homebased workers do not get a break here; in fact, they must pay into their accounts at a higher rate than regularly-employed workers, and the percentage is increasing all the time.

In 1985, employees paid 7.05% while self-employed workers paid

---

*1988 Update on
Sales Tax Laws*

Several states have now formed compacts with surrounding states in an attempt to force sellers to collect sales tax from customers in states other than their own. Individual states are thus sending letters to everyone who presently collects sales tax, suggesting that they "voluntarily register" to avoid possible problems later. Once registered with another state, companies can be held liable for collecting taxes under that state's law.

This kind of taxation is a nightmare for both small and large mail order companies since different states charge a different rate of sales tax, and sellers are expected to inform consumers exactly what they're supposed to pay.

As near as I can tell, the penalty for not registering voluntarily is that you might be audited and, if "nexus" (business presence for tax purposes) is established, you would be liable for all unpaid use tax and interest plus "substantial penalties." If you do not have nexus, your customers could be contacted for payment of use tax, penalty and interest, the states advise (which might sound good to them in theory, but would be difficult to do in practice). Generally, "nexus" has always meant that one has buildings or employees in a state; now state tax collectors are saying that merely advertising in the local media constitutes presence. (This has not yet been upheld in court, however.)

You should know that many companies are simply ignoring these new state sales tax laws in the belief that they are unconstitutional. A few states have begun legal proceedings against major catalog mailers in an attempt to collect such taxes, but it seems unlikely that any state would have the time or staff to pursue small

(. . . more)

(more . . .)

mail order businesses based at home. A trade magazine said of this matter that "there is an element of bluff here," and one tax examiner in Minnesota said they were primarily interested in collecting taxes on higher ticket items — "certainly not on $10 items, because it's not worth the trouble."

In time, these state sales tax laws may be replaced by a federal sales tax law, and if so, it will probably affect only multi-million-dollar companies. Read trade magazines in the direct mail (mail order) industry to stay informed on this topic.

Notes

11.8%. In 1986, these figures increased to 7.15% and 12.3% respectively. By 1990, they are expected to be 7.65% and 15.3% respectively.

You should periodically request a statement of the earnings shown on your social security record. To get it, simply send a letter to Bureau of Data Processing, Baltimore, MD 21235.

State Laws Restricting Homework

Still more laws? Yes, and if you've read this far, you're probably ready to throw this book at me. It was so much more comfortable not knowing all this stuff, wasn't it? But as a writer, my job is to present facts and information that will enable you to make intelligent, *and financially safe,* decisions. As a home business owner I, too, resent the way government sticks its nose into the homebusiness arena, and the state laws I'm about to bring to your attention will probably surprise and upset you as much as they did me when I first learned about them.

These "homework laws" have never been discussed in the hundreds of how-to-make-money-at-home books published in the past, except in passing, such as " . . . be sure to check on any state laws which may apply to you." They have come to light now only because of their similarity to the Labor Department's "sweatshop law," which has been receiving publicity in the national media since early '83.

Ironically, some of these laws have been on the books for years, and although people have been breaking them right and left, no one has done much about them until recently.

For example, I heard about a woman in California who is being sued by the state for violating its homework law, and when the state is through with her, the Department of Labor will probably file suit as well. *So this situation is real, and really dangerous if you're working in a restricted industry.* If so, please consult an attorney at once — one with experience in labor law.

Now, before you read the information which folows, keep this positive thought in mind: In some states, at least, the situation may not be as bad as it appears on the surface. For instance, even though the New Jersey state law prohibits the manufacture of toys, dolls, and infant's and children's wearing apparel (using homeworkers to produce goods), a close reading of this state's law suggests that these items are prohibited only by unlicensed manufacturers, particularly those in "tenement houses." The law actually reads: *"Purpose of Industrial Home Work Law was to abolish plants known as 'sweatshops' whereby work was 'farmed out' to be done in homes in which unsanitary conditions often prevailed, and in which the aged, infirm and very young were often required to work long hours."*

Perhaps the key lies in whether you are a licensed manufacturer or not. To be safe, you *must* obtain a legal opinion about the law in your state. Although the law may appear to be the same in several different states, the specific articles of each state's law may say entirely different things.

If certain state and federal laws seem to violate your constitutional rights, you'll ave to fight to correct the situation. One way to do this is to join and support the national organizations who are now fighting on your behalf. Also support the efforts of The Center on National Labor Policy, which is working to get outdated Labor Department laws changed.

State Homework Laws

Several states have "homework laws" which affect *employers of homebased workers*. Following is information about items which cannot be manufactured at home, along with each state's employer registration requirements, and penalties for violating the law. The name and address of the enforcement agency to contact for additional information has also been included. (Note: Other items — cigars and tobacco, drugs and poisons, bandages and sanitary goods, and explosives and fireworks — are also prohibited by most states, but have been omitted from the list since it is highly unlikely that they would be considered for manufacture by this book's readers.)

All of this information has been provided by attorneys at The Center on National Labor Policy, Inc.

State	Enforcement Agency	Prohibited Articles	Registration Requirements	Penalties
CALIFORNIA	Division of Industrial Welfare 2422 Arden Way Sacramento, CA 95825 (916) 920-6116	Food and drink Wearing apparel Toys and dolls	All homeworkers must obtain a certificate, valid for a period of one year. Employers of homeworkers must obtain a license. Information must be furnished on materials to be provided, the rates of pay, and descriptions of the final articles to be made. License fee is $100, valid for one year.	*First offense* — Fine not to exceed $1,000, imprisonment for not more than 30 days, or both. *Second conviction* — $5,000 and 6 months. *Third conviction* — $30,000 and 1 year.
CONNECTICUT	Department of Labor and Factory Inspection Labor Department 200 Folly Brook Blvd. Wethersfield, CT 06109 (203) 566-5160	None Listed	Permits issued to homeworkers unable to work in factory because of handicap, illness, old age, or to care for invalid. Employers must obtain a license — $25 per year.	Fine of $25 per day for each day of violation or imprisonment for 30 days, or both.
D. of C.	D. C. Minimum Wage Board (Wage & Hour Division) 614 H Street, NW Washington, DC 20001 (202) 727-2118	None listed	None indicated	None indicated

State	Enforcement Agency	Prohibited Articles	Registration Requirements	Penalties
HAWAII	Department of Labor and Industrial Relations 825 Mililani Honolulu, HI 96813 (805) 548-2211	No homework in garment industry without a special certificate	Certificates issued to homeworkers unable to work in factory because of age or physical or mental disability, to care for a child under 6 or an invalid, or is undergoing vocational rehabilitation. Employers must obtain an industrial homeworker certificate from the Director of Labor and Industrial Relations.	Employers violating provisions of special certificate are subject to fines up to $500 or imprisonment up to 90 days, or both, for each offense.
ILLINOIS	Department of Labor 100 North First St. Springfield, IL 62702 (217) 782-6206	Food and drink Toys and dolls Manufacture of garments	Homeworkers must obtain a certificate. Employers must obtain a license. The original permit is $200; renewal is $50 if no more than 100 homeworkers are employed during the year; $100 if more than 100, but less than 300; $200 if more than 300.	Violations of provisions are punishable by a fine of $10 to $500 each day of violation.
INDIANA	Division of Labor 100 North South Ave. Indianapolis, IN 46204 (317) 633-4473	Coats, Vests, Trousers, Knee-pants, Overalls, Cloaks, Furs, Shirts, Purses, Feathers	Employers must obtain a permit.	None listed.
MARYLAND	Division of Labor and Industry Department of Labor 501 St. Paul Place Baltimore, MD 21202 (301) 659-4191	Restrictions on apparel, feathers, fur, artificial flowers.	Rooms for homework must be licensed and are open for inspection anytime work is being carried on. Employers need not have a license. Homeworkers must have a certificate.	Fine of $5 to $100 or imprisonment from 10 days to 1 year, or both.

State	Enforcement Agency	Prohibited Articles	Registration Requirements	Penalties
MASSACHUSETTS	Department of Labor and Industries 100 Cambridge St. Boston, MA 02202 (617) 727-3454	Apparel items *(except for hosiery and women's millinery)*	Homeworkers must obtain a certificate, good for one year. Employers must obtain licenses, valid for one year. Original fee is $50. Annual renewal is $50 plus $2 for each homeworker from previous calendar year.	Fine of from $50 to $500 or imprisonment up to 2 months, or both.
MICHIGAN	Department of Labor and Industry 309 North Washington Square Lansing, MI 48933 (517) 373-3580	Strict compliance with employment conditions required to manufacture the following: Apparel, Purses	Permit granted after inspection to ensure proper working conditions.	Seizure of goods deemed made in unhealthy workplace.
MISSOURI	Division of Industrial Inspection Department of Labor & Industry Relations 421 East Dunklin Jefferson City, MO 65101 (314) 751-4091	No room may be used by more than 3 persons for the following: Apparel Purses Feathers Artificial Flowers	None listed	Fine of $10 to $50 or imprisonment for 10 days, or both for manufacturing home goods under unclean conditions.
NEW JERSEY	Department of Labor and Industry John Fitch Plaza Trenton, NJ 08611 (609) 292-2323	Food and drink Toys and dolls Infants' and children's wearing apparel	Homeworkers must obtain a certificate, at no cost, valid for one year. Good for one employer only. Employers must obtain an annual permit. License fee is $40 for the original and for annual renewal is $50 for under 25 homeworkers, $100 for 25 to 100 and $200 for more than 100. Employers and homeworkers in the *hand knitting* industry must keep a daily record of work done and maintain records for 2 years	Any *person* who refuses to allow investigation or violates any provision — $100 to $300 fine or imprisonment for not more than 6 months, or both. Any *place* where work is carried on in violation — $200 to $500 fine or imprisonment up to 2 years or both.

State	Enforcement Agency	Prohibited Articles	Registration Requirements	Penalties
NEW YORK	Industrial Commission Dept. of Labor Building State Campus Albany, NY 12240 (518) 457-2741	*All homework* is prohibited in all industries, except where the Industrial Commissioner, after proper study, determines such work may be permitted *without unduly jeopardizing factory workers.* Homework orders, containing special provisions for homeworkers, have been issued for the following industries: Men's and boys' outer clothing Men's and boys' outer neckwear Artificial flowers and feathers Gloves	Permits and licenses are restricted to industries in which the Commissioner determines homework may be permitted without unduly jeopardizing factory workers or unduly injuring the health of homeworkers.	Civil penalty on employer — not more than $1,000 for each violation.
OHIO	Industrial Commission 2323 West Fifth St. Columbus, OH 43204 (614) 466-3271	Restrictions on dwelling (must be used only by immediate family) for: Apparel	None listed	None listed
PENNSYLVANIA	Department of Labor and Industry 1800 N. Second St. Harrisburg, PA 17102 (717) 787-5279	Food and drink Toys and dolls	Homeworkers must obtain a certificate — only issued to those unable to leave home to work because of physical handicap, illness, or to care for an invalid. Employers must obtain permits, to be renewed annually. Original fee: $500. Renewal fee: $100 for under 100 homeworkers; $200 for 100 to 300; $300 for 300 or more.	Fine up to $1,000 or imprisonment for up to 6 days, or both.

State	Enforcement Agency	Prohibited Articles	Registration Requirements	Penalties
P U E R T O R I C O	Commonwealth Department of Labor (809) 751-5353	Food and drink Toys and dolls Cosmetics Pipes and articles for use of smokers	Homeworkers must obtain a certificate and be a resident of the home in which the work is done. Employers must obtain a permit, valid for one year. Original fees: $10 for less than 7 homeworkers; $15 for 8 to 15; $25 for 16 or more. Renewal fees: $5 for less than 7; $7 for 8 to 15; $10 for 17 or more.	Delivery of articles or materials for home-work manufacture without a valid permit is punishable by a fine of up to $1,000 or imprisonment for up to 6 months, or both.
R H O D E I S L A N D	State Department of Labor 220 Elmwood Ave. Providence, RI 02907 (401) 277-2744	Jewelry, including accessories, garments.	Homeworkers must obtain a certificate. Employers must obtain a license if homework in the industry is customary or if homeworkers are physically handicapped or over age 50.	Fine of $100 to $300 for each day for each offense.
T E N N E S S E E	State Department of Labor 501 Union Building Nashville, TN 37219 (615) 741-2582	Restrictions on dwelling.	Persons having control of home work-shops must notify the Board of Health within 14 days of location, nature of work and number of homeworkers.	Any noncompliance subject to a fine as a misdemeanor.
T E X A S	Board of Health 1100 West 49th St. Austin, TX 78756 (512) 458-7111	Any work deemed injurious to health of homeworkers or to health of general public.	Homeworkers must obtain a certificate, good for one year, at a charge of 50¢. Applicant must furnish health certificate. *Nonresident* employers must obtain a permit for $50 for one year.	Fine of $25 to $200 or imprisonment from 30 to 60 days, or both.

State	Enforcement Agency	Prohibited Articles	Registration Requirements	Penalties
West V I R G I N I A	State Department of Labor 1900 East Washington Street Charleston, WV 25311 (304) 348-7890	None listed (besides tobacco, explosives, etc.)	Homeworkers must obtain a certificate, good for one year. Employers must obtain a permit, good for one year, at a fee of $50.	None listed.
W I S C O N S I N	Department of Industry, Labor and Human Resources 201 E. Washington Ave. Madison, WI 53703 (608) 266-9850	Homework may be prohibited to protect health.	Employers must secure permits upon compliance with minimum wage law. Also, a license must be obtained from the local health officer after inspection. The license is $300, good for one year.	Revocation of permits and a fine of $100 for each offense.

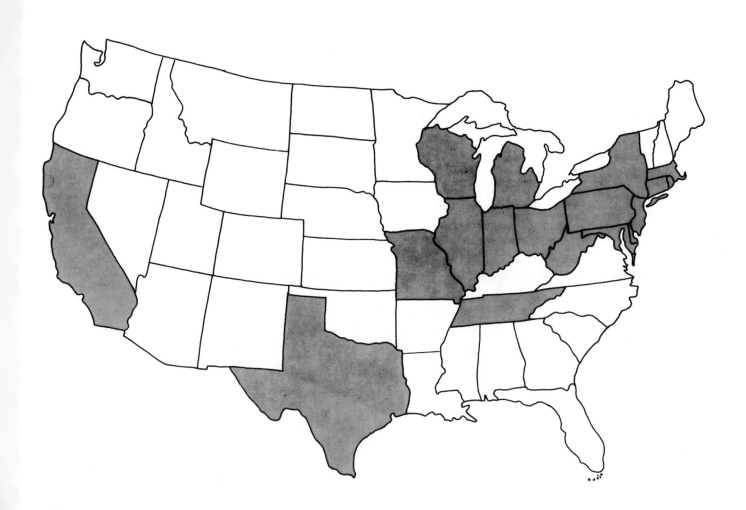

Taxes

As a business owner, you need to be concerned about several kinds of taxes, more if you're an employer than if you're not. Those taxes include:

Federal Taxes. Owner-Manager's Income Tax, or
Corporation Income Tax
Social Security Tax (FICA)
Employee Income Tax (if you have employees)
Unemployment Tax (if you have employees)

Elsewhere in this section, under "Employees," "Labor Laws," and "Social Security Taxes," you found information about the above taxes. Not discussed earlier, however were *Estimated Tax Payments,* which are due from self-employed individuals. These payments are due quarterly, on the 15th of April, June, September, and January. Naturally, there's a penalty for not paying taxes when due, as well as for underestimating them. An accountant will help you figure out the amount you need to pay each quarter, and additional information is available in IRS publication, "Tax Withholding and Declaration of Estimated Tax."

State Taxes: Income Tax
Sales Tax
Unemployment Taxes (if you have employees)

Most states have an income tax. Like the federal income tax, it's calculated on your net income or profit and is generally due at the same time you file your annual federal tax return.

See discussion of sales tax elsewhere in this section and note that, in addition to state sales tax, there may be local sales tax as well. All are calculated together and paid to the state either on a monthly, quarterly, or annual basis, depending on the size of your business and the amount of tax collected.

Local Taxes: Inventory tax

In addition to certain local taxes, your state or local governments may impose an inventory tax — a property tax, actually — on business equipment and inventory, such as the for-sale goods you're holding, or the large supply of books you've just self-published.

For more information about your tax obligations, obtain the free SBA management aid, "Steps in Meeting Your Tax Obligations," and the IRS publication, "Tax Guide For Small Business."

Telephone, Use of Personal Phone for Business

Most homebusiness owners list their personal telephone number on their business cards and stationery, not realizing this may be a serious violation of telephone company regulations. Each state has a separate commission that determines the usage of a residential phone, and you'd be wise to check on this matter. In some states, a stiff fine may be imposed for improper use; in others, you may only be asked to stop doing this. Still others may simply start charging you business telephone rates.

First and foremost, do *not* answer your residential phone with your business name. If you don't want to just say "hello" you can always give your name, saying, for example, "This is Barbara Brabec, may I help you?"

You cannot advertise your personal phone number in connection with business, but you can receive business phone calls on it and make outgoing calls, of course. (The IRS may question large deductions of this nature, so keep a daily telephone log of all your calls.)

Investigate the various long-distance systems now available since service rates and charges vary considerably. Note that only phones with touch-tone dialing will work with the new systems.

Trademarks

A trademark "includes any word, name, symbol, or device, or any combination thereof adopted and used by a manufacturer or merchant to identify his goods and distinguish them from those manufactured or sold by others," according to the Trademark Act of 1946. The primary function of a trademark is to indicate origin, but in some cases it also serves as a guarantee of quality.

Generic and descriptive names in the public domain cannot be trademarked, nor can one adopt any trademark that is so similar to another that it is likely to confuse buyers. Trademarks thus prevent one company from trading on the good name and reputation of another.

To establish a trademark, you first decide which mark you want to use, do preliminary research to be reasonably sure no one else is using that mark, and then start using it on your goods. You cannot file for a federal trademark until the mark has been used in interstate commerce at least once. In other words, *you establish your trademark simply by using it.* Then you take steps to prevent others from also using it on the same or related goods by filing an application for trademark with the Patent and Trademark Office in Washington. (This will cost $175 and take several months to accomplish.)

If your application qualifies for registration, you will be able to use the mark for 20 years and renew it thereafter. Once the trademark registration has been confirmed, you place the notice of trademark, an R with a circle around it, after every use of the trademark word or symbol. (You may also use the words, "Registered in U.S. Patent and Trademark Office" or "Reg. U.S. Pat. and Tm. Off.")

Companies who have not yet filed for a trademark often use the letters "TM" to indicate they've claimed that mark. But one can use these letters even if they have no intention of registering for a federal trademark.

For more information, order the booklet, "General Information Concerning Trademarks," from the Superintendent of Documents.

Trade Practice Rules and Regulations

Write to the Federal Trade Commission and ask for their free booklets on trade practice rules and regulations. Mention your type of business and specifically ask for information about rules relating to it. For instance, there are certain rules for industries such as jewelry making, leather, ladies' handbags, feathers and down, the catalog jewelry and giftware industry, millinery, photography, furniture making, and mail order. In the latter, you need to be especially concerned about such things as the use of customer testimonials, guarantees and

---

Trademark Register

An annual Trademark Register *of the U.S. is published, and may be available in larger libraries.*

The 30th edition of this directory covered the period of 1881–1988 and included 800,000 registered trademarks in use.

Notes

warranties, plus the 30-day rule about shipping orders. (I can't go into all of this here, but if you're in the mail-order business, or plan to start one, you must read a few books on the topic. I've listed several good ones in the resource chapter.)

When an FTC rule has been violated, it is customary for the Federal Trade Commission to order the violator to cease the illegal practice. No penalty is attached to most cease-and-desist orders, but violation of such an order may result in a fine.

United Parcel Service (UPS)

You probably don't need an introduction to UPS, surely the most economical and dependable shipping service in the country. UPS packages are rarely lost or damaged, and delivery halfway across the country takes only a few days. ("Blue Label" service is available at extra cost for packages that need even faster delivery.)

UPS will pick up packages anywhere with just one day's notice — and that includes your residence. There is a weekly pickup charge, presently $3.75, which applies to the first pickup of the week and covers all other packages and pickups in that same week. Packages must be weighed beforehand by the mailer, who then calls the nearest UPS office (toll-free numbers provided) for postage applicable to each package. A simple form, plus a check for total postage completes the process. Packages are automatically insured for up to $100 and additional insurance may be purchased if desired.

Call your nearest UPS office and ask for information about their "Ready Customer Pickup Service."

Zoning

What you don't know about zoning can put you out of business. On the other hand, what zoning officials don't know about you can often remain a harmless secret. The "twilight zone" is nothing as compared to being lost in the "zoning zone," say some homebusiness owners who have fought for the right to work in their own homes. Some have obtained special permits or zoning variances, while others have gone to court to defend their position, and lost.

Many homebased workers seem to be walking a thin line between being legal in the eyes of the IRS, and illegal in the eyes of their local zoning boards. The problem is that most zoning laws were written in horse-and-buggy days when no one could have imagined the millions of people who would someday be working in homebased occupations or businesses. If home businesses are prohibited in your town or city, you have only two choices; work underground or organize homebased workers in the area and fight for changes in the zoning laws.

National homebusiness organizations are fighting right along with you. For instance, in May, 1982, Marion Behr, Founding President of The National Alliance of Homebased Businesswomen was invited on behalf of President Reagan to discuss the administration's proposal for the creation of rural and inner city enterprise zones. She was given an opportunity there to state the organization's interest in seeing tax benefits provided for homebased business people living and working within designated zones. This was the first time homebased business was mentioned in the framework of these discussions.

By 1985, NAHB had circulated its Model Zoning Regulations Set nationally to help members of local zoning and planning commissions make necessary changes in outdated laws.

Notes

Author's Note

The national association mentioned at left is no longer operating.

Activities ceased in June 1988 due to declining membership and lack of operating funds.

One Woman's Zoning Battle

Janet Hansen, owner of Koole-wong, Ltd., a homebased publishing company, has been waging a small zoning war in her community of Mt. Prospect, a Chicago suburb. Her efforts to change zoning laws were discussed in a feature newspaper article that broadcast the illegality of her homebased business to everyone in the community. Curiously, nothing adverse has happened as a result of this visibility and Janet's many meetings with city officials. (It doesn't hurt that she is on the Board of Directors of the local Chamber of Commerce, and President of its Entrepreneur Council.) In short, everyone knows what she is doing, but no one is doing anything about it. It's almost as if this kind of visibility is a form of protection.

Janet reports that she has met with the Chamber of Commerce in her city in an attempt to get their support in changing the residential zoning ordinance. A meeting with the Mayor was fruitless, however. All she said was that she had had no complaints against homebased businesses to date, and would not instruct the Village to go after those running a business.

— Reprinted from National Home Business Report

Endnote: A note from Janet after this article was published reads: "The Village Manager finally got back to me saying they definitely do not want to change the zoning laws. He more or less indicated that the people with offices and stores would be our biggest opponent. I'm still assured that they won't go after the homebased business owner unless a complaint is received."

Leaders in the home-business movement believe that, within a few years, some of the zoning laws in the country will fall or be amended due to the impact of flexible worksites, the electronic cottage, and the work-at-home movement. But what do you do in the meantime to solve your particular zoning problem? First, find out how you stand by reading a copy of the zoning regulations, either at City Hall or the library. Find out what zone you're in, and read the section that pertains to home occupations. Remember that it's your right to see this information without explaining your interest in it.

Zoning officials do not go around checking to see who's violating zoning ordinances. In fact, the only time they do anything about this is if they receive a complaint. Thus, most homebusiness owners have found it best to "keep a low profile." They avoid loud noises, strong odors, obvious customer traffic, and they don't tie up neighborhood parking places, use business signs, or do anything else not in keeping with their particular residential neighborhood. Some people keep their businesses a complete secret, in fact.

The trouble with keeping a low profile is that you can't advertise or publicize your business without attracting undue attention to the fact that you work out of your home, which is one reason some people use post office box addresses.

After reading your local zoning ordinance, if you decide that your business is violating the law but isn't going to create any problems for your neighbors or the community at large, you might want to ask for a variance, or, more likely, some kind of "conditional use," or "special use," or "special exemption" permit. This is generally issued following a public hearing about which your neighbors must be informed. If you can get support from neighbors, the special permit may be easy to obtain.

If you think you may eventually want to fight to change outdated zoning laws in your area, start now to build a list of all known homebased business owners who can give support or testimony when the time is right. (See boxed info left, for the story of one woman who has "taken up the zoning sword" in her community. The results (or lack of them) are both interesting and surprising.)

One last thought: If you rent, or live in a condominium, be sure to check your lease, apartment regulations, or condominium covenants for any clause that may prohibit a homebased business. A business in one unit of a co-op apartment, for example, can affect the tax-deductibility aspects of others in the building. So even if local zoning ordinances aren't a problem, this sort of thing could stop you dead in your tracks.

Someone asked me recently why so many homebased businesses are located in small towns and communities, or out in the country. Maybe it's because zoning ordinances are less of a problem there. If a home business is important to you, and it's currently prohibited by zoning ordinances, perhaps a relocation to another area is your best solution.

Worksheet #1: Concerns or Problems

If you have been making notes in the margins as you have been reading this book, now would be a good time to go back and recap those notes by categories. Use this worksheet and the three that follow to list: (1) your business and legal concerns or problems; (2) the specific questions you should ask your advisors; (3) the resources listed in *Homemade Money* that can help you answer all your questions and problems; (4) the short and long range goals that will key the development and expansion of your homebased business.

Concern or Problem	Action to Take	Action Completed

Worksheet #2: Special Questions

List the specific questions you plan to ask your accountant, lawyer, banker, insurance agent, or other business advisor.

Question to Ask	Person to Ask	Call	Visit	Write

Worksheet #3: Information to Send For

Use this page to list the book and periodical publishers, organizations, and individuals you want to contact for information. Keep a record here of everything you have sent for (as listed in the Resource Directory, starting on page 283) and note when you have received a response.

Name or Title	Resource page #	Date Requested	Received
_____	_____	_____	_____
_____	_____	_____	_____
_____	_____	_____	_____
_____	_____	_____	_____
_____	_____	_____	_____
_____	_____	_____	_____
_____	_____	_____	_____
_____	_____	_____	_____
_____	_____	_____	_____
_____	_____	_____	_____
_____	_____	_____	_____
_____	_____	_____	_____
_____	_____	_____	_____
_____	_____	_____	_____
_____	_____	_____	_____
_____	_____	_____	_____
_____	_____	_____	_____
_____	_____	_____	_____
_____	_____	_____	_____
_____	_____	_____	_____
_____	_____	_____	_____
_____	_____	_____	_____
_____	_____	_____	_____
_____	_____	_____	_____
_____	_____	_____	_____
_____	_____	_____	_____
_____	_____	_____	_____
_____	_____	_____	_____
_____	_____	_____	_____

Worksheet #4: Short and Long Range Goals

Use this page to list your short and long range business goals. Note any particular action you should take to achieve those goals.

Short term goals	Long term goals	Action to take

Pricing
for
Profit

5.

PRICING IS EVERY SELLER'S PROBLEM. It always has been; it always will be. Unless you are involved in a business where the retail price of the merchandise you sell already has been set or suggested by someone else, you are going to have pricing problems of one kind or another throughout the life of your business.

Product and service sellers alike need to be concerned with the same basic pricing factors; the value of one's time, profit, overhead, labor costs, and so on. In addition, there are a number of intangible factors to consider, such as the way price affects one's image (and thus the growth of a business), the preconceived notions buyers have about the worth of certain things, and market trends, among others. Product makers/manufacturers have yet another major factor to consider: the cost of raw materials and their availability at wholesale prices.

As a consumer with a lifetime of shopping experience behind you, it's only natural to ask yourself how much you would be willing to pay for your product or service if you were the buyer instead of the seller. This kind of common-sense logic in evaluating the prices you set is fine, if you happen to be selling to a market of buyers much like yourself. But unless you're rich, or at least a "free spender," you may find it hard to believe that some people might actually pay the price you need to make a profit on whatever it is you are selling. People in this category tend to keep their prices low because they are afraid no one will buy at a higher price.

This is just one of the little traps sellers, myself included, sometimes fall into. Time and again I have heard people say, "But no one will pay more than this for what I offer." Sometimes that's true; but often this statement is based on belief, not fact, and this belief is directly tied to one's own pocketbook and spending habits. While fearful sellers sit around complaining that no one will pay more, smart entrepreneurs come along and offer almost the same thing at two or three times the price — and get it. Why? Because they know some things fearful sellers do not. They know their marketplace, they have marketing savvy, and they know exactly what it takes to get people to part with their money.

> *"Pricing can make you or break you. If your price is wrong, it hardly matters whether you do everything else right."*
>
> — *Michael Scott, editor,*
> The Crafts Report

Notes

The Value of Your Time

Few people seem willing to set a price on the worth of their own time, yet everyone in business must do this, and soon. Most people who work at home don't have enough time to begin with. As their home business workload increases, each hour seems more precious and fleeting.

The decision as to what one's time is worth is a very personal one. It is influenced by many factors, including one's education or degree of skill, age, professional reputation (if any), amount of salaried job experience, level of confidence, and degree of boldness or nerve. Where a person lives also has much to do with the pricing of a product or service, as does a person's need for money, or lack of need for it.

Women who have been homemakers all their lives may tend to think their time is of no value, particularly if they have little or no salaried job experience. But *this* has absolutely nothing to do with anything. It is *not* this job experience that determines the worth of one's time in a home business, it is what one does with that time that counts. It's what you know, and what you know you are capable of doing. If this happens to describe you, don't sell yourself short. Your time is worth as much to you as it is to the richest businessman in America.

People with full time jobs naturally equate the value of their time to their present salary, while others may decide on an hourly rate by asking themselves what they could earn if they went out and got a job. This is a good place to start, but Kate Kelly, author of *How to Set Your Fees and Get Them,* reminds us that self-employed people always should multiply the hourly rate they receive in a salaried job by at least 2.5. In her book, she explains.

> "Let's suppose that you're making $16,000 per year on staff. That means you earn approximately $308 per week; $62 per day, and $8 per hour.
> "To arrive at a starting figure for your hourly rate once you are self-employed, multiply $8 by 2.5 (some even say by 2.8 or 3). This means that you would use $20 an hour for your initial estimate as to what you might charge.
> " . . . the true reason for the multiple figure is overhead."[1]

I can just hear some of you product makers hollering, "But I can't charge $20/hour for my time. That would put the price of my products totally out of reason." If you're making all the products you sell, you probably are right. But this only emphasizes the fact that it is difficult, if not impossible, to make a large amount of money when you — the entrepreneur — are also the entire labor force of your business. In that case, maybe what you ought to do is set several different hourly rates for the various jobs you do; perhaps $20/hour for design time or marketing, and a much lower rate for labor (based on whatever you would have to pay to hire a production worker).

Remember that while owners of product businesses can make a profit from the individual items they sell, owners of service businesses must include in their hourly price whatever profit they hope to realize at year's end. In truth, the only product they have

---

[1]© 1982 by Kate Kelly. Used by permission of Visibility Enterprises.

to sell is their time and expertise, and it must be valued accordingly.

In this light, then $20/hour isn't much money at all, especially when one considers what professionals in many fields currently receive. I think one problem here is that many of us are still living in the past (particularly if we have been out of the job market for some time), before inflation took its toll and dramatically increased the price of everything. Often it's hard to believe that some businesspeople — particularly those who work at home — are able to command and get $60 or more an hour for their time. But of course an hourly rate like this is based on many years of experience in a particular field. You may have a long way to go before you reach this point . . . or maybe you already are there and just have not realized it yet.

The Profit Factor

"Profit" and "wages" are not the same thing, though most of us working at home tend to forget this fact. After you have paid all the expenses related to your business (including your own salary and any wages paid to others), the idea is that there still should be something left over as profit for the owner or company. But there won't be if you forget to include profit in your pricing formula.

Product sellers, in particular, often fail to add profit into their price. They simply set wholesale and retail prices based on the cost of materials, labor, and overhead. But this can be an expensive mistake, says Ambrose J. Rouble, a CPA in Dearborn, Michigan. "If you base your price on costs alone, you're foolish. Put something in for profit, too," he emphasizes.

For example, once you have set your wholesale price on a product, try adding a 10-20% profit margin. Let's say you have picked $18 as the wholesale price. The examples below show how the profit calculation affects the figures:

10% profit: $18 wholesale price × 10% = $1.80 + $18.00 = $19.80 adj. wholesale
20% profit: $18 wholesale price × 20% = $3.60 + $18.00 = $21.60 adj. wholesale

While this small hike in the wholesale price may mean little or nothing to the buyer, it can mean a lot to you. For example, if you sell 500 units of this item in a year, look what happens:

10% profit: $1.80 × 500 units = $900 profit for you
20% profit: $3.60 × 500 units = $1,800 profit for you.

And while you are thinking about that, here's another thought to ponder: if you work on a 10% profit margin, you will have to sell $1,000 worth of goods to offset a $100 loss; or, on a 20% profit margin, $2,000 worth of goods to recoup a $200 loss.

Since profit is so closely tied to both sales and costs, you must consider both of them whenever you are looking for ways to increase your business profits. Selling more goods won't mean much if your costs also increase to any degree. On the other hand, if you can lower your costs, your profits will increase even when you don't make additional sales. An accountant once told me that it was a lot easier to increase profits by decreasing costs than by increasing sales, because of the high cost of marketing and obtaining each new

Notes

customer. I certainly can see the wisdom of that remark from a study of my own business records.

As you might suspect, the only way to assure continued profits for any business is through a constant analysis of what's happening in that business. Whether you are selling products or services, it's important for you to study all the sales and cost figures relating to your business. In them you will discover the clues to what you must do to increase profits each year. Sometimes it means increasing the price of certain products or services; sometimes it means adding something else to your line (which, incidentally, may have little effect on your overhead costs); and sometimes it means dropping a product or activity that clearly is proving to be unprofitable.

I worked at my present business for almost two years before I "found the time" to get really serious about my books and the information in them. What I finally learned came as a real surprise. A thorough analysis of your books after a year or so will no doubt surprise you, too, particularly if you make and sell a variety of products, or if you are involved in a diversified business involving both products and services. For example, I write articles and books, self-publish books and a newsletter, present workshops and seminars, do some consulting, and have a couple of sidelines going as well. Each of these activities takes a certain amount of my time; a factor that is fairly easy to estimate on an annual basis. Although I always have kept track of the income each of my business activities has generated each month and year, it was not until my third year in business that I decided to break down all the business expenses and overhead costs relating to each of these income categories. Suddenly I could see what really was happening with the business. Then I knew the direction I had to take to realize greater profits in the years ahead.

It was then I also began to analyze the income and expenses related to each item in my product line, and I saw clearly that some products which seemed to be making money (based on gross sales) were really not profitable at all in terms of their material and handling costs. As a result, I dropped some of them.

Perhaps a fictionalized account of a business that involves the sale of both products and services will give you a better idea of what I'm talking about. Let's assume that a business grosses $36,000 one year — $30,000 of which is from the sale of products, the balance from some service; let's say teaching, or consulting. Here's how the figures might look on the Schedule C tax report:

Gross receipts or sales	$30,000
Cost of goods (labor + materials)	−13,500 (45% of total sales)
Gross profit	$16,500 (55% of total sales)
Other income (services)	+ 6,000
Total income	$22,500
Less business deductions	−10,500 (35% of total sales)
Net profit before taxes	$12,000 (40% of total sales)

Not let's break down the income and expense figures into two separate categories:

Product Portion of Business		Service Portion of Business
$30,000	gross receipts	$6,000
–13,500 (45%)	labor + materials	– 100 (2%)
$16,500 (55%)	gross profit	$5,900 (98%)
– 9,750 (32.5%)	deductions	– 650 (10.8%)
$ 6,750 (22.5%)	net profit before taxes	$5,250 (87.5%)

$12,000

Although the "bottom line" is still the same — $12,000 — the service portion of the business is obviously the most profitable in terms of labor, materials, and other expenses. But, to really "see" what's happening in this fictional business, one would need to continue the analysis by separating all the income and cost figures for each individual product or service. Although there might be ten or twelve products in a line, such an exercise might show that one of them was generating 50% of the income, and one or more were, in truth, costing more to inventory and ship than they were worth.

Whether this fictional business owner decides to expand the service area or the product area would have much to do with the particular business and the market for the products or services it offers. If it is a one-person manufacturing company, and no plans are being made to hire employees to increase productivity, then perhaps it would pay to drop part or all of the product line and concentrate on providing additional services. Choosing the right direction for this business may not be a simple matter, but with figures to work with, at least the owner will not be making plans in the dark.

Try this kind of income vs. cost analysis for each product and service in your business at least once a year; quarterly, if possible. The answers you get not only will help you evaluate the correctness of all your prices, they will give you the comfortable feeling that at least you know where you're going and why (even when the profit picture is not as rosy as you would like it to be).

Bringing Overhead Into the Picture

"Overhead" includes all the operating costs of a business that are not directly related to the production of a specific product or service. Such costs are generally fixed, monthly expenses. Even when a business is generating zero income, overhead costs will be adding up. Specifically, overhead includes rent, utilities, telephone, insurance premiums, car expense (or other transportation costs), employee expenses, maintenance, cleaning and repairs, packing materials, freight charges, office equipment and supplies, and other miscellaneous costs that may be related to the overall operation of your particular business.

If you have been in business for at least a year, it will be fairly easy for you to pull all these overhead figures together to arrive at an average monthly cost. But if you are just starting, you will have to do some fancy guessing and estimating. To illustrate how

A Checklist of "Overhead" Items

In trying to determine your business's overhead costs, remember to include all of the following:

☐ *rent*
☐ *utilities*
☐ *insurance premiums*
☐ *car expense*
☐ *other transportation costs*
☐ *employee expenses*
☐ *maintenance*
☐ *cleaning and repairs*
☐ *shipping*
☐ *packing materials*
☐ *freight charges*
☐ *office equipment and supplies*
☐ *other miscellaneous costs related to the overall operation of your particular business*

Notes

Hangtags . . . the professional touch that often increases sales.

These hangtags illustrate the variety of sizes and shapes one can use. (They're shown in reduced size, of course.) Note that tags can provide information about one's business, how products are made (with loving care, etc.), type of materials used, care and cleaning instructions, or technical information about the manufacturing process. Or, tags can simply convey a whimsical note designed to tug at the buyer's heartstrings.

Hangtags courtesy of: (A) Flo Hoppe; (B) Johnny Kearney; (C) Julie Larson; (D) Bobbie Irwin; (E) Susan Johnson; (F) Sara Thill; (G) Marjorie Turner; (H) Pat Cody.

BASKETS
by FLO HOPPE

A.

overhead figures fit into the pricing picture, let's assume that your annual business overhead costs are $3,000, and you're working 1,000 hours per year on your business. That means your hourly overhead rate is $3.00 per hour. Now, you can either add this hourly figure to the one you arrived at earlier for your time, or, if you make goods for sale, you can apply it proportionally to each product on a percentage basis.

Assume for example a $3.00 per hour overhead cost. If you can make three of something per hour, you would add $1.00 to the labor and materials cost for each of those three products. Or, if it takes two hours to make a product, you would add $6.00 in overhead costs to each product.

Some production workers use a different method based on the total cost of labor plus materials. For example, if you spend $15,500 to produce your goods in a year, and you have $3,000 in overhead costs, you would divide $15,500 into $3,000 to get a percentage of overhead to production. In this example, it's 19%. That translates to 19¢, which is the amount that should be added to every dollar of production costs on an item.

Example: An item costs $10.39 in labor and materials. Add 19% of this figure ($1.97), increasing total cost to $12.36.

Start now to document all the overhead costs that will affect the profitability of your business in the months and years to come. You might set up an "overhead notebook," one with 13 columns so you can record expenses by month and then total them at year's end. At the beginning of each new business year, you could refer to these figures to see how much your overhead costs had increased because of inflation and other expense factors, then increase your prices accordingly.

The Game of the Name

You will recall that I talked about positioning in the preceding chapter, explaining how this affects the marketability of certain products. (Remember the candymaker who sells in gift shops instead of food shops?)

Through the ages, people have collected shells from the seas and used them in various ways. Some were used for food, as medicine, jewelry, dye, for trading, ornaments, tools and many other uses.

We have collected shells from around the world and used them to make music boxes. This one is made from a

SCALLOP

shell from THE ATLANTIC OCEAN

The tune is "LARA'S THEME"

We hope you enjoy it as much as we enjoyed making it for you.

Richloy crafts

P.O. Box 337
Sparks, Maryland 21152 (301) 628-0167

B.

whenever our missouri raised grandmother thought something was especially delightful she said she was in "goose heaven"; that's how we feel about simple country things.

C.

← fold

Fiber Content — Care & Cleaning

Warp:

Weft:

Yarn ends may appear on the surface of this fabric, especially after cleaning. Do not cut the ends; pull them to the reverse side with a crochet hook.

Do not bleach.

You may wish to use a stain repellent on this item.

D.

Closely tied to this idea is what you call your product or service. In fact, there is quite a game to this business of a name, and it can greatly affect your ability to wholesale a product successfully. A common complaint from many product makers is that they can't find the right market; or worse, they have the right market in mind, but their pricing structure will not allow for wholesaling to it. If this is your problem, one solution might be to change the name of whatever you're selling and offer it to a different market.

For example, if you call a garment a "patchwork vest" and offer it for sale at a local crafts fair or shop, it might command a price in the $35–$65 range. But if this same item happened to be of unique design, labeled "One-of-a-kind Wearable Art," and marketed in an exclusive designers' clothing shop in New York City, it might command a price of several hundred dollars.

To further illustrate, consider the following list of craft items now being made for sale in countless homes across America. Merely by changing the names of such items — and thus suggesting greater consumer benefits — higher retail prices can often be commanded.

- *Candles* can be sold at higher prices when their image is not merely functional, but decorative, as in *Wax Sculptures.*
- *Folk paintings* may seem more valuable to buyers if they are called *Early American Folk Art.*
- *Crude wood carvings* will attract a more affluent buyer if they are called *Primitives,* and sold in art galleries instead of craft or souvenir shops.
- Large *cloth dolls* can command higher prices when they become *life-size sculptures* or *manikins* for use in fine shops and stores.
- *Found-art jewelry,* made from pieces of wood, bone, shell, etc. has brought higher prices in specialty and department stores when labeled *Folkloric Jewelry.*
- *Sewing machine embroidery* takes on a new image when it is called *Machine Artistry.*
- *Quilts* will sell for more when they are offered as *art,* suitable for hanging.
- *Replicas of antiques* may be worth more in buyers' minds if they are called *Authentic Period Reproductions.*
- *Knick-knacks* of all kinds will be worth more to buyers if they are identified as *collectibles.*

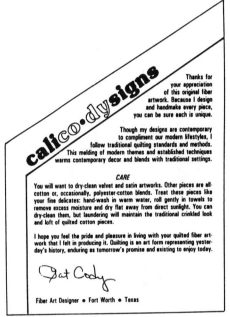

H.

E.

F.

G.

Notes

Back in the days when I was selling handcrafted and handpainted boxes and other decorative woodenware, I had an interesting shop experience that taught me a valuable lesson. I took several of my boxes to an exclusive shop on the north shore of Chicago and was amazed when the manager opened them and said, "But there's nothing in them." I naturally replied that they were supposed to be empty, so people could put things into them, but she just was not interested.

I got to thinking about her remark and came up with an idea. When I went back a few weeks later, I presented the same line of boxes, with one difference: this time, each one had a musical movement in it. "Ah!" she exclaimed. "What lovely music boxes these are." Voila! The same boxes I could not sell empty at prices of $7.50 to $22.59 could now be sold at three times the price, simply because the name of the item had been changed, and had taken on new importance in the minds of buyers. Yet my only extra cost was about 15 minutes labor per box, plus the movement, which in those days sold for as little as $2.75.

You don't have to make boxes to apply this kind of thinking to your product line. Just look at everything you make and ask yourself what changes or additions you could make that might enable you to call things by a different and more expensive-sounding name.

A simple hang tag with the right "sales message" on it, or a message written on the product itself, often can double the worth of an item to the buyer who is looking for just the right gift for a friend. I'm reminded of a little handpainted picture my husband and I once bought. It was just a sailor standing by a rowboat, and we never would have thought it worth more than three or four dollars, except for the fact that it bore this message: "Old sailors never die; they just get a little dinghy." It was the perfect gift for Harry's old school chum, and we happily paid $10 for it.

Here is another tip for product makers. Instead of trying to market all your products on an individual basis, take a look at what you have and see if you can't come up with some kind of special gift package, kit, or coordinated ensemble. Think about offering a "Holiday Gift Pak," a "Gourmet Selection," a "Beauty Care Kit," a "Designer Bathroom Ensemble," a "Mother's Sanity Kit" (things to keep kids out of mischief), or a "Special Gift for Baby," and so on. You not only will sell more products this way, you also will get a higher price for them.

What you call yourself, and the way you promote your business, has a lot to do with the prices you can command, too. For instance, are you a "legal typist," or the best professional in town whose motto is "The Lawyer's Best Friend?" Are you the fellow down the street who fixes old furniture, or are you an "Old World Artisan" who offers expert refinishing of antiques?

Businesspeople often speak in terms of the "business package" they offer. Remember that you can offer a business package, too. You either can present it in plain brown wrapping paper — for "a plain brown price" — or you can add some glitter and ask a higher price for it.

A service may be easier to sell if it is presented as a "package." For example, if you plan parties, you are not just a "party planner," but a packager of several, separate services that probably include every little detail; from sending invitations to planning the menu and decorations, to finding just the right entertainment. So present your business package with flair! Offer a little pizzazz and *charge* for it.

In trying to sell a "service package," you need to identify its true customer benefits. Why should people use your service instead of that of your competitor's? Do you have more experience, a better business reputation, do you offer special guarantees of satisfaction, faster service, more attention to detail . . . what? Remember that buyers often will pay extra for intangible benefits like these. (How many times have you heard yourself saying things like, "Well, you only get what you pay for," or, "This is important to me, so I want the best I can find. Price is no object.")

> *"Never charge a client what you think you're worth; charge what you think he's worth."*
>
> *— Anonymous*

Notes

How to Quote a Job

For some great advice on how to quote a fee or price any kind of service, I urge you to read Kate Kelly's book, which I mentioned at the start of this chapter. One thing Kate stresses is to give yourself plenty of time to figure the price you need. "No matter when the subject of money comes up," she says, "make it a practice of getting back later with a figure. Unless you're simply quoting an hourly or daily rate which you've set in advance, or if it's a fee on a proposal you've written (when you've had ample time to consider how much work is involved), then it's too early to talk money."

Different jobs will require different rate structures. You will need to consider quoting by the hour, versus by the day, per head, or per project. Some jobs lend themselves to a flat rate charge, while others need to be charged on a retainer or contingency fee basis.

Some professionals charge by the hour when their services are required for only an hour or two, and offer a more economical hourly rate for a full day's work. In setting a daily rate, much has to do with the amount of preparation time that is required, plus travel time, in some cases. As a workshop leader, for example, I charge a flat fee for a one-day workshop. While my fee may seem high to some, one must consider that a one-day workshop actually takes almost four days of my time: a day of preparation (planning the program, gathering handout materials, packing, etc.); a day of traveling (poor plane connections often require leaving in the morning to get somewhere by 5 in the afternoon); the day of the workshop, and the return trip home.

Some jobs are better quoted by the project, particularly if the job is one you know you can do easily and quickly, but which may seem difficult to the client. As Kate points out, people often react poorly to knowing how much she earns an hour. "When they compute and compare their hourly staff pay with mine, they tend to forget that I must pay for my own insurance, set aside my own pension benefits, and budget for any vacation time I take. What's more, I couldn't possibly bill out forty hours a week, so my overall income is almost surely less than they expect."

In setting fees of any kind, remember to consider your overall experience and expertise. Just because you may be able to do a job in a day doesn't mean someone else could do it that quickly, or as well as you. The client, after all, is buying *your* experience and expertise. You are not obligated to tell him how quickly you have done the job. There are definite advantages in not delivering a job too quickly, lest the client thinks he has, indeed, been overcharged. As Kate confirms, "Recently I billed $1200 for a project due in seven days' time, and the client never knew whether I polished it off in

Notes

a day or burned the midnight oil for a week, though I feel quite certain that he preferred to think the latter."

Setting fees and quoting on specific jobs is both an art and a skill, and a topic I can only touch on in this book. But the help you may need is readily at hand in Kate's book, *How to Set Your Fees and Get Them.* I urge you to read it if you are in a service business of any kind.

Some Pricing Formulas to Try

Before any pricing formula will work, you have to come up with some kind of hourly rate for your time or labor. Here is one of the most sensible formulas[2] I have ever found. It can be applied to any kind of business.

1.

Hourly Rate Formula

Desired annual net income ÷ by number of working hours per year + annual expenses ÷ by number of working hours per year = hourly rate needed to realize desired annual net income.

Here, the hourly rate is determined through a calculation based on time and expenses. Decide how much you would like to net for the year, then estimate the number of working hours per week and multiply this figure by 50 weeks (giving yourself two weeks vacation). Then add your fixed, variable, and selling expenses for the year and divide by the number of working hours per year. Add this hourly figure to the first hourly figure to get the final hourly rate you will need to charge to realize your desired net income at year's end.

EXAMPLE: Let's say you desire $10,000 net income, and you work part time 20 hours per week × 50 weeks, or 1,000 work hours per year. Divide net income by 1,000 work hours to get a $10 hourly rate for your time. Now add up expenses for the year. Let's assume they are $8,375. Divide this expense figure by 1,000 hours to get an hourly expense rate of $8.38. Add this to the $10 figure to get a total of $18.38, or the amount you must charge per hour to realize $10,000 net income at year's end.

Before I present some pricing formulas for manufacturers, let me share these comments, which I turned up in an old magazine article in my file:

"New product pricing is one of the few areas of management in which there is virtually no organized body of knowledge based on practical operating experience. There is a wealth of abstract economic theory on pricing in general, but it is too far removed from the realities of new product introduction to be of much help. When the marketing executive faces his first experience in pricing a new product, he thus finds himself relying almost entirely on his own intuition."[3]

[2]Libby Platus' Pricing Principle, as noted in *The Crafts Report.*

[3]from the article, "Hardwork, Experience Bring Direct Mail Lesson," in *Direct Marketing* magazine, February, 1981.

2.

Classic Formula for Manufacturers

Cost of labor + materials for one unit × number of units to be produced in a year + estimated annual overhead costs + desired annual profit ÷ by number of units to be produced in a year = wholesale cost per unit × 2 = retail price.

Here, the idea is to get into the price of each item not only all the costs and expenses, but the profit as well. Whether you are planning to produce several thousand units per year, or a limited edition of 250 handmade items, this formula clearly will show you any pricing problems you are going to have.

EXAMPLE: Let's assume that you're going to make laminated walnut-and-pine breadboards. Based on your time it takes to make one, you figure you can make 800 a year. Let's then assume that you will have to invest a total of two hours' time in each breadboard, and that you want at least $8/hour for your labor. Materials cost will be $1.25 per board (you have a good source for scrap lumber). That gives us a total labor + materials cost of $17.25/unit.

Let's also assume that you will have $3,000 overhead costs for the year, and that you would like at least $2,500 profit from your money-making enterprise. Here's how the figures would work out:

$17.25 × 800 units = $13,800 + $3,000 + $2,500 = $19,300
÷ 800 units = $24.12 (wholesale price) × 2 = $48.25 (retail price).

Logic tells us that $48.25 is too high a price for a breadboard, even one that is to be offered as an exclusive hand-made item in a gourmet catalog. (At least I never would pay that much for one.) What this exercise has done, then, is point out that you either will have to be satisfied with a lower hourly labor rate or less profit. It's clear you would not be able to reduce your materials cost much, if at all. On the other hand, if you could produce this item in half the time, the figures would change considerably, as follows:

$9.25 (labor + materials) × 800 units/year = $7,400 + $3,000 + $2,500 = $12,900 ÷ 800 units = $16.12 (wholesale price) × 2 = $33.25 (retail price) — a more reasonable price.

If you think the price still is too high, you will have to sacrifice profit, trim your overhead costs, or do something to the product itself to give it a higher worth in the customer's mind.

If you want to work with this formula, but have no idea what overhead costs and profit might be, simply begin with what you know a product will cost you in labor and materials, then estimate how many you can produce and sell. The difference will be what's left to cover overhead and profit.

EXAMPLE: Let's suppose you want to write and publish a book, and you plan to do all the layout and pasteup work yourself. You find from a printer's estimate that it will cost you $938.11 to print 1,000 copies of a 64 page, perfect bound book, or $.94 each. To this per-book print cost, you must also add production costs, including graphic art and cover design ($250), typesetting ($896), and something for all the hours you

Notes

are going to spend putting the book together: let's say 80 hours at $6/hour, or $480. (Don't count the time you spend writing the book, however.) Production costs thus add up to $1,626. Now divide this cost by the number of books you plan to print (1,000), to arrive at a cost of $1.63 per book. Add the print cost of $.94 per book to get a total book cost of $2.57.

Now let's assume you can sell 1,000 copies of this book on the retail level for $5.95. Multiply that figure times 1,000 books for a gross income of $5,950. Deduct your costs of $2.57 per book, or $2,570 and you have $3,380 left. The question is whether this is enough to cover your time in writing the book, plus the overhead costs connected with your endeavor. And don't forget all the marketing costs and time that will be required to advertise and sell the book by mail. The arithmetic looks like this:

(a) $938.00 ÷ 1,000 books = $ .94 per book (print cost)

(b) $ 250.00 — art and design
    896.00 — typesetting
    480.00 — labor
    $1,626.00 ÷ 1,000 books = $1.63 per book (production cost)

(c) $ .94 print cost + $1.63 production cost = $2.57 total book cost

(d) $5.95 (sug. retail price) × 1,000 books =
    $5,950.00 gross income

(e) −2,570.00 ($2.57 × 1,000 books)

(f) $3,380.00 left.
    Is it enough?

Note: Trade book publishers figure that the retail price of a book needs to be from 6–8 times the total production cost to make it a profitable title. Self-publishers rarely are able to set retail prices this high because their print quantities are too low. Also, there seldom is enough room in their pricing formula to allow for wholesale prices, so they must sell the book only by mail, a costly marketing method.

Craftsellers and other "thingmakers" often use simple pricing formulas like the ones that follow, but only as a general guideline. In the end, they know a thing is worth only what it can be sold for, and a pricing formula is worthless whenever it yields an unrealistic retail price. But just for fun, let's apply the same basic figures to each of the three formulas below, to see how they work.

Without identifying the object we are making, let's assume that our materials cost is going to be 86¢, we can make three units an hour, and we want $6/hour for our labor. (Labor cost per unit, then, is $2.00.) In the first formula, we also will add 20¢ for overhead and a 20% profit based on the wholesale price.

3.

A. Materials + Labor + Overhead + Profit = Wholesale price × 2 = Retail Price
$ .86 + $2.00 + $ .20 + .61 = $3.67 × 2 = <u>$7.34</u>

($3.06 × 20% = $ .61)

B. Materials + Labor × 3 = Wholesale price × 2 = Retail price
$ .86 + $2.00 × 3 = $8.58 × 2 = <u>$17.16</u>

C. Materials × 3 + Labor = Wholesale price × 2 = Retail price
$ .86 × 3 = $2.58 + $2.00 = $4.58 × 2 = <u>$9.16</u>

Interesting, isn't it? Now if the item we were making happened to be a clothespin doll, all three retail prices would be out of line. But if we were making designer coffee mugs, price A. would be quite acceptable as far as consumers were concerned, price B. would be much too high, and price C. questionable. (It would have to be some mug before I'd pay $10 for it, although I've seen many mugs with higher prices than this.) The point I'm really trying to make is that formulas may be fun, but they are often impractical, and the retail price still has to be adjusted to whatever consumer market one is trying to reach.

Now here's one of my favorite formulas, from Raymond Martell, a jeweler in New Jersey. It's offered for comic relief.

4.

Cost of materials + labor (at the rate it would cost to pay someone to replace owner at the bench) + 40% of the labor-plus-materials figure + 10% of the labor-plus-materials figure for overhead × 2 = retail price.

"Then," quips Ray, "I throw the whole thing out and figure what I can *get*."

In the end, common sense must take over and the retail price must be set by the maker based on what the market will bear. If the maker cannot realize a profit in addition to his or her wages, perhaps the product should be dropped from the line.

The following comments from a Department of Labor booklet seem especially appropriate here:

"No matter which method is used to monitor costs, costs alone are insufficient to fix a price. Expenses must tell the entrepreneur one important fact: the price below which he is losing money. Costs only set a floor. Consumer demand will set the ceiling. In between, the business person must fix a cost-competitive price. In the last analysis, your price must lie somewhere between a product's cost and the ability of the buyer to get it somewhere else."

In trying to set the best selling price possible, remember also to consider industry guidelines. For example, if you are in catering, you may learn from a book, as I did, that caterers all over the country just sigh when asked how they figure prices. Many say the question is too hard to answer concretely, but they do use a couple of "rule-of-thumb" formulas. In large cities, like New York, for example,

Notes

caterers multiply the cost of ingredients by four or five, which amount is said to allow for all overhead, profit, and labor costs. Other caterers, in smaller cities, multiply the cost of ingredients by three, then divide by the total number of guests the client plans to invite.

Similar guidelines for other professions and industries will be found in books, several of which I've listed in the resource chapter. In particular, there are special pricing guidelines available for people who offer typing, business, and computer services, as well as those whose businesses include cooking, consulting, teaching, herbs and gardening, animals, music, child care, fine art, crafts, design, graphic arts, photography, repair services, and so on. In short, you do not have to work in the dark. You just have to do a little research.

The "Break-Even Point"

This is the point at which your annual income from sales covers your costs. The income received after this point is profit.

The Break-Even Point

Sometimes the price decision on a product can be made as a result of a break-even analysis. Let's suppose that you plan to sell a new toy, and you want to price it at about $25. You estimate you can sell 300 toys in one year. You know your direct costs per toy (materials, labor) will be $10, and you estimate your annual fixed expenses for the business (overhead) are about $3,000. Here's how to find out how many toys you would have to sell to break even:

1. The difference between the selling price of $25, and the direct costs of the toy ($10) is $15, which is your "contribution to fixed costs per item." Up until your break-even point, every penny of this amount has to go toward covering your fixed expenses.

2. Now apply the following formula to find out how many toys you have to sell to break even:

$$\frac{\text{total fixed costs} \quad \$3,000}{\text{contribution to fixed costs per toy} \quad \$15} = 200 \text{ toys, or number of sales needed to break even}$$

3. To prove the calculation:

$$200 \text{ toys} \times \$10 \text{ direct costs} = \$2,000 \text{ direct costs}$$
$$+ \,\$3,000 \text{ overhead}$$
$$\$5,000 \text{ total costs}$$
$$\text{or } 200 \text{ toys} \times \$25 = \$5,000 \text{ total sales}$$

Thus, if you have built in all your direct costs and other expenses related to this particular item, you would break even for the year when you had produced and sold 200 toys. (For more information on break-even points, see the SBA management aid, "Business Plan for Small Manufacturers.")

Markups and Discounts

The pricing formulas I gave you earlier were all based on the idea of doubling the wholesale price to get a suggested retail price. While a 100% markup is standard for many retail outlets, other markets, such as chain stores or mail-order catalog houses, need larger markups than this, anywhere from 150% — 400%. Thus, the product you make and the wholesale price you set may or may not permit selling to certain markets. (In the following two chapters, you will find more about the markups and discounts normally taken by certain buyers.)

If a buyer tells you he needs a three-times markup in order to accept your product, you can figure out easily enough if your wholesale price is low enough to still yield a retail price that consumers will accept. For example, let's say you offer a hobby kit with a $2.00 cost in materials and labor. A general rule of thumb is that you must mark up this price five times to realize a profit, which means your wholesale price must be $10. You may be able to sell the kit in a store that marks up your price 100%, but will your kit sell for $30 or $40? The answer you get to this question, then, tells you to which wholesale markets you can sell.

Sometimes a buyer will tell you that a discount of 50% is needed. That's easy enough to understand — just divide the retail price in two. (Actually, this is the same as a 100% markup of your wholesale price.) But you may become confused when buyers start talking about discounts of 50+10%, or worse, 50+10+10+5%. A 50+10% discount is standard for many distributors, but in certain industries, distributors try to get additional discounts. I have heard of some that are 50+10+10+10+5%, in fact. Here is the way to figure such discounts, so you will know what these buyers are talking about:

> EXAMPLE: Suggested retail price of item is $20
> Buyer wants a 50+10+10+5% discount.
>
> 1. First turn the percentage figures into decimals:
>   50% = .50; 10% = .10; 5% = .05
>
> 2. Multiply $20.00 × .50 = $10.00 (equivalent to a 50% discount)
>
> 3. Multiply $10.00 × .10 = $1.00
>   Subtract $1.00 from $10.00 to get $9.00
>   (equivalent to a 50+10% discount)
>
> 4. Multiply $9.00 × .10 = $ .90
>   Subtract $ .90 from $9.00 to get $8.10
>   (equivalent to a 50+10+10% discount)
>
> 5. Multiply $8.10 × .05 = $ .405 (round off to $ .41)
>   Subtract $ .41 from $8.10 to get $7.69
>   (equivalent to a 50+10+10+5% discount)

And now, a few general comments about markups. If you sell products directly to consumers, as well as to wholesale buyers (shops and stores), *do not* sell these products at a lower retail price than your retail outlets sell them for. If you do, you not only will jeopardize the retailer's business, you will hurt your own as well, because the retailer will stop buying from you.

In other words, if you make something that wholesales for $10.00 and retails for $20, don't sell this item to a shop for $10, then go to a crafts fair and also sell it to the consumer for $10.00. That is extremely unprofessional.

If you sell wholesale to a shop or store figuring your price will be marked up 100%, as is the normal custom in such outlets, but you later find the shop has marked up the price by 200%, do not

---

Elements of a Successful Kit

"For a kit to be successful, the pattern has to be unique in some way, and also economical. You don't want customers looking at the contents of the kit and thinking they could pull all the components off the shelf for less than the cost of the kit. Good packaging is also essential when marketing to retail outlets (not as critical when selling by mail)."

— Susan Foote, Co-owner of Knot House Industries (from Sharing Barbara's Mail)

Notes

Notes

get angry. It is none of your concern at what price the shop sells your wares. The only thing that should concern you is the fact that you are receiving a fair wholesale price for the merchandise. Some shops price items for what the traffic will bear, and they have every right to do this. However, if you notice that shops and stores in different parts of the country consistently mark up your products more than 100%, it probably is a sign that you are wholesaling them at too low a price. Maybe you don't know the value of what you are selling and should raise your wholesale prices.

Buying Materials Wholesale

Next to labor, the cost of materials is the most important consideration in setting the price on any product. Small manufacturers and other individuals who create a limited number of products for sale each year often run into trouble when it comes to obtaining wholesale prices. Manufacturers and distributors in certain industries (the crafts industry, in particular) simply will not sell to anyone who is not a "qualified dealer;" to them, this means owning a retail store. It doesn't matter whether a buyer can meet their minimum quantity order requirements or not. It simply is an unwritten law in this particular industry: suppliers will not sell at wholesale to homebased manufacturers. (The one exception seems to be manufacturers and small craft sellers who have mail order businesses.)

In other industries, however, suppliers could care less whether one is a homebased business or not. Mostly what they care about is the fact that you are in business, have a resale tax number, and can meet minimum order requirements. Small budgets, however, sometimes make this impossible. And whenever any material used in the production of goods for sale has to be bought at retail prices, a lot of the maker's profit goes right down the drain.

Finding reliable and affordable suppliers is a major challenge for all business owners regardless of size or type. It is a job you must do for yourself. It may take a couple of years before you finally have solved most of your supplier problems.

One of the easiest ways to find the special suppliers you need — a way often overlooked by business novices — is to obtain copies of the Yellow Pages from large cities such as Chicago, New York, or Los Angeles. Call your telephone office for information on how to obtain the directories you need.

To locate other suppliers, see the resource section of this book for directories that will be helpful to you, such as the *Thomas Register of American Manufacturers* and the annual directories published by magazines such as *Gifts & Decorative Accessories* and *Profitable Crafts Merchandising*. Some directories are available in libraries, others can be ordered at reasonable cost. Also note that a number of special business and office suppliers are also listed. You can order by mail from all of them.

Since manufacturers, wholesalers, and distributors do not sell to hobby businesses or individuals, your first job in obtaining wholesale prices is to convince suppliers that you are in business. Do this by having a professional letterhead, and send well-typed letters requesting catalogs. Don't give explanations. Just say, "Will you please send me a copy of your current catalog? Thank you." The businesslike appearance of your letter should do the rest. (If you don't know the proper format for typing a business letter, obtain a secretarial how-to book from the library. If you don't have a typewriter, plan to buy one and learn how to use it; or find someone to type your letters for you. Few businesses can function without a typewriter or other word processor.)

When you receive a catalog and decide to order, be prepared to meet the company's minimum quantity requirements without question. If you are concerned that you might not qualify in their eyes as a legitimate dealer, send your first order on a purchase order (get them at any office supply store), include your resale tax number, and enclose a check for the total amount of the order. (Few companies will turn away an order with a check attached.) You might also send a cover letter saying you are enclosing payment because you need the materials quickly. If you plan to continue ordering from this company, ask for a credit application at this time so you can be invoiced the next time around.

Some manufacturers sell to dealers, bypassing wholesalers and distributors entirely, while others sell only through wholesalers and distributors. When you find a manufacturer who will sell to you at dealer prices, but whose minimum quantity requirements are too high, ask for the name of the distributor nearest you. If you cannot meet the distributor's minimum quantity requirement, the next thing to try is to approach a dealer who carries the materials you want. Ask for a 20% "professional discount." Don't do this within earshot of customers, however, or you'll get a fast turn-down. Instead, telephone for an appointment to discuss a "matter of business." Explain your situation. You may find that the dealer (also called retailer) is interested in selling to you because this will enable the store to buy in greater quantities and thus get a greater discount on the material or item in question.

Another way to find the special suppliers you need is to network with others in your industry, through membership in professional or business organizations, as well as through subscriptions to newsletters and trade periodicals. Sometimes members of an organization band together to buy supplies on a cooperative basis, and this is something you might want to explore.

Good luck!

> *"Networking is vital. Isolation is sure business death. 'Keep in touch' is more than a polite phrase this year. It has become a principle of a healthy business."*
>
> — Decor *Magazine, January, 1982*

Notes

Pricing Worksheet

Referring to the pricing formulas and other information in this chapter, check your prices on specific products or services.

Direct Selling to Consumers

6.

THERE ARE ONLY TWO WAYS to get a product to the ultimate consumer: directly or indirectly. Most small businesses begin by selling directly to buyers on a person-to-person basis through fairs or shows, party plans, home sales, open houses, in-home demonstrations, and door-to-door sales (now called person-to-person selling). What we are talking about, then are over-the-counter sales, personal calls to prospective customers or clients, and all other merchandise or service transactions that involve face-to-face meetings with prospects.

As a business grows, indirect and less personal methods of selling are usually employed, including sales to consumers through retailers, mail-order dealers, trade shows, and a variety of special markets. Retailing is *direct* selling; wholesaling is *indirect* selling. The adjacent chart shows your marketing opportunities in both areas.

This chapter will address the ins and outs of selling at the retail level. The following chapter will discuss the wholesale marketplace; the chapter after that will explain the advertising techniques that can be used to sell on both the retail and wholesale levels, including direct mail promotions, two-step advertising, space ads, and special distribution programs.

But, first things first. If you are a marketing novice, I want to emphasize that certain products traditionally sell best when marketed to certain audiences in a certain way. You will be wise to follow the guidelines given in this and the next two chapters because a lot of marketing experts already have done the expensive trial-and-error testing to prove these theories.

Since entire books have been written on practically every topic I am about to discuss, my primary objective is to cover the basics; to awaken you to market opportunities and alert you to pitfalls which may be inherent in each market or method of selling. You can continue your education on each topic by studying the special resources I have included in each section. All are detailed in the resource chapter. With all this information at your fingertips, there is no reason why you should fail in your attempt to market any good service or product.

> *"No matter what you are selling — service, product, or yourself — you have competitors. The only sure way to outsell them is to give your customer service. Not just ordinary service, but something extra, something over and beyond the call of duty."*
>
> — *Dottie Walters,* The Selling Power of a Woman
> © *1962 by Royal Publishing, Inc. Reprinted by permission.*

Retail and Wholesale Markets to Explore

RETAILING

Direct Selling to Consumers

This is *personal* selling, involving face-to-face meetings with buyers or the public at large through:

1. Arts and crafts shows/fairs/festivals

2. Flea Markets

3. Other consumer shows

4. Home sales, shops, and studios

5. Open houses

6. Party-plan sales

7. Person-to-person selling and in-home demonstrations

(These markets are discussed in Chapter 6.)

WHOLESALING

Indirect Selling to Consumers

This is *impersonal* selling, involving sales to consumers through retailers, dealers, and other distribution methods, such as:

1. Retail outlets:

   (a) gift shops, card shops, boutiques, and other specialty shops

   (b) craft shops and galleries

   (c) museum shops

   (d) department stores

   (e) other mass merchandisers

   (f) florists and garden centers

   (g) hobby and craft supply shops

   (h) needlecraft supply shops

   (i) bookstores

2. Mail order catalog markets

3. Trade shows/Sales Reps/Merchandise Marts

4. Institutional buyers

5. Premium sales

6. Government market

7. Foreign markets

(These markets are discussed in Chapter 7.)

Sections of the text are numbered to correspond with the items above.

Note: The terms *retailer* and *dealer* are interchangeable, as are the terms *wholesaler* and *distributor*. They simply are called by different names in different industries.

Direct sellers in multi-level marketing plans also are called distributors, even though they sell directly to consumers instead of retailers or dealers.

1. Arts and Crafts Shows/Fairs/Festivals

No one knows this precisely, but there probably are as many as 10,000 arts and crafts fairs, shows, and festivals in America each year. Some are annual events which have been held for twenty years or more, while others are brand new. Often staged in parks, shopping malls, or community buildings, these colorful shows attract millions of people, some of whom go to buy, others to sell.

This market is supported by individuals who appreciate handmade/handcrafted goods, most of which are produced in limited quantities, if not one-of-a-kind editions. Whether sellers call themselves amateur or professional artist, craftsman, designer or hobbyist, all have one thing in common: they love to work with their hands to make things of beauty. The joy of creating often exceeds the satisfaction of selling, which accounts for why so many of these sellers are not much concerned with business. They work first for love . . . and then money. The fact that so many buyers know this has a lot to do with the prices they will pay for handcrafts.

Because there are so many shows and so many sellers, competition truly is keen. It takes much more these days than just a good product to realize sales success at a fair or show. The profit-oriented seller will thus read marketing guides and trade periodicals to stay informed of opportunities and to learn the inside tips and tricks to financial success at a show.

Many shows are "juried," which means hopeful exhibitors have to submit slides or photos of their work to prove it is of a type and quality desired for a particular event. Annual shows of long-standing have a loyal buyer following because of their reputation for high quality and a certain kind of product. This is particularly true of the shows sponsored by the American Craft Enterprises, Inc. and other artist/craftsmen/designer guilds and associations throughout the country, in which only members may be allowed to exhibit and sell. (See related article in next chapter.)

Other shows are open to sellers nationwide, but because of their high quality and buyer following, they, too, have more applicants than exhibit booths or spaces. Thus it pays to know about such events far in advance. Subscriptions to show calendars make this possible. There are non-juried shows, too, including church bazaars and a variety of "arts and crafts" fairs that have become annual celebrations in many communities across the country. It should be noted, however, that such events are often populated by hobby sellers who are exhibiting as much for the fun of it as for the sales which may result. Senior citizens, in particular, often enter such shows to earn supplementary income.

Regardless of the type of show a seller enters, this kind of market offers advantages no other retail market can provide. Here, beginning sellers can get their first sales experience, gain confidence in dealing with the public, test prices and salability of products, meet others who share their interests and concerns, and have a good time in the bargain. Historically, many people who begin selling at a small fair soon go on to sell to retail outlets and, in time, develop profitable part- or full-time home businesses.

For additional information on this topic, see show calendars and related periodicals such as *Art & Crafts Catalyst,* and *The Crafts Report.*

Six Guidelines for Sales Success at a Show

1. A good display is critical to one's sales success. If you plan to do a number of shows, your display needs to be light enough for you to move it from place to place, yet strong enough to stand up to strong winds or the press of a crowd. It has to be collapsible to fit into your vehicle, too. A-frame structures which bolt together are a popular choice for things that must be hung, as are folding pegboard units. Many exhibitors build their own interesting shelf arrangements, display cases, and background walls to accentuate their particular art or craft. In total, the overall display must not only be eye-appealing, but inviting as well. Make it easy for people to walk in, browse, and get out without feeling trapped.

2. Create a professional image by being well groomed and appropriately dressed. Many sellers wear special costumes in keeping with their total display or line of goods. Have business cards and brochures to promote your business.

3. Even if you hate to sell, remember, that is what you're there for. Salesmanship involves looking people squarely in the eye, smiling at them, talking to them. Above all, don't sit around reading a book or looking bored.

4. Be prepared to handle any and all questions that may arise, from "Do you sell on consignment?" to "Can you make it in blue, instead of red?", and "How soon can you deliver twelve dozen?"

5. Brace yourself for negative feedback from critical people who do not appreciate fine craftsmanship. It's part of the business, and one of the few disadvantages of direct selling you must learn to accept. Listen carefully to your critics, though, to get new ideas on how to improve your work or make it more salable.

6. Money tips: If you take a check for merchandise, be sure to ask for identification, and note the individual's driver's license number on the check. Also get their telephone number and address, if it's not printed on the check. Don't cash checks for anyone, and don't let them write a check for an amount larger than the purchase, requiring you to give change. To protect the checks you do have, endorse them on the spot, "For deposit only."

When customers pay with cash, never put a large bill into your cash box until change has been given. Don't give them an opportunity to say, "But I gave you a twenty, not a ten." Prove the fact by showing them the original bill, still lying on top of your money box. (Remember, there are con artists everywhere.)

Ten Questions to Answer Before Entering a Show

1. *How many people are expected to attend?*

2. *What kind of sales has this show generated for past exhibitors?*

3. *If the show is not juried, how does my work compare with other work in the show?*

4. *Are my prices right for this area?*

5. *How will I display my work? Can pegboard or other wall units be rented? Are tables and chairs furnished?*

6. *What kind of help do I need to do this show (set up, take orders, watch the booth during my breaks, tear down, etc.)?*

7. *Am I all set up to keep track of sales, with sales book, money box, collection of sales tax, etc.? Do I have sacks and wrapping paper for customer purchases?*

8. *Can I increase sales by demonstrating my art or craft during the show? (And is this allowed?)*

9. *If my display must be left overnight, what protection will I have against theft or damage? Do I have insurance for any kind of loss?*

10. *If this is an outdoor show, am I prepared for bad weather?*

2. Flea Markets

Flea markets are comparable to craft shows in that no one knows how many there are, or how much money is being generated at such events. But one thing is certain: flea markets are big business, and they are gaining in popularity as marketplaces for small business owners. An article in *Collectibles Illustrated* emphasizes this point: "The indoor markets, open daily, are packed with dealers. Drive-in movie theaters are running flea markets on their lots during the daylight hours. Buyers are flocking to the western 'swap meets' for new merchandise."[1]

This same article also indicated that the large outdoor shows are most popular, and that flea markets, in general, are appealing to buyers because they are seen as "a return to the traditional trading marketplace of old."

Flea markets also are popular because they offer bargain prices and a chance to barter, an activity which is enjoying a revival in America. The consumer's acceptance of flea markets literally has forced some discount chain stores to start offering "flea market prices" and sales in their parking lots, according to an article in *The National Flea Market Dealer*.

Obviously, flea markets are not for the same sellers who go to art and craft fairs. Primarily they are for those who deal in new or used goods for resale — from individual dealers who trade in antiques or second-hand merchandise, to highly-commercial enterprises which sell everything from food to foreign imports. It has been said that a lot of stolen merchandise ends up for sale in flea markets, and that may be true; but it also is a fact that many reputable dealers market here, too, apparently on a profitable basis. No doubt much of the merchandise offered for sale at flea markets has been obtained at close-out prices from companies who want to dump excess or damaged inventory. But there also seems to be a growing number of wholesalers who specialize in offering new "flea market merchandise."

Charles Clark, publisher of a flea market directory (see adjacent article) estimates there are at least 4,000 flea markets throughout the country, so millions of dollars no doubt are changing hands annually at such events. Such sales probably account for much of the under-the-table income being generated by entrepreneurs today. But state governments are getting wise to all this. They eventually will figure out how to trace this kind of income and prevent the movement of stolen goods as well.

As indicated in the *Collectibles Illustrated* article, California now requires that all flea market merchandise be registered with local police. And in New York, several bills which will affect both show promoters and exhibitors are currently being considered by the Legislature. It has been proposed that vendors maintain detailed records and descriptions of all merchandise for sale, giving receipts to customers. Also being considered is a requirement that centralized check-out facilities be used to record all sales at such shows. It probably is only a matter of time before other states introduce similar bills which will affect consumer markets nationwide, and the under-the-table income they generate.

Because no two flea markets are the same, it takes a special kind of savvy to buy and sell with success. Thus, the wise dealer

---

[1]from the article, "Flea Market Fever," by Jamie Trowbridge, September/October, 1983.

Flea Markets: Last Remnants of Free Enterprise in U.S.

No one knows for certain, but Charles Clark estimates that there are at least 4,000 flea markets throughout the U.S. And Mr. Clark should know as well as anyone, since he publishes a quarterly directory called Flea Market USA. *The directory lists about 2,500 locations.*

The Clarks got into the flea market arena in a roundabout way. When the county in central Florida rezoned his land, he had to sell his equipment business, but kept a school bus and trailer in which he and his family traveled to Spokane, Washington. While there and without a job, he started going to flea markets — eventually setting up a route that took them up and down the West Coast. He kept saying that someone should put together a directory of flea markets — before finally doing it themselves. (Besides the directory, they also have a sideline business in recycling cans, paper, and other salvageable materials.)

A single flea market with 700 to 800 dealers can yield a $150,000 profit for sellers in a single day. Said to be the nation's largest, the San Jose Flea Market, Inc. attracts an average weekend flow of 65,000 with 2,500 dealers paying $13.50 a day for table space. The Englishtown, NJ Auction — which dates back to 1929 — has an attendance of up to 40,000 many weekends. Dealers are described as ranging from the retired elderly and the unemployed to stockbrokers and government workers. "Today, with mortgages the way they are and with unemployment running high, the people out there are doing this for a living. It's probably one of the last remnants of free enterprise in the nation," says Clark.

— from Sideline Business newsletter, August, 1983 issue. Reprinted by permission.

Notes

will avail himself of periodicals and books related to this field to learn the tricks of the trade, the best sources for merchandise, and the most profitable shows to enter.

For more information, see the books, *How to Make Money in the Antiques & Collectibles Business* and *The Flea Market Entrepreneur*. In addition to *The National Flea Market Dealer*, also see the directory, *Flea Market, USA*.

3. Other Consumer Shows

Without getting too precise in this definition, I'll just say that this category includes every other consumer show you can think of; all of them commercial events which are staged purely for profit by show organizers and exhibitors. Shows run the gamut from commercial exhibits at county or state fairs to sleek expositions held in convention halls. Merchandise includes everything from fine antiques, paintings, gemstones and stamps, to hobbies, housewares, food, and collectibles of every kind and description. By and large, such shows are for manufacturers, wholesalers, and dealers, rather than small, homebased businesses.

For more information, check with your Chamber of Commerce for a listing of shows in your area, or read trade and professional magazines for announcements of national consumer shows.

4. Home Sales, Shops, and Studios

Many people who produce products for sale set up private studios in their homes where they work, teach, and sell on a custom-order basis. Where zoning laws permit, individuals may elect to open year-round retail shops in their homes to sell their wares and possibly other products as well.

Additional uses of one's home include sales or "holiday boutiques," as they are often called — events generally held on a one- or two-day basis in one's home or garage. Sales like this are particularly popular among sellers who make gifts and decorative accessories, crafts, toys, dolls, and related items. Christmas sales are the most common — and the most profitable — but home sales often are held in the spring and fall as well. Such sales often are given interesting names which lend themselves to publicity. Others are very quietly produced (because of zoning regulations), with private invitations being sent to a select mailing list of people who have attended earlier sales.

In effect, these home sales serve as temporary retail shops. Often set up to run on a weekend, they provide an interesting and profitable alternative to selling at fairs or through local shops. Surprisingly, twenty or thirty exhibitors can ring up total sales of as much as $10,000 in a couple of days, particularly if the sale has become a regular annual event noted for high quality merchandise.

Unlike fairs and shows, however, which often are announced in periodicals to enable interested sellers to participate, holiday boutiques and other home sales usually are organized and coordinated locally by one or two entrepreneurs (almost always women), who have determined a need for this kind of market. Usually, the show organizers produce goods for sale and are unhappy with local retail outlets which may be inadequate or even non-existent.

Such sales are easy to organize and generally cause few, if any, problems with local officials since they seem to be viewed in the

Holiday Bazaars Generate Attractive Profits

Marj Sparks of New Philadelphia, Ohio, and Lynn Ocken of Cedar Rapids, Iowa have a lot in common. They are entrepreneurs who have established annual shows in their communities to serve as holiday markets for local artists and craftspeople.

Marj's event is called *Harvest Time Craft Sale.* It is held the first weekend in October to capitalize on early buyers' Christmas gift needs. Lynn's show, *Heatheridge Holiday Boutique,* is held the first weekend in November. It also is designed to capture Christmas shoppers.

Both shows run for two days and each generates similar dollar amounts. Lynn's 1982 show, with 28 participants, grossed almost $10,000, as did Marj's 1982 show, which had 25 participants.

Both women charge a small exhibitor's fee (under $10) to cover advertising and refreshments. Exhibitors of both events are required to share in the work of the boutique, before and during the event. Individual jobs might include such things as making and distributing posters and flyers, setting up the show, manning the cashier's table, taking custom orders for individual exhibitors, serving refreshments, and so on.

The advertising methods used by both women include:

- Flyers distributed by participants. (Lynn, however, has discontinued this practice, finding that postcards to her customer list of more than 1200 names are more effective advertising.)
- Ads in local papers, including "pennysaver" publications.
- Posters with tear-off, take-along reminders attached.

Marj also uses announcements on cable television, and rents a billboard at the fairgrounds for a week.

Both show organizers accept only the highest-quality merchandise because they know this is what their customers have come to expect. To keep them coming back year after year, they must continue to present merchandise that is new and different.

What else do these two women have in common? Both have diversified their home businesses by becoming self-publishers of special reports which tell other women how to duplicate their success. These reports, of course, automatically have put both women in the mail-order business as well.

Notes

same light as ordinary garage sales. There may be exceptions, however; it always is best to check with local authorities before organizing such an event.

5. Open Houses

This kind of sale differs sharply from the home boutiques just described because it usually is associated with multi-level marketing and the sale of commercial products such as cosmetics, housewares, cookware, jewelry, and so on. Often, the salesperson will send information about products for sale to a select list of prospects, then follow up with phone calls to invite them to an "open house," at which the seller can announce a company's latest products, show sample merchandise, and pass out a catalog or brochure.

Visitors at an open house either can place orders for later delivery, or take a catalog home with them. Mary Kay Cosmetics, Avon, Amway, and a host of other products are sold in this manner, often in conjunction with party-plan sales, person-to-person selling, and in-home demonstrations. (See following sections.)

Note: Check with local authorities about zoning regulations which may prohibit you from using your home in this manner. In some areas, zoning laws prohibit any kind of business that involves inventory. Or you may find that you can take orders in your home, but that you would violate the law if you let customers walk out the door with merchandise you sold to them during the open house. (Later deliveries may be a simple solution here.)

6. Party-plan Sales

Many people are involved in party-plan selling, offering a wide variety of products — everything from commercial items like Tupperware, to handcrafts and custom-designed/personalized items. Basically, a party works like this: A salesperson arranges for parties to be held by friends or relatives, who in turn suggest the names of other friends and relatives who might like to hold a party. A host or hostess at each party supplies refreshments (generally cake and coffee) and earns points according to the sales volume of the party and the number of additional parties booked.

The salesperson plans the presentation, supplies any necessary game or door prizes, and displays wares for sale. Orders are taken, but merchandise is not delivered until later. This job falls to the host/hostess, who also must collect payment for the seller. (A deposit, especially on custom-designed or personalized items, is recommended to discourage later cancellations.)

Jewelry, cosmetics, household products, crafts, and gifts — all make good products for party-plan sales. Many companies are eager to work with sales-oriented people to build profitable part- or full-time businesses. In deciding which products to sell, be sure to compare the offers of several companies, noting especially:

(1) start-up costs
(2) cost of promotional catalogs, brochures, delivery bags, etc.
(3) whether you have to pay for merchandise in advance of receiving payment from your party customers, and
(4) local competition. (Ask companies for the names of dealers in your area.)

If you do not produce your own merchandise, and don't want to sell commercial products, you might consider acting as a sales

Missouri Homemaker Scores with Mary Kay

"When I joined Mary Kay Cosmetics as a Beauty Consultant in 1981, I had no idea of the possibilities! I was only interested in making the same amount ($200 weekly) I was earning at my 40 hour-a-week job. I discovered I could do that with only 6 to 8 hours a week in Mary Kay. So, that was the extent of my activity for the first year.

"Then I attended our annual seminar in Dallas, Texas. There the number one gal in all of Mary Kay made the statement that if we would hold three beauty shows a week *consistently*, as well as some time on the phone, there was no limit to the possibilities for us in Mary Kay.

"I stepped up my activities to three shows per week, and obtained Directorship nine months later! As a Mary Kay Director, I receive a 10-13% Director's check on every member of my unit in addition to my 8% commission check on those people I have personally recruited. My income is not limited to what I, alone, can produce.

"The money has been a great blessing to our family. We won the pink car three months after forming our unit — Menzies Mountain Movers. Since debuting as a Director in October, 1982, my unit has gone from 24 to 63 members, with several of the girls headed toward Directorship for themselves.

"I appreciate the principles on which our Company is founded, and I count it a great privilege to represent the Mary Kay Company."

— Twyla Menzies
Springfield, Missouri

* * * * * * * * * * *

Author's note: Twyla emphasizes that this kind of business is great if you have a family. She has two children, one three, one ten, and schedules her work around them, often giving facials or beauty shows when the younger child is napping. The beauty shows, by the way, generally are held for three to six people, either in Twyla's home or somewhere else; they demonstrate the skin care program and teach a woman how to give herself a facial.

Twyla adds that it is not necessary to buy an inventory of products, but that profits will be greater if you do.

Although large profits are possible in direct-sales companies like Mary Kay Cosmetics, few sellers get rich quick. Like all other businesses, the amount a person can earn is directly tied to the amount of time and effort expended. As reporter Laura Green stated in her article about the Mary Kay Company (August 28, 1983 issue of the *Chicago Sun Times*), " . . . of the nearly 200,000 beauty consultants (mostly women, many working part time), only 358 earned more than $30,000 in commissions and prizes last year. Of those, 166 earned more than $50,000, and 45 made more than $100,000. The odds of growing rich are no higher at Mary Kay than they are elsewhere."

Free Complimentary Facial To Bearer Of This Card

Mary Kay
Independent
COSMETICS

TWYLA MENZIES, Director
(417) 882-0179
2033 E. Wayland   Springfield, MO 65804

Diane Kruger sold her business (see right) in mid-1985.

Update

Diane Kruger sold her business (see right) in mid-1985. The new owners, Carolyn Isaak and her sister, Mary Zachry, sent this note in mid-1986:

"We operate the business as Diane was doing, giving home shows or parties in individual homes and also holding several open house events each year.

"We now have representatives selling for us in several additional states.

"Our new 15-page catalog is in full color, and includes many additional items. Because we cannot keep all of our items current in our present catalog, our representatives purchase samples of their choice to display at the home parties they give.

"We warehouse our merchandise in the basement of one of our homes, thus enabling us to deliver customer orders in about two weeks."

Carolyn also indicated that the forms and cards illustrated on the next page have been changed to some degree, and they're presently selling to individuals by mail. Their impressive catalog is $2 ppd. (refundable with first purchase).

Successful Party-Plan Business Makes Home a Daily Stop for UPS

"Before originating Home Country Fair, a party-plan business, my husband and I had taught in our local high school for twelve years. When he took a job that required him to travel, I felt the need to be home more for my two children. Two weeks later, at our weekly coffee session, some friends and I began to talk about selling crafts through home parties. Home Country Fair was introduced to the public on April 17, 1982 with an open house. Our sales totaled over $1,000, we booked eleven parties, and it was hard to catch our breath for awhile after that.

"We had intended for this to be a part-time occupation, giving parties only the first week of each month, but in June, we had to hire another representative to help give parties, and by August, still another was hired. By October, every night was booked through November, which was the last party date for guaranteed delivery before Christmas. Not having enough to do, I opened a local Christmas shop from November 6 through December 28.

"By this time we had outgrown many of our craftspeople who were supplying us. Realizing that if I were going to expand I would need people who could supply in quantity, I attended the January Gift Market at the Atlanta Merchandise mart, searching for high-quality handcrafted gifts and accessories. I found just what I was looking for. Now the Home Country Fair line includes items from the Merchandise Mart, items from local craftspeople, and items found at craft fairs wherever I go. I currently have eight representatives giving parties for me, seven in Illinois, one in Missouri. I have interested people I'm talking to in Ohio, Indiana, and Tennessee. I see no limit to the growth of the business. I'm still learning, experimenting, changing, wondering, and it's WORK, WORK, WORK!

"My home is perpetually full of boxes, my bedroom has become an office, and my home is a daily stop for the UPS man. When the semi pulled in front of my house with seventeen boxes of sacks, the driver's first comment, after asking if he had the right address, was, 'What are you going to do with all of these sacks?' I, of course, replied, 'Oh, I have a home business.' I don't think he understood.

"At first, I found myself embarrassed when someone asked me where I worked and what I did for a living. But now I hold up my head, smile, and say, 'I'm in the business of selling unique handcrafted gifts and accessories through the home party plan. Would you be interested in having a party or seeing our catalog?' "

— Diane Kruger, Home Country Fair
Carlyle, Illinois

"Happiness Is Homemade!" This motto reflects the "back to basics" trend sweeping the country today. The term hand-crafted brings to mind a time in our history when people lived a more leisurely life at a slower pace. Most of the items in the home were hand-crafted with loving care and pride.

This loving care and pride is reflected in the excellent workmanship of the craftspeople represented in this catalog. Home Country Fair has consolidated and made available to you the best of the crafts on the scene today. We are dedicated to providing quality crafts that can be purchased in the comfort of your home at a reasonable price.

Home Country Fair representatives are qualified spokesmen on the newest in crafts and decorating and gift ideas. Our items reflect the nostalgia of the past while keeping current with the newest trends in hand-crafted creations.

We do not sell kits—we sell the "finished product," ready to hang, display, or give. And nothing makes the recipient feel more special than a hand-crafted gift which can become a family heirloom.

The Home Country Fair Catalog, created by Diane Kruger, measures 5-1/2" x 6-7/8" and is 14 pages of photographs, each illustrating a variety of handcrafted items.

New craft business is starting in Carlyle

A unique craft business is opening in Carlyle April 17. The business, Home Country Fair, will be operated by Gail Greer and Diane Kruger. Its motto is "Happiness is Homemade."

The talents of local craftspeople will be utilized in making available to the people of Carlyle and the surrounding area unique, individually handcrafted items made to order.

According to Mrs. Kruger and Mrs. Greer, "There are so many talented craftspeople in this area who display their skills only through occasional craft shows. Home Country Fair gives them the opportunity on a year-round basis to earn money doing something they love ... and at the same time provide a service to the community."

More than 20 craftspeople are contributing to Home Country Fair. Their talents include tole painting, counted cross stitch, macrame, crochet, woodworking, applique, quilting, sewing, pen and ink, quilling and caligraphy.

Items will be sold through the home party plan, where they can be displayed and individual orders placed in the comfort of a home.

A grand opening "Open House" with refreshments and door prizes is being held at 971 Mullikin in Carlyle on Saturday, April 17, from 10:00 a.m. to 4:00 p.m. and on Sunday, April 18, from 12:00 noon to 4:00 p.m. At this time the handcrafted items will be on display and orders can be placed and parties booked.

The ad (above right) launched the business, and publicity in the local paper brought additional response.

The invitation at right is a postcard measuring 5-1/2" x 4-1/8". (The reverse side includes a bulk rate indicia and the business return address.)

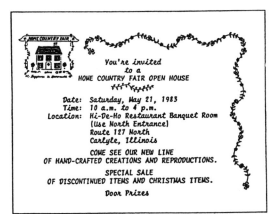

The professional, 3-part order form (above left) enables customers to have a good receipt for orders placed at a show. It includes a legal notation about buyer's right to cancel: " . . . at any time prior to midnight of the third business day after the date of this transaction."

Notes

agent for a group of sellers in your area who produce quality goods and need marketing outlets. You could work out your own terms as to the percentage of profit you would take on merchandise sold in this manner, but make sure it covers your time and expenses and yields a satisfactory profit for your entrepreneurial ability.

To connect with companies such as Amway, Tupperware, Shaklee, Mary Kay Cosmetics and others, check business directories in the library or request a free directory listing of members who belong to the Direct Selling Association. (Also refer back to chapter two for general information about multi-level marketing plans, which is what most of these companies are really offering.)

To set up your party-plan system, offering your own products or those of individual creators, see *The Craft Party Plan Report* and *A Guide to Marketing Crafts Through a Home Party System*.

7. Person-to-person Selling and In-Home Demonstrations

This used to be called door-to-door selling, but the phrase has become outdated inasmuch as most sales today are generated by appointments arranged by telephone, instead of by door-knocking. Besides, say companies involved in this field, the new phrase has more sales appeal.

The main difference between person-to-person selling and open-houses or party plans is that person-to-person selling is more personal. For instance, a Mary Kay Cosmetics salesperson may invite a number of people to her home for an open house, or meet them at a party. Later, she may call these people one by one to set up appointments for in-home demonstrations and perhaps a free facial (which is bound to sell a few products). Or, prospects may simply drop by the seller's home to place an order after having received a catalog or brochure.

Other salespeople, such as those who sell vacuum cleaners, encyclopedias, housecleaning supplies, cookware, and a variety of other merchandise, may distribute flyers or catalogs on a house-to-house basis or by mail, then follow up with telephone calls to evaluate the level of interest. (Note that flyers placed in mail boxes violate postal service regulations.)

Not too many years ago there were a lot of door-to-door sellers, but somehow they seem to have gotten lost in the shuffle. As a little girl living on a farm, I remember "The Rawleigh Man" and other peddlers with great affection. Maybe it's time to get back to basics. With so many of us now working at home, we are not getting out to shops and stores as much as before, and the right products delivered to our doors at the right time, in the right way, would be a time-saving convenience to say the least.

Whether you call it "door-to-door" or "person-to-person" selling, any kind of product, and many kinds of services, could be marketed in this fashion, so consider the possibilities.

As you have seen, there are a number of markets to explore, even if you find you can sell only at the retail level. And remember this: for every product imaginable, there probably is at least one group of consumers who would have an intense interest in buying that product *if only they knew it existed*. And as you'll discover in chapter eight, reaching such buyers is not as difficult as you might think.

But before we get deeply involved in advertising methods, let's take a look at your wholesale market possibilities. I hope your pricing will allow for sales to at least some of them.

Notes

Retail Marketing Worksheet

List the retail marketing methods you plan to explore in the future, with any questions you have that require further research. (Be sure to check all the related information sources listed in the Resource Directory.)

Marketing Method	Comments
_____	_____
_____	_____
_____	_____
_____	_____
_____	_____
_____	_____
_____	_____
_____	_____
_____	_____
_____	_____
_____	_____
_____	_____
_____	_____
_____	_____
_____	_____
_____	_____
_____	_____
_____	_____
_____	_____
_____	_____
_____	_____
_____	_____
_____	_____
_____	_____
_____	_____
_____	_____

Exploring Wholesale Markets

7.

ALTHOUGH SOME OF YOU may be importers or distributors who are buying merchandise for resale, I suspect many of you are individuals who are creating self-made (or manufactured) goods such as those described on the product business chart in chapter two.

If you are a small manufacturer, you may think you cannot sell at the wholesale level because of pricing or problems of limited production. Often, this is true. Other times, however, a product can be changed or redesigned in some way to permit increased production at a retail price that's high enough to allow for wholesaling, at least to some markets.

Whether you're an importer, distributor, or manufacturer, once you decide to enter the wholesale marketplace your thoughts probably will turn to retail shops and stores, mail-order catalogs, trade shows, and a variety of other markets which are discussed in this chapter. As before, my goal is to bring several market possibilities to your attention, tell you how to penetrate them, and warn you of any pitfalls inherent in the process. The rest is up to you.

One point I would like to stress is this. You will find it impossible to crack certain wholesale distribution channels unless both your product and its pricing structure are right for those markets. For example, individuals who publish their own books often think they can sell directly to bookstores and certain other retail outlets when, in fact, this is almost impossible because of the way books are normally discounted and distributed by trade publishers. Thus, self-publishers who do not do their marketing homework before they go to press are apt to end up storing most of their press run under the bed, in their closet, in the garage, etc. Often, the only way to sell a self-published book is by mail; and, just as often, the small and inexperienced publisher has no real understanding of what it takes to sell anything by mail, especially books.

> " . . . of all the hats the small entrepreneur must wear, none is more deserving of time and attention than that labeled 'Marketing/ Sales Manager.' "
>
> — *Herman R. Holtz,* The Secrets of Practical Marketing for Small Business

How to Shift Gears from Retailing to Wholesaling

With few exceptions — sales representatives, party-plans, and in-home demonstrations, to name three — the same marketing methods are used to sell on both the retail and wholesale levels. The primary difference is that, in wholesaling, the marketer has to shift mental

Retail and Wholesale Markets to Explore

RETAILING

Direct Selling to Consumers

This is *personal* selling, involving face-to-face meetings with buyers or the public at large through:

1. Arts and crafts shows/fairs/festivals

2. Flea Markets

3. Other consumer shows

4. Home sales, shops, and studios

5. Open houses

6. Party-plan sales

7. Person-to-person selling and in-home demonstrations

(These markets are discussed in Chapter 6.)

WHOLESALING

Indirect Selling to Consumers

This is *impersonal* selling, involving sales to consumers through retailers, dealers, and other distribution methods, such as:

1. Retail outlets:

   (a) gift shops, card shops, boutiques, and other specialty shops

   (b) craft shops and galleries

   (c) museum shops

   (d) department stores

   (e) other mass merchandisers

   (f) florists and garden centers

   (g) hobby and craft supply shops

   (h) needlecraft supply shops

   (i) bookstores

2. Mail order catalog markets

3. Trade shows/Sales Reps/Merchandise Marts

4. Institutional buyers

5. Premium sales

6. Government market

7. Foreign markets

(These markets are discussed in Chapter 7.)

Sections of the text are numbered to correspond with the items above.

Note: The terms *retailer* and *dealer* are interchangeable, as are the terms *wholesaler* and *distributor*. They simply are called by different names in different industries.

Direct sellers in multi-level marketing plans also are called distributors, even though they sell directly to consumers instead of retailers or dealers.

gears because dealers and retailers don't think about merchandise in the same way as consumers.

Whereas you have to sell a consumer on his or her need for your product, you have to sell dealers and retailers on this point plus one other: *why the consumer will want to buy your products from them.* That's one reason why wholesalers and manufacturers work so hard to make it easy for their dealers to sell, and why they offer them free or inexpensive counter display racks, finished samples (to sell kits), promotional literature they can give to consumers, camera-ready advertising copy, and so on.

In trying to find new wholesale markets for your products, shift your thinking by looking for the wholesale counterpart of each retail market you are now selling to. With few exceptions, you will find both consumer and trade shows, magazines, and organizations for each industry and each specific interest. This kind of "detective work" is what good marketing is all about. The sharpest marketers are those who not only dig around to find just the right distribution channels for their products, but also the most efficient and cost-effective way to use them.

Before continuing, let me stress that I do not pretend to have all the answers about wholesaling. The following information about several markets is by no means the total extent of your wholesale opportunities. Rather, it is simply a reflection of what I have learned from on-the-job experience as an entrepreneur, and through research and networking with successful sellers in various industries. With additional research on your part, coupled with actual marketing experience, you are likely to turn up other markets and a number of "trade secrets" still unknown to me.

If the nearby chart looks familiar, it's because it also appeared in the preceding chapter. It is included again for your convenience, providing at a glance your primary retail and wholesale marketing opportunities. Again, note that the various sections of this chapter are numbered to correspond with the numbered items on this chart.

1. Wholesaling to Retail Outlets

This is a huge market that includes many different kinds of shops and stores. Some retailers will be less likely than others to buy from you because of bad experiences they may have had with other, less professional sellers in the past. Craftsellers, in particular, are notorious for accepting orders beyond their production capabilities, then shipping short or late at the expense of a shop or store. Some sellers also pack things poorly, resulting in damaged goods which create return headaches for store buyers or managers. In addition, too many inexperienced sellers are concerned only with getting that first order. They do not produce, or sell, with reorders in mind, and reorders are a primary concern of most retailers.

a.) Gift Shops, Card Shops, Boutiques, and Other Specialty Stores

This is an enormous market, accessible through direct mailings to rented lists (one company offers a mailing list of 63,670 gift, novelty, and souvenir shops), as well as through direct-response postcard mailings, trade show exhibits, merchandise marts, and sales representatives. Most gift shops buy merchandise outright, marking it up 100% or more, depending on what their traffic will bear. Few shops in this category take merchandise on consignment, although many buy handcrafted/handmade merchandise from trade show and craft fair exhibitors.

Author's note:

Even though 2,000 less visitors were attracted to the 1983 fair, sales exceeded projections, reaching $6.1 million. Wholesale buyers from major department and specialty stores were hosted for two days before the show opened to the general public, and a special "Collector's Evening" was held on June 23rd.

Other shows similar to this one, but smaller, are held annually in Dallas, San Francisco, and Baltimore. Competition is incredibly keen, and only the most professional and skilled sellers will gain admittance. One need not be a member of the American Craft Council to submit slides for the jurying process, but if accepted into the show, membership becomes mandatory. (Note: Rhinebeck's 500 applicants were accepted from some 2,000 entrants.

Today's Collectibles, Tomorrow's Antiques

(From a 1983 press release by American Craft Enterprises, Inc.)

Collectors from all over the United States will be drawn to Rhinebeck, New York, June 23 through June 26 for the ACC Craft Fair, held at the Dutchess County Fairgrounds, sponsored by American Craft Enterprises, Inc. The country's finest craftspeople, selected by their peers, will exhibit, and collectors will have the opportunity to expand their ceramics, glass, wood, jewelry, and fiber collections.

"The collecting of crafts has grown over the past ten years, just as the craft movement as a whole has developed," said Carol Sedestrom, President of American Craft Enterprises, the marketing arm of the American Craft Council, and operators of the event.

The first A.C.E. Fair featured 65 craftspeople and produced $18,000 in sales. This year's Fair will include more than 500 craftspeople, will attract more than 50,000 collectors and visitors, and will produce sales estimated at $5,500,000.*

This will be the Fair's last year at Rhinebeck. In June, 1984, it will move to the Eastern States Exposition Center in West Springfield, Massachusetts, a facility that allows for growth, easy accessibility by car, train, or plane, and extensive accommodations for visitors.

Modern crafts have become a legitimate art form, recognized by museum, corporate, and private collectors. According to Sedestrom, "Today's craftspeople have attained new levels of expression and sophistication, and are creating 'tomorrow's antiques,' both a wise investment and a source of pleasure."

Business writer Sylvia Porter agrees. In her widely read newspaper column, she noted, "If an American living in 1980 had had the good fortune to choose ancestors who had admired crafts and had purchased the production of Paul Revere or Chippendale, that individual could be immensely wealthy. (He or she would have needed the sense to hold on to the crafts bought by the talented ancestor.) Similarly, the crafts you pick up so inexpensively today may be priceless items in tomorrow's market. And you can enjoy them, too."

Read magazines such as *Gift & Tableware Reporter* and *Gift & Decorative Accessories* to connect with this industry. (The latter publishes an annual directory which lists manufacturers, importers, and distributors, plus information on trade shows and industry organizations.)

Also included in this category of retail outlets would be souvenir shops and concessions in over 300 national parks. You may be able to obtain a mailing list of such buyers. Check catalogs of various list houses.

b.) Craft Shops and Galleries

This is a much smaller, and more select, market which is accessible primarily through wholesale buyer's markets, ads in periodicals which serve this industry, or direct mail. Some sellers compile their own lists of shops from advertisements in such publications as *The Crafts Report.*

While many craft sellers complain they cannot find an appreciative market for their work, other, more professional sellers literally are cleaning up at wholesale buyer's markets — such as those produced by American Craft Enterprises, Inc. and other show promoters. (See the related article in this chapter, *"Today's Collectibles, Tomorrow's Antiques."*)

As you might suspect, craft shops usually are started by individuals with a special interest in handcrafts and the people who make them. Unlike gift shop owners, craft shop owners are often craftspeople themselves; thus they tend to be more receptive to beginning craft sellers than buyers in gift shops. Some shops and galleries operate strictly on a consignment basis while others mix consigned merchandise with goods purchased at wholesale. Still others buy everything outright.

Though considered impractical by gift shop owners, consignment selling is a perfectly acceptable form of marketing in the crafts industry. In fact, without it, few of today's finest shops and galleries could have opened, and fewer still craftsellers and artists could have launched careers or home businesses. I suspect there always will be another new consignment shop opening somewhere, to the delight of a whole new audience of novice sellers who need such a marketing outlet. But such new shops do represent a pitfall to beware. The hazard lies not with consignment, per se, but in the fact that new shop owners are likely to be as inexperienced as the sellers with whom they are dealing. Often, it's a case of the blind leading the blind. With good management, however, many of these same shops grow and flourish, so don't ignore them as a market for your work, especially if you still are trying to "get your feet wet." Do be cautious, however, about dealing with new shops on a consignment basis until you're satisfied you have a good thing going. Be especially wary of dealing with such shops by mail, when it's impossible to keep tabs on what is happening. (For more information, see my list of tips for success in consignment selling elsewhere in this chapter.)

By the way, note that there are two kinds of "craft shops": Those just mentioned, and those you will find described in section 1(g). There also are two kinds of galleries. One kind offers only fine art while the other sells both fine art and crafts, including sculpture, weaving, woodworking, pottery, glass, metalwork, and stitchery. Special exhibitions and sales are often held in galleries

Consignment Selling
Pros, Cons, and Tips for Success

Advantages: Consignment selling enables individuals with limited capital to open shops that may provide important marketing outlets for local producers. Such shops, in turn, enable beginning sellers to get started, and provide a good way to test prices and the marketability of a wide range of goods. In particular, consignment selling enables artists and designers to sell expensive, one-of-a-kind items which cannot be sold at wholesale. Some sellers prefer consignment because they can market merchandise of their choice without pressure of deadline dates on orders.

Disadvantages: Consignment selling means increased bookkeeping and paperwork for both shop and seller, and for the latter, merchandise is tied up, but not sold, which presents cash-flow problems. Common consignment hazards are shopowners' lack of concern for goods they do not own, which may be left to fade in sunny windows, become shop-worn, or simply "lost" due to shoplifting, breakage, or mishandling. Furthermore, new shops have sometimes been known to close suddenly, with owners and stock disappearing overnight, leaving many sellers "holding the bag." Others simply go bankrupt, with consigned goods being seized by creditors.

Consignment Laws: In some states, artists and craftspeople have lost all their merchandise due to such seizures. In one case I recall, an artist actually had to pay $10,000 to retrieve her own paintings from a bankrupt gallery.

Theoretically, consigned goods remain the property of the seller until they are sold to the retail customer, and in normal situations, there are no problems. According to the Uniform Commercial Code (which has been adopted by most states), if an establishment goes bankrupt, consigned goods may be subject to the claims of creditors, and be seized by such creditors unless certain protective steps have been taken by consignors. (A standard consignment contract is not enough to protect one in this instance.)

Several states now have adopted consignment laws designed to protect artists and craftspeople; these include California, Colorado, Connecticut, Illinois, Iowa, Kentucky, Massachusetts, New Mexico, New York, Oregon, Texas, Washington, and Wisconsin. Each state's law offers varying degrees of protection, so obtain complete details about this law from your own state legislature for maximum protection of your goods.

Note: Some state laws protect "art" only, excluding protection to items which fall outside the area of painting, sculpture, drawing, graphic arts, pottery, weaving, batik, macrame, quilting, "or other commonly recognized art forms."

Tips for Success

1. Avoid consignment to shops that normally buy most of their merchandise at wholesale. Such shops who offer to take your work only on consignment may believe that your products are unsalable for one reason or another, and they will not work very hard to sell them for you.

2. Never consign more than a few items to a new or unknown shop until you have developed a satisfactory relationship with the owner or manager (based on prompt payment after the first merchandise has been sold) and see other indications that the shop is being well managed.

3. Never consign merchandise without a consignment agreement. Standard forms are available, if not provided by the shop. The consignment agreement should address such things as insurance, pricing and commission, payment dates, how merchandise is to be displayed and maintained, and how and when unsold merchandise will be returned.

4. When you do establish a good consignment outlet, support it in every way possible, and never compete with it by selling the same items it carries at a price lower than what the shop offers. For example, don't wholesale a $20 item to a shop for $10, then go to a local crafts fair and sell that same item to consumers for $10.

to promote the work of the artists and designers they represent. Due to the high cost of most gallery items, consignment selling is the primary method of operation. Commissions from architects and interior designers, as well as custom orders from private collectors, are just some of the special benefits connected with gallery exhibitions. Prestige is another.

Consignment selling is neither fish nor fowl (neither retail nor wholesale), but it is appropriate to discuss it here since so many people sell this way as an alternative to wholesaling. Interestingly, switching from consignment to wholesale selling may be more profitable than you realize. You may think you will make less money because you'll get only half the suggested retail price instead of the usual 60–75% you ordinarily might get from consignment. However, you will gain in other ways, especially in the time department. You will have fewer cash flow problems, too, as Dorsey Moonen, one of my newsletter readers, explains:

> "Instead of consigning $300 worth of merchandise to one shop and receiving $10–$75 monthly checks trickling in over a year's time, I can now send three shipments, each worth $100 to three different shops and within a month have $300 in hand.
>
> "Within a couple of months after switching to wholesale, my monthly gross sales literally doubled. And my bookwork decreased by 80%. That's because an invoice can be prepared in less than five minutes, whereas the paperwork for a shipment of consigned merchandise might take an hour, what with all the numbering, listing, and describing of merchandise in the package.
>
> "True, wholesaling requires more outlets than consignment selling, but there are a lot of shops who want quality merchandise and who are willing to pay for it. All you have to do is look for them."[1]

c.) Museum Shops

Certainly there are many museums in this country, and, accordingly, a number of museum shops. But this is not an easy market to crack, from what I have read, and it has its own peculiar problems. Handmade items are a logical thing to try to sell to this market. However, many museum shop managers are not educated to the value of American handcrafts and thus do not always pay the price craft sellers need to realize a profit. And price obviously is an important factor since many low-priced items are offered to museum buyers by low cost, skilled artisans in underdeveloped and developing countries.

You may have noticed that much of the "art" being exhibited in museums and museum shops actually is what we call "crafts" — everything from wood carvings from Africa to ceramics from the Orient and blown glass from Italy. If you are thinking about importing such items for resale to museums, explore the market thoroughly before you buy. Since museum shops can buy from these same sources, they would have no reason to buy from you. This may seem logical, but it is exactly the kind of pitfall a beginning seller is likely to overlook.

There is a trade organization and a trade show for this industry, and it appears that membership in the organization (*The Museum Store Association*), and exhibitions at its trade show have a lot to do with selling to this market.

---

[1] from *Sharing Barbara's Mail* newsletter.

*How to Get Orders from
Store Buyers*

• *Drop-in calls may be fine for
local or small shops and stores;
however, if you are planning to call
on major department store buyers,
or the buyers of exclusive specialty
shops, telephone for an appointment. Some of these buyers see
sellers only on certain days of the
week.*

• *Whenever possible, "case the
joint" before trying to sell to it.
Make sure your products fit into the
line of merchandise it already
carries.*

• *Create a professional image
that will leave no doubt in any
buyer's mind as to your ability to
produce and deliver an order on
schedule. This image will largely
be created by your personal appearance, so present yourself as a well-
groomed professional. Dress in a
manner that is in keeping with the
atmosphere of the shop or store,
and be on time for your
appointment.*

• *The manner in which you
present your line is as important
as the manner in which you present
yourself as a salesperson. Design a
good-looking sample case or display board – whatever is appropriate for your products; something
that can be set up in a jiffy in a
small place, and packed away just
as quickly. Individual items in your*

(more . . .)

Notes

d.) Department Stores

This is a much easier market to penetrate than museum shops. As with the gift and craft shop market, markups of 100% and more are the rule. Trade shows and wholesale buyers' markets are an excellent way to connect with buyers. Personal calls on individual stores or buying offices work well, too, as do professional presentations by mail.

As a consumer, you certainly are aware of the kind of merchandise found in department stores, so you also realize what might sell. Note that fine handcrafts are now part of the inventory in many stores. J. C. Penney and Lord & Taylor, recently have moved into the crafts market. In an article in *The Crafts Report*, the merchandise manager for Neiman-Marcus said that decorative objects with strong design concepts were of greatest interest to his buyers, but that functional objects with good design were also marketable. This viewpoint seems to be held by many department store buyers today.

In addition to a store's own buyers, it may also have "Resident Buyers" or "Market Representatives," according to Marvin David, publisher of *Quality Craft Market* (QCM), a publication which gives attention to the architectural and department store markets.[2] "These people work from centrally-located offices," he says, "most often in New York and California, covering the market for the stores they represent. Some of these representatives actually place orders while others make recommendations to buyers in their member stores." If this is a market you want to explore, you might check the directory of department store buyers available from *Chain Store Age Magazine.* (It's unlikely that such a specialized directory as this will be available in your library.)

For maximum sales success in the department store market, add these tips to the ones already given for other retail outlets:

• Know the store's buying calendar. If you don't know, ask. For example, Christmas goods are bought in early spring, for fall delivery. The larger the store, the longer the lead time. Use this as a guide for judging when other seasonal merchandise may be ordered.

• If you are marketing garments, note that there are four seasons, and merchandise is shown to buyers in the month indicated in parentheses: Summer (January); Fall (March); Resort/Holiday (August); Spring/Summer (October). (For information on trade shows, read *Women's Wear Daily.*)

• Contact the Merchandise Manager's office for the name of the specific buyer you should use — jewelry, home furnishings, apparel, etc. — then call that buyer. If you fail to connect, don't leave a message; just call again, as often as necessary. (Buyers are hard to catch; many do not return calls.)

• When you do get an appointment, be organized and ready for your sales presentation. It may be "short and sweet," so show your best things first.

• When making presentations by mail, include photographs or good drawings of your products. Make sure they are properly identified and accompanied by detailed description

---

[2]1988 update: This periodical is no longer in print.

lists and a price list. (Note: do not send slides unless requested. Buyers may not have a viewer for them.)

- A sample may sell the order for you, but sending free samples to all buyers is impractical since they won't be returned. One option: You might offer a sample at a special price that will at least cover your actual production costs.
- When you do get an order, don't start production until you have a written confirmation on the store's own order form. Take nothing for granted.

e.) Other Mass Merchandisers

I must confess I do not know much about selling to this market. However, I do know that few small, homebased businesses can produce in the quantity and price range demanded by buyers in the mass merchandise field. There are exceptions, of course. I can think of at least one homebased kit manufacturer who now sells to chain stores through sales representatives. If this is your market, you will need to make contact with the trade industry appropriate to your product line. Also investigate trade magazines such as *Chain Store Age* and *The Discount Merchandiser*.

f.) Florists and Garden Centers

I do know something about this market, as I used to sell books to them when I was with a publishing company. Most of these retail outlets (called ''dealers'' in this industry) work through distributors, although some also buy direct from manufacturers and publishers. Like many bookstores, these are slow-pay accounts.

Distributors in this industry generally want 50+10%, maybe 50+10+10%; dealers buy at 40% discounts. For more information, see trade magazines such as *Garden Supply Retailer* and *Lawn & Garden Marketing*.

g.) Hobby and Craft Supply Shops

This is a market I know especially well. A lot of beginning sellers with craft-related products (kits, tools, books, etc.) think they can sell easily to craft supply shops around the country. Hobby shops, perhaps, but not craft supply shops. There are approximately 20,000 of these shops in the country, and it is standard practice for all of them to buy *only* from distributors in the industry. Thus, to sell to retail craft shops, you must first sell to distributors who want the same kind of discounts as lawn and garden distributors. Regrettably, few small manufacturers or self publishers seem able to give them.

If you are an exception, you can easily break into this industry by exhibiting at the regional or annual HIA shows (Hobby Industry Association). Don't enter a trade show, however, until you have contacted a couple of craft distributors to test interest in your product. If you have at least one large distributor, an exhibit at the HIA show would be a great way to promote your products to retailers and encourage additional distributor sales of your line.

For more information about this industry, subscribe to *Profitable Craft Merchandising* magazine. They also publish an

---

(. . . more)

display should be tagged with pertinent sales information, such as the wholesale price, sizes and colors available, your order or stock number, and any minimum or maximum quantity requirements.

- *If you happen to make limited-edition items, don't apologize for this fact. Instead, emphasize the uniqueness, rarity, or exclusivity of your products. Even large department stores are buying one-of-a-kind originals and limited editions these days.*

- *Acquaint yourself with the business terms and forms you must know and use to do business. You will find a list of each on an adjacent page.*

- *Don't try to sell anything to anyone until you have good printed materials: catalog sheets with photographs of your products (or at least a brochure), a wholesale and retail price list, business stationery, and cards. Such materials are vital for selling to store buyers. You always should leave sales material with each retailer you call upon.*

- *Buyer resistance? Try offering a ''trial sample selection'' at a special introductory price. And when you do get an order, be prepared. Have your own order pad in hand in case the shop or store does not use its own purchase order forms.*

Notes

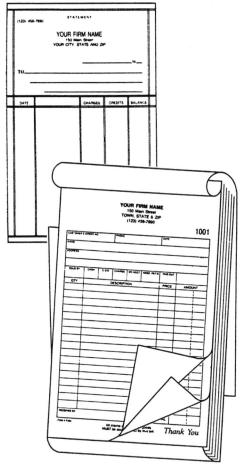

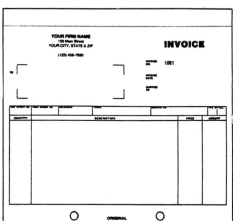

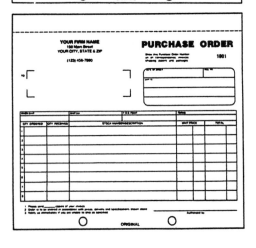

Six Necessary Business Forms

- **Sales Order Form.** If you do not wish to use a sales order book, simply write an order on your business letterhead, making a copy for the buyer. Some buyers, of course, will give you their own purchase order. Make sure that it is signed by the buyer, and that he or she agrees to all your terms and conditions as stated on your price list.

- **Price List.** Do not place retail and wholesale prices on the same sheet, but print individual price sheets for each. Your wholesale price list should state your conditions for new customers (your need for credit references or check with first order, etc.), your guarantee (if one is offered), and your shipping charge policy. (Some sellers charge the actual postage or shipping costs incurred while others work on a certain percentage of the order — such as 5% — which few buyers would question. The latter charge probably would help offset your overhead costs in packaging orders.)

- **Packing List.** Buyers need some kind of checklist when they are unpacking a shipment. The packing list serves this purpose by describing the contents of each box or carton in the shipment. The packing list must agree in description and number with the information shown on the invoice, which is why some standard invoice forms include a packing list as one of the copies in the form. Obviously, this saves time by eliminating the typing of a second business form.

- **Invoice.** Standard invoice forms are available in three, four, or five-part sets and generally include the following information: Seller's name and address, buyer's name and address; ship-to address (if different from sold-to address); date of invoice; date of shipment; method of shipment (parcel post, truck line, UPS, etc.); invoice number; customer's purchase order number; terms of payment (Net 30 days, etc.); quantity and description of items shipped, their unit price, and total amount; plus shipping charges.

- **Statement.** A statement shows an account's balance at month's end. If an account does not pay your invoice, send another invoice, not a statement. Unless you are making several shipments to major accounts each month, statements should not be necessary.

- **Purchase Order.** You may receive purchase orders as well as send them. A purchase order received from a shop or store should be acknowledged either with immediate shipment of the order, or by an order confirmation that indicates when later shipment may be expected. When you use a purchase order for your own suppliers, it signifies that you are a businessperson, not a hobby business, which is why the use of this form may help you in getting wholesale prices or credit. Purchase order forms are also helpful inner-office records that enable you to keep track of incoming supplies, invoices that must be paid, and the volume of business you are giving each of your suppliers.

Note: All of these standard business forms can be purchased in local stationers stores or ordered by mail from office supply catalogs listed in the resource chapter.

annual directory that lists all the manufacturers, wholesalers, publishers, distributors, and dealers in this industry, along with a directory of supplies by product category. Also contact the HIA for a complete schedule of hobby and craft trade shows nationwide.

h.) Needlecraft Supply Shops

You may be surprised to learn that the needlework industry is a separate and very large industry which operates quite differently from the hobby and crafts industry. Many needlework manufacturers and publishers are now involved in craft industry trade shows. Needlecraft shops may buy from craft distributors, but, unlike craft retailers, they also buy directly from manufacturers and publishers, usually at a 40–50% discount.

There are all kinds of needlecraft trade shows, just as there are different craft and hobby industry shows, and many small, homebased businesses have been launched as a result of exhibiting in just one of them.

It may surprise you to learn that many of the needlecraft how-to instruction booklets for sale in needlecraft shops have been published by women working at home. Beginning as needlecraft designers, they have discovered the profits that can come from self-publishing a line of design books for the consumer market. This is not something everyone should jump into, but it is nice to know that hundreds of homebased publishers have succeeded in this industry. It's just the opposite story in the crafts industry. Authors who have published their own books have learned the expensive way that, because of the distribution system in this industry, they cannot get their books into the shops where they would be most likely to sell. The reason is usually price-related, and sometimes the book's format is a problem, too. That's why most of the craft how-to instruction booklets in retail shops are published by industry publishers.

To get a better feel for the needlecraft market, investigate The National Needlework Association (TNNA), which sponsors one of the industry's largest trade shows. A subscription to *Sew Business Magazine* also will give you an excellent overview of the needlecraft/sewing/quilting industries, as well as listings of all related trade shows. Finally, membership in the Society of Craft Designers will benefit everyone who is trying to introduce needlecraft or craft supplies, kits, tools, books or other publications to the crafts and needlecrafts industries.

For an overall education in how to sell to the craft and needlework industries, as well as how to profit from sideline activities related to these industries, see *Creative Cash — Making Money with Your Crafts, Needlework, Designs, and Know-how.*

i.) Bookstores

As a former trade book publisher, I have had considerable experience with bookstores, much of it frustrating. If you are a self-publisher, you won't want to sell directly to this market. The book trade's purchasing and payment practices can aggravate even the largest trade publisher. Independent bookstores generally order only one or two copies of a book at a time, then take 60 to 90 days to pay. They also retain the right to return books up to a year after date of invoice if the books don't sell. Even more frustrating, the books are not always returned in resalable condition.

> ### *Tips on Setting Prices*
>
> *If you do not establish a high enough minimum order for dealers, you may find, especially at Christmastime, that the owners of shops will buy your work at wholesale prices for themselves or for personal gifts. While this may not bother you, remember that very small orders can be a nuisance when you're primarily wholesaling your work, and you may want to discourage such sales with a higher minimum order.*
>
> *To increase dealer orders from new shops, consider offering a special "get acquainted" sampling of products at a lower price – something you can afford to do because this would be a standard order that could be prepackaged in advance. Suggested price might be in the range of $50–$100, depending on what you sell.*

Notes

Notes

If you are a one-book publisher, as so many self-publishers are, you'll find it nearly impossible to get into major bookstore chains like B. Dalton and Waldenbooks; they do not like to establish accounts with one-book suppliers. On the other hand, I do know several small publishers who have broken the barrier simply because they promoted their books so well that a public demand was created for them; they "pulled" people into bookstores. If you create a demand, many stores will "special order" a book for their customers.

Of course, your troubles may only be starting once you get onto a computerized system like B. Dalton's. Their policy is to punch in automatic orders for each store in their system, and then send from one to six books at a time to each of these stores. (Quantity depends on the size of each store's market area.) Then, periodically, reorders go out again to the same stores, often at the very moment the same stores are packing up the first order for return to the publisher. The computer does not always keep track of returns.

Book publishing is a risky business at best. While I heartily encourage self-publishing for those who want to sell by mail, I never would encourage a small publisher to enter the bookstore market. Ignore this advice, however, if you really are serious about becoming a *real* book publisher, and if you have the necessary stamina, patience, and financing to survive this business. Good books will sell, if they are attractively designed — cover especially — and promoted effectively.

For a small book publisher, the best distribution system is a larger publisher who will sell to bookstores and wholesalers for you, doing the warehousing, invoicing, and so on. But such distributors may demand a large discount — usually 65%, sometimes more — which puts most small publishers right out of the ballgame. (You may have to print 10,000 copies of a book to get a production cost that will allow for this kind of discount, and only an entrepreneurial daredevil would take that kind of financial risk on a self-published book.)

But I know some of these daredevils: a few have achieved financial success. Dan Poynter is one of them. *The Self-Publishing Manual,* one of Dan's many books, has become the "bible" in its category. I recommend it heartily. Dan is now producing computer and word processing books and enjoying similar sales success with each new title.

Peggy Glenn is another entrepreneur who had the courage of her convictions. Her manual, *How to Start and Run a Successful Home Typing Business,* is now in its second printing, principally because of nationwide publicity obtained through the author's fine promotional efforts. This book also served as a springboard for other books Peggy and her husband have written and published.

There is an exciting new possibility for self-publishers — a new book distribution plan that was introduced in January, 1984. Conceived by authors William F. Buckley, Jr. and Stuart W. Little, it is designed to help authors everywhere protect and extend the lives of their out-of-print books. Frequently, when publishers decide to let books go out of print, they "remainder" all copies in their inventory (which means, simply, to sell them cheaply to discount houses who specialize in selling marked-down books by mail or through retailers, including the book chains, who promote remaindered books). Authors often prevent this kind of sale by buying the inventory themselves for selling by mail. Unfortunately, this doesn't solve the problem of people going into bookstores to buy them as a result of publicity generated by the author. But The Buckley-Little Book Catalog may solve this problem. It contains listings of books available directly from authors, and it will be circulated to bookstores and libraries, enabling them to order directly from authors. Although this plan was originally designed to help authors who have been published by trade publishers, I inquired and was advised that self-publishers also are invited to participate in this unique program. Stuart W. Little explains: "The criterion for being listed in the catalogue is that books are to be made available through the authors themselves. On this basis, I should think many self-publishers would qualify."

For more information, see "Marketing Aids" in the resource chapter. And for more about the crazy-but-wonderful book publishing industry, read *Publishers Weekly,* and study *Literary Market Place,* both available in most libraries.

2. Selling to Mail Order Catalog Houses

Catalogs have been popular with Americans since Aaron Montgomery Ward published his first one in 1872. Although it was only a single sheet of paper (much like some of the catalogs issued by today's small entrepreneurs), it was obviously an idea whose time had come. Since then, thousands of small and large businesses, corporations, institutions, and organizations have jumped into the multi-billion-dollar mail order industry with catalogs of their own. Five billion catalogs were mailed in the United States in 1982 (an average of 40 per household), generating sales of over $40 billion, according to *Direct Response* newsletter. Experts predict that by 1990, 20% of all merchandise will be purchased from catalogs.

There are as many kinds of catalogs as there are retail outlets. For a good, overall look at them, see the directory offered by the National Mail Order Association, which lists 6,300 firms. Gift catalogs are particularly popular, and especially suited to the kind of products generally produced by homebased manufacturers and product makers. Anything and everything seems to be selling, from $3 kitchen gadgets to $100,000 jeweled necklaces.

Craft, needlework, and hobby catalogs also abound. You will find many of them simply by reading ads in craft consumer magazines. These catalog buyers are likely to be interested in kits, books, tools, and supplies. For yet another listing of mail order catalogs, see *The Great Catalogue Guide,* which lists more than 600 mail order catalogs published by companies who are members of the Direct Marketing Association.

So what does it take to get into this great marketplace? Basically, a product that is suitable for mail-order marketing. Study a few catalogs and you soon will have the idea. You do need an item you can produce in quantity, and the right wholesale price is essential. My experience in selling books to mail order catalog houses indicates that you will need to allow for a three- or four-times markup. For example, if your product has a suggested retail price of $25, the catalog house may be interested in it only if you can sell it to them at between $6–8. The question is whether *you* can make a profit at this level.

You can see at once that the product you offer ought to be one of your higher-priced items. If you are timid about setting prices in the $50 and higher range, just read some of the exclusive gift catalogs now in the mails. Consider, too, that you may be willing

(. . . more)

get away with this kind of shenanigan. (They may not pay your invoice for the 2%, but at least they'll know you mean business and may abstain from this practice in the future.) If you prefer not to offer a discount, but simply want full payment within ten or thirty days, you would write on your invoice, "Net 10 days" or "Net 30 days," whichever is desired.

• F.O.B.: Means "Freight, or free, on board." These initials with the name of a city immediately after them indicate the point to which the seller will pay the freight. If the customer is to pay freight, the notation would read F.O.B. your city; if you are paying the freight, it would read F.O.B. his city. This F.O.B. notation could be important in the event goods are lost or damaged in transit since, legally, title of the goods changes hands at the F.O.B. point.

• Pro Forma: If you are uncertain about the credit worthiness of a new outlet, do not ship and bill, but sell your first order to them on a "pro forma" basis, which means you want your money in advance. Simply send a Pro Forma Invoice for the merchandise that has been ordered, and ship the goods when payment has been received.

Notes

Notes

to settle for a smaller per-piece profit simply because you will be selling in greater quantities. I know some kit manufacturers who have sold thousands of kits to mail order catalog companies over a period of time. Initial orders probably will be for a few dozen — maybe a gross (144) — with reorders on a regular basis if the item sells well. Buyers usually give their suppliers notice of the approximate quantities they plan to buy. They naturally want assurance of your ability to deliver before they put an item in a catalog.

How do you approach catalog buyers? Try querying the catalog houses of your choice by phone, asking for the Director of Merchandise, or the Catalog Merchandise Buyer. Initially, try to determine if there is any interest in the product(s) you offer; if so, follow up immediately with a good information package. A glossy photo is a must for your presentation package, but don't send samples unless they are requested. Like department store buyers, catalog buyers will not pay for samples, nor will they return them.

You also can introduce your products to thousands of mail order dealers by advertising in publications like *Mail Order Product,* where, for $35–$50 you can reach 3,000 direct marketers and catalog buyers with a feature on your product. Also contact Gift Finders International, a company that publishes a wholesale catalog that's distributed to approximately 1,000 companies, many of whom are mail-order catalog buyers. Other prospective customers are premium sales buyers or fund-raising groups.

For more information on penetrating this market, see the booklet, *Selling to Catalog Houses.*

3. Trade Shows/Sales Representatives/Merchandise Marts

Small manufacturers and publishers often consider exhibiting in trade shows to reach new markets, and well they should. Although trade show exhibiting is neither simple nor inexpensive, it can often be the most important marketing move a small business can make.

Fairs, shows, and exhibitions of products are held periodically by many industries. Some hold annual shows in the same city each year while others hold three or four shows a year, each in a different city. These shows, which may last for a few days or possibly a week, offer a tremendous opportunity for manufacturers to make contacts with wholesalers, retailers, and interested sales representatives. In addition, trade shows are the best way to find out what your competition is doing.

But doing your first trade show can be something of a shock, particularly if you are not prepared with the right pricing structure, type of display, or promotional materials. Trade show novices often attend their first show fearful that they will be bombarded with so many orders they will be unable to produce and deliver goods on schedule. Worse than too many orders, however, are none at all. This is more apt to be the result when one enters a trade show without knowing the ropes. If and when orders do pour in, the smart marketer will have a plan in the wings which will allow for an immediate increase in production (cottage industry, help from sheltered workshop workers, etc.), or at least be smart enough to know when to stop taking orders.

Another important consideration, in the event orders do pour in, is the capital that will be needed to buy the necessary raw materials to fill orders, plus the time it may take to collect on such orders once they have been shipped.

The cost of doing trade shows often is prohibitive to many small businesses. In addition to high booth fees, there are all kinds of extras because unions do all the set-up and dismantling work and charge highly for it. Before doing a show, make sure you calculate all the costs that will be incurred, from laying down a carpet or installing an electric outlet, to moving boxes to and from your exhibit area. Display design and construction costs often are expensive, too, yet they are critical to one's success at a show. You probably will save a bundle if you can design and build your own exhibit, as well as the shipping crates you'll need to get it from place to place. (You may save money by buying some of the lightweight and highly portable show exhibits now offered by many manufacturers, and regularly advertised in trade magazines.)

Because of the high cost of trade show exhibiting, many small businesses find it better to use sales representatives who not only call on certain retail outlets but regularly exhibit in certain trade shows as well. Some reps also have permanent exhibits in merchandise marts (discussed below.) One either can elect to work with one or more independent representatives, or with a rep organization. The latter often offers national coverage of a particular market. (In working with independent reps, be careful about establishing the territories they will handle for you. You may hire a rep to cover one state, only to later discover that this state is part of the regular territory handled by another group of reps you would like to hire.) On an adjacent page you will find a sample sales rep agreement that may be helpful to you.

If a product can be sold in more than one market, a manufacturer or publisher may need two or three different kinds of reps or rep organizations. For example, there are reps who call exclusively on bookstores, others who call exclusively on needlework shops, still others who call on gift shops, lawn and garden outlets, and so on.

How do you find trade shows and sales reps? As already indicated, there are trade shows for most industries. Your first goal should be to locate the trade magazines for each industry of interest to you. (The library is the place to go to locate periodicals for any industry not mentioned in this book's resource chapter.) In addition, publications such as *Convention World* and *Exhibits Schedule* list and describe thousands of trade shows each year to help exhibitors determine which shows are worthy of consideration. If you live in or near a large city, be sure to contact its trade mart or merchandise mart for a list of all trade shows presented there each year.

Trade periodicals usually carry classified ads from manufacturers and sales reps alike to aid connections between the two. Reps also can be found at trade shows or in merchandise marts. In addition, the Manufacturers Agents National Association publishes a monthly magazine in which many reps and manufacturers advertise their availability.

What you may not realize about sales reps is that they only want to deal with companies who can produce in volume. For instance, many established reps can't afford to take on a line unless it grosses at least $100,000 a year for them; that automatically eliminates most homebased manufacturers. And since a sales rep's commission is dependent on gross sales, this definitely is a figure with which you must be concerned. If you do find a rep willing to handle your line, he or she probably will want a commission of at least 15%. (Commissions actually may range from 5% on items with huge

MEMORANDUM OF AGREEMENT

Made ___(date)___ between ___(name of sales representative or organization)___ (hereinafter referred to as the Associates), of ___(address of sales representative or organization)___ and ___(your business name and address)___.

This agreement shall be in force for the period of one year and shall continue thereafter for one-year periods unless either party gives notice to the other in writing six months in advance of the renewal date or on that date for a date six months hence.

The Associates shall be our exclusive representative to the ___(specify trade area or industry)___, both retail and jobber, in the following states or parts thereof:

(list states here)

We expect the Associates to give this territory diligent and intensive coverage for which a commission of _____% will be paid on all invoices of sales made by the Associates.

Commission payments will be sent to you on the 15th of each month, accompanied by copies of invoices for all the billing to trade accounts in your territory. All expenses of travel and maintenance will be paid by the Associates. You will call on major accounts ___(specify how often, based on discussion with rep)___

We grant the right of access at all times to our files of copies of all invoices to enable you to ascertain the correctness of our commission payments to you.

We agree that your services to this company are not exclusive (meaning that the Associates will continue to represent other companies).

Please indicate your acceptance of this agreement by signing and returning the attached copy of this agreement.

Sincerely,

___(your signature)___

FOR: ___(your business name)___

Accepted:

___(signature of sales rep)___   DATE: ___(date signed)___

This sample memorandum of agreement may help you prepare one for the sales representatives you may hire. It is similar to an agreement used by a book publisher, and it can easily be adapted to fit the needs of any product business. One thing it does not cover, however, is the availability of product samples — how many will be provided as "selling tools," and provisions for replacement of samples that become damaged. Also make it clear whether you, too, are entitled to contact the same accounts being called on by the rep. For instance, will you be making mail order promotions? If so,

will a commission be paid to the sales rep on such invoiced orders? (Some reps may demand a commission on any order from an account in their territory, whether they had anything to do with getting the order or not. In other words, they may not want you to "compete" with them for orders. This can be a touchy area, so make sure it's clarified in the beginning.)

For your added protection, you might let an attorney check the agreement you create. (The fee for this would be much smaller than if you asked the attorney to actually write the document.)

sales potential to as much as 20–30% on low-ticket items with limited sales potential.)

In addition to regularly hosting trade shows, several cities, such as Chicago, Atlanta, New York, and Los Angeles, have permanent merchandise marts, apparel centers, or gift marts which enable manufacturers and sales representatives (or other wholesaling middlemen) to rent space and exhibit throughout the year. Such showrooms are not open to consumers, of course, but manufacturers are welcome to visit.

4. Institutional Buyers

Depending on your product, institutional buyers may be a market worth exploring. In particular, book and periodical publishers will want to investigate sales possibilities with schools, colleges, universities, and libraries. These buyers like to receive a 20% discount on books, but often buy them, and subscriptions to periodicals, at full retail price. They prefer that you ship and bill, often asking for from three to five copies of an invoice (which can be aggravating to the small business). But these accounts almost always pay promptly and are worth the effort it takes to sell to them.

Mailing lists of institutional buyers are readily available from list houses, or can be compiled from directories in the library.

5. Premium Sales

Premiums are marketing tools often used by companies to entice buyers into purchasing some product or service. This is a difficult market to crack, but any product or publication that can be produced in quantity may have premium appeal to buyers. Companies who specialize in offering premium products exhibit at premium and incentive shows. Smaller businesses could connect with interested premium buyers by working with marketing firms who specialize in premium offers, or by placing ads in certain publications that reach catalog buyers, premium users, and fund raisers. (*Direct Marketing* magazine often publishes notices of such offers.)

What are some typical premium situations? Banks often use premiums to entice people to open savings accounts. Manufacturers use premiums to lure customer prospects into their dealer's shops to look at the newest model now being offered (television sets, sewing machines, equipment, etc.), and publishers use premiums as bonus items for new subscribers or as a renewal incentive. In other words, when thinking of premium sales, try to relate your product to some other product or service already on the market, then think of a way in which it might be used by that seller to increase his business. Since premium sales may involve thousands — even hundreds of thousands - of units, your discounts will vary considerably.

Another kind of premium arrangement involves coupons. For instance, you might buy a sack of lawn seed and find a coupon or order form on the back of the bag that promotes a booklet on lawn care. The seed manufacturer has not gone into publishing as a sideline; the company is simply working with some publisher on a premium deal. This kind of thinking can be applied to many products and services. There is no reason why small, homebased manufacturers and publishers cannot approach one another and work out their own special premium arrangements to boost the income of their businesses.

Notes

6. The Government Market

I know nothing about selling to this market, but I know someone who does, and I am simply going to introduce you to him. If this is your market — or could be — you can take it from there. Herman Holtz is the author of *The $100 Billion Market,* a book that explains how to do business with the U.S. government. He knows what he is talking about. In his capacity an independent consultant, he has won several million dollars' worth of contracts for his clients. In his book, he shows you the mistakes he has made and how you can avoid them, and he includes all the hard-won inside facts behind his success.

You don't have to be General Motors to do business with the government, says Herman. In fact, the climate has never been better for small businesses to get their share of government contracts. It is not the size of your company that counts, it's the way you compete for the contracts.

7. Foreign Markets

Exporting to other countries is not something the average small business wants to do, but some readers of this book may find this activity of interest, so I'm including enough information to give them direction.

To avoid the specialized paperwork (including export licenses) involved in exporting, it probably is best to work with agent-buyers or bonafide distributors. The Department of Commerce is the place to start when you want more information on this topic.

First, however, you must decide if your product has overseas sales potential. If so, you then must weigh sales opportunities against the complexities of exporting. It is expensive and time consuming to develop overseas customers; because of the time it takes to receive mail or shipments, it can often take months to consummate a business deal.

How do you find customers abroad? One way is to send a letter to the foreign embassies in Washington, or to their commercial offices, which often are located in New York City. Or, information can be sent to U.S. embassies in countries that offer a market possibility.

In looking for overseas distributors or sales agents, try placing ads in publications circulated in England and several European countries. And, if you are looking for international mailing lists and a way to get books into English-speaking libraries throughout the world, contact IBIS Information Services, Inc.

I suggest you carefully analyze these markets to determine which ones seem to offer profitable opportunities for you. I think you will agree that you have some interesting work ahead of you. In the next chapter you will learn some special marketing techniques that will enable you to communicate with the specific wholesale markets you have decided you want to penetrate.

Direct Response Advertising

8.

T HE LAMENT OF BEGINNING ADVERTISERS everywhere seems to be: " . . . but I expected a much greater response than I got. I don't know what went wrong." A *lot* of things can go wrong in advertising, and experienced marketers are as likely to encounter problems as beginners. The only difference is that the former can more easily afford mistakes than the latter.

Large corporations obviously believe the old saying, "You always buy familiar names/the ones you recognize; that's why the adman always claims/it pays to advertise." Certainly the big companies spend millions of advertising dollars each year just to remind consumers they are in business. (Food and drug product companies, insurance companies, car manufacturers, and oil and utility companies come readily to mind.) Because of exposure to intense media advertising, consumers often are subconsciously persuaded to make certain buying decisions.

Even on the smallest scale, homebased business owners cannot afford this kind of image advertising, unless it comes in the form of publicity. Actually, many small business owners believe they cannot afford to promote their goods or services at all, but if a business is to grow, it must be promoted. If there isn't money for ads, then one quickly must become a publicity expert to survive. (The how-to's of this are described in the next chapter.)

Although I have placed the advertising chapter first (because of its linkage with preceding chapters), I urge you to exploit your publicity opportunities fully before you spend much money on advertising. Many small businesses can travel as far and as fast on publicity as they can on paid advertising; if your dollars are limited, you'll want to hang on to each one of them as long as possible.

When you are able to make funds available for advertising, investigate the direct response advertising methods described in this chapter. (Note that each can be used to sell to both consumers and wholesale buyers.)

> *"If you want to learn how to sell, you should emulate the examples of people who know how to sell."*
>
> — *John Caples*, Direct Marketing Magazine

1. Direct Mail

I believe in direct mail advertising. But the only way to learn how to sell by direct mail is the expensive way — through trial and error. You can save money and heartache by giving yourself a thorough education before you "drop" your first bulk mailing, but there are no guarantees of success here, even for the most experienced advertisers.

Notes

Check List of Mailing Lists You Can Rent

List rental houses offer thousands of categories of lists. These may be rented for $35/M and up, generally in minimum quantities of 5,000 names. One does not have to mail to all the names rented, however. Following are just a few categories of lists that will be of interest to small mail-order businesses. Whether or not you plan to rent such lists, you will find these market categories helpful in determining the most likely groups of buyers for your particular product or service. Check those of interest to you.

- ☐ Associations, cultural & trade
- ☐ Boat Owners
- ☐ Book Buyers
- ☐ Bridal Shops
- ☐ Bridge Clubs
- ☐ Business Executives
- ☐ Business Opportunity Seekers & Self-Improvement Buyers
- ☐ Clubs, Organizations, Societies
- ☐ Collectors (Limited edition plates, coins, stamps, gems)
- ☐ Colleges & Universities
- ☐ Day Care Facilities
- ☐ Doctors
- ☐ Editors, newspapers & periodicals
- ☐ Farmers
- ☐ Fundraising Prospects
- ☐ Garden Clubs
- ☐ Gift Shops
- ☐ Gourmet Food Shops
- ☐ Hobbyists
- ☐ Knitting & Yarn Shops
- ☐ Libraries
- ☐ Mail Order Firms
- ☐ Mail Order Catalog Buyers (by category of goods purchased)
- ☐ Music Teachers
- ☐ New Mothers
- ☐ Owners of Small Businesses
- ☐ Pet Shops
- ☐ Religious & Ethnic Groups
- ☐ Senior Citizens
- ☐ Subscribers of most magazines
- ☐ Sweepstakes Entrants
- ☐ Teachers (by grade or subject)
- ☐ Typing, Addressing & Mailing Services
- ☐ Wives of Prominent Businessmen
- ☐ Women (in communications, in the arts, in education, etc.)

See the resource chapter for a list of companies which sell mailing lists such as these. A larger list will be found in the free SBA publication, "National Mailing List Houses."

* * * * * * * *

Here's how to build a mailing list of potential customers in a specific market area:

Cities have directories called "criss-cross directories" or "cross reference directories." Call the Chamber of Commerce or the reference librarian at your city library to find out which publisher serves the market area you want to reach. These directories can be leased, or used free of charge in a library.

With a local criss-cross directory in hand, you can establish a mailing list of apartments and homes within specific areas. You cannot get individual family names, but you can address your mailing to "Occupant," at each address on your list.

To find companies who already have compiled such lists, check the Standard Rate and Data Service publications available in libraries.

Direct mail is the preferred choice of all major mail-order marketers. You need only look at your daily mail to realize the wide variety of products being offered by direct mail, and the competition your mail piece will have in the average person's mailbox.

For the small, homebased entrepreneur, direct mail provides an excellent way to reach any category of buyers (consumer or wholesale) in the nation, yet it may be less expensive to reach these same buyers through display advertising in special-interest or trade publications. Always compare costs carefully before deciding on the direction you should take.

On the other hand, certain items, such as books, magazines, and newsletters, do not sell well through display ads because prospective buyers need a lot of information to make an intelligent buying decision. Many other products fall into this category, too. Only a direct mail piece can effectively convey the advertising message needed to generate a sale.

Publishers traditionally have advertised expensive books and periodicals in impressive (and expensive) direct mail packages. These generally consist of a color brochure (often quite elaborate), a cover letter, an order form, and a postage-paid reply envelope. Such mail pieces are always sent to specific, targeted audiences such as those indicated on the adjacent page: "Examples of Mailing Lists You Can Rent."

Mail packages less expensive to produce may be used to offer less-expensive books, newsletters, and magazines, as well as clothing, jewelry, housewares, and a variety of other mail-order merchandise.

Since direct mail advertising is the most expensive method of selling by mail, and certainly unpredictable in terms of order response, beginners are cautioned to make small mailings in the beginning. It's one thing to advertise a new product or service to your own small mailing list of satisfied clients or customers, and quite another to rent 5,000 customer prospect names from a list house, and send them an expensive mail piece promoting a single product.

And if you do rent 5,000 names (the usual minimum test) don't feel that you must mail all of them at once. Mail only 1,000 or 2,000 initially if you can't afford to do the whole mailing. While it may be necessary to test a 5,000 sampling when a list has more than a million names in it, you often can get accurate response readings from much smaller tests, particularly if the total list is small in size or highly specialized.

Your Direct Response Advertising Opportunities At a Glance

1. *Direct Mail*
   a.) *Average Response from Direct Mail Promotions*
   b.) *Timing of Mailings*

2. *Two-Step Advertising*
   a.) *Average Response from Classified Ads*
   b.) *Figuring per-inquiry/per-order costs*
   c.) *Step Two: Getting response to your Follow-Up Mail Piece*

3. *Space (Display) Ads*
   a.) *Using Ad Agencies and Other Freelancers*
   b.) *The Importance of Good Copywriting*
   c.) *Other Tips for Display Advertisers*
   d.) *In-House Advertising Agency*

4. *Other Media Ads*

5. *Special Distribution Programs*
   a.) *Package Inserts*
   b.) *Direct Response Postcard Mailings*
   c.) *Per-Order (PO) Arrangements*
   d.) *Per-Inquiry (PI) Advertising*

Sections in this chapter are numbered to correspond with numbered topics above.

Notes

---

a.) Average Response

The most important thing to remember about direct mail is that a 1% response is considered good by major mailers. They would be ecstatic with 3–4%. One percent, of course, translates into only 50 orders on a 5,000-piece mailing. You need not be a mathematician to see how easy it would be for the inexperienced direct mailer to lose his shirt the first time out. It can easily cost 50¢ per contact (list rental, addressing charge, printed materials, preparation of mailing, postage, etc.) for even the most ordinary direct mail package; the four-color mail packages mentioned earlier cost much more than this.

Now you know why only the more expensive products are offered by major direct-mail marketers. In fact, a product with a retail value of less than $50 probably would not be profitable to them, given the high costs of direct mail and the average response

Notes

typically received to a "cold mailing list," which is all that rented lists are.

A "hot mailing," on the other hand — meaning a mailing to qualified buyer names generated from publicity or advertising — is something else entirely. And you don't have to offer a $50 product to make money on a direct mailing to this kind of list. In fact, we never have lost money on a direct mailing to our house list, even when the offer was for one book priced at $8.95. So much depends on the product, the quality of the names on your list, and how well your offer matches their interests.

If you do test a list, you may wonder what results you need from such a test to indicate whether you should purchase more names from that same list. One authority says that if you get back at least 100% of the direct costs of your first promotion, you should try another mailing of the same size to the same list. If you get the same response twice, this would indicate that you would get a similar response to even larger mailings of the same list. In other words, the results of one test are never conclusive, but similar results from two test mailings to the same list could be a strong indication that a larger mailing to the same list would bring similar results. Still, *there are no guarantees;* these are merely guidelines.

After you have made a mailing, how soon can you tell if it's going to produce a good response? In doing my research (and checking my own files) on this topic, I found several guidelines proposed by industry experts. Here they are:

- One expert says that the heaviest day's response to a mailing will come the second Monday after the first order arrives.
- Another says that half the total response to a direct mailing should be within the first 13 days of returns.
- Others suggest that, by the fifth or sixth day (after the first response has been received), you will have about 30–35% of the total response you are going to receive. By the end of two weeks you will have about 75–80% of the total response you're going to receive.

These figures also offer guidelines to response from publicity and display advertising in magazines. (In an adjacent illustration, you'll find a form you can copy to help you tabulate your response to ads or publicity.)

b.) Timing of Mailings

In addition to having a good mail list, one of the most important considerations in planning any direct mailing is when to mail. Direct mail marketing experts have all kinds of theories about when certain people will buy certain products. Experience has shown that January and September are good months to mail a variety of consumer offers, but response naturally depends on type of product being offered. (Obviously, one does not mail information about gardening in September, nor Christmas offers in February.)

Robert Jay, publisher of *The Copley Mail Order Advisor* (no longer in publication), learned from research and experience that retail merchandise and giftware seem to sell best in these months (listed in order of priority): October, January, February, November, September, March. Money-making offers, he said, do well if mailed in February, January, September, October, March, and August. These are only guidelines, of course. The results of one mailer may have little bearing on the results of another.

For instance, one report I read said that July was a good month to mail to hobbyists and crafters, but the crafts field has been a specialty for me. I can assure you that both July and August are terrible mail-order months for me (and a lot of my mail order networking pals, as well). That's because most of my buyers are women, and their buying habits are closely tied to what their children are doing. My sales always drop off when school lets out, and pick up again when it starts. What this proves is that no one knows it all, and all direct mailers have to test to determine the best mailing months for their particular products.

If you are selling to consumers, you might put yourself in the buyer's position, and ask yourself what you normally would be doing at a certain time of the year if you were that buyer. Then ask yourself if you would buy your kind of merchandise at that time of year.

Do remember that bulk mailings can take anywhere from 10–30 days to be delivered, regardless of what the post office may tell you. Ten-day delivery these days is pure fiction, from my experience; and many people in my network have confirmed that they, too, are getting reports of 30-day delivery on mailings. Plan accordingly, and build plenty of time into your schedule, especially if you are offering seasonal items such as Christmas merchandise. If you pay careful attention to the mail you receive, you will notice that major catalog companies start sending Christmas catalogs as early as September. They continue to mail them throughout the month so the catalogs will arrive in our homes toward the end of September and throughout October. (It is October 5 as I write this, and so far we have received about fifteen Christmas catalogs.)

Note that the mailing date you select will depend on whether you are mailing to consumers or wholesale buyers. For instance, if you're offering Christmas merchandise to retail shops, you must mail months in advance of the season. The same is true for all holidays, and for wholesalers in all fields. The best way to learn the buying season of any particular market is to telephone a couple of buyers and ask.

> *Advertising Tip for Catalog Sellers*
>
> *When offering your catalog in an ad that may be read by consumers, be sure to indicate that it will be sent ONLY to qualified wholesale buyers who write to you on their business letterhead.*
>
> *Otherwise, you may end up sending a $3 catalog to a lot of curiosity seekers who only want to study your catalog for ideas.*
>
> — *Tip from* Sharing Barbara's Mail

Notes

2. Two-Step Advertising

This is the preferred method of advertising for all businesses with limited budgets, but it works so well that major marketers also use it to build mailing lists of qualified customer prospects.

"People who can't do a complete selling job within the limitations of space ads are using the unique reach of these ads to draw thousands, even millions, of interested inquiries," says the author of a marketing article in *Zip* magazine. "They then follow up these inquiries with catalogs, or elaborate and sometimes personalized mail packages, and occasionally telephone calls."

While major companies may place expensive display ads to attract buyer prospects (manufacturers trying to interest dealers, for instance), smaller businesses are more likely to think in terms of placing classified ads in a number of magazines. And for as little as $500, one can run quite an effective campaign.

	# OF INQUIRIES		# OF ORDERS		# OF DOLLARS	
DATE	Daily	Total	Daily	Total	Daily	Total

ONE MONTH RESPONSE RECORD FOR:

[] CLASSIFIED AD in:

_____

Date of Issue: _____

Number insertions: _____ Key: ____

Cost: _____

Item advertised: _____

[] DISPLAY AD IN:

_____

Date of Issue: _____

Number insertions: _____ Key: _____

Ad size: _____ Cost: _____

Item advertised: _____

[] DIRECT MAILING   [] Individual
                    [] Cooperative

List used: _____

Quantity mailed: _____
       [] Bulk mailing [] First class
Date of mailing: _____

Mail piece used: _____

[] PUBLICITY in:

Source: _____

Date of publicity: _____

Key: _____

Item publicized: _____

COSTS and ANALYSIS information:

This typewritten form, created to size 8½″ × 11″, had to be reduced somewhat to fit space in this book. If desired, readers may photocopy this form for their own use, or simply use it as a guideline to prepare original typewriter artwork for a printer.

a.) Average Response from Classified Ads

In this type of advertising, the idea is to go fishing, but forget about catching fish for awhile. First, just try to get a nibble.

The first key to success here is a careful matching of your product or service with the right publication or audience of readers, whether trade or consumer. Another key to success is learning to write the kind of ad copy that entices readers to respond. What you have to do is learn how to "dangle the carrot," while also being careful not to give so much information in an ad that readers can say, "Oh, I know what this is, and I'm not interested." Instead, you want them to think, "I wonder if this is what I have been looking for? Guess I'll have to write for more information to find out."

The response to a classified ad, then, brings a number of "hot prospects;" people who obviously are interested in learning the details of your offer, as opposed to the "cold prospects" you normally would reach in a direct mailing. (The latter prospects, never having asked to receive your literature, may simply throw it in the wastebasket when it arrives.)

Since all ads attract a certain number of curiosity seekers, don't expect to sell more than 5% of your hot prospects with your first promotional mailing, and be satisfied if you get an order response of even 2–3%, which most mailers consider good. (Again, much depends on what you are selling, and to whom. I have received order conversion rates everywhere from 3% to 18% in the past few years, but my average at present is 10%. I have noticed a steady increase in this average, which seems to be related to the length of time I've been in business.)

About six to eight weeks after your first mailing to a list of prospects gained from a classified ad, send a follow-up mailing, and keep on mailing these prospects as long as you get back enough orders to cover all your costs. In my experience, repeated mailings to a good prospect list will generate orders every time. This seems to hold true even if you mail the same people the same offer over and over again.

b.) Figuring Per-Inquiry/Per-Order Costs

If you wonder whether a display ad or the two-step method, would be best for you, try a test and evaluate the results on a per-inquiry/ per order cost basis. This is far more important than the cost of an ad or mail promotion. For example, if a classified ad costs $60 and generates 75 inquiries, your per-inquiry cost would be 80¢.

If you were to place a display ad in the same publication — one that cost $250 and brought in 197 inquiries — your per-inquiry cost would be $1.27. In this instance, then, classified ads would certainly be the most cost-effective way to generate inquiries *in this particular magazine*. (You might get an entirely different response from a different magazine.)

To illustrate the above figures:

Classified Ad	Display Ad
Cost of ad: $60	Cost of ad: $250
Number of inquiries: 75	Number of inquiries: 197
Per-Inquiry cost:	Per-Inquiry cost:
$60 ÷ 75 = $ .80	$250 ÷ 197 = $1.27

Notes

Your per-customer (or per-order) costs are even more important to you. Let's say that you send a catalog to customer prospects. The catalog costs you 18¢ to print and 25¢ to mail first class. Using one of the examples above, let's assume that you send this catalog to the 75 prospects who have responded to the classified ad, for a cost of $32.25. Add to this the cost of the ad itself, which was $60. If you were to get an 8% order response (conversion of prospects to customers) — only 6 new customers — your per-customer cost would be $15.38, as illustrated below.

Depending on the cost of your product, or the size of your average order, you can easily see whether you're going to make or lose money in this kind of situation, and determine whether you should be charging some kind of fee when you "fish for prospects." As you know, many advertisers charge from 50¢ to $3 for brochures or catalogs, depending on how elaborate or expensive they are to print and mail. If you were to place the same $60 classified ad and ask 50¢ for your catalog, you might get only 50 prospects, instead of 75, but they would probably be better buyer prospects, and your order response might increase from 8% to 10%. On this basis, your actual ad investment would be $60, less the $25 your customer prospects send you for postage and handling, or just $35. To this, add $21.50 in costs to send them a catalog, and you've lowered your costs to just $56.50. On the basis of a 10% order response — 5 customers — your cost per customer now drops to $11.30, instead of $15.38. Quite a difference, isn't it, from an ad that reads, "free catalog," to one that reads, "send 50¢ for catalog." Certainly you'll be money ahead whenever you can break even on your classified ads by charging for your promotional literature. Just don't charge too much and stop response altogether.

To illustrate the above figures:

Step One of Two-Step Advertising Method

Ad reading "Free Catalog"		Ad reading "50¢ for Catalog"	
Cost of ad:	$60.00	Cost of ad:	$60.00
		Less 50¢ sent by each of 50 prospects	−25.00
		Adjusted ad cost	$35.00
Per-Inquiry cost: $60 ÷ 75 = $ .80		Per-Inquiry cost: $35 ÷ 50 = $ .70	

Step Two of Two-Step Advertising Method

Cost to send catalogs to 75 prospects:		Cost to send catalogs to 50 prospects:	
75 × .43	$32.25	50 × .43	$21.50
Plus ad cost (above	60.00	Plus ad cost (above	35.00
Total invested in this ad promotion	$92.25	Total invested in this ad promotion	$56.50
If 8% response (6 customers), per-inquiry cost would be:		if 10% order response (5 customers), per-inquiry cost would be:	
$92.25 ÷ 6 = $15.38		$56.50 ÷ 5 = $11.30	

Instead of asking for money, some advertisers ask interested prospects to send a SASE, a Self-Addressed, Stamped Envelope. In doing this, remember the importance of making it easy for people to respond to your offer. Sometimes the extra effort involved in getting an envelope and finding a stamp kills the impulse to order at all. In fact, experts say that a request for a SASE will automatically decrease by 25–35% the total number of responses you may receive. "You're cutting your own throat to save a first class stamp and an envelope," says one mail-order seller. A little arithmetic exercise proves his point:

> If you could get 100 inquiries from an ad that didn't require a SASE, but would lose 35% by asking for the SASE, that would cut the number of prospects to 65. If you were selling a $10 item, and you normally get a 5% order response, on 100 prospects that would mean you'd get 5 extra orders × $10, or $50 worth of business, and five customers who would probably order from you again. But 5% of 65 prospects is only 3 customers, or $30 in orders. For the cost of $10.50 (35 × .30 for a stamp and envelope), you might have had two more customers, more money in orders, and more prospects for future sales. Think about it.

c.) Step Two: Getting a Response to Your Follow-up Mail Piece

Obviously, the material you send to your best prospects has a lot to do with the number of orders you'll get. The easier you make it for people to order, the more likely they are to respond to your offer. That's why flyers or brochures without any kind of order form do not pull as well as a catalog with an order blank; better yet, a standard direct mail package with a cover letter, separate order form, and postage-paid reply envelope. In the beginning, your goal should be to get started with the best package you can afford; test the response to each mailing you send out, and test a number of direct mail pieces. Then decide which kind of mail piece works best for you. (See sample order forms in nearby illustration.)

Note that handcrafts and gifts, in particular, will *not* sell well to consumers through inexpensively-printed, black-and-white brochures or catalogs with line drawings or poor photographs. One reason is because buyers easily may be able to buy such items locally, where they can see every little detail. When ordering by mail, however, they have no visual assurance of the color, texture, and quality of such products. Conversely, the same products that will not sell this way may sell beautifully if they are featured in a full-color catalog produced by a nationally known company, such as Horchow or Lillian Vernon. The difference here, of course, *is buyer confidence in the company making the offer.* This is just one more key to success in selling by mail. Guarantees also go a long way in mail order, as do testimonials from satisfied customers. (It is said that a money-back guarantee may increase order response by as much as 40%.)

For more information about direct mail and two-step advertising, read any of the mail-order books and publications listed in the resource chapter, such as *How to Start and Operate a Mail-Order Business, Mail Order Moonlighting,* and *Mail Order Know-How.* Also see the book, *Elephants in your Mailbox,* which tells the success story of the Horchow catalog.

(more . . .)

Really successful ads of mail-order sales are placed in many magazines. They seldom are changed because they work. What you want to do is find the common denominator in the ads that appear to be successful, and emulate it. You probably will note such words as "new," "free," "Order now," and so on. That's because words like these are proven response stimulators. (My tips on copywriting offer other motivational words you can try.)

In studying display ads, note if advertisers have increased or decreased the sizes of their ads, whether they use order coupons in the ad, offer bank charge card services, or toll-free telephone numbers.

In particular, pay attention to the headlines of all ads. When advertisers do decide to make changes in their ad copy, it often is the headline they experiment with first.

Note: Many advertisers place ads for a three-time run, so in studying the repeat patterns of ads, you need to be looking for ads that have been repeated, say, six months down the road after the first three-time run. That probably would indicate the ad pulled well. (Because of the long lead times of magazines, it probably would take this long for the advertiser to get back into the magazine.)

Notes

Order forms courtesy of Marjorie Turner, Marg Hyland and Carol Carlson.

There are no "rules" for order forms. You simply create one to suit your specific needs. The M. J. Hand Works order form is a 4-part, carbonless form — expensive, and not recommended until you have many orders on a regular basis. The other two forms are single-sheet forms, a kind most often used by small businesses.

Federal Trade Commission Rules

Truth in Advertising: It is not what you say in actual words that counts, but what people believe after they have read your ad. In evaluating whether an advertisement has the tendency or capacity to deceive, law enforcement officials and the courts apply certain standards involving: (1) the message as a whole (the impression left by the total advertisement); (2) the "average person" standard (ads must be viewed from the perspective of the "average" person, not the sophisticated or skeptical person); and (3) deceptive non-disclosure (giving selected information or omitting facts the average person would need to know to make an intellient purchasing decision).

Use of the word, "new" is restricted. As a general rule, a "new" product can only be advertised as new for a period of six months. An older product, although new and unknown to a particular market, may not be advertised as "new" insofar as it gives the impression it has just recently been discovered, developed, or invented. It can, however, be advertised as being new to a specific market area.

Use of Endorsements and Testimonials: These must be based on actual use of the product and the endorser's informed knowledge of the field. Statements of opinion should be so identified to avoid the impression that they have a scientific or other authoritative basis.

If you publish a periodical, you cannot use testimonials from readers whose subscriptions have expired. Endorsers must actually use the advertised product. Also, do not use people's names without written permission.

Warranties and Guarantees: *Warranties* inform buyers that the products they are buying will perform in a certain way under normal conditions. An *implied* warranty means that a product will perform as similar products of its kind under normal conditions, while an *express* warranty states a specific fact about how the product will perform. Claims made in advertisements may constitute an express warranty that imposes legal obligations on the advertiser.

Guarantees must clearly disclose the terms, conditions, and extent of the guarantee, plus the manner in which the company will perform the guarantee. FTC standards require not just a statement, such as "Satisfaction guaranteed, or money back," but a detailed explanation, such as: "If not completely satisfied with the merchandise, return it in good condition within ten days to receive a complete refund of the purchase price."

For more information about all of the above, see the free booklets from the U.S. Department of Commerce: "Advertising, Packaging & Labeling," and "Product Warranties and Servicing."

FTC 30-Day Mail Order Rule

It is extremely important to comply with this rule because it is strictly enforced with penalties up to $10,000 for each violation.

The FTC says it is unfair or deceptive to solicit any order through the mails unless you believe you can fulfill the order within the time you specify. Or, if no time is specified, then you must ship the order within 30 days after receipt of customer's order. You are not affected by the 30-day rule if you 'invoice orders after shipment, or if you specify a particular length of time for delivery, such as "Allow 6 weeks for delivery."

If you are unable to ship within the specified time, or within 30 days if no time has been specified, then the FTC ruling demands that you notify the buyer of the additional delay, and enclose a postage-paid reply card or envelope. You must give the buyer the option either to cancel the order for a full and prompt refund, or extend the time for shipment. If the buyer does not respond, the FTC ruling states that you automatically get the delay, as silence is construed as acceptance. For additional information, ask the FTC for their bulletin on this topic.

Notes

> *The 10 words that spell direct mail success are said to be:*
>
> *Free . . . You . . . Now . . . New . . . Win . . . Easy . . . Introducing . . . Save . . . Today . . . Guarantee*

Notes

3. Space (Display) Advertising

Few small businesses can afford the incredibly high advertising rates of most national magazines. Those who decide to risk such an ad often lose their investment. An ad can fail even when the product being advertised is salable and correctly priced. Most ads probably fail either because they are placed in the wrong publications, or are poorly written or designed. There's so much more to preparing an ad than just making it look good. If the advertising copy doesn't motivate people to buy, they simply will not respond. I must repeat for emphasis: *do not spend money on display advertising until you know something about graphic design and ad copywriting.* And if you don't know, and feel you can't learn, hire a professional to do the job. You will save money in the long run.

Fortunately, novice advertisers can "test the water" with less expensive display ads in a variety of special-interest periodicals which may actually pull better for them than some of the national magazines. The resource chapter lists some of these publications, and many more will be found in the resource chapters of the various how-to books I've listed. The library also has periodical directories, classified by category, to help advertisers find just the right magazine for their advertising message.

a.) Using Ad Agencies and Other Free-Lancers

Beginning advertisers often feel they should consult an advertising agency when they get ready to place their first display ad. While this may be a good idea, it can also be an expensive one, as Colleen Bergman, publisher of *The Cloth Doll* magazine, explains: "Advertising agents can be extremely helpful; however, let's remember that they are there to sell advertising. It is of no concern to them that you had to borrow money at incredible interest rates to place your first ads or perhaps took money out of your hard-earned savings (which was supposed to go toward a down-payment on your first home or your child's education fund), or even took out a second mortgage on your home. Too often they do not realize what the small business person stands to lose. They tend to give you the same advice they give the large company executives who have an unlimited advertising budget."

In picking an advertising agency, use the same kind of logic you would use in picking an accountant. You need an agency that (1) understands how limited your funds are, (2) has experience in working with small business owners, and, most important (3) has some understanding of your product and your market.

Harry and I once went to the best agency we could find for help in creating a direct mail piece, and we really got a beautiful mail package from them. But it failed to draw orders. Although we had explained our product and our market, they had failed miserably in the job of copywriting, did not truly understand the benefits of what we were selling, nor how to sell to the market we wanted to reach. Actually, we knew these things better than the agency, but we lacked confidence at the time. It was an expensive lesson, and one I fear many readers of this book may eventually have to learn for themselves.

Often, large agencies will not even consider working with a small business, so that leaves small agencies as your only choice. These tend to be more oriented to creative services than marketing, but this does not mean they can't do a good job for you. Graphic arts businesses and commercial artists who offer typesetting and design capabilities to advertisers often work with capable freelance copywriters who can do a good job for you.

You also may find help as close as your local newspaper office. Someone on the paper's staff may be interested in working with you on a free-lance basis, to help you plan the layout and design of your ad and provide illustrations. And, if you live near a college, you may find students specializing in advertising or marketing who would be delighted to earn a little extra income by working with you.

If you can write your own ad copy, note that many magazines will typeset it for you and lay it out according to your instructions. Telephone the advertising manager about this. He may even do this without charge, especially if your advertising program looks promising for the future. If you pay for the typesetting, the ad artwork becomes your property, so request the original art back after the ad has been run. (You probably can get it whether you pay for the typesetting or not.)

b.) The Importance of Good Copywriting

It is more important to hire a good advertising copywriter than it is to hire an expensive advertising agency to create the graphics for your ad. A good ad copywriter will create a dummy copy of the entire ad for you; all you have to do is order the typesetting and paste it up. You can find copywriters by reading periodicals like *Writer's Digest, Direct Marketing,* and other business-related publications. To economize, support the efforts of a homebased copywriter who, like you, may be struggling to succeed in business. Connections like these are made easily through home business newsletters like mine, or through membership in professional organizations.

Because good copywriting is so important to the overall success of your business, you should make it a point to acquire some skill in this area. You do not have to be "a writer" to do this, but you do need to acquire some of the writer's skills. Probably the best way to learn ad copywriting is to study the advertisements of other advertisers. As indicated at the start of this chapter, if you want to learn how to sell, emulate the examples of people who know how to do it. The same thing applies to copywriting.

Make it a point to study the promotional materials of other businesspeople in your field. Subscribe to marketing magazines such as *Direct Marketing,* which includes regular articles on how to write better direct response ad copy. Read *Persuasive Writing* and other books listed in the resource chapter. Like every other skill the homebased business owner must acquire, this one just takes a little time and effort.

c.) Other Tips for Display Advertisers

As emphasized earlier, it's important to calculate the per-inquiry cost of your advertising efforts. The earlier example was a comparison of costs of a display ad versus a classified ad, but you should also compare the pull of various sizes of display ads. As one mail-order authority points out, a one-column inch ad might draw 150 responses for a per-inquiry cost of 75¢ each, while a 3″ ad might draw twice as many responses but have a per-inquiry cost of $1.10. And a full-page ad could be the least cost efficient

> *The 12 most persuasive words in the English language, according to ad copywiters, are:*
>
> *You . . . Save . . . Money . . . New . . . Love . . . Easy . . . Health . . . Safety . . . Results . . . Discovery . . . Proven . . . Guarantee*

Notes

Tips in Writing Classified Ads

- *Eliminate every unnecessary word. Write in telegraphic style. Use as many one-syllable words as possible.*
- *Don't try to sell two things in the same ad because the average reader can only retain one basic idea at a time.*
- *Close classified ads with a phrase that prompts action. Give readers something to write for or do. Examples: (1) For information write; (2) Send for free details; (3) Catalog, $1.00; (4) Order NOW!*
- *Use the A-I-D-A formula in writing ads:*

  A = ATTRACT your reader
  I = INTEREST him by appealing to one of his wants or needs
  D = Stimulate DESIRE for your product by listing benefits to be derived from it.
  A = Demand ACTION by asking for the order, stating your guarantee, and emphasizing the ease with which the buyer can obtain your product, and what he may lose by not purchasing it.

General Copywriting Techniques

- Use everyday language. Short sentences. Short paragraphs. Don't ever try to be funny. Just be sincere and conversational.

- People like to deal with people, so establish a personality, flavor, and atmosphere by your name, concept, and what you are trying to do.

- Speak to your audience as if you were speaking to one person. Use the words "you" and "your" often. Avoid "We-centered" remarks.

- Make your offer believable by avoiding exaggerated claims and words like "astounding," "unbelievable," or "sensational." Be prepared to prove any claim you make.

- Don't use opinionated phrases like, "You'll love it," or "It's really beautiful." Instead stress the product's benefits, such as "comfortable," "practical," "lasting." Remember that people have basic wants and needs. Among other things, they want to save time and money, worry or discomfort; and they want to be successful, healthy, informed, and attractive. They also want more money, security, confidence, and a feeling of importance. (Note: In a *Reader's Digest* ad test of two different headlines, the "save time" ad outpulled the "save money" ad.)

- Speak always in positive terms. Do not say, "You will not be disappointed," because this is a negative thought. Instead, say "Satisfaction assured," or better yet, "Satisfaction guaranteed."

- People often are motivated to buy out of greed or fear. Whenever you can inject these elements into your advertising message, you will increase response. For greed, stress what people will gain from your product (money, getting ahead in business, envy of neighbors, etc.), and for fear, tell people what they will lose by not ordering. (Loss of time, money, convenience? Will price soon increase? Is this the last chance to order?)

- Make a special offer. Examples: Buy three, get one free. Free (product) if you order within ten days. Buy one at full price, get the second at half price. Free freight on all orders over $100. Free lesson to first ten people to respond. Save 20% by ordering our "Early Bird Selection." And so forth.

Headline Ideas for Ads or Flyers

The headline is all important, because this often is the only thing people read. According to ad experts, five times as many people read headlines as read body copy.

Try to incorporate some of the 12 most powerful words in your headline copy (see elsewhere) and use action verbs for more power, such as : How to . . . GET, BE, DO, SAVE, MAKE, STOP, WIN, HAVE, START, etc.

If you study full-page display ads, you'll note that many headlines (proven to be successful) begin with the words, "How I . . ." BECAME . . . MADE . . . STARTED . . . SUCCEEDED . . . IMPROVED, and so on. A variation on this theme is to speak directly to the prospective customer by saying, "How you can . . . " BECOME . . . MAKE . . . START . . . SUCCEED . . . IMPROVE, and so on.

Other successful headlines for ads and flyers often involve numbers, such as "10 ways to . . . ," "25 tips for . . . ," "100 ideas on how to . . . "

Use good typography in setting your headline. Help people read your ad more easily. Avoid use of all capitals as this is said to retard reading speed. Never use the kind of flowery typeface that makes readers have to look at it twice to be able to make out the letters.

Display Ad Construction Tips

The construction of a full-page ad or promotional flyer often breaks down like this:

- Headline: This usually is a short and powerful group of words which make a sweeping product claim or otherwise attract attention.
- Main Sub-headline: Set in smaller type, this is an additional or substantiating claim or statement.
- Documentation of claims: This kind of information is often put in a "box" near the top of the ad or page.
- Picture or illustration: Often placed in upper right-hand corner, it should show, if possible, how the product or service can be used by buyer. Use copy under the photo — and even add a headline above the photo if appropriate — to help move reader along to the rest of the ad copy. (One large picture is better than several smaller ones.)
- Guarantee: Another "box" or certificate (often quite small), placed near the order coupon.
- Testimonials: Also placed near the order coupon.
- Order Coupon: Should be rectangular or square-shaped, and bordered with a dashed line that clearly indicates the reader is supposed to cut it out.

Note: Increase response to any ad or offer by giving customers the option of charging an order to a bank credit card. The average mail order by credit card is said to be 20–40% higher than a cash/check order.

Powerful Words and Persuasive Phrases

The following words and phrases are used regularly by successful advertisers. Incorporate them into your advertising copy whenever possible.

Bargain	Learn
Bonus	Love
Check	Money
Compare	New
Complete	Now
Confidential	Offer
Discover	Personalize
Earn	Popular
Easy	Profit
End	Profitable
Exciting	Proven
Facts	Quick
Free	Refundable
Fun	Reliable
Gain	Safe
Gift	Save
Guaranteed	Stop
Helpful	Successful
Here	Tested
How-to	Try
Important	Wanted
Improved	Your
Informative	YOU
Interesting	

Act NOW
A Special Invitation
Buy three — Get one free
Do not delay
Free details
Get started today
Here's news
It's easy
Judge for yourself
Never before
Proven results
Save time and money
Send no money
There's no risk or obligation
Three good reasons
Trial offer
You can trust

Notes

of all, even though it draws thousands of quick responses. It's best to start with small display ads and classifieds to minimize your financial risk, and test several publications. As you increase the size of your ads, keep analyzing response and measuring actual results against the cost of each ad.

If you have a mail-order business, always indicate that you want the mail-order ad rates of the magazine you are contacting. These rates are lower than regular ad space; for many advertisers they actually pull better because they're placed in a special mail-order section of the magazine where interested mail-order buyers are most likely to look.

Also ask about the availability of "remnant space," which usually is offered at highly discounted rates and available only for a short time. Sometimes a magazine will sell a particular page of an issue to an advertiser who wants distribution only to certain sections of the country. This means that this particular page for the remaining sections of the country must be filled. Major consumer magazines would be a logical place to find such space.

At a seminar I attended, the advertising director of a trade magazine offered the following comments and tips which may be helpful to you:

1. In planning an ad campaign, set objectives and plan well in advance, making sure your strategy is consistent with your objectives. Don't view advertising costs as an expense, but as an investment. Always follow up on the leads and inquiries generated by your advertising, and have a plan to evaluate the results of each ad.

2. Few readers are motivated by one ad only, so one ad in one issue of a magazine is probably a waste of money. When running an ad more than once in the same publication, you can figure that the response will peak somewhere between the second and third insertion of the ad, and be "worn out" by the fourth exposure.

3. Ads placed on the right-hand side of a page will get 5–10% more attention from readers, and if you can get the top corner of the right-hand page, you may attract as much as 25% greater viewing attention. (You may not get such preferred positioning when you place an ad, but always ask for it.)

4. There is no right or wrong way to write an ad, but there are five basic elements of a good display ad: (1) Heading, (2) Sub-Head, (3) Body copy (details of offer), (4) a "call to action" (coupon, toll-free number, or anything else that motivates response), and (5) the company's signature (name and address).

5. You'll increase the pull of an ad if you add a second, "spot color" to it. This will cost about half again as much as a regular black and white ad, but considerably less than a four-color ad.

6. If you use a toll-free number in a display ad, you can figure that you probably will be able to make a sale to at least half the people who call.

d.) In-House Advertising Agency

Smart advertisers who regularly place display ads will form their own in-house advertising agency and thus save 15% and more on every ad they place.

Advertising rate cards generally include a note to the effect that a 15% commission will be allowed to "recognized advertising agencies." Actually, any agency can be "recognized." All magazines know that advertisers set up their own agencies to save money. There is nothing shady about doing this. But magazines don't like you to be obvious about such in-house agencies. They will "look the other way" and not make waves about the "recognized agency" clause in their rate card if you at least make your agency appear to be independent of your regular business.

As one ad manager told me, "We're not concerned that people use their own agencies as much as we are concerned with receiving camera-ready ad copy. We appreciate agencies of any kind or size whenever they save us the hassle of production costs by sending ad copy ready for printing."

So, if you can prepare your own ad copy, you might as well earn the 15% commission on each ad you place. Actually, you can save even more by paying the invoice within ten days and taking the additional 2% discount that's always offered. In addition to these savings, an ad agency gives you longer use of your money. The average display advertiser may have to send payment with an ad, and since there may be two or three months' lag time between placement and publication of an ad, you can see the advantage of being billed on publication, a normal procedure for agencies. Therefore, when placing your first in-house agency insertion order with a magazine, either include some excellent credit references or bluff your way to a credit okay by looking so affluent that no one would dare question your credit to begin with.

4. Other Media Ads

If you watch television, you probably have noticed that a certain kind of product is traditionally advertised for delivery by mail; for example, records, cutlery, household gadgets, tools, and magazines, to name a few. Since few homebased businesses have the right product for this kind of national marketing, let alone the funds for it, my discussion of national television advertising is brief. (If you are the exception to the rule, you'll find more help from specialized marketing publications listed in the resource chapter.)

I have concluded, both from my own experience and what so many qualified people have told me, that local radio, television, and newspaper advertising may be good ways for certain retailers and business professionals to promote their businesses, but few people can successfully sell any kind of mail-order product this way. That is why you ought to place your limited mail-order advertising funds in other areas.

If you have a service business, you probably can get more mileage from radio and newspaper publicity than advertising. Do experiment, however, to see if a modest newspaper or radio advertising campaign will work for you. One thing you might try with a newspaper ad is to offer some kind of money-off coupon (such as an introductory offer) readers can clip and use for your services.

5. Special Distribution Programs

Few small businesses know about the distribution programs I am about to describe, and that's a shame because they offer an affordable way to reach mass consumer markets, as well as selected trade buyers.

Notes

Included in this category are package inserts, postcard mailings, and per-order/per-inquiry advertising.

a.) Package Inserts

Although one can use package inserts to sell to both consumers and wholesalers, I believe that this book's readers will be most interested in reaching the consumer market, so I will concentrate on that.

This is not an inexpensive way to advertise, but it's an exciting one to consider. The right product, matched to the right audience, could really take off in this kind of promotion.

Many package insert programs have to be purchased in minimum quantities of 100,000, but companies like Larry Tucker, Inc., and Leon Henry, Inc. offer interesting markets with minimum test quantities of between 10,000 and 25,000.

For example, Larry Tucker claims to have the largest distribution program in the college market. This system employs traveling fieldmen who distribute literature on college campuses throughout the United States, utilizing "take-one" posters or flyers placed under students' doors in dormitories. This same company also offers cooperative mailings sent to families at home addresses where a new birth has occurred within the past twelve months. An optional package, the New Mother Hospital Sampling Program, distributes polybag packages to new mothers while they still are in the hospital. These contain product samples or inserts and coupons supplied by advertisers.

Leon Henry offers several package insert programs of special interest to marketers of craft, hobby, and needlework products. Here your insert can be included with the actual shipments of merchandise purchased by customers of Saddle Valley Stitchery, Annie's Attic, Herrschners, Inc., and Lee Wards. Other programs enable you to reach buyers of "Shopsmith," a multi-purpose power tool, plus buyers from the Brookstone catalog, which features hand and power tools, garden products, gourmet kitchenware, and unusual gifts for men and women. Leon Henry also offers, for a minimum test of 100,000, mailings to the readers of the *Sunday New York Times,* and a "Coupon Carousel" cooperative mailing to a California audience of homemakers. (The next time you receive one of those 6″ × 9″ advertising envelopes stuffed with about 24 flyers promoting a variety of products, you will have in hand a perfect example of this kind of marketing.)

While the cost of package insert programs may compare to the cost of large display ads, there is a big difference in the kind of response you can expect to receive. Being able to get your material into the hands of a customer prospect is a big marketing plus, so take this into consideration when comparing costs of both types of advertising.

In addition to the per-thousand price, of course, you must add the cost of your printed insert, which could run anywhere from 2–10¢ per piece, depending on the kind of insert you elect to use. (Under "Printers" in the resource chapter, you will find the names of companies who specialize in printing package inserts.) If you elect to test, say, a quantity of 10,000 at a price of $35 per thousand, you'd have a cost of $350 plus your package insert at, say 6¢ each, or $600, for a total of $950, or 9½¢ per customer prospect. When you compare this to the 75¢ or more you might pay to get inquiries through classified or display ads, and the

25¢ it now costs to mail a first-class letter, you can see that this kind of advertising is well worth considering.

For information about other special distribution programs of this kind or nature, see the *Standard Rate & Data Service* (SRDS) publications available in libraries. Here you also will find a listing of more than 3,000 business, trade, and technical publications categorized by market area served. *Direct Marketing*, a trade magazine, offers information on distribution programs. Finally, if there is a particular market you would like to reach, such as the buyers of a specific mail-order catalog, simply write to that catalog company and ask about any package insert programs that may be available.

b.) Direct Response Postcard Mailings

This is a popular marketing tool often used by sophisticated marketers to generate leads for salesmen or to develop interest among consumer prospects for a variety of high-priced products and services. These typically include electronics equipment, investment opportunities, expensive business books, and so on. My research indicates there are about 600 card decks with an annual circulation of over 125,000,000. These decks are targeted to specific audiences in both consumer and business sectors. Lists commonly used include subscribers to business and consumer magazines and newsletters, mail order buyers, schools, churches, and individuals in a variety of professional fields.

The idea behind card deck mailings is the same as with the two-step advertising method. A typical card deck might include 25-40 postcards, so there always is competition to contend with, as with classified advertising. But there is a lot less competition in a card deck than in the classified ad section of a magazine; and, since the customer prospect actually has an advertiser's material in hand, response is always higher. The advertiser's ultimate goal is to get a direct response from an interested prospect so he can send more information by first class mail, or perhaps follow up with a telephone call, depending on what is being offered on the card.

What kind of response is average for card deck mailings? A fellow who used to direct such mailings says that the greatest response one reasonably should expect to receive from a cooperative mailing like this is about 6%, although some advertisers have told him their response went as high as 7½%. On a mailing to 50,000 prospects, then, we're talking about a response range of 3,000-3,750.

As with all advertising, the first key to success is to have good selling copy on the card — a selling message that motivates the prospect to return the card for more information. And, says one expert, "the less the individual has to do to get that card in the mail, the greater the response will be. In addition to good 'sell copy,' a postcard would have to offer prepaid postage to command a 6-7% response. If you ask the prospect to 'put stamp here,' you'll probably cut your response in half. Of course, you'll also end up with more serious prospects, since anyone who wants your literature badly enough to pay for the stamp is more likely to order than the curiosity seeker who sends for anything that's free."

Most of the deck programs I've seen are either inappropriate or too high priced (because of volume mailed) for the average small business owner. But there are exceptions, and a search of

Notes

A.

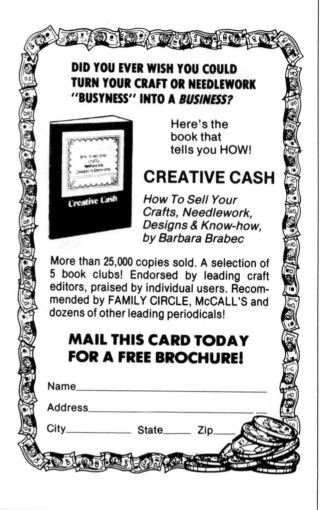

B.

Cards are shown in actual size: 3½″ × 5½″

The above cards were tested in a single mailing to 40,000 arts and crafts consumers (in a card deck no longer available). The cards were distributed equally on a national basis to give an accurate reading of response. The "test" was to determine whether people were more likely to respond to a *book*, or *information* on the topic of how to make money.

As you can see from the figures below, "information" won; however, a higher *order response came from the people who responded to the book card*. Here are the actual response and order figures two months after the mailing was dropped:

Card "A"

608 cards received — a 3% response

24 orders received from the 608 names mailed, for a response of 3.9%, and total dollar sales of $262.80

Card "B"

239 cards received — a 1½% response

21 orders received from the 239 names mailed, for a response of 8.8%, and total dollar sales of $229.95.

Note that Card B, with fewer responses, pulled almost the same number of orders as Card A. In other words, a "vague" ad tends to attract curiosity seekers who may not buy, while a specifically-worded ad is more likely to attract serious customer prospects.

available card decks may yield the right one for you. Following is one some of you might consider.

Paul Foght, publisher of *Creative Products News,* a trade periodical for the crafts industry, offers a dealer card deck aimed at retailers and distributors of craft and art materials. For just 2¼¢ each, a postcard will be printed and mailed to 40,000 prospects, which (at this time) includes 16,700 outlets for crafts, 17,900 for needlework, and 11,300 for art materials. Foght indicates that his "Quick Order Card Advertisers" are reporting responses of from 200–800 cards per mailing (.005 to 2% response), which is higher than the normally anticipated response rate of .33% to 1¼% for most card decks. (The latter information is taken from business publications.)

In my capacity as publisher of Barrington Press book division, from 1979 through 1981, I used postcard mailings to sell two special-interest books. One was a landscaping book, which was promoted to lawn and garden dealers; the other was *Creative Cash,* which was offered to craft consumers. In checking my files, I turned up samples of two postcards I once tested in a split-run mailing to 40,000 arts and crafts consumers. Perhaps these sample cards, and the results I received, will offer additional perspective to the figures offered above.

As you can see in the nearby illustration, 20,000 individuals received each card, and the response and order figures indicated beneath each card give a realistic idea of what your own advertising might generate. Both cards, by the way, asked recipients to add the stamp. (Note: This particular deck is no longer published.)

Postcard mailings are not recommended to anyone who has only one product to sell. Instead, they are designed to help a business develop a customer prospect mailing list which will respond to other offerings in the future. Even when a postcard mailing does not prove profitable initially, it may pay off in the future.

Remember that, because of limited space for copy, it's difficult to sell products directly off a card. Strive instead to elicit a response from individuals whose names can be added to your permanent mailing list. They may well buy later when they have received your complete advertising package.

If you plan to use a postcard to solicit an order, not just an inquiry for more information, be sure to make it easy for customers to pay, offering later invoicing or charge card privileges. Many post card advertisers also offer toll-free numbers to encourage the placement of orders.

In designing a direct response postcard, think in terms of offering special products and deals, such as your "best buy" offers, your newest catalog, announcements of new products, and so on. Say, "This is new!" and use cards to offer customer prospects a first look at what you're offering.

In the illustration right, you will find several cards from a cooperative mailing issued by *Creative Products News.* Each card's format will suggest ideas on how to create a card of your own. Note the various headings used: "Introductory," "Back to School," "Big Savings," "New," and "Special Offer."

For more information about other card deck programs, visit the library and see *Book Marketing Handbook,* published by R. R. Bowker Company. It has one of the best source guides to

Notes

card deck mailings I've seen. Categories include accounting, business and finance, architecture, electronics, medicine, packaging, real estate, and veterinary medicine, to name just a few. Cost per mailing varies from about $450 to $1,680.

For more information about the companies mentioned in this section, see "Mailing Lists & Distribution Programs" in the resource chapter.

c.) Per-Order (PO) or "Drop-Ship" Arrangements

PO advertising is free, no-risk advertising that is offered by many magazines, particularly the small, special interest publications. The only problem with PO advertising is that it never is invited by publishers. The only way to turn up such opportunities is to do some sleuthing on your own. For example, if you would like to have a large display ad in a certain, specialized publication, but just can't afford it, call that publication's advertising manager and propose a PO arrangement. Don't ask for this kind of advertising; simply propose a business deal that will sound profitable to the magazine. Whether your offer is accepted or not will depend on your product or publication and how well the publisher thinks it will sell, as well as the amount of financial risk he has to accept.

Major magazine publishers accept PO advertising, too, though few will admit it. You always can spot PO ads, however, because the publisher will list its own address as the place to send orders. (Some will try to avoid detection by setting up a special post office box number to throw you off the track.)

What it boils down to is whether a publication has unsold advertising space or not. If so, they may be interested in including a PO advertisement from time to time. You may have to wait until some unsold ad space appears, but it would be worth it to get such no-risk advertising.

Remember, too, that everyone wants to make money. If you have a "sure-fire" product or publication that's going to sell, the smart advertising manager may see this as an opportunity to make extra money (and also convince you that you can afford regular display advertising in the future).

If you intend to work with anyone on a drop-ship basis, you will need to establish a "drop-ship policy." It should include:

1. Your discount. You generally have to offer 50%, though some publishers will accept less.

2. Your drop-ship charge — something to cover your postage and handling costs, usually $1.35 to $2.00, depending on the publisher's overhead.

3. Your label requirements. Generally, typed address labels with the publisher's name and address as the shipper are required. (The idea is that the buyer has ordered from the publisher, thus expects to receive the order from the same place. All you're doing, in effect, is sticking a label on a package and dropping it in the mail for them.) Your own sales literature should not be included in drop-ship packages like this. Such customer names belong not to you, but to the publication with whom you are working.

d.) Per-Inquiry (PI) Advertising

These ads are similar to, yet different from, PO arrangements. In PI deals, you make some kind of arrangement with a publisher whereby you will pay so much for each inquiry received from the ad he places. This might be anything from 25¢ to $10.00, depending on the publication.

An excellent example of PI advertising is the "Information Center" advertisement that runs periodically in *Parade, The Sunday Magazine*. You may have noticed it — a full-page offering free brochures and booklets, as well as certain items for $5.00 or less. Consumers simply circle numbered items of interest, adding any money that may be required; *Parade* refers these inquiries or orders directly to advertisers.

This listing is free to advertisers, but if you advertise a free brochure, you must pay 40¢ for each response you receive; $1.50 for each response if the reader is asked to send money. Because *Parade Magazine* is one of the most widely-read weekly publications in the world — going to over 22 million households — advertisers offering free literature can expect to receive up to 20,000 inquiries; but perhaps only 3,000 if readers are required to send money. As you might imagine, space is limited. A lot of advertisers are competing for it. (At present, this feature runs only five times a year.) Note that while the right offer could be extremely profitable, the wrong offer could bankrupt you.

Let's see now . . . if I offered a $3.00 booklet with helpful information on how to make money at home (actually a promotional tool for my books), and I got 3,000 orders, I'd receive $9,000 less *Parade's* cost of $4,500, for a profit of $4,500 on my booklet. And I would have all those great customer prospects! But if I offered a free brochure, got 20,000 requests for it, and had to pay out 40¢ each . . . whew! — that's $8,000! And I still would have the cost of my brochure printing plus first class postage to mail to 20,000 people. Nope, this kind of marketing is for the big guys, not me. I like the idea of a for-sale booklet. How about you?

Note: Both PI and PO advertising are also available on radio and television, with stations being paid a commission for each inquiry or order they secure. Some stations apparently seek this type of advertising, but there is only one way to find out: call station managers and ask. As always, this kind of deal will require some selling ability on your part. You will have to convince the station that your product will sell, and show them how profitable this kind of advertising might be for them. If you feel you have the right kind of offer, it's worth trying.

Author's Note — October, 1988

For your added information about the pulling power of Parade *Magazine: I was fortunate to be quoted in a full page article, "When You Start Your Own Business" in the August 21, 1988 issue. A sidebar in the article recommended* Homemade Money *and listed its availability by mail, giving a postage-paid price and coded address.*

Orders were still being received in late December, by which time total sales had passed the 500-mark.

Notes

Wholesale Marketing Worksheet

List the wholesale marketing methods you plan to explore in the future, with any questions you have that require further research. (Be sure to check all the related information sources listed in the Resource Directory.)

Marketing Method   Comments

The Publicity Game

9.

"**H**OLLER" IS ONE of those quaint old words few people use any more, but the technique of hollering is well known to publicity experts. Whether one is calling the hogs, or people in the media, the idea is the same: *to get attention.*

Unlike advertising, which is the expensive way to get attention, publicity is virtually free. (Your only costs, in addition to the time you spend on your publicity campaign, will be for printing and mailing press releases or media kits — plus some follow-up telephone calls.)

Although few small businesses can hope to get publicity on national television, many will find opportunities on cable TV. Anyone with a message of interest to a large audience of consumers can get publicity on major radio stations, and even the smallest business can attract the attention of local radio or television program directors. The print media are the easiest of all to crack; small and large businesses alike are mentioned with regularity in the nation's most prestigious newspapers and consumer magazines; trade and professional magazines are generous in giving publicity, too.

What does it take to get your name, or that of your business, into print? What do you have to know to get an interview on radio, or a news story on television? What are the tricks of the trade, the rules of the game, the keys to getting publicity? This chapter answers those questions.

How Publicity is Generated

Publicity can be generated in many ways, using techniques that run the gamut from a simple letter or telephone call to expensive campaigns involving publicists and high-priced media kits. This chapter concentrates on the inexpensive and practical methods an individual can use to increase the visibility and income of a homebased business. As with advertising, the primary goal of small businesses should be to get the kind of publicity that will generate a direct response from customers or prospects.

Regardless of the publicity method you use, remember that editors and program directors are not interested in giving you free advertising. What they want is news or information that will inform, benefit, or at least entertain their readers and listeners. Actually, all publicity pivots on the answer to one question: *Is your information*

Contact: Meg Jones
The Office Center
115 West 10th Street
Portland, Oregon 97201

(503) 555-8642

FOR IMMEDIATE RELEASE

NEW EXECUTIVE SHOPPING SERVICE--DESIGNED TO SAVE TIME

FOR BUSY EXECUTIVES--BEGINS AT THE OFFICE CENTER

Portland--An Executive Shopping Service, designed to save time for busy executives, is now being offered by The Office Center.

"Shopping can be very time-consuming," says Meg Jones, Manager of the Executive Shopping Service and former merchandise manager for Flatt's Gift Shop. "Most executives can't spare the time to shop, and some have trouble deciding on the right gift for the right person. Our service provides consultation, leg work, a recommendation and the final purchase. In other words, we take care of everything from planning to wrapping and delivery."

Ms. Jones will consult with clients on the type of gift, the occasion and the price range. After that, a search is made for the right selection. A final check with the client guarantees satisfaction.

Charges for the service are 25 percent over the gift price, with a minimum gift order of $35. There is a one-time registration fee of $10. Once a client is registered, the Executive Shopping Service will keep track of birthdays, anniversaries, holidays and special occasions and provide reminders and gift suggestions well in advance of any special date.

The Office Center, located at 115 West 10th Street, is Portland's one-stop business resource for office space, secretarial help, printing and messenger service. Phone Meg Jones at 555-8642 for more information on the Executive Shopping Service.

-0-

A sample press release announcing a new service. From The Publicity Manual *by Kate Kelly. © 1980 by Kate Kelly. Used by Permission.*

or news "newsworthy" or at least interesting to a large number of people? If the answer is yes, you'll get your publicity. If it's no, the wastebasket will get your press release.

Thus, publicity is most often generated by people who send newsworthy press releases to the media. If you create self-serving press releases which blatantly advertise your product or service, you won't get publicity. A press release does not have to be filled with actual news to be newsworthy, but it must be worth publishing as news because it cannot be published as advertising.

What editors want, more than anything else, is a "news peg," on which your story can be hung. Actually, the key word here is "new," not "news." Anything that's new is likely to be newsworthy, as in a new business just starting, a new product that offers some special benefit to consumers, a new achievement of some individual in a community, locality, or industry, a new twist to an old idea, and so forth. The news peg or hook for a story can be almost anything. Sometimes it is the very thing that makes you, your business, or product stand out from the rest; often, it's the benefit offered to consumers in your press release.

All businesses have characteristics or qualities that lend themselves to a press release, but not all press releases are appropriate for all media. In fact, it may take several different releases to get all the publicity that's available to you. If you shoot a shotgun loaded with buckshot, you will get an interesting scatter effect; aim a rifle, however, and you hit one target dead center. In thinking about publicity, you need to consider both approaches. Different products and businesses require different approaches, and you should be prepared to adjust your thinking and strategy at any time.

For instance, the press release that is designed to attract attention from local media — newspapers, radio, or television — probably will not work for a national publication or station because the news impact is not the same. It can work just the opposite, too. I am reminded of a story heard on radio. A woman was stopped in a parking lot outside a bowling alley by a would-be robber who demanded all her money . . . or else. Obviously a quick thinker, she put a stop to his plan by dropping her bowling ball on his foot, so disarming him that she was able to get away. Curiously, this story was not noticed by local newscasters in my city, but National Public Radio heard about it and presented it as an amusing anecdote, just as I have done.

Thus, information that is news to one editor is not news to another. For this reason, small businesses which may be taken for granted in their own community may find it easier to get publicity in national media. (Ironically, national publicity for your business easily could lead to a feature story in your hometown paper along the line of "Local business featured in national magazine." That, you see, is newsworthy.)

> *Getting publicity is as easy as one, two, three . . .*
>
> 1. *Publicity is generated by people who send press releases to the media.*
>
> 2. *"The media" include newspapers, magazines, newsletters, radio, and television.*
>
> 3. *Within the media are individual editors, publishers, journalists, reporters, freelance writers, syndicated columnists, book reviewers, news broadcasters, and program directors who work very hard constantly to turn up story and article ideas that are new and different.*
>
> *Whenever you can send them a well-written, newsworthy press release, it will be used to your advantage.*

Notes

Creating a Newsworthy Press Release

Before you can make publicity work for you, you have to ask yourself what you expect to gain from it. First, are you seeking local, regional, national, or international publicity? Do you want the names of interested prospects so you can send them your brochure or catalog, as in two-step advertising? Or, better yet, are you hoping for orders with payment enclosed? Maybe your primary goal is to get people

NEWS/CROWN

Atlanta Market Center News

Atlanta Apparel Mart

Suite 2200, 240 Peachtree
Atlanta, Georgia 30043
(404) 688-8994

Befo

News

20,000 LETT

BEST-SELLING C

Maybe it's the economy, or maybe

NEWS
from R. & E. Miles

From G. P. Putnams Sons, 200 Madison Ave., New York, N.Y. 10016

FOR IMMEDIATE RELEASE
From: Barbara Hendra
Contact: Susan O'Connell
          212/576-8854

From THE ILLUMINATED BOOK OF DAYS:

"With the old Almanack and the old year,
Leave thy old Vices, tho' ever so dear."

      -Benjamin Franklin,
      January 17

"In the 14th century, under Bavarian law,
women were given the right to duel men to
settle disputes."

      -May 22

"Wedding rings go on the fourth finger because
the ancients believed it contained a nerve
going straight to the heart."

      -June 21

"In Kentucky there is a folk belief that if you
can break an apple in half with your bare hands
you can marry anybody you want..."

      -October 23

Greenaway and Grasset Illustrate THE ILLUMINATED BOOK OF DAYS
By Kay and Marshall Lee

OF DAYS by Kay and Marshall Lee

ober 23, $14.95) is a timeless

which every day of the year is

eric and exotic facts, verse

d with voluptuous illustrations,

s to the paintings of the

ntury illustrator Kate Greenaway,

s of Eugene Grasset, an

e.

framing

recipes

licious

ke to

g dew,"

The experts say press releases should be kept plain and simple, but many companies obviously pay little attention to this "rule," as you can see from the eye-catching letterhead designs above. Press releases issued by book publishers are especially interesting. They occasionally include artwork, are often printed on 8-1/2" x 14" ivory or buff-colored paper, and the letterhead may incorporate colored ink. There's no reason why you can't design a similar eye-catching press release if you plan to do regular promotional mailings.

Cr

A Patchwork Year should

not easy in these diffi

to look for your product in retail shops and stores, either locally or nationally. Or perhaps you are seeking publicity that would generate telephone calls from prospective clients locally or nationally — calls that might lead to freelance assignments, consulting jobs, speaking or teaching engagements. Or maybe you just would like to get your name in the paper so your mother will be proud of you.

Before I discuss the seven basic elements of a good press release, let me explain the proper form a press release should take. (The examples in this chapter will help you to visualize the following instructions.) Above all, a press release must look "crisp," and be easy to read. Typed, of course, and double spaced, with margins of about 1½" all around.

Releases can be printed on white paper, on your business letterhead, or on a special news release letterhead you may wish to design. (Other samples nearby will give you ideas on this.) Publicity experts say you should not use fancy paper because editors are not concerned with how "pretty" a press release is — only how interesting. But many publicity directors obviously believe otherwise because a lot of colorful releases cross my desk every month. Personally, I think a touch of color on a news release is going to make any editor look at it twice. But use your own judgment here.

In writing copy for the release, use simple English and short sentences. Avoid flowery phrases and words like "fantastic," and "very unique." (Before using the word "unique" in any of your copy, check the dictionary. This is one of the most overworked and abused words in use today.)

You can talk about yourself in a press release, but always write copy in the third person, as though someone else had written it about you. This makes it easy to quote yourself, which is important. Since publicity legitimizes information, you can make strong statements about your business or yourself through quotes in a news release, and people will believe them simply because they have appeared in print. However, if you said the same thing in a sales brochure, it would be suspect, simply because *you* said it. Example:

Brochure copy:

I believe my service is the only one of its kind. Give it a try. I'm sure you'll benefit from it because I get thank-you letters from satisfied customers every week.

Press Release copy:

To his knowledge, the service offered by Bob Jones is the only one of its kind. "I know it helps people, too," says Jones as he shuffles through the week's stack of thank-you letters. "I get mail like this every week."

If your press release runs to more than one page, write "MORE . . ." in the lower right-hand corner of the release, and print the second page of the release on a second sheet of paper. (Press releases never should be printed on both sides of the same sheet.) Staple all pages of a release together in the upper left-hand corner.

Although 8½ × 11" paper is standard for press releases, book publishers often use legal-size paper and write very long material. This often results in the placement of feature articles. Such releases are a combination news release and biography press release, or a

Two Important Promotion Rules

• *Don't communicate with any audience unless you can afford to repeat your presentation at least three times. As with advertising, only a small fraction of any audience is paying attention to a promotion at any given time, and only a percentage of that fraction will take action on the first contact. Repeat your message at frequent intervals to find automatically a different fraction-of-a-fraction who will respond to each mailing.*

• *Always promote to your best audience on a regular and thorough basis before spending any money on your second-best audience. (As true in advertising as it is in publicity.)*

Notes

Contact: Dorothy Glenn
           Moss, Finley and Tupper
           510 Court Street
           Cleveland, Ohio 44114

           (216) 555-3267

RON FINLEY

By day, Ron Finley sits in a wood-paneled office meeting with clients, discussing financial planning and poring over figures. By night, Finley dons make-up and costume and assumes any number of roles.

When meeting Ron Finley, a partner in the accounting firm of Moss, Finley and Tupper, one would hardly suspect he is the same Ron Finley who performs professionally in many productions at the Hayden Playhouse in Cleveland. At 6'2", Finley traditionally wears pin-stripe suits and sports a distinguished salt-and-pepper beard. He looks far more the businessman than the actor.

To Finley this split life is the most natural thing in the world. "I love my work at the office. I enjoy meeting with people and solving the complexities involved in managing money," he says. "But at night I become a very different person--taking on new roles is a challenge I enjoy immensely."

Finley's schedule is a challenge as well. Hayden Playhouse performances are held Friday and Saturday nights and Sunday afternoons. Each play usually runs four weeks. Prior to the run, Finley's evenings are filled with rehearsals. "Tax time is the only time when I can't work at the Playhouse. We're just too busy here," he explains. "Otherwise I love the schedule. I can't think of a better place than the theatre to spend the rest of my time."

Finley was bitten by the acting bug six years ago while helping the Playhouse with its initial fundraising drive. It was the classic cliché when director Alfred Bush asked, "Ron, have you ever considered acting?" Finley has been at it ever since. His most recent role was as the doctor in A Doll's House.

Ron Finley helped form Moss, Finley and Tupper twelve years ago. A 1946 graduate of Ohio University, he is single and resides on Northridge Drive.

-0-

A sample of a "feature bio," a special release which often accompanies a news release. Its purpose is to encourage a feature article instead of just a news announcement. From The Publicity Manual. © *by Kate Kelly. Used by permission.*

"bio," as it is called in the trade. Other businesses might do well to send this kind of release, too. If a separate biographical press release and a photograph accompanies a news release, you will greatly increase your chances of getting a feature article in newspapers and magazines. Basically, the "bio" tells who you are and why your business is interesting. It generally reads exactly like an article, the idea being that a busy editor can simply run it as is, or a lazy reporter can submit it under his byline. (See a sample bio release nearby.) Many writers, of course, use bios to form the basis of their own, lengthy feature articles. If you can't write this kind of story about yourself, hire a freelance writer to do it. (For a one-page bio, you might expect to pay about $50.)

Press releases should be printed, not photocopied. If you can't afford to print 100 copies of a release, forget it. Editors are not going to pay any attention to a release that looks as though it has been done by an amateur. The only exception to this rule would be if you're using the "rifle shot" technique and aiming for one particular magazine, radio station, etc. In that case, a letter, accompanied by the bio and other background material, probably will be just as effective. Another option is to hand type one release and mark it "EXCLUSIVE TO (name of publication.)" (This is the technique I used to get publicity in *Family Circle*, a topic discussed later in this chapter.)

The Seven Basic Elements of a Press Release

The seven elements are (1) source information, (2) release date, (3) headline, (4) basic facts, (5) important details, (6) supplementary information, and (7) the "for more info" line. Let's discuss them one by one.

Source Information. This information, which should be placed near the top of the release either to the left or right side of the page, gives the media the name and telephone number of the person to call should more information be desired.

Release Date. Most news releases carry the line, FOR IMMEDIATE RELEASE (always typed in capital letters) on the right-hand side of the page, positioned just above the headline. But I also have seen this line positioned to the left. This date tells the media that the release can be used immediately upon receipt, or at their earliest convenience.

Headline. The headline, also typed in capital letters, should be neatly centered on the page. It should summarize the content of your press release. Although most editors will write their own headline, the one you put on your release may have a lot to do with whether it's read or not. Following are some example headlines to help you get started (notice the consumer benefits in most of them):

COUNSELING FOR HOME-BUSINESS OWNERS
OFFERED BY LOCAL AUTHOR

NEW DAY CARE SERVICE HELPS WORKING MOTHERS

SENIOR CITIZENS BENEFIT FROM NEW
"MEALS ON WHEELS" SERVICE

Notes

LOCAL TEACHER STARTS BUSINESS —
ATTRACTS NATIONAL PUBLICITY

LOCAL CRAFTSMAN DESIGNS
NEW ENERGY-SAVING PRODUCT

FIBER ARTIST'S QUILT TOURS
STATE OF MARYLAND FOR TWO YEARS

INFORMATION IN NEW REPORT COULD
SAVE HOMEOWNERS HUNDREDS OF DOLLARS

HOME COMPUTER BUSINESS THREATENED
BY OUTDATED ZONING LAWS

(I just threw in that last one to see if you were awake. Actually, if some law did threaten to put you out of business, you could easily use it as a publicity gimmick to win support for your efforts, attract the attention of other business owners in the area, and perhaps start a movement to get the outdated law changed.)

Basic Facts. The first paragraph of your press release should include the most important facts the media should know — the who/what/when/where/why and how of your story. If you can't get all of them into the first paragraph, get them into the second one.

Examples:

A. New York, N.Y., August 29 — More than 100 giftware manufacturers and distributors from around the world have previewed a unique year-round display facility in one of New York City's most prestigious Park Avenue office buildings.

Worldwide Business Exchange (WBE), a new concept for showcasing products to the trade, had its first preview this month during the 105th Semiannual New York Gift Show held at the New York Coliseum.

B. In a bold and unprecedented move, *TIME* chose the computer as its "Man of the Year" — or rather, "Machine of the Year" — for 1982.

"It is an information revolution," states *TIME*, and it's dramatically changing the way we live, work, and think. The sales figures for a personal computer leaped from 700,000 units sold in 1980 to an estimated 2.8 million units in 1982.

Personal computers are finding their way into thousands of homes. And thousands of consumers are trying to find the right personal computer, relying mostly on advertisements and salesmen. Dona Z. Meilach, contributing editor of *Interface Age,* a leading computer magazine, and the author of *Before You Buy a Computer,* recommends homework, research, and preparation — *before* you buy.

C. Columbia MD — On July 20, 1983, the winners of the Mayor's Quilt Contest were announced in Baltimore by Mayor William Donald Schaefer. After touring the state of Maryland for two years for the Baltimore Museum of Art, and even making a tour to California, the quilts are coming home for a final show that opens in City Hall Galleries, Baltimore, MD on October 18, 1983.

One of the artists, Nancy Smeltzer, did a seven and half foot tall quilt of the Arts in Baltimore. This particular quilt won first place in the Arts Division of the contest. The quilt was done in the style of a medieval tapestry, since Baltimore is undergoing its own Renaissance. Eight of the city's cultural institutions are depicted doing what would have been appropriate had they been around during the medieval period. An adaptation of the state flag borders each square. In the corner of each flag square is a piece with the embroidered signatures of the then directors of the various institutions. Black-eyed Susans, the state flower, complete each row and border.

Go back and read the copy in each of the three examples, and look for the "news peg" used. In Example A, the news is that manufacturers and distributors from around the world have gathered in New York. In Example B, the news is that *Time* magazine has named a computer as "Machine of the Year," because computers are changing the way we live, work, and think. In Example C, the news is that a quilt exhibit which has been traveling for two years is coming home for a final show.

In each example, the additional news in the press release also is newsworthy, giving editors a double reason to publish it: (A) a new concept in trade showrooms; (B) a new book to help consumers learn to use computers; and (C) a local resident honors the city of Baltimore with a prize-winning work of art.

This kind of copywriting is what it takes to get publicity. No matter how small your business, when you learn to write copy like this, you'll get publicity, too.

Important Details. In addition to the basic facts of your press release — the news peg and vital news — a good press release will include other details as well, the kind of material that might prompt a feature story instead of just a short announcement. For example, the important details in press release (A) included the benefits exhibitors would enjoy (cost-effectiveness, convenience, atmosphere of restrained elegance, etc.) then went on to explain why the showcase concept is unique, how products are displayed, and so on.

In press release (B), the important details were tips on why consumers should be cautious about buying a computer, an explanation of the costly mistakes people often make, and several quotes from the author designed to encourage beginners to give computers a try.

In press release (C), the artist dropped the ball by omitting additional information that could have brought her commissions for custom-designed work. She could have included a paragraph that talked about her business, but she didn't. The release may still lead to feature articles, however, if editors have time to contact her for more information.

Supplementary Information. When the press release reaches this point, we're talking about the kind of background information that adds color to a feature story. In press release (A), this information included comments about the showroom from foreign companies, described the various product categories to be highlighted in the showroom, and ended with a quote that stressed the economic benefit this facility will have for manufacturers from around the world.

In press release (B), the supplementary information included a "homework assignment" for prospective computer buyers, with a number of tips from the author. In press release (C), the artist included a closing paragraph and a quote that probably made a lot of editors smile:

A Press Release Copywriting Exercise

Below is a copy of an actual press release (shown in reduced size) I once received from a new self-publisher who was struggling to learn the many things she needed to know for success. She asked for suggestions on how to improve her copy, and I made several of them, as indicated in the revised example on the next page (also shown in reduced size). By studying both examples,

you'll have a better idea of how to strengthen the copy in any press release you may write.

Note: Charlene has since enjoyed success both as an author and designer. Her work has been featured in several leading craft and needlework publications since 1981.

Keepsake Designs
571 North Madison
Ogden, Utah 84404
(801) 782-6369

Best to delete entirely

(Add source information here)

November 5, 1981 *delete*

FOR IMMEDIATE RELEASE

A NEW TECHNIQUE FOR SEWING MACHINE ENTHUSIASTS

Charlene Miller of Keepsake Designs, 571 North Madison, Ogden, Utah, 84404, has written a book on the technique she developed for using the sewing machine to make lace. The book is due to be released for distribution on November 10, 1981. The book has full size patterns and easy to follow directions for making a variety of lace including yokes, medallions, inserts, collars and cuffs.

The book is 48 pages long and is soft bound. The book sells for $11.95, postpaid, and may be ordered from Keepsake Designs, 571 North Madison, Ogden, Utah, 84404.

This is not important...

...But this is. this is the "news"

Common error of beginning writers. Avoid repetition of the same words.

Avoid hyphenations in a press release.

```
              For more information, contact:

                 Charlene Miller
                 (801) 782-6369

                                            FOR IMMEDIATE RELEASE

     1.              A NEW TECHNIQUE FOR SEWING MACHINE ARTISANS

                     Many women sew, but few know how to make lace with their sewing

               machines.  This little-known technique is now clearly explained in a

     2.        new book by Charlene Miller, a designer in Ogden, Utah.

                     In HOW TO MAKE LACE WITH YOUR SEWING MACHINE, Charlene includes

               easy-to-follow, full-size patterns and directions for making a

               variety of lace, including yokes, medallions, inserts, collars,

               and cuffs.

     3.              "This is the only book of its kind," says the author, who has

     4.        written and published two other special technique books for home

               sewers.  Both have enjoyed good reviews and sales in the home

               sewing market.
     5.
     6.              A free brochure detailing all three of the author's books is

               available on request.  HOW TO MAKE LACE WITH YOUR SEWING MACHINE

               may be ordered by mail for $11.95 ppd. from Keepsake Designs,

               571 North Madison, Ogden, UT 88404.



     7.        HOW TO MAKE LACE WITH YOUR SEWING MACHINE

               by Charlene Miller

               $11.95 ppd., paperback, 48 pages

               Publication Date:  November 10, 1981
```

1. "Enthusiast" is not as desirable a word as "Artisan."

2. By adding the phrase, "a designer in Ogden, Utah," the author's identity and credibility are strengthened.

3. By adding a brief quote by the author, it adds to the illusion that someone other than the author has written the release.

4. Whenever you're promoting a new product, also promote whatever you've done before. Buyers are more receptive to a new product if they know a company or business has a "track record."

5. This would be a good place to add whatever good review comments the publisher has received on earlier books, such as " . . . Miller presents clear instructions and challenging designs." — MACHINE ARTISTRY NEWS. (Even better would be an early review comment on the new book by some leading authority in the field.)

6. In offering a mail-order product through a press release, it's a good idea to offer something free, such as a brochure. Reviewers of consumer magazines probably won't list the price, but they may mention a free brochure as a service to readers. (Generally, book reviews given by magazines are designed to steer people into bookstores for the book, so unless a book is available in bookstores, there's no point in offering self-published books for review — *unless you can get your address mentioned in connection with a free brochure.*

7. It is standard practice for book publishers to include information at the bottom of their releases. Releases for other products do *not* use such a notation.

Notes

The piece took approximately three months of countless hours to execute. Applique and quilting were all done by hand. When asked about the time required to complete the piece, Ms. Smeltzer commented that her "life's blood was in the piece, literally, because I forgot to use a thimble."

"For More Information" Line. Not all press releases include this line. In fact, none of the above releases did. But small businesses who send press releases should always include a last, short paragraph that gives their name and address and offers any promotional material that may be available free, or at a fee. After all, a direct response from consumers is a primary goal of publicity for the small business.

Although the "for more information" line definitely is advertising, editors often will include this information, *particularly if it will benefit readers to have it*. Here are some examples of closing paragraphs you might use.

For more information, send for the free brochure, (title), available from: (name and address).

or

(name of product) is available in (kind of retail outlets), or directly from the (manufacturer, publisher, etc.) for (postpaid price) from: (name and address).

or

The artist welcomes commissions from architects and interior designers and may be reached at (phone or address).

Getting Local Publicity

The first trick in getting local publicity is to study local media. Notice the kind of story that makes the evening news. Which local businesses have been mentioned, and why? What consumer benefits are indicated in each story? If none, then what else about the story interested you?

Analyze articles in the newspaper the same way. In particular, note the special sections of the paper and try to relate your business to one of them. For instance, in the home section, small businesses often get publicity by offering tips related to the care or maintenance of one's home (such as how to clean a chimney or carpet, be a better landscaper or gardener, or make general home repairs). Any business that offers a related product or service that can be promoted in a free brochure should explore the possibilities of either writing a short how-to article for the paper, or asking that the brochure be mentioned as a reader service.

Similarly, the business or marketplace section of the paper is the perfect place to promote business-related products and services; the lifestyle section appropriate for things related to weddings, anniversaries, entertainment, and so on.

Note especially the regular columns in each section of the paper. Such columns are generally written by freelance writers who are always looking for interesting people and things to write about.

A lot of small businesses have found that publicity in the local paper is as easy as picking up the telephone, or stopping by the newspaper office to talk to a reporter. You have nothing to lose and everything to gain, so make a little effort here by deliberately seeking such publicity.

You may have noticed that retailers often get newspaper publicity around the holidays by announcing such things as a "gala celebration," or "festive sale." A shop owner of my acquaintance received excellent publicity for her shops by announcing a "Make It With Felt Easter Design Contest," which offered prizes to winners and a guarantee of local publicity and recognition. Many people entered the contest, which not only brought new customers into the shop, but increased its visibility in the community. Furthermore, the prize-winning local residents were also benefited through recognition for their talents. This kind of thinking always can get publicity for a small business, no matter where the business is located.

Often, press releases are hung on national holidays or other proclaimed events. When September was proclaimed by the sewing industry as National Homesewing Month, it provided people in sewing businesses across the country a wonderful "excuse" to send press releases announcing this fact, and also mentioning the availability of their workshops, classes, custom sewing services, new products, supplies, and so forth.

"Anniversaries of major events and days or weeks established to commemorate certain causes are a publicity seeker's dream," says Kate Kelly, author of *The Publicity Manual*. "If you can tie your business in with one of these occasions, then you will likely have a good chance for additional press coverage." To find dates which might be used for your business, Kate suggests that you consult an almanac, or obtain a complete listing of dates in *Chase's Calendar of Annual Events*. This is just one of many excellent tips to be found in Kate's manual, which contains many helpful examples of press releases and an extensive media resource list. (Kate kindly agreed to let me use press release samples from her book. You will find them elsewhere in this chapter.)

There is one week in particular that you should capitalize on: That's National Small Business Week, proclaimed by the U.S. Small Business Administration. (The exact dates of this week in May vary from year to year, so check with the SBA for exact dates. You can use their toll-free number indicated in the resource chapter.) This would be a perfect time to issue a press release that "hooks" your business on this important "news peg." Newspapers across the country are currently running feature stories about local residents who have turned hobbies into home businesses, or people who are combining occupations to make a living, and this trend is likely to continue in view of the current "home-business boom." To give you an idea for a publicity slant of your own, here are the opening paragraphs of three such articles I found in my files:

from *The Quincy Herald-Whig:* "Gail Dee Intertwines Crocheting and Singing," by Betty Moritz

When singer Gail Dee was traveling with her own band in Europe, the Orient, Viet Nam in 1969, and around the states, essential part and parcel of her baggage were a skein of yarn and a hooked needle. "I always carried a bag of yarn and crochet needles."

Blues rock singing around the world and looping threads into fanciful designs may appear a bit incongruous to most but to Dee, now living at Town and Country Estates, Quincy Route 9, crocheting has become both a pre-stage prescription for relaxing and a flourishing livelihood.

WARNING!

Before you seek local newspaper publicity, be sure that your business is operating legally as far as zoning ordinances and licenses are concerned. Zoning officials and other local authorities may pick up on such publicity and pay you an unexpected call.

Notes

Contact: Cheryl Jackson
           My Best Baby
           2311 South Drive
           New Orleans, Louisiana 70140

           (504) 555-6908

                                        FOR IMMEDIATE RELEASE

ADVICE FOR NEW MOTHERS OFFERED

DURING NATIONAL BABY WEEK, APRIL 21-28

New Orleans--There comes a time when every new mother asks herself:

"Am I doing the right thing?" "Is this really what my baby is asking for?"

       To mark National Baby Week which runs from April 21-28 this year,

My Best Baby, a clothing store specializing in the needs of infants,

is offering tips on a multitude of subjects. Among them are a few

pointers on a baby's cry:

       -The tone of the cry is what to listen for. Crying is a baby's only

        way of saying he needs you, and the tone tells you how great his distress.

       -When a baby is allowed to cry for a long time, he can become so

        exhausted that it will be difficult for him to sleep even after

        you've seen to his needs.

       -But don't go running every time your baby cries. Soon he'll be

        crying more frequently--sometimes just to have company.

       These and 100 additional tips for new mothers are in a brochure being

distributed by My Best Baby during National Baby Week. Customers will also

receive a discount slip for 10 percent off any future purchase.

       My Best Baby specializes in clothing needs for the newborn to the

3-year-old. All layette needs can also be found here. My Best Baby is

located at 2311 South Drive and is open from 10-6 Monday through Saturday.

Phone 555-6908 for more information.

                              -0-

A sample press release which illustrates "timely news." Note how the store tied its line of babywear into National Baby Week. From The Publicity Manual *by Kate Kelly. © 1980 by Kate Kelly. Used by permission.*

from *Fort Lauderdale News and Sun-Sentinel:* "Rugs and Hangings Cover Bills," by Dorothy Anne Flor

When Harriet Mathis' job as office manager of Fort Lauderdale's Center for Pastoral Counseling and Human Development was eliminated in November, she decided to turn adversity into advantage.

Hours of solitary late-night thinking convinced her to turn her hobby into a cottage industry. "I plunged in knowing that once the little seed money I had was gone, I might have to bite the bullet and go back to being a secretary," she says. "But now, three months later, I think I have every reason to be encouraged."

from *The Wichita Eagle-Beacon:* "More and More Folks Are Deciding Home is Where The Job Is," by Lindsay Peterson

There's a clattering in the background as Patti Mann speaks, "That was a truck going across the kitchen floor," she says, chuckling into the phone. "One of the slight disadvantages of having a business at home."

Her voice turns muffled, "Please kids, Mommy's doing business . . ."

Mommy is an entrepreneur, making a living without leaving home every day. She has two businesses in fact: Patti Mann Designs, for which she designs and markets decorative needlework, and Basketful, a gift-basket delivery service that she runs with her partner, Nancy Compton. Mann's kitchen is the headquarters of each.

Yes. I realize these examples all feature women. But women obviously get more publicity for home businesses than men, simply because more women than men have home businesses; also because they probably tend to seek publicity more than men. (It also is easier for women to get publicity, in view of the many women's magazines and home sections in newspapers which currently carry this kind of article.)

In all three cases, it's easy to see that the "news hook" relates to the fact that more and more people — especially women — are starting home businesses, and the special-interest angle of each article is: (1) Gail Dee's interesting mix of activities; (2) Harriet Mathis's ability to turn adversity into advantage; and (3) Patti Mann's humorous approach to doing business with kids underfoot. All three articles provide "human interest material," always needed by newspapers and magazines alike. People simply are interested in what other people do. If you are doing something interesting, you can bet there are people in your community who would like to know about it.

Try for publicity on local television stations, too. Often, interesting news stories are aired locally, then picked up for broadcast nationally. For instance, on television recently, we enjoyed a story on a new service business in California. It not only is unique, it also is afffordable, time-saving, and thoroughly appealing to a large segment of the population; specifically, everyone who has a dog. Although the service is simple — just a dog wash — it's the kind of business that literally commands publicity in local and national media alike. Why? The name of the business, for one thing; the business idea for another.

Called "Shampooches," it is a dog wash service that operates on the same principle as a car wash. Drive up, run your dog up a ramp and into a tub of warm water for a fast shampoo (given by the dog owner), then a brisk dry with a towel or blow dryer, and out the other end, fresh as a daisy. This obviously is an idea

Notes

whose time has come because it benefits busy people who love dogs — and that's a big market. There isn't an editor in the country who could pass up a story idea like this. As sure as I'm sitting here, the television coverage received by "Shampooches" will lead to additional publicity in both business and consumer publications.

Cable television is something else you should explore. I have noticed on some of the local cable shows that people often are interviewed, and, at the end of the show, there is a special offer made to viewers. For example, although I have done nothing about this yet, it has occurred to me that I could suggest that I be interviewed as a local expert on home business and offer to send viewers a copy of my home business resource list. This would cost me little, yet would put me in touch with people who are known to be interested in starting a home business. These are obviously the people with whom I want to communicate. This kind of idea surely would work for you, too.

A letter from Cathy Gilleland, who organized a cooperative in Chelmsford, Massachusetts, explains how an organized group might obtain publicity on cable television. She writes: "Our community is preparing to start broadcasting on its own station, and The Crafters is going to be doing a regularly-scheduled series of craft programs. I'm excited about the potential of using this medium, and I'm sure this opportunity exists in other towns."

Cathy told me that various members of the cooperative will demonstrate techniques and give how-to instructions. The tapes of each show will be kept on file at the local library for additional viewing after each broadcast. Although commercial aspects will be downplayed, this will provide wonderful exposure for each craftsperson. "Names and addresses can be given at the end of each show, and inexpensive instruction sheets can also be offered," says Cathy. "This not only helps viewers, but gets the craftperson's material into community mailboxes."

To increase your chances for publicity on television, study shows the same way you study newspaper articles. Learn what kind of guests are interviewed on each show, what topics are discussed, and what kind of promotional literature, if any, is offered at the end of each show. When you think you have an idea of interest, write or call the show's producer or interviewer and explain it.

Shooting for Publicity — Like Shooting Pool

I have a special fondness for pool because it was one of the first games my husband taught me after we were married. We don't play that game anymore, but in my mind I can still hear the delicious clicking sound the pool balls made as I broke them with that first thrust of the stick. It's rather like the "good vibes" I get now when I put new press releases into the mail. "Click, click, click," they go, as they land on editor's desks across the country.

In pool, if you're good, your first shot will knock a few balls into pockets and position the rest near other holes for easy tapping in later. The same kind of thing can happen with a press release, once it is mailed. For a moment, think of yourself as the pool stick, and the white cue ball as the press release. Let's imagine you have just sent a couple hundred copies of it to your publicity list (by first class mail, of course), which may include local papers, a few major newspapers, regional and national magazines, special-interest publications, radio stations, organizations, and so on.

One of your releases — let's relate it to the number three ball that just rolled into the center pocket — has landed on the local newspaper editor's desk. He decides that what you are doing is worth at least a short article. On publication, it brings you to the attention of the president of a local organization (the number four ball), who asks you to speak at the next meeting. This will be an excellent publicity break for you. Hard to tell what opportunities await you here.

Meanwhile, you have other balls on the table — or, a lot of press releases still circulating — just waiting to be knocked into pockets. In pool, you often have to shoot two or three times to pocket a ball. The same thing is true when you shoot for publicity. Your first release may work beautifully, resulting in publicity in several publications, or it may just fizzle out. Or so you may think. What you may not realize is that your "publicity push," like those pool balls on the table, is in a state of limbo, waiting for yet another push from you. Maybe it's a follow-up telephone call, another press release, or some additional attention you are able to get for yourself. Often, these things work together to trigger other publicity you could not have received if the first publicity effort had not been made.

Publicity Breeds Publicity

I am reminded of Rebecca Townsend of North Edgecomb, Maine, a reader who once took the time to send me a letter about her business. I later used some information from that letter in my regular column for *Crafts* magazine ("Selling What You Make"). On seeing this publicity, Rebecca's mother was so pleased that she called the local paper and told the editor about it. He sent out a photographer and a reporter who wrote an article that promoted Rebecca's business and brought in some good sales.

And Rebecca still is getting mileage out of that original letter she sent me, substantiating a fact you must always remember: *publicity breeds publicity.*

I am walking proof of that statement. *Creative Cash* was published in 1979. There has not been a single month since then that I have gone without publicity of one kind or another, either for my book, my newsletter and related publications, or for myself and my business. Yet, I have sent very few press releases to get this publicity.

What I have done, and what you can do, too, is a lot of *networking* with people in my field. Early on, I made it a point to get acquainted with people who were in a position to help me. I sent letters, made telephone calls, and mailed thousands of brochures to anyone and everyone who might conceivably be interested in what I was doing. In short, as a beginner in my field, I did a heck of a lot of hollering to get attention — and I got it.

In recent years, I have received publicity in hundreds of consumer, trade, and professional publications, given interviews on radio stations across the country, and been quoted in such prestigious publications as *Woman's Day, Family Circle, Time, Parade, The New York Times, Inc.,* and *Money.* The latter magazine provides a specific example of how publicity breeds publicity. At just the

Notes

1375 S. National
Springfield, MO 65804
866-3743
National Art Shop
Art, Drafting and Graphic Supplies

A Potpourri of Promotional Ideas

In addition to the publicity opportunities discussed elsewhere in this chapter, check the promotional ideas below that might work for your business:

☐ Tell friends, neighbors, relatives, and business acquaintances what you are doing so they can help spread word of your business. Make it easy for them to do this by giving them some of your cards or other promotional printed materials.

☐ Print an inexpensive flyer and distribute it in your neighborhood on a door-to-door basis, using energetic kids for "manpower." (Do not put such flyers in mailboxes, however, as this is a violation of postal laws.) If you are trying to reach the general consumer, you might consider placing flyers under the windshield wiper blades of cars in shopping center parking lots.

☐ Create an oversized business card — one that might serve as a bookmark — and put useful information on it that will encourage people to keep it close at hand. A local art shop created a cardboard "pencil," size 2″ × 8¾″, and had a 6″ ruler imprinted on it. (See illustration nearby, shown in reduced size.)

☐ If you live in an out-of-the-way place, think about a postcard — one that has a map on it. (See illustration of the card used by Joanne Rammer, Puddledock Crafts, in Portsmouth, NH.) Joanne says she uses the card to notify customers when custom jobs are completed, when open houses are being held, and so on.

☐ Speak about your business whenever you get the chance — free, if necessary. Members of local groups and organizations will provide considerable word-of-mouth advertising for you.

☐ Just speak up, in general. A teacher who went to a national conference casually mentioned that she would like to teach a class the following year. She got the job as a result. When she got home, she mentioned this news to the owner of a local shop, who promptly hired her to give a workshop at the store. This, in turn, led to other teaching jobs.

☐ Consider publishing a simple newsletter or regular bulletin to promote your business or the products you sell. Distribute it free to customers and prospects.

☐ Join organizations so you can network with people in your field. They may become your strongest supporters, steering a lot of business your way.

☐ Donate your products or services to charity or fundraising groups to get your name mentioned.

(more . . .)

Notes

(. . . more)

☐ Get involved in community projects, which automatically draw attention to your business. Example: a shop owner and her partner volunteered to decorate a well-known museum in their city which was open normally for special tours during the Christmas season. By giving something special to the community, they received considerable publicity for their decorating efforts, and a great deal of attention for their shop as well. You wouldn't have to be a retailer to benefit from this kind of "rub-off publicity" idea.

☐ When you do get print publicity, "merchandise" it by having it reprinted as a promotional flyer. (Paste the article to an 8½″ × 11″ sheet of white paper, include the name of the periodical in which it appeared, and have copies made as needed.) Stuff the reprint in all your outgoing mail, in customer's packages, etc.

☐ Post notices about your business on community bulletin boards.

☐ If you offer a business service, create a promotional brochure with business tips of one kind or another that will appeal to the market you're trying to reach. In other words, give people something they can use — something that also carries your advertising message. Other service businesses can create pieces related to their specific businesses. For example, a catering service might create a brochure that contains a few recipes. This printed piece could be distributed in local shops as a customer handout. (To get the cooperation of retail stores, make sure your recipes include ingredients carried by the stores, or tie in to their product line in some other way.) The brochure could be a simple 8½″ × 11″ sheet folded in thirds, with a subtle but effective advertising message on the back: " . . . these recipes are just a small indication of the good things in store for you at (name of your business.) Call us at (number) to discuss how we can help you with your next party."

☐ You might also think about creating a for-sale booklet that will work for you in the same way. Give your customers or clients some useful information which merely emphasizes services. (I'm reminded of a little booklet offered by a magazine publisher that tells how to write a good classified ad. Obviously, the idea is to get you to send your well-written ads to this magazine. And it works.)

☐ If you sell hobby or craft patterns of one kind or another, you might offer a free pattern to consumers, something simple that can be printed on one side of a sheet of paper and inserted at no extra postage cost in the brochure package you normally would send to interested customer prospects. A press release offering this free pattern probably would be used by every how-to publication in the country because editors like to offer their readers "freebies." Use the free pattern to entice people to order additional items in your line.

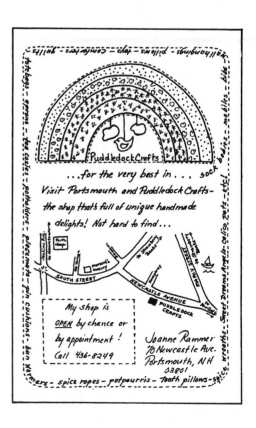

Notes

right time, I happened to connect with a free lance writer who was doing a story for *Money*. After he received my press release, he phoned for an interview, and included several of my comments in his article. After the article was published, I got a call from the magazine's publicity director who wanted to know if I would like her to arrange a few live radio interviews for me. "Sure," I said, trying to sound confident while shaking in my boots. (Having never done this before, I naturally was uneasy about it.) As it turned out, each interview was easy and fun, just like talking to an interesting friend on the phone. Some conversations were only minutes long, others ran as long as an hour. Like everything else in business, doing this kind of thing just takes a little getting used to. Experience breeds confidence.

After I had done four or five interviews, I wrote a press release and sent it to several stations, which resulted in still more interviews. The opening paragraphs of my release read:

> Millions of Americans have a leisuretime interest in arts or crafts, and a growing number of them are currently wondering if their craft or hobby could be turned into a profitable home business.
> Barbara Brabec, author of the best-selling book, *CREATIVE CASH — HOW TO SELL YOUR CRAFTS, NEEDLEWORK, DESIGNS & KNOW-HOW*, has the answer to that question, and she welcomes telephone interviews on this topic.

You, too, can get radio interviews for your business using this kind of press release, and you do not have to be an author to do it. What you do need to be, though, is "an authority" on some topic likely to be of interest to a lot of people. You realize, I'm sure, that many "authorities" you hear on radio and television are just ordinary people with a passionate interest in some particular topic; people who have made it a point to learn everything they can about it. If such people have a flair for talking, they make excellent subjects for media interviews. And such interviews are a great publicity technique for anyone who has anything to sell. In every interview I have given on radio, the announcer always has included a generous mention of my book, either directing people to bookstores, or sending them directly to me. (I also advise the station that I have free information to send to interested listeners. This often gets my address mentioned during the interview.)

How to Develop Your Own PR List

You should have your own PR (public relations) list, even if you also plan occasionally to rent special media lists or use distribution services to print and mail press releases for you. Only with your own list can you be sure your message is reaching the individual editors and program directors most likely to respond to your press releases or media kits.

Developing and maintaining a PR list can be a never-ending job (1) because new opportunities for publicity are always presenting themselves, and (2) editors tend to move around a lot, which means constant corrections to your list. If you have a computer, the job will be a snap; if you don't, you will have to set up a 3 × 5 index card file (or see the Flexilist system described in the resource chapter under "Office Supplies & Equipment").

Depending on what you are promoting, your media list probably will be divided into basic categories, such as: newspapers, radio & television contacts, consumer magazines, special-interest publications, trade press, and so on. Once you have developed a card deck, you will need either to hand-type the list each time you make a mailing, or get the names onto some kind of list addressing system. If you don't have a computer, try using white paper masters which can be photocopied onto adhesive labels.

Build your media list in keeping with your business and publicity goals. If you are trying to reach the mass consumer market, you will want to concentrate on getting publicity in national consumer magazines, major newspapers, and radio and television stations across the country. If you're interested in reaching a specific segment of the consumer market, such as collectors, gardeners, new mothers, hobbyists, etc., you must first identify the periodicals these people normally read, and learn about organizations to which they might belong. If you are a manufacturer trying to stir up interest in your newest product, you'll need to promote not only to the trade publications your dealers might read, but to the special-interest publications related to your field of business. And where do you find all these names and addresses?

Local media lists can be compiled from your telephone book. Directories from major cities can easily be obtained, as previously discussed. You probably subscribe to a number of periodicals which should be on your PR list. Others can be found in library directories. Many directories can be ordered by mail.

One of the niftiest directories I've seen is *All-in-One Directory*, published by Gebbie Press. It lists, in alphabetical order by category, the names and addresses of daily and weekly newspapers, AM-FM radio stations, television stations, general consumer magazines, business papers, trade press, black press, farm publications, and news syndicates. With this directory (and others like it) you easily can zero in on a specific category of interest, be it art, babies, cooking, golf, travel, or dozens of other special-interest areas. Listings include circulation information, type of readership served, and more.

In addition to standard media directories like this one, consider writers' publications, which are often-overlooked sources of media contacts. Many of my best names have come from *Writer's Digest* and *The Writer*, magazines which regularly print market information and special market lists. (Once you know the kind of editorial material an editor wants, you also will know the kind of press releases most likely to attract attention.)

Writer's Digest also publishes an excellent directory, *Writer's Market*, which is a tremendous source of information for anyone who wants contact with publishers in both the book and periodicals fields. (If you are trying to find a publisher for the book you have written, this is where you'll find the most up-to-date information on who wants to publish what.) For publicists and others who are building PR lists, this directory lists periodicals in dozens of categories within two general sections: consumer publications, and trade/technical/professional journals.

More Ideas That Have Worked for Others

- *A publisher of books on the art of silhouette cutting promoted a new book by sending press releases to the craft media offering consumers a free holiday design, ready to cut and mount. All they had to do to receive it was to send a self-addressed, stamped envelope, which would be stuffed with the publisher's flyer — and an order form for the new book, of course.*

- *A printer of business and social stationery has her name and phone number imprinted on the fine side of emery boards. She says they are a good promotional tool for her business because almost everyone uses this item sooner or later.*

- *A crochet designer and newsletter publisher (Gail Dee, mentioned earlier in this chapter) came up with a clever publicity idea last October after rumors began about the possibility of Halloween candy being poisoned. She decided to give money instead of candy, and she whipped up a "60-second crocheted pumpkin" that held a coin in its mouth, then phoned her local television station to see if they would be interested in announcing this alternative to candy. She said she'd give the pattern free to all those interested. The TV station sent out a video crew and did a 2½-minute tape that aired on the 6 and 10 o'clock news. The station received many calls from people who wanted this clever crocheter's address.*

Magazine Publicity

Radio publicity adds to your credibility and boosts your ego, but it seldom produces more than a couple dozen inquiries for the publicized product or service. Newspaper publicity is nice, too, but it

Notes

dies overnight. You are lucky to end up with a nice clipping for your scrapbook and perhaps an article that can be reprinted as a promotional handout. In short, radio and newspaper publicity does not motivate people to respond the way a printed article in a magazine does. This does not mean you should not seek such publicity — because it often works for you in other ways — only that you should place maximum effort on getting publicity in magazines.

Magazines can generate actual business for you (orders with checks enclosed), and it works for a long time. That's because magazines tend to be saved in doctor's offices, beauty shops, libraries, and home collections. Major consumer magazines actually can generate mail for years. Professional and special-interest publications also work for you long after information has been published because people tend to trade or share such publications with others in their field.

I think magazine publicity is easier to get than publicity on radio or television because editors are conditioned to receiving, and using, the thousands of press releases that cross their desks each year. It's their *job* to print the information in them so long as it benefits their readers. But there are other ways to get magazine publicity besides through press releases. Sometimes a letter to the editor (for inclusion on the mailbox page), or to one of the magazine's individual columnists or freelance writers works just as well. The trick here is to carefully study each magazine in which you would like publicity, then try to relate what you're doing to the individual "departments" and columns in that publication. If other people are receiving publicity in them, you may be able to get it, too. But in considering such columnists or writers, don't say, "I would like some publicity in the magazine." Instead, stress that the information you can contribute for use in the publication " . . . would be of value to the magazine's readers because . . ." and you would be glad to do this in exchange for having your name and address mentioned.

To make publicity work best for you, you may have to create some special "package" that can be offered in your press releases or promotional letters to publicity decision-makers. Information sheets of one kind or another often work here. For example, as I am writing this chapter, I have some new publicity breaking in *Family Circle* magazine (circulation seven million). It is giving me and my business a tremendous boost, and I got this publicity because (1) I was persistent in trying to get it, and (2) I offered *FC* readers a benefit in the form of a list of publications and home-business information resources for only a dollar. The editor knows this is valuable advertising for me, but she also knows her readers want this kind of information and will get much more than a dollar's worth. My package contains an 8½″ × 11″ home resources sheet (it lists 20 books, a dozen periodicals, and other information sources), a sample copy of my newsletter, and a copy of my catalog, "Information Resources for Home Business Owners and Dreamers." Mailing this information is a break-even proposition for me; as with two-step advertising, I am hoping for a good order response. (Conversion of prospects to customers.) I have every reason to expect it, too, based on past response figures on publicity in this magazine. Let me add to your education by sharing them with you.

The earlier publicity came in the form of a review of my book shortly after it was published. The March 11, 1980 issue of *Family Circle* gave the book a one-paragraph mention and offered readers the option of ordering it from the publisher at its postage-paid price, or receiving a free, descriptive brochure. As indicated in the advertising chapter, the heaviest day's response to a mailing or publicity is supposed to come the second Monday after the first response is received, and that's exactly what happened with this publicity. A few orders dribbled in at first, and the first Monday's mail contained 75 letters. The second Monday's mail, however, brought 536.

Thereafter, for several Mondays in a row, a larger-than-usual surge of mail was received, in comparison to daily response figures on Tuesday-through-Friday. The Monday figures looked like this: 464, 301, 219, 122, 92, 52, and so on. After one full month's response, there were 2,970 brochure requests and 930 book orders, which represented 66% of the total inquiries and orders by mail that would be received the first year. (Those totals, rounded off, were 4,500 brochure requests, and 1,400 book orders.) Over a period of time, 18% of the inquiries were converted to book orders. An added benefit, of course, was that many consumers went into bookstores to buy the book. (This was evidenced by increased orders from the publisher's bookstore and library distributors.)

Although the tally of responses was discontinued in May, 1981, inquiries and orders continued to arrive throughout that year. Even now, more than 3½ years later, each week's mail brings a couple of letters with the old *"Dept. FC"* code in the address. As you can see, publicity in *Family Circle* is the kind of gift that keeps on giving. And if you think it's great to receive more than 6,000 letters from this kind of mention, consider that some businesses have received more than 20,000 letters.

Although you should try to get publicity in major consumer magazines, it is very difficult to obtain. Don't expect it. Much easier to get is publicity in special-interest periodicals, newsletters, professional journals, and trade magazines. Make it a point to obtain and read at least one issue of every trade or professional magazine related to your field. Study every section of each magazine to find the names of the special editors or "departments" that obviously are giving publicity. Most trade magazines have *New Product* departments which make it easy to get publicity. You will increase your chances here if you send a press photo with a good caption.

A press release for a trade publication should include technical information that will be of interest to readers in that trade. Publicist Dorothy Doty recommends the use of an accompanying fact sheet that includes such pertinent information as engineering design, efficiency of operation, model sizes available, prices, distribution information, weight, and any other specific information buyers will want to know. Dorothy also suggests that you expand your thinking when considering which publications to add to your PR list. For instance, in addition to trade magazines that directly relate to your new product and its obvious uses, look for other publications that indirectly relate to it. When you find them, write a different press release that presents your product from a new viewpoint and in a way that will appeal to the new audience of readers.

If you happen to be involved in the crafts field, there is a goldmine of publicity awaiting you in the approximately 250 periodicals now serving this field. Almost without exception, the editors and publishers of these magazines, newsletters, and newspapers are extremely generous in giving publicity to anyone with a product or service of interest to craft consumers (which includes everything you can think of that relates to the word *handmade*). To build a PR list of such periodicals, see the resource chapter of *Creative Cash*.

Notes

Some periodicals in this field, such as *Crafts, Needlecraft for Today, Quilter's Newsletter, Crafts 'N Things,* and others, have circulations from 100,000 to half a million or more readers. Anyone with a business service of any kind also is likely to get publicity in such periodicals since so many readers have home businesses of one kind or another.

Another way to get publicity in special-interest magazines like the ones above is to write articles for them. If you don't feel like "a writer," don't worry; most of the people writing for these magazines began as hobbyists with something interesting to say or share. In fact, this is one of the easiest fields beginning writers can break into.

Wire Services & Syndicates

Instead of sending press releases to newspapers across the country, try first to get your story picked up by a wire service, such as Associated Press (AP) or United Press International (UPI), or news syndicates such as King Features, N.Y. Times News Service, and the Los Angeles Times Syndicate.

You have to have interesting, well-written material to get their attention, but once you do, it could mean that your story would appear in newspapers or on radio stations across the country. You will find a list of news services and feature syndicates in any of the media directories I have mentioned. There seems to be no end to the kind of material that will be considered. Many syndicates seem to be interested in material related to "living and lifestyle," which includes everything from cooking to car care, from contemporary living to coping with old age, from growing plants to raising a family. Health, food, nutrition, and money topics also are of interest.

Note that many of the regular columns in newspapers are syndicated. If you can connect with a syndicated columnist who will mention your product or service, you may derive huge direct or indirect benefits. I struck paydirt in late 1982 because I happened to connect with a writer, Vivian Doering, who had just agreed to do a special article on cottage industries for King Syndicates. Vivian quoted me and other home business authorities in an article entitled, "The Cottage Industry: Rural Explosion," which was syndicated in newspapers nationwide. Regrettably, my address did not appear in this article, so all I gained was an ego boost and perhaps some help in establishing recognition of my name. Sometimes this kind of publicity is the very thing that makes people order later when they run across your product in a store. Perhaps they buy because they think, " . . . seems I've heard this name before." (At least we publicity seekers like to think this is what happens.)

One thing is certain: people tend to do business with people they know. If you have limited funds for advertising, make sure people hear about you through publicity. This chapter serves as an introduction to the art and craft of getting publicity, but you should continue your education by reading available books and guides. If, in the end, you feel publicity just is not "your thing," hire some capable help in the form of a publicist or good freelance copywriter. It could be one of the best investments you'll ever make.

Diversify and Multiply

10.

YOU MAY NEVER make a million dollars from your home business, but you certainly can increase your income through diversification. This chapter shows you how.

Why is diversification so important to the small business owner? Because, often, only a certain amount of profit can be realized from a particular endeavor, no matter how hard one works. Yet if that endeavor is tied to one or more closely-related activities, one's profits may increase dramatically while overhead costs stay virtually the same.

In addition to being important to the financial success of a business, diversification also can be an antidote to business boredom. An interesting mix of activities not only adds spice to one's home business life, it may be crucial to certain businesses; mail order and seasonal operations, for example, which die down in certain months of the year. Clearly, something else must be done if income is to roll in regularly.

If your particular business does not lend itself to diversification into related products or services, you may need to start two or three separate businesses to bring in the dollars you desire. At the very least, strive for diversification in your product line if you happen to be in manufacturing or sales; if you make or sell only one type of product, your business might not survive if the bottom were suddenly to fall out of that product's market. Especially in product-related businesses, remember that consumer interests change constantly and you may have to keep changing your product line, possibly your marketing methods as well, to keep up with their fickle buying habits.

Above all, don't overlook the economy, which can be a fierce foe or a staunch ally, depending on your particular business. Certain products and services may be in greater demand when the economy fluctuates, or not needed at all. It is never too early to start thinking about an "understudy" product or service — one that could go on stage should your star performer suddenly fail to perform.

As I see it, one of the real formulas for success in a home business is:

Diversification of Business = Multiplication of Dollars

What's fascinating to me is the way different people use this formula. For instance:

> *"Does a million-dollar industry mean one million GROSS, one million NET, or one million OWED?"*
>
> *— Kaye Wood, owner of a diversified home business*

Notes

Five Businesses and How They Diversified

- Rex Allan has a full-time job and a sideline chimney sweep service called SonShine. Recently he and his wife, Carol, decided to diversify by starting a small mail order bookselling business, specializing in titles related to the home business industry. Says Rex, "We see these two businesses as being very compatible, because (1) peak seasons for each are different times of the year, resulting in steady income through the year, and (2) we are not overburdened with work involved in two simultaneous peak seasons."

- Ciya Stuart and her husband, Scott, own and operate The Country Craftsman, a woodworking studio, publish an annual regional directory for craft sellers and buyers, and offer marketing workshops and consulting to small businesses. Ciya also is a freelance writer, a sales representative for 15 artisans, and a psychologist with a private practice. Unquestionably, she's also an expert on time management, a topic she writes about frequently.

- Glen Baker owns the Pine Ridge Vineyard and Clock Works, a business that supplements his retirement income. Vineyard activities are planned for the spring and summer months, with clock-making activities in the fall and winter. Members of a local winemakers club are providing a word-of-mouth demand for Glen's grapes, and he plans to soon offer winemaking ingredients, chemicals, and accessories — items which would extend the vineyard income period beyond its usual September–October season. Glen's clock business at present is mostly Christmas sales, but lately he has been taking custom orders for clocks, music boxes, and weather instruments as birthday and anniversary presents. To make the best possible use of his woodworking equipment, he also buys small antique restorations, custom furniture, and bookcases.

- Pam Young and Peggy Jones, authors of *Sidetracked Home Executives* and its sequel, *The Sidetracked Sisters Catch Up On The Kitchen,* sell their books by mail along with a line of products directly related to their books. These include a series of cassette tapes, a "Home Executive Kit," a bimonthly newsletter, *S.H.E.'s On Track* (which promotes all of the above), and inspirational 3 × 5 cards containing information gleaned from back issues of the newsletter. The sisters frequently lecture on their favorite topic as well.

- Susi Torre-Bueno and her husband, Jose, own two home businesses: Rainbow Designs, a book publishing company, and American Innovations, a computer-design company. Rainbow Designs first published Susi's needlework design books, then issued the first annual *Index of Counted Thread* (now in its fifth edition) which enables needlework shops nationwide to connect with the more than 4740 book publishers in this field (most of them home-based women). The directory required the talents of Jose, who turned his many years of computer experience in a new direction. Now Rainbow Designs has diversified into the list rental business. The couple's second business, American Innovations, evolved because of their joint interest in computers, and they work in partnership with a computer designer to create custom-designed parts for computer systems that solve the specific needs of individual companies.

- People in service businesses often expand by adding related products to their line, which may then lead them into mail-order businesses. As they become known as experts in their field, they may be asked to speak about their business, which in turn may lead to consulting jobs, or the writing of articles or books.

- People with product businesses may decide to diversify by adding other lines, and possibly importing a line of supplies or finished merchandise. Others start their own party-plan businesses to move merchandise, and many end up in the mail order business as well.

- Craftspeople may begin by selling their wares to shops or at fairs, then go on to teach or write about their craft. Some get into self-publishing or kit manufacturing. Others go into show promoting, or become sales representatives for other sellers.

- Designers often end up publishing their own pattern or design books, which leads them into the mail order business. Then, to sell more of their books, they may begin to give workshops. Some eventually add supplies to their line.

- Authors tend to diversify into the seminar/consulting area, and often end up writing and publishing their own books or newsletters. Many go on the speaker's circuit.

- Publishers who start out with the idea of issuing one publication may buy a computer to help do the job, then end up selling computer programs and services, or possibly getting into the list rental business.

In brainstorming for ideas on how to diversify your business, try this "recipe." First take your primary product or service and add to it a list of other products and services related to it. Then stir in your knowledge about all of these things and mix well with the experience you have in all areas related to them. Add any business, professional, or marketing contacts you may have, and season with such intangible things as your personality and long-range business goals. The resulting mixture is sure to lead you to an interesting discovery about what you might do to "diversify and multiply."

Diversification Ideas and Techniques

Interesting ideas for business diversification usually come as a result of stretching one's imagination and asking, "What if . . . ?" Do you recall the lady I talked about earlier, the one who works all day on Saturdays to make bread which she sells for 70¢ a loaf? Let's use her as an example of how to expand and diversify a simple product business. In addition to selling bread on an occasional basis to a country store, the local restaurant, or a few neighbors, this homebased worker might consider such things as:

- A "Bread Subscription Service," whereby regular Saturday deliveries would be made to homes, restaurants, or stores in the community for a flat monthly fee; an echo of the golden days of daily milk and bread deliveries.

- A "Bread-of-the-Month Club." What works for fruit might work with bread. The month's "special" could be delivered on the first Saturday of every month to buyers themselves, or to their friends and relatives who may be unable to bake their own bread.

- A Party Service — Ethnic or gourmet bread products for cocktail parties or holiday celebrations.

Notes

- A "Season's Greeting Gift Pak" — a unique bread assortment, beautifully packaged in a basket or box, which executives and local merchants could give to their best customers as a special thank-you at Christmas or New Year's. (This package might include some of the products mentioned below.)

- A related product sideline, like homemade jams and jellies, handcrafted cookie trays, bread boards, baskets and tea cozies, all made by people in the community who need a marketing outlet for their products.

- A cookbook — a published collection of holiday or fancy bread recipes, in booklet form suitable for sale in local shops, by mail order, or for use as a fund-raising product for local organizations.

- Speaking engagements. One could talk to local groups about the history and lore of bread or the art and craft of bread baking itself. (Speaking is an excellent way to promote any business.)

- Classes in bread baking. There always will be people who want to "do it themselves;" smart entrepreneurs tell them how, for a fee. Such students often become regular customers for other products and services.

You don't have to sell bread or other edibles to apply the kind of logic suggested here. Just put your "thinking cap" on and start looking at your product or service from a new angle.

Ideas for Service Business Owners

A study of your particular service business will surely reveal ideas for related services that might be offered. (The service business chart in chapter two will help stimulate your mind.) In trying to determine the new services you might offer, you really have to work backwards by first thinking of your market possibilities. Who needs what? What else might you offer that would help or benefit your clients or customers? If you presently are selling to consumers, could you modify your service in some way to make it salable to the business community, or vice versa? For example, a writer might sell individuals the service of writing family memoirs, and also offer creative copywriting services to businesses. A dressmaker might work with women in the community, or contact restaurants to see if they need uniforms for waitresses. And so on.

Some service businesses can diversify by adding a retail product line. For instance, a calligrapher who does diplomas or scrolls might create a calendar, print quotes on parchment paper suitable for framing, or design a line of greeting cards. A wedding consultant might commission local artisans to create handmade garters or embroidered handkerchiefs to serve the "something blue" needs of brides, or perhaps offer handmade cake ornaments. Commercial items such as bride's books or paper products (napkins, nut cups, etc.) could also be purchased wholesale for resale to clients. A teacher might elect to sell books; a hairdresser, related hair care products, etc.

If your service business is unusual, and proves successful, you might want to investigate franchising it. You will find books in the resource chapter to give you guidelines in this area.

Ideas for Product Business Owners

Anyone who creates products for sale can easily come up with new designs for additional products, and people who buy goods for resale can always find other products related to their line. Product sellers can also offer custom design services, become a sales representative or marketing agent for other product makers, coordinate shows or sales, or start a marketing cooperative.

Sometimes a product business diversifies its operation merely by changing its marketing methods — moving from direct selling to consumers to wholesaling to shops, or perhaps establishing a mail order catalog division.

Importing is another option. Unless you have found a source of supply on your own by visiting a foreign country, you'll need to connect with agencies that can provide the names of firms that export products. Each country has a consulate office in the United States, many of which are located in New York, Chicago, or Washington, DC. (The National Mail Order Association sells mailing lists of foreign trade associations which may be helpful to you.)

If you are importing raw materials, you may be able to deal with individual firms in other countries. But if you are interested in importing handmade goods, you probably will have to work through special marketing organizations for each country. For example, all goods from Poland must be channeled through Cepelia in New York, handmade items from Greece are marketed through the National Organization of Hellenic Handicrafts, and so on. Each country's consulate office will put you in touch with the specific marketing contacts you'll need.

When merchandise from a foreign country arrives in this country, it must go through customs, so consult a customs broker in advance of ordering any goods. There is a certain dollar value of shipments that you can clear through customs yourself, and this may affect the quantity of merchandise you order at one time. In addition to customs regulations, there are state and local requirements about licensing and the payment of sales tax. Check with the State Treasury Department about this.

Mail Order

Mail order is not a kind of business, per se, it is just one good way to market goods. It is also a good way to diversify an existing product business. Since I already have discussed this topic in other sections of the book, I'll add only a few additional comments here.

A proven way to success in mail order is to start with a line of related products that appeals to a well-defined market, one that easily can be reached through classified ads or direct mailings of one kind or another. However, if mail order is going to serve merely as a sideline to your mail business, you may be able to realize good profits by creating a simple flyer that promotes one product. Then work with other mail order sellers to market it. If you can "ride along," in their cooperative mailings, or interest them in selling for you on a drop-ship basis, you could increase your income while incurring few extra costs.

What kind of product is best suited to mail order? Here are ten characteristics of a good mail order product:

Notes

How One Mail-Order Business Started and Grew

Below is the message I found on the inside cover of Herbal Concoctions' catalog, which features herbs, herb blends, and homemade soaps. It illustrates the kind of warmth and personality that so many of today's mail-order catalogs project. I believe it is this kind of sincerity that encourages so many buyers to order with confidence from small companies that are unknown to them:

"Herbal Concoctions began with three potpourris, a summer craft show, and a long history of loving and working with herbs. One new herbal concoction just naturally led to another, until we grew to be a home business with the support and help of our families.

Just as herb gardens mature, so has our involvement in this business. Our children have taken over certain whole parts of the gardening, as well as the mixing and packaging of herbs. Our daughter is growing herbs and making herb vinegars and has written an article on them;* another is concocting potpourris. All pitch in and help package, and they've become terrific sales people at shows and hostesses at open houses. We are pleased to present the third printing of our catalog."

In 1979, Carolyn Loughridge and Liz DeCleene of Littleton, Colorado, each invested $250 in Herbal Concoctions. They were operating in the black by the end of their first year. Their first catalog was a "hurry-up job" with dessert spelled wrong throughout the catalog. "We still have customers who ask for 'Desert Blend'," says Liz.

"Carolyn is the soapmaker, and I'm the herbalist," she adds. "Neither of us has a business background, so we've had to work through our mistakes. Fortunately, our instincts have led us in the right direction most of the time."

---

*The Mother Earth News, July/August 1983 issue.

1. It is a product not readily available elsewhere, either in retail stores or from other mail order firms. The more exclusive the product, the better.
2. It will appeal not to a wide universe of buyers, but to some special-interest group of individuals; a relatively narrow market that large companies are not interested in because profits aren't great enough. (Sales that would be "peanuts" to them might represent a substantial amount of money to you.)
3. It is an item in which people will not quickly lose interest.
4. It is an item people can use, appreciate, and understand; one that offers a benefit of one kind or another.
5. It is easy to describe in writing.
6. It photographs well and looks good when pictured in a catalog.
7. It is easy and inexpensive to pack and ship for arrival in customer's hands in undamaged condition. (Postage should cost no more than 10% of the retail price.)
8. It is small, so many items can be stored in a minimum amount of space.
9. It retails for less than $25 and has a profit margin of 65–70%.
10. It is a product of high quality. (While you always can sell a bad product, the customer who bought it won't buy from you again. This is vitally important, since the real profits in mail order come from repeat sales to satisfied customers.)

Writing and Self-Publishing

After a while, anyone who operates a business naturally acquires certain information and insights that would be beneficial to others. Some people elect to share this knowledge through consulting, teaching, or lecturing, while others prefer to put it into written form and publish it as information sheets, special reports, or booklets. Others decide to publish periodicals or directories. Still others write magazine articles or books.

Some writers, like myself, combine self-publishing with the writing of books that are published by trade publishers. Since I know how to publish and market books, people often ask me why I don't publish all my own books. The answer is simple. Writing and publishing a newsletter is a full-time job. So is book publishing. And so is marketing. One person cannot do everything, so I do the work I like best, and leave the publishing of my major trade books to those who specialize in this field. That does not mean I don't work hard to promote and sell all my books, however.

For the benefit of those who may be confused about the difference between self-publishing and being published by a trade publisher, let me explain briefly. If you write a book that is accepted for publication by a trade book publisher, your job will be almost finished by the time you have written the book and typed the manuscript. Your next job will be to read the galley proofs (the sheets of typeset copy) for last minute corrections. You may or may not be involved in the preparation of the index. After that, you have no further responsibilities to the book, except to help publicize it whenever you can. You just sit back and wait for your royalty checks to roll in, which often takes a long time. (Royalties generally are 5–15%

Notes

of the wholesale price, depending on whether it's a paperback or hardcover book.) It is the publisher's responsibility to pay the printer, send out press releases, place advertising, and handle distribution of the book. If you are working with the typical book publisher, you will have absolutely nothing to say about any of this, nor will your suggestions even be welcomed. (I'm happy to say that I don't have that kind of publisher.)

As a self-publisher, however, you are in total control from start to finish, and you assume all financial responsibility for the book. You not only write it and see that it is typeset, proofread, and prepared for printing, but you also have to pay the printer, get out the publicity, place advertising, and figure out how to get the book distributed to the general public. This is not easy for even the most skilled person to do alone. But when it's done right, it's truly exciting, and often quite profitable.

If you think you have a book in you, the first thing you should do is read *How To Get Happily Published*, my all-time favorite in this field. It will give you a well-rounded education in the craft of writing, the kind of books trade publishers want to publish, and your self-publishing options.

Not everyone can write a book worth publishing, but almost everyone has information or knowledge worthy of publication in the form of a special report or booklet. That's what I want to concentrate on now. When you reach the point in your business where you think you know something that other people might want to know, or you have gathered hard-to-find information that others might pay to receive, you are ready to think about putting this material into written form. (Ideally, you already will have access to the market most likely to buy it.)

What kind of information will sell? Anything and everything. People are hungry for information of all kinds, the more specialized, the better. They are willing to pay for it, too. A lot of material from self-publishers crosses my desk every month, and it generally falls into one of the following categories:

- **Special Reports.** Usually on topics related to business, special reports often take the form of loose 8½″ × 11″ sheets stapled together. Some are printed on 11″ × 17″ sheets and then folded to 8½″ × 11″. Number of pages may vary from perhaps 4 to 20, depending on the topic. Because such reports generally contain highly specialized information, prices are always based on the value of the information, not on how fancy the report looks in printed form. Prices of between $1 and $10 are common.

- **How-To Books and Booklets.** These generally are of two sizes, 5½″ × 8½″ or 8½″ × 11″, and usually have white paper inside and a heavier, colored stock for a cover. The number of pages varies from 12 to 84 or more. Larger books may be spiral bound, soft bound, or placed in special three-ring binders. Prices vary from $2.95 to $29.95, depending on how much the publisher had to pay to get the work into print, and how valuable he believes the information happens to be.

- **Directories.** These publications usually are 5½″ × 8″ with white paper inside and a heavier, colored stock for a cover. They are either saddle stitched or spiral bound. All kinds of information lends itself to publication in directory form, from collections of supplier names and addresses to artists and craftsmen who are seeking buyers. There are directories of craft fairs and shows, flea markets, home business owners, local shops and stores, community events, and special-interest periodicals, among other things. The common denominator, of course, is a listing of names and addresses which certain people desire either for business or personal reasons. Directories seem to sell best if they're priced in the range of $3.95 to $6.95.

Some directories are distributed free of charge, with the publisher making his profit from advertising placed in the directory by listees. Naturally, when the publisher charges for ads, distribution must be sufficient to produce a satisfactory response for advertisers, else they will not pay to be in future editions.

• **Newsletters.** According to the Newsletter Association of America, the definition of a newsletter is " . . . a specialized information publication which is supported by subscription sales and doesn't contain advertising." But there are many newsletters that do contain advertising (usually classified ads only), and not all newsletters are published on a paid subscription basis.

For instance, some people diversify a small business by starting a newsletter that's designed to promote their products or services. It may be sent free of charge to a business's customer or client list, or distributed in retail shops and stores. Or, it may be offered to readers at a nominal charge to cover postage and handling.

A newsletter also can become a profitable sideline or full-time business, but it takes skill, time, and money to make a newsletter pay off. Whether it is profitable or not depends first upon the market for it, and second, upon the creator's ability to write well enough to hold the interest of his or her audience. There are thousands of newsletters in print today, many dealing with finance, investing, and business. Periodicals in this category are often quite expensive, from around a hundred dollars per year to more than a thousand, depending on the type of information being presented and, more important, the expert who is presenting it.

Many other newsletters are produced by "kitchen table entrepreneurs," free-lance writers, and other professionals who serve a small, but select readership. Here, subscription rates may be as little as $6/year or as much as $96/year. A lot of people think newsletters are a quick way to make money, but I can assure you that this is not true. There is more to newsletter publishing than meets the eye. If you are planning to start a newsletter, you owe it to yourself and your subscribers to get started on the right foot. You can start small and grow as you go, provided you have a way to obtain at least a couple hundred subscribers to begin with and enough money to pay for the printing and mailing of the first few issues. Additional capital will be needed for advertising and promotion, because without a steady flow of new readers to capitalize the rest of the first year's issues, a newsletter will not long survive.

The one thing all newsletters have in common is specialized information that appeals to a specific audience of readers. If you can identify a universe of at least 20,000–30,000 possible subscribers, and you have a way to communicate with them, you may be able to make a go of a newsletter. Conventional wisdom says, however, that you will be lucky to get more than 10% of this universe as subscribers; and once you have them, you have to keep them. This isn't easy, even when you have a terrific newsletter. Even the most skilled publishers are lucky to get a 60–65% renewal rate, according to Frederick D. Goss, author of *Success in Newsletter Publishing*, and second year renewal rates are not likely to go higher than 85%. If you cannot keep at least half of your first year's subscribers, something is definitely wrong, either with the editorial content of your newsletter, or your promotional renewal efforts.

Notes

As you will recall from an earlier chapter, you have to send mailings to a lot of people to get even a few orders. The same thing is true of newsletter subscriptions, which are best obtained through direct mailings and the two-step advertising method. Each new subscriber easily can cost $10 or more, so first-year profits usually are nonexistent. And if you're going to lose 35–50% of your subscribers every year, you can see that you have to hustle just to stay even. For that reason, a lot of publishers quit about the middle of their second year.

- **Magazines.** Magazine publishing is not a way to diversify a business because it is a full-time business in itself — and a complex topic that cannot be covered adequately within the confines of this book. Although I know many people who have started magazines on shoestring budgets and achieved financial success, this is not something I would recommend to everyone. From experience, I can tell you that magazine publishing makes newsletter publishing seem like child's play.

To be a success in this field, you need many special skills and a considerable amount of time and money. To my knowledge, there is no good book still in print on how to succeed in the magazine publishing business, but you might check your library for *How to Start Your Own Magazine*, which was first published in 1953 and reprinted in 1978 by Contemporary Books. There is also *Folio*, a trade magazine for magazine publishers, but this publication is directed to major publishers who have a lot of money to spend. For that reason, small, homebased publishers will find it of little value. The book on newsletter publishing I mentioned earlier will be helpful, though, since much of its content also is applicable to magazines.

Freelance Writing

If you have the desire to write, but not self-publish, you might be able to add to your income through the sale of articles to magazines. Many craftspeople and designers, for instance, sell how-to projects to consumer magazines or write personal profile articles. Others write regular columns for newspapers or magazines. There are dozens of excellent books on how to be a successful freelancer, and you can find them by visiting a library or by contacting *Writer's Digest,* which has a good book club.

Like any other seller, a writer must be able to deliver the kind of material that currently is in demand. Beginners usually are advised to write about what they know; however, there also has to be a need for information, or it won't sell. To be a successful writer, you must first be an avid reader and subscriptions to writer's magazines are a must.

Speaking/Lecturing

If you have the "gift of gab," you may be able to earn additional income as a speaker or lecturer, talking on topics that relate to your home business or personal interests. To get started, you'll need a brochure or flyer that describes your act (which is exactly what it ought to be. Good speakers are entertainers, first and foremost.) In your brochure or flyer, include a description of your talk, colorful background information on yourself (for example, why you are so knowledgeable about your topic), and your experience as a speaker or "authority" in your field. As soon as possible, get letters of reference from groups you have addressed. This will help you get additional engagements. Word-of-mouth advertising also works well here.

Send your brochure or flyer, with an appropriate cover letter, to local organizations, clubs, societies, and other groups that might be interested in your topic. In the beginning, charge according to a group's ability to pay, (or whatever the going rate happens to be in your area), as well as on the basis of your time and experience. To reach a broader market (do you want to travel?), subscribe to *Sharing Ideas*, a newsletter written by and for speakers nationwide. This will connect you with booking agents and other groups who may hire your services.

Teaching/Workshops/Seminars

Anything you do well can be taught to others. This is an excellent way to diversify a home business and increase one's annual income. Organized people with enthusiasm, patience, and the ability to communicate their knowledge to others make the best teachers. A college degree or teacher's certificate seldom is required, but it may help command higher prices. (So will experience. The more you have, and the better a teacher you become, the more you can charge.)

To get started, read a couple of how-to guides (such as *Yes, You Can Teach!* and other books by the same author), and let your friends and neighbors know what you're planning to do. Contact schools in your area to see if they would be interested in an adult education class or workshop. Offer to give a free talk at the library or to some organization to step up interest in your topic. Try for newspaper publicity as well.

Whether you will be teaching at an institution or in your own home, set your per-student or per-day price according to what others are charging for similar classes. If no standards exist, set a price you feel is fair, based on what you might pay if someone else were giving the class. (So much depends on the area in which you live and the demand for your particular knowledge or skills.) To find more students, try classified ads in the local paper, post notices on community bulletin boards, and print flyers for distribution throughout the area.

If tutoring individual students is more to your liking, establish an hourly rate per student, keeping in mind that you are providing a special service that may be unavailable elsewhere. Charge accordingly.

In addition to teaching in your home or at other locations in the community, you might also consider giving workshops or seminars in other parts of the country. In setting a fee for a day's work, be sure to cover not only the time you spend on the actual day of the workshop or seminar, but your preparation and travel time as well. It is customary to receive a daily fee (or honorarium, as it is sometimes called), plus all expenses. Or you may prefer to work on the basis of so much per person attending.

For additional information, see the books, *Advice: A High Profit Business,* and *How to Organize and Manage a Seminar.*

How Nancy Dorman Got Started Teaching

"A friend who admired my Christmas ornaments got my 'teaching career' started. She had the coordinator of a local adult education program contact me about teaching. The once-a-year, six-weeks' session of classes was supposed to be expanded into three, six-week sessions. The following year I got started at a local community college, too, and the same thing happened again.

Programs of this type are great. They provide the advertising, space, etc. It's practically hassle-free. I love it, and not a session goes by that I don't learn more than the students. This keeps my designs fresh and workable from a construction point of view (a big factor in the salability of a design), and the pay is good."

— *from* Sharing Barbara's Mail.

Notes

Consulting: A Definition

"If defining consulting is important to anyone, I would define it as 'Helping clients through the application of your own special skills, knowledge, and abilities, whether that help consists of advice, doing for the client, guiding the client's hand, or some combination of these services.'"

— *Herman Holtz, from* Sharing Ideas Among Speakers & Friends

Notes

Consulting

To become a consultant in any field, you first must have special knowledge about this field, and a market willing to pay for it. Anyone who knows something that other people want to know probably can offer that knowledge through consulting. Maybe it's how to organize a home or office, plan a wedding, pick the best school for Junior, plan investments, or get a government grant. Or maybe your field of expertise lies in the areas of advertising, marketing, public relations, communications, or sales. Pick any field you can think of, and you will find consultants specializing in it. There even are consultants who teach people to become consultants.

If consultants seem to make a lot of money for very little work, it's only because they have spent years acquiring the kind of knowledge and experience that can command such fees. "Consulting on a full-time basis is a time-consuming venture that requires not only expertise in one's field, but also a creative and skillful marketing approach," says Jack K. Mandel, an assistant professor of marketing at Nassau Community College in New York, and owner of a consulting firm. "Professional consulting can only be achieved after years of careful planning," he adds.

As jobs become more specialized, professions often require the individual to specialize within a specialty, notes Herman Holtz, author of *How to Succeed As An Independent Consultant*. Today's complex, technological society means that more specialists will be needed to handle specific jobs. But it does you no good to have the skills of a consultant unless you also know how to market them, adds Holtz, whose book contains practical guidelines on how to do this.

If you are looking at consulting as a possible sideline for an existing business, you may find it an easy thing to market. You may already have customers or clients who would welcome this additional service. As soon as you have developed special expertise in any given field, you'll be ready to consider a consulting sideline. You will know when it's time to do this because people will start coming to you, asking questions about how to do this or that. And as soon as they start asking for advice, you had better start thinking seriously about charging for it. Every hour you give to someone else is one hour you cannot devote to your own business.

All of us who work at home need to constantly share our knowledge and experiences with others in our industry if we hope to make gains and stay abreast of our competition. But the busier we become in our own businesses, the more selective we must be about the time we give to others. It's one thing to network with other businesspeople, and quite another to freely give to a curious beginner (who may become a competitor in short order) all the information it has taken you years to acquire on your own. At least charge that person for the privilege of picking your brain.

I have always believed in sharing what I know, as this book proves, but the demands of my business now make it impossible for me to help people on a one-to-one basis unless they pay for my time as a consultant. The more successful you become in your own business, the more you will be asked for help and advice from others who would follow in your footsteps. Sooner or later you, too, will have to draw the line between how much you can share gratis, and how much you offer for a fee, through writing, teaching, speaking, or acting as a private business consultant.

In the end, the determining factor probably will be whether you are working for love, or with the idea of becoming, and staying, a profitable and self-supporting business. Time is your most precious possession. If you give it away, you will find it difficult to succeed in business. As a part-time, paid consultant, you will be helping your business to succeed while also helping others.

The Advice Business

Many of the foregoing topics fall neatly into one area called "The Advice Business." Because the foundation of the economy is now shifting from an industrial base to one of information and service, that makes the advice business one of the hottest home-business bets around. There are great opportunities for profit in this field, and several good books to help you realize your potential and find your niche as an adviser or information-giver. It all boils down to the same thing, regardless of whether you call yourself a writer, publisher, speaker, lecturer, teacher, seminar leader, or consultant.

Let me introduce you to two author friends who are nationally recognized experts in this field. Their books are considered to be among the best ever published.

Herman Holtz — a man who has been called "the guru's guru" — has been mentioned elsewhere in this book, and several of his titles are listed in the resource directory. One of his latest books is *Advice, A High Profit Business* (Prentice-Hall). This concise guide zeros in on a market Holtz says is wide open to professionals, technicians, managers, and individual entrepreneurs of all kinds.

As Holtz points out, advice is not a regulated business, and anyone can sell advice in any form (except for advice in some regulated or licensed professions). "And even in these fields," says Holtz, "one is free to sell general *advice* to the public at large (rather than to individuals) because it is then *information.*"

This is an important point, Holtz emphasizes. "Any layperson is free to write, lecture, and otherwise render advice in general for fees as long as the advice or information is general and not offered to an individual." For example, you may write or lecture about legal matters in the abstract, says Holtz, "but unless you are a licensed attorney, you may not counsel a person in legal matters for a fee."

If you think you have to be an expert in order to sell your advice, you're wrong, says Holtz. " . . . in many cases, simple access to or even the ability to gain access to useful information is ample underpinning for selling advice profitably."

If you plan to educate yourself to the possibilities in this field, you also need to study the books of Jeffrey Lant, who is known nationally as "the unabashed promoter," (also the title of his successful publicity book). In *Money Talks,* Lant discusses how to profit from the lucrative world of talk with workshops, seminars, lectures, institutes, conferences, and more. Says Lant, "If you know something and can open your mouth, this book is for you."

In *Tricks of the Trade,* Lant zeros in on what advisers of every kind need to know to profit from what he calls "the remarkable

Notes

transformation of the American economy" and to launch profitable advice and consulting practices in any field.

"The trick to building a practice in its early stages," says Lant in one of his books, "is to find a specific service which produces for the client a disproportionate benefit compared to your fee and to leverage each individual success to get further clients." And don't be sheepish about your fees, he adds. "Your ability to deliver success to your clients, a disproportionate benefit compared to fee, entitles you to raise your prices. A client is not merely paying for your current time, but all the years, the effort, the intense mental concentration, the innovation, the creativity, and patient practice and determination it took you to get to this point." (He adds that it's a pity so many client prospects fail to understand this, but counters with the kind of information you can use to get the message across.)

Lant's books, all of which he has published and successfully promoted himself, have enjoyed excellent sales. "That's as it should be," he says. "I remain an unreconstructed believer that we who assist other people, who do good, should do well in the process. Keep this belief as your credo and you, too, will do well."

I'll buy that.

As you're about to discover in the chapter which follows, the computer is a valuable tool for anyone in the advice/information business. In addition, I think it is probably the ultimate business expansion/diversification tool. You'll soon be reading about some people who found themselves on exciting new business roads as a result of computerizing their businesses. Frankly, the potential of a computer in your home-based business is unlimited. Whether you're a frightened computer novice or a seasoned pro, I know you'll find the next chapter as fascinating to read as it was for me to write.

Computers in Homebased Businesses

11.

THE PURCHASE OF A COMPUTER is likely to lead the average home-based business owner down many new roads of discovery, particularly those which reveal heretofore hidden abilities and new business opportunities. Given that fact, why, then, do most home-based business owners continue to operate without a computer? I think it's because technology is moving faster than most people. For example, when this book was first published in 1984, microcomputers were still too expensive to be practical for most homebased business owners and, even if affordable, were considered by many to be a luxury they could do without. Few small business owners even understood what a computer might do for their businesses.

Now, however, microcomputers are within the financial means of even the smallest business, and anyone with the desire to become "computer literate" can do so in a short while, given the wealth of published information and computer classes available.

The problem, however, is that all this information tends to frustrate as much as it helps. The more you learn about the different computers, software, and peripherals now available, the more confused you become about what you should actually *buy*. Should you buy the Macintosh in order to get its graphic capabilities, or buy an IBM because of the name, or select a less-expensive (and, many will tell you, just as good) IBM-clone because everyone says the best business software is produced for this market? And then should you buy the model that's available now, or wait for the improved version that is almost guaranteed to appear the minute you sign a purchase agreement? And do you need two floppy disk drives, or one floppy plus a hard disk with 10, 20, 30, or 40 Mb . . . and should it be internal or stand alone? And how about the backup system you'll need? Streaming tape, cassettes, or Bernouli box? Should your monitor be color or monochrome? If monochrome, should you buy green, amber, or white on black? Oh yes, the printer. Do you want a fast dot matrix (they're so much better now), or will you consider ink jet, thermal or daisywheel printers? Or maybe you should buy that expensive laser printer you want so badly . . . except if you wait 'til next year, prices will surely be lower. And so it goes.

It's rather like being told that we have access to the world's greatest candy store, yet once inside we find we can select only half a dozen pieces from the wide array available. And, furthermore, for every week that we wait to make our selection, we can add another

Statistics on Computers Used in Homebased Businesses

In a few words, exact figures do not yet exist. Since no one even knows for sure how many home-based businesses there are, it's anybody's guess as to how many of these businesses are now using computers.

A Family Circle *survey of home-business owners in its readership in 1985 did reveal, however, that only about one-fourth of those who made money at home (about 7,400) used computer equipment.*

The recent home-business survey conducted by Joanne H. Pratt Associates for the SBA (mentioned earlier in this book's introduction) states:

"There may have been substantial growth in work at home since 1980. In late 1984 nearly three million people were using a computer in their home or job- or business-related activities. Very preliminary estimates from the Current Population Survey show over 15 million people doing some job-related work at home in 1985. Fifteen million is a very sizable number of people working at home. In this population there is bound to be a large number of homebased businesses that remain to be identified . . ."

There were about 5,000 desktop computers in the U.S. in 1978. By 1982 there were three million. By 1990 there will be 80 million, according to Michael Crichton, author of Electronic Life – How to Think About Computers *(Alfred A. Knopf). Crichton maintains that since computers are changing every aspect of human life, we cannot afford to turn out backs on them.*

* * * * *

Cray Computers, each costing about $5 million, are capable of performing 100 million operations in a second, a feat that has been likened to reading Gone With The Wind *in the blink of an eye. (From the* Chicago Tribune.*)*

Notes

piece of candy to our sack, as a reward for waiting it out. It's not surprising, then that some conservative individuals have delayed a computer purchase in anticipation of getting more for their money.

Another thing that holds many potential computer users back is the matter of time. Certainly that was my problem for a long time. My regular work has always kept me so busy I couldn't imagine where I was going to find the extra time needed to learn how to use a computer and then enter all the necessary data. (Of course I wouldn't trust anyone else to do it for me.)

When this chapter was added to the 1987 edition, I did not yet have a computer system, so I called on friends in my network for help in writing it. What follows is the result of their enlightening and informative replies to my questionnaire. Of special interest will be their viewpoints on time — the amount it takes to learn how to operate a computer system, as well as whether computers do, indeed, save time for a business or demand more of it.

Before I get to the nitty-gritty of this chapter, I want to tell you what it isn't about, and why. It isn't about the technical side of computers — what they are and how they work — because dozens of books have been devoted to this topic and you can find them anywhere books are available.

What this chapter *is* about is *people* — how they relate to computers, and how their personal lives and homebased businesses have been impacted by them.

In short, what you have here is a personal peek over the shoulders of 37 individuals who have learned from frustrating trial-and-error experience exactly what computers can, and cannot, do for them. Their comments are informative, revealing, and often amusing. To my knowledge, they are also the first of their kind to be documented in a book about homebased businesses.

Computer novices will find the following material helpful and encouraging as they make plans to computerize their own businesses, while computer pros will no doubt do a lot of smiling and head-nodding as they read the remarks of others who have had experiences similar to their own.

General Information
Gleaned from Questionnaire

Most of the individuals who answered my questionnaire have had homebased businesses for two to five years, with several being in business for six to ten years. Most of these business owners have been using a computer for business for more than two years, although a few have only recently purchased their systems.

In instances where a computer purchase was delayed until after the business had been operational for some time, users gave as reasons, in this order: (1) didn't think they could afford exactly what they wanted; (2) were not convinced a computer would do that much for them; (3) didn't think they had enough time to learn to use a computer because their business kept them so busy; (4) were concerned about their ability to learn to use a computer.

When asked if initial concerns, worries, or excuses for not purchasing a computer were justified, most said they were not.

Most respondents said that, in shopping for a computer, they first talked to other computer owners, read books, and studied available literature before going out to see various computers demonstrated. Several also took special classes on computers. Only five said they did little research beforehand and simply went shopping, listening to what the salespeople told them. (Elsewhere, see comments from users who think this is the worst possible way to buy a computer.)

Those who studied before shopping said their study definitely influenced their decision to buy, and they found they knew as much, if not more, than most computer salespeople.

When asked how many service calls were necessary in the first year of operation, most said none or one, with a few reporting two or three at most. Apparently breakdowns which require service calls are no longer much of a problem. (A few people did report that their hard disk drives had "crashed," however.)

When computer users in my survey were asked if they had software needs not allowed for in packaged programs, most said no. Those who said yes indicated it was not that software wasn't available, only that it either would not work on their machines, or it cost more than they wanted to spend.

When asked if a computer consultant or specialist was ever considered, all but a few said no. Interestingly, most of the users in my survey group had spouses, children, or friends who gave them learning assistance and any programming help needed. This may indicate that the homebased business market for computer consultants is quite limited.

When asked for what uses computers were originally purchased, most users said, in this order: (1) word processing, (2) writing articles or books, (3) managing a mail list, (4) organizing data, (5) accounting/bookkeeping, (6) desktop publishing, and (7) graphics, research, or programming.

When asked how usage changed *after* the computer was up and running, there was little change, except that list management moved up one position, and more people reported using their computer system for desktop publishing.

Finally, when asked if the computer had been purchased for business use only, or a combination of business and personal use, answers were fairly evenly divided between the two. However, those who use the computer only part time for business use it heavily: from 75–90% of the time.

> ### Author's Note
>
> *When writing about the brand names of computers, such as "Apple" or "IBM PC," it's proper for writers to add the word "computer" after these names because they are all protected by trademark law. Using brand names without the appropriate descriptive word after them — or the trademark sign (an R in a circle) is something all manufacturers try to prevent in order to keep brand names from becoming generic terms.*
>
> *However, since brand names of computers are used repeatedly throughout this chapter, and since it seems redundant to use "computer" or the trademark sign after every mention of such brand names, both have been omitted for the sake of expediency.*
>
> *This in no way indicates the author's or publisher's lack of regard for such trademarked names, of course, and we trust the individual computer manufacturers will understand.*

Notes

An Imaginary Networking Session

If I could have brought together the many individuals who contributed to this chapter, and we all sat around talking about computers, the conversation might have gone something like this:

In looking back to life before the computer, who among you can imagine working without one now?

Carol Moore: "Not me. My computer eliminated boxes and boxes of index cards. I wouldn't like to return to that."

Liz DeCleene: "Me, neither. If you're a lousy speller and worse typist, as I am, the computer makes you look great."

Janet Attard: "I wouldn't attempt to work without a computer; in fact, I couldn't work without one. Some of my clients require their work be transmitted over the modem and phone lines. We have two computers in the house, now. By the end of the year, we'll have at least three, and maybe four, since I plan to buy an IBM clone

"Computers are nothing more than tools. Most people still don't understand that. They have changed the way we do things just like movable type, sewing machines, and the cotton gin changed the way we did things a hundred years ago.

"For most home businesses, a computer could not be considered a necessity. The exceptions (yes, there are many) include businesses that offer computer-related services such as bookkeeping, software developing, word processing, etc.; work which allows disabled people to work; businesses which are information-related; and any business that does extensive word processing, number crunching, or has a lot of data on file (such as a large customer base or mailing list).

"A computer can be used to increase productivity and efficiency and thereby save a lot of time, but only after a great deal of time has been spent learning how to use it."

— *Lynie Arden, Editor*
Worksteader News

Notes

with a hard disk. My daughter would also like her own computer."

Lu Anne Ruttenberg: "A good portion of my business is custom programming, so I definitely could not get along without one. I also do all my bookkeeping, billing, and customer info with a computer — which saves me a great deal of time."

E. S. Matz: "I'm a publisher who sells books by mail. For a long time it was only me and my computer. In a sense, the computer took the place of an employee."

So far, the feeling seems to be unanimous. A computer has become a necessity for most of you.

Bobbie Irwin: "Not exactly. I always hated computers and probably would not have gotten one except that my husband was so anxious to have one for the computer-oriented thesis he's working on. My attitude has changed since I've been using it, but it's still just a tool, and I do not see it as a necessity."

Tom Ellison: "For some applications, like word processing, it's possible to get by with a typewriter. But trying to manually maintain a mailing list with thousands of names is crazy these days."

Charlene Anderson-Shea: "I agree! Even using it for my small (600) mailing list makes it worthwhile. I have tried designing on the computer, but find that I do better with graph paper. Keeping the books is a snap, and my accountant loves the neatly printed, balanced books."

Herman Holtz: "As a former electronics engineer with ample experience and familiarity with big computers, I was not impressed with, nor in awe of, the 'gee whiz' aspects of word processing, as so many writers were. But there are so many other things this magic machine does that I could not imagine now ever going back to the old ways."

Eileen MacIntosh: "I'm with you, Herman. There's not a chance that I could live without my computer. As an artist used to dealing in graphic concepts, the idea of using a system based on logic — a foreign subject to me! — was intimidating. However, once I discovered that my computer could easily reduce my paperwork, streamline my correspondence, and generally minimize my tedious, overwhelming, administrative work . . . well, my life changed."

I've heard it said that everyone loves a computer, no matter what kind it is, simply because computers make life easier. How many of you agree with this statement?

Lynie Arden: "Not me. There are thousands, maybe more, of computers sitting on closet shelves because their owners believed that kind of hype."

Ed Simpson: "Right. Some of the cheap computers are essentially useless for business purposes."

Lu Anne Ruttenberg: "Agreed. Not every computer is sophisticated, versatile, or reliable enough to necessarily make things easier."

Charlene Anderson-Shea: "That's true. In some instances, using a computer is not the best or easiest way. Some things are more trouble than they're worth."

Janet Attard: "Not only that, if a computer doesn't do what you want it to do, and do it the way you want it to do the work, it can create more problems than it solves."

Arlene Biales: "I think computers do make life easier, but unless you jump in with an expensive setup, you will find limitations to what you have, which can be frustrating."

Mary King: "Frustrating isn't the word for it. If the computer cannot do what you need, you can't help but hate it."

Tom Ellison: "You're right, Mary. I know many people who hate their systems. Computers can be incredibly frustrating."

E. S. Matz: "That's true, but when you have invested the time it takes to learn a particular computer, with all its eccentricities, it takes a lot of nerve to learn to use another."

Your answers emphasize the love-hate relationship that seems to be typical of most computer owners. Anyone want to add anything to the discussion?

Susan Anderson: "I have mixed feelings about this. I love my computer system, but it is rather like the love a mother has for a child who has been wayward at times and lovable at other times. I believe that you love the things you invest the most time in. I have invested enough time in my computer system that I have to love it a lot, like a child I've raised who has both good and bad traits. Some days it behaves and works well with me; other days it is all headaches and problems. As with a child, it takes a lot of time and maintenance for it to become worthwhile to have around. A potential computer owner should never go into that ownership believing that the computer will do all the giving. The computer takes a lot before it ever gives, and then requires a lot of loving care besides."

Bobbie Irwin: "I like my computer but refuse to love it, probably because I'm stubborn and have never been one to follow fads. Not that computers are a fad, but the idea that it's something you have to have makes me cringe. It's a useful tool, and while I enjoy its benefits (along with those of my dishwasher and microwave oven), I could get along fine without it. (It was all my husband's idea, you see . . .)"

Susan, your comment about time prompts me to ask how long it took you to get your system fully operational?

Susan Anderson: "I did not have an appreciation for how many hours it would take to get our IBM PC-XT to the point where it became a workhorse for me instead of me being a nursing mother for it. During the first six months of computer ownership, I spent many, *many,* nights working through computer problems, installing new software, restoring destroyed data, learning new computer programs, investigating breakdowns, and just plain getting acquainted enough with the computer and operating system to be able to really control the computer. It still needs more hours of maintenance than I originally thought it would — backups, updating programs, learning new programs, etc. We now have about 200 floppy disks full of data, plus a 10 megabyte disk completely full — which means I have to continually dump data to make room for more.

I might add that this computer was installed in my husband's dental office two years ago. I'm also using a PC Designs FD-1000 (IBM clone) in my new homebased business."

Carol Moore: "Susan's experience is obviously unique. My husband and I also use an IBM PC-XT and three programs to handle our correspondence, filing, and bookkeeping needs. I did not spend

---

Before & After Comments of a Computer User

August, 1983

"I took an adult school class on 'How to Buy a Computer for a Small Business' and decided I cannot afford to have one and cannot afford to be without one. As a stop-gap until I make up my mind, I bought a Royal 5030 typewriter with a computer in it and proportional spacing that looks like typeset. It is serving my immediate needs."

July, 1986

"Knowing what I know now, I would certainly recommend a computer, if only for its mailing list capabilities. We got ours 2½ years ago with a lot of hesitation on my part. We feel that in the mailing list alone, we have saved the cost of the computer in labor time. We see a lot of potential for more uses, such as bookkeeping and word processing, which we plan to do as soon as possible. Now we feel we would really be handicapped without a computer."

— *Janet Stocker, Editor*
Treadleart

Notes

"This is probably a typical good news/bad news story from yet another computer junkie. The good news is that I have the ability to do twice as much work in half as much time. The bad news is that I actually try to do twice as much work in half as much time, not realizing that simply keeping track of all the projects I dream up eats up even more of my time.

"My four-year-old dedicated word processor isn't really a PC-style computer. It's a stand-alone word-processing system designed to make working with words easier. That it does, and it does it so effortlessly that I have still not found a PC-oriented word processing program that I like.

"My system also has an excellent records processing program for maintaining mailing lists and merging text with those lists. The biggest drawback to my system is that I currently have no way to purge duplicate names from my databases except by doing time-consuming two-person eyeball checks on the various lists.

"The only other drawback to my system is that by today's standards it was rendered obsolete three years ago when the manufacturer quit making it. There have been no adjustments to the system's existing programs, and it appears that the system is not programmable by outside means.

"In summary, I love the ease with which I can move, store, retrieve, and rearrange words and information via computer technology. As a writer and communicator, this has made my professional life wonderful. I only wish I could develop the personal restraint to harness my entrepreneurial and creative energy when it starts to get out of line and drive me instead of letting me drive it. Last, since my system is so simple to operate, I am still computer illiterate when it comes to understanding the leading edge of today's computer technology."

— *Peggy Glenn, author and owner of Aames-Allen Publishing Company, Huntington Beach, CA*

more than two days studying my manuals and learning the programs. When questions did arise, I simply called IBM's support system for help in solving the problem."

As I see it, Carol, the real difference between you and Susan is that Susan's involvement from the beginning was much more than that of "computer operator." She was fascinated by her ability to comprehend the solutions to difficult programming problems, and decided early on to become an expert. That automatically takes a lot of time. Also, to date she has mastered at least ten programs.

Julie Ann Allender, Ed.D.: "Even if you don't decide to become an expert, it takes hours to fully master any computer system. I use an AT&T 6300, with 20 Mb hard disk. When I first got the computer, it was a disaster. I thought it would be a simple process and I would be able to do it within a short amount of time. Instead, I found that, on the average, I have had to spend 20 hours to learn the basics of any new program such as WordStar, WordPerfect, Lotus, or DBase, and even with this amount of time per program, I have barely touched the tip of the iceberg. I found that it was helpful to take an advanced beginner's computer course, but that I had to spend from 8 to 10 hours straight at the computer figuring things out.

"I have now had the computer over six months, have probably put in a minimum of 200 hours learning time, and feel quite comfortable with it. I am aware, however, that I really know very little compared to what it can do. But at least I am no longer threatened by the computer and it no longer takes me 20 hours to replace my hard disk after I accidentally wipe it out. I can now do it in two."

E. S. Matz: "There is definitely no general agreement that computers are faster. Some folks consider the learning time, the "bugs," and the mental discipline involved in computer use not worth the trouble."

Susan Boykin: "She's right. I have been unwilling to spend the hours needed to learn how to use our data base program, R Base 5000. We added so much to our system when my husband was setting up his data processing business that it's been overkill for me."

Janet Attard: "May I offer a quick tip here? I think computer novices should start with a word processing program first. It's usually the simplest program to learn to use, and once you've mastered that, learning other programs tends to be less confusing."

Jeannie M. Spears: "I can certainly relate to everything that's been said here. When I brought my computer home, it was like being dropped in a foreign country without knowing the language. But I did learn it, and it was worth it, and every day I learn a little bit more."

As we're all learning, it takes a lot of time to fully master a computer system, which leads me to ask how much business time all this learning time eventually saves?

Tom Ellison: "You're likely to be disappointed if you really expect your computer to save you a lot of time. Any time saved will automatically go into new tasks you hadn't realized you needed to attend to before getting your computer. The net result is that you improve your control of the business and probably increase your chances of succeeding at it, but you won't save any time that you'll notice."

Lynn Ocken: "I was afraid it would take more time to learn the computer than time it would save. Not the case! I thought a typewriter was easier — wrong. In short, the computer has saved me countless hours — which, as Tom just explained, I can now put to more profitable use."

To summarize, then, we're saying that the time-saving aspects of a computer are something of a "Catch 22." Any time one saves is automatically gobbled up by more work. The real benefit, then, is that more work may mean additional profits for a business.

Bobbie Irwin: "Not always. I think it takes me longer to compose a letter on my computer simply because it is so easy to go back and change errors and rearrange paragraphs that I actually spend more time at it."

Eileen MacIntosh: "Maybe the best way to summarize this topic is to say that a computer doesn't necessarily give one more free time; it merely allows one to make different use of their time. In my case, the computer has freed up enough time that I've been able to write not just articles, but novels. And the computer makes work so much fun that I find myself wanting to work more hours."

How Computers are Helping Some Business Owners

I'm going to break our networking session for awhile so I can tell you more about some of the businesses owned by individuals mentioned to date. Obviously, the kind of business one operates has a direct bearing on one's approach to a computer, as well as the amount of time it may take to input data and learn the number of software programs that may be needed to do an effective job.

For instance, several of the above-mentioned individuals are periodical publishers. Ed Simpson, Lynie Arden, Jeannie Spears, and Eileen MacIntosh all use their equipment primarily to create their individual publications, manage their growing mail lists, maintain necessary information databases, and handle the usual recordkeeping and word processing jobs, including the writing of freelance articles or books.

Ed, who publishes *Home Business News*, says he wouldn't be in business if not for his computer. Lynie, whose special comments appear as sidebar information elsewhere in this chapter, publishes *Worksteader News.*

Jeannie, publisher of *The Professional Quilter*, says the thing that sold her on a computer was the fact that she could hook it to a typesetter (through a device called a modem), and set type for quarterly issues of her periodical. Beginning with a Kaypro II, she gradually updated the equipment as later models were introduced. "The software that accompanied our computer purchases filled most of my needs; public domain programs filled remaining gaps."

"My initial purpose for the computer was to get my mailing list and business records under control," says Eileen, who frequently writes articles for craft periodicals and publishes a newsletter. "Secondary was the ability to edit articles on the word processor. Once I got the computer, however, (an Apple IIc), I discovered that entering my mailing lists would not be such a quick little task, done right. I stress that because I could have just typed in the names and addresses and been done with it, but I chose to "code" my list according to individuals' interests, so I could select a certain cate-

---

Have You Named Your Computer?

Henry Kisor, whose "Personal Computers" column appears in the Chicago Sun-Times, *noted that many computer owners, especially first-time users, have named their computers. Names tend to reflect the owner's love/hate relationship with the machine, he said, and run the gamut from "Slippery Sam" to "Old Lovable."*

In doing research for this chapter, I naturally asked my computer friends if they had named their machines. Most said no. Several said such things as "The names I call it aren't fit to print." One said she called hers GDSOB when it didn't work. Margaret Boyd calls her Kaypro "Buster," as in "Listen, Buster!" When E. S. Matz became a grandmother at about the time she became a computer owner, she dubbed her Apple II "Granny Apple." Janet Hansen, who likes to play around with her MacPaint software, calls her Macintosh computer "Figment," as in figment of her imagination.

And Janet Stocker's IBM is named Bufford. "He has a definite personality, and has grown people talking silly to him," she says.

Notes

TODAY'S CHILD

YOU'RE
INVITED
TO AN

EDUCATIONAL
SENSATIONAL
TOY SALE

Come see our unique
toys that develop the
intellect, imagination, and
love of learning!

OPEN HOUSE
Sunday, February 16
1 p.m. to 4 p.m
San Carlos Townhouse, #5
Bring a Friend!

Your Hostess_____
Presented by
TODAY'S CHILD

"Our Apple home computer has been invaluable for making letterheads, signs, and invitations to home parties," says Ursula Sarli, owner of Today's Child. "I used THE PRINT SHOP program to create the above illustrations and type."

(Shown here in greatly reduced size. Original invitation measures 5½ × 8½ in.)

What a Computer Can Do for the Small Entrepreneur
by Herman Holtz

The microcomputer is particularly appropriate to mail order enterprises because of its facility for doing all the following important things for the entrepreneur:

- Setting up, maintaining, and printing out mailing lists on labels, or directly on envelopes.
- Typing and addressing sales letters individually from a stored list.
- Invoicing customers.
- Maintaining various useful files, such as these:
  a) Customers and what they bought in the past (plus any other information you might want in each file).
  b) Current orders, with pertinent data — prepaid, to be billed, source of the order, size of the order, etc.
  c) Accounting — receivables, payables, journals, balance sheets — whatever you need.
  d) Inventory, with trends, balances, projections, costs, etc.

- Doing analyses of various kinds, such as these:
  a) Tabulating sales of various items for any period, to show trends and/or make projections.
  b) Tabulating costs in any/all categories, for any period, to show trends and/or make projections.
  c) Marketing analyses — tracking results of advertising, direct mail, other marketing/sales efforts.
  d) Do spreadsheet ("what if") projections.

Any one of these services provided by your computer can make the investment a profitable one in time and money saved, not to mention improvement in marketing and sales, among other benefits. But even that is not all; there is at least one more consideration: the computer can itself provide additional profit centers. Consider these possibilities:

- Most successful mail order entrepreneurs earn extra income by renting out their own mailing lists, when they have built those lists up to enough volume. The microcomputer can not only print out the lists on labels, but can also manage the effort, keeping track of all such transactions.
- Many owners of microcomputers operate computer services for others who do not have their own systems or who do not have time to do their own mailings.
- Train others in how to use a microcomputer to do all the things mentioned above.
- Write articles about how to do all these things.

Sooner or later you will probably reach the conclusion that having a microcomputer is an absolute necessity for success in your enterprise. In any case, it won't hurt to begin studying the situation now, and gather up some information likely to be useful when you are ready for that step.

— Excerpted from the article, "The Inevitability of the Personal Computer," in *National Home Business Report.*

gory of people each time I had a special mailing. Thus, in my third month as a computer owner, I'm still entering names."

Incidentally, that kind of list coding is critical if you ever plan to sell your mailing list. The more information that can be supplied to prospective list renters — such as individual's sex, source of name, number of orders to date, total purchases (dollars) to date, special interests, etc. — the more marketable a list will be.

Tom Ellison and E. S. Matz are book publishers who use their computer system in much the same way as the periodical publishers just mentioned. Both sell books by mail — their own as well as books by other publishers. Both use a Macintosh desktop publishing system. Publishers have a great need for printed forms of all kinds, and E. S. says she uses her Datastar database to create and print as many copies as needed of customer and general business or advertising records, as well as bibliographies and craft show information used in the show guide she also publishes.

Herman Holtz and Janet Attard are both freelance writers and authors whose special words of advice appear as sidebar information elsewhere in this chapter. Herman uses his Morrow MD3 primarily for writing books; Janet says her Sanyo 1000 is used not only for word processing, but indexing her files and keeping track of expenses.

Five of the individuals mentioned to date are in craft-related businesses. Bobbie Irwin, who teaches weaving and sells handwoven goods, yarn, and equipment, uses her Morrow MD computer and printer setup to make single copies of things like workshop descriptions, which look professionally printed. "That way," she says, "I can change the wording to slant it for a particular need or institution to which I might be applying. This has saved printing expense; rather than printing several hundred copies of a workshop list in advance, I can do personalized copies one at a time." Interestingly, Bobbie still does her bookkeeping manually, partly because she enjoys it, and partly, she says, because the computer doesn't seem to save her any time here. She does, however, use the computer to keep track of inventory records. Her system is not designed to handle graphics — a point, she says, for others to consider if they plan to draw electronic pictures. "If I did have this capability," she adds, "I might use it to plan weaving patterns (software is available). With such equipment, I could also start teaching computer-design workshops, except that I have no real interest in doing that."

Like Bobbie, Charlene Anderson-Shea uses her computer to manage a weaving business, which involves the design and production of handwoven clothing, plus sales of weaving supplies and equipment. "I have tried numerous software packages on my Apple IIe to assist me in my designing of handwoven clothing, but I still have not come up with any that really suit me. Dazzle Draw has come the closest, and would probably be acceptable for most people. I'm on the lookout for a program that will show a grid on the screen and allow you to fill in the design square by square." Charlene also uses the computer to manage her mailing list, create flyers, signs, and other graphic needs and handle recordkeeping and general word processing functions.

Susan Boykin is a basketmaker who did not give me specific details on how she uses her Compaq Deskpro 2, but did tell me about some of the problems she encountered when she went shopping for a system. Those remarks appear later in this chapter.

Mary King works a full-time job and runs a small crafts design business as well. She uses her Tandy Color Computer 2 for all

---

Computers Do NOT Cut Paperwork

"A computer generates paperwork at a speed and in a quantity never before possible," says James Colwell, a veteran of 18 years in the office products industry. *"Through the magic of semantics the Great Lie is revealed as a self-fulfilling prophecy: a computer always cuts paperwork, since it is no longer called paperwork. Now it is known as hard copy. And the fact that it is printed on paper is merely coincidental.*

"Computers store information on magnetic media, not paper. Thus through another example of semantic sleight-of-hand, computers do, indeed, reduce paperwork. That the paper is replaced by tape or discs — which must themselves be handled, filed, and stored — is easily overlooked."

Colwell added that what computers do save is time. But the more time saved, the more work done, which only means more paper (discs, etc.)

— from an article by Colwell in the Chicago Sun-Times

Notes

Are You Computerphobic?

According to one survey, 30% of the population is computerphobic, according to Mark Fuerst & Sanford Winberg, authors of Computer Phobia, *(Banbury Books, 1984).*

"These people manifest varying degrees of anxiety, from simple dislike of the machines to, in the severest cases, nausea, fainting, high blood pressure, dizziness, or chills when forced to deal with computers," the authors maintain.

Notes

her letter writing, income and disbursements, and designing: "I'm happy with my setup, but I don't have the amount of time to spend on it that I would like," she says.

Arlene Biales manufactures and sells functional quilted accessories, and she uses her Commodore 64 to manage her mailing list and handle general word processing functions, including some article writing.

The foregoing information has given you a good idea of how homebased businesses in the writing, publishing, and crafts industries use a computer for business. Now let me tell you how six individuals in other fields have put the computer to work for them.

Carol Moore and her husband, Rich, manage condominiums, requiring financial reports, management reports, budget projections, capital reserve schedules, and so on. "These are infinitely easier on the computer," says Carol. "It adds up all the columns, brings balances forward, etc. It also gives us a printout that looks professional, and professionalism is the word in this competitive market. When we bid on a new condo job and present our very professional package — done on our IBM PC-XT computer — we usually get the job. Rich discovered he can do a monthly update on a financial report in about fifteen minutes, rather than the two hours it used to take when figured on a calculator and typed."

As a psychologist in private practice, Dr. Julie Ann Allender uses her AT&T 6300 equipment to make her own forms and receipts, plus handle all her secretarial and recordkeeping needs. In addition, she maintains a mailing list and database related to her profession.

Liz DeCleene, who sells herbal-related items by mail and is also beginning to write articles and columns about the use of herbs, seems most grateful to the computer for freeing her from the restrictions of the typewriter, which always locked in creativity, she says. She uses her Apple II for writing, list management, and the preparation of printed pamphlets, newsletters, and price lists.

Lynn Ocken, whose earlier activity as a producing craftswoman eventually led her into the publishing of special reports for organizers of home boutiques, has recently branched out into teaching, consulting, and the management of art workshops for a local gallery. She uses her IBM PC for writing, accounting, and organizing information.

That brings me to Lu Anne Ruttenberg and Susan Anderson, both of whom are computer specialists. For the consulting end of her business, Lu Anne uses her Zenith Z-150 and Z-160 computers to keep track of the different brands of hardware and software she may recommend to her clients. "I can sort on the type of software, for instance, and list out all the packages for word processing and the functions they offer. Or I can list out all the IBM compatibles and their included features. I also use my database program to maintain my client file and do my bookkeeping."

Susan, as you recall, set up the computer for her husband's dental business before getting involved in her own homebased computer consulting business (a direct result of all that learning experience). She uses the IBM PC-XT to do accounts payable, manage mailing lists of patients, do graphs and charts, handle payroll, accounting, checkbook records, prepare tax returns, make signs and posters, and much more.

Perhaps I should emphasize, for the benefit of the computer novices in my readership, that the computer by itself is useless without the right software (programs) to do the work. For more information on the specific software used by some of the business owners I've

How to Determine Your Computer Needs
Advice from Janet Attard
Writer/Editor

After gathering information about what a microcomputer can do, as prospective purchaser you should make a list of all the jobs you'd like a microcomputer to do for you. Keep a notebook near your work area and jot down the different tasks you do each day. Keep adding entries to the list for at least a month to be sure to include all the jobs you're likely to do frequently. Try to include descriptions of all the steps necessary to complete each task.

The purpose of this list is to get a complete picture of what you want the computer to do and how you want it to do your work. The more details you know about how information is used and processed in your business, the better are your chances of getting the right computer system for your needs.

For instance, do you need a word processing program simply to type short letters and memos, or do you need one which will allow you to boldface words for emphasis, change margins frequently, print out your work in columns (like a newsletter) or perhaps add up columns of figures within a document or report you are typing? Will you just use your customers' names and addresses to print mailing labels, or will you want to use your customer list to print personalized letters, to prepare invoices, or to track sales? Will spreadsheets you prepare have to be inserted into typed reports? Will you require any special printing features such as the ability to print Greek or other alphabets, footnotes, page headings, etc.?

You should also try to estimate how much information the computer system will have to process and store. For instance, how many names are on your mailing list? What is the longest document or report you're likely to type, etc.?

Use your list of what you want the computer to do to help you determine which software programs you'll need. (A good reference guide is Alfred Glossbrenner's *How to Buy Software*, [St. Martin's Press, 1984].) When you look at software programs, try to find out what other programs they will work with. For instance, can the word processing program you like read files created by the database or spreadsheet program you want? Also note what brands of computer the programs run on, how much computer memory (RAM) the programs require, and whether or not a hard disk is recommended.

As for memory and storage space, my advice is this: if you will be using the computer for several different tasks, have a large number of customers (or expect to have), or if you prepare lengthy typed documents (such as a book), buy as much memory and as much storage space as you can afford. Minimum memory I'd recommend is 256K (640K is desirable); minimum storage space for efficient business use is two, 320K floppy drives. However, one floppy and at least a 10-meg or 20-meg hard drive would be better for businesses that plan to do many tasks or have large volumes of information they want to work with on the computer. A lot of the better programs on the market now require a lot of computer memory to function efficiently. As for storage space, it's much more efficient to have the files you work with regularly available on a hard disk, than to have to keep switching floppy disks in and out of your drives.

These illustrations (reduced from their original size of 7½ × 6½ in.) are examples of the designs created by Vicki Powers on her IBM PC computer, using the COLOR PAINT program.

just told you about, see the special chart I've included later in this chapter. Its purpose is to give you an idea of what software does what jobs, and also what software runs on which hardware. By no means is this information complete, however, it merely reflects usage by some of the computer owners in my network. Study available reference guides for more detailed information about the complete capabilities of specific computer programs mentioned.

Hazards of VDT Terminals

Many computer users have reported difficulties with their vision after a long session at a video display terminal (VDT). The most common complaints include blurred vision, itching and burning eyes, eye fatigue, flickering sensations, and double vision.

There is also something known as "The McCollough Effect" — where people who use VDTs with luminous green characters on a dark background see white as pink when they stop working at the screen. Though not dangerous, this aggravating effect may last for hours. (From an article in the New England Journal of Medicine.)

A pamphlet published by the American Optometric Association, St. Louis, MO suggests that eye problems can be greatly relieved merely by taking the following precautions:

1) Properly position the VDT unit and reference materials in such a way that the eyes won't have to change focus when looking from one to the other.

2) Have proper lighting, with windows and sources of bright light shielded and sources of screen reflection eliminated.

3) Take regular breaks every two hours to rest the eyes, and whenever possible during work, look away from the screen.

4) Finally, if you have eye problems of any kind, consult a doctor to have the problem properly diagnosed and treated.

(more . . .)

The Computer's Impact on a Homebased Business

On my computer questionnaire, I naturally asked people to tell me how the computer had impacted their home-business lives. Had it increased their efficiency and productivity, I wondered? Enhanced their business or professional image? Enabled them to increase knowledge or business connections? Cut costs or improve profits? Diversify present businesses or start new ones? What, exactly?

The encouraging and thought-provoking replies indicate that a computer can easily do all these things and more. Regardless of the kind of business owned, most respondents pointed to ways in which the computer had increased efficiency and productivity. As you might suppose, writers, publishers, and others deeply involved in word processing were especially quick to sing the praises of a computer.

"Owning a microcomputer has tremendously increased my productivity and has allowed me to take on jobs that were once too time-consuming to be profitable," says Janet Attard, homebased writer and editor. "Additionally, since I am a fast but sloppy typist, having the computer has greatly enhanced my professional image by allowing me to turn in attractive-looking finished copy to my clients.

"The most recent addition to my computer system — a modem — is proving to be indispensable. Now, instead of having to print out and deliver ad copy, newsletters, and the like to some of my business clients, I send finished copy over the telephone lines directly to their computers. With the modem, I've also been able to tap into commercial networks and local bulletin boards to gather information for some of the articles I write."

Herman Holtz sent similar comments. "The computer has vastly improved the quality of my work, as well as my productivity because it encourages rewriting and revision in many ways. I now do far more rewriting than ever, and that is nearly 100% of the secret of quality writing for most professional writers. Talent helps and an 'ear' for language is a great asset, but it is almost impossible to write well; most of us *rewrite* well."

Like Janet, Herman also uses a modem, which he says opened a new dimension for him. "Through computer-to-computer communication via my modem and telephone, I can now do research without leaving my desk. I am in regular touch with others via electronic bulletin boards."

As a book packager-agent-writer, Elyse Sommer finds that the computer has not only saved her time, but cut down on expenses for typing, copy editing, manuscript styling, and indexing. "My computer has also provided some unanticipated benefits: I was able to use my word processor to make illustrative charts for a crafts book (a tremendous aid for my illustrator). By hooking a modem to my computer, I've also been able to instantly transmit material, do research without leaving home, and make business contacts via electronic bulletin boards.''

Elyse adds that her office, while still not paperless, is much more so, a comment several people made to me. "The computer has helped me sharpen my business correspondence and get my desk organized,'' says Marion Boyer, co-owner of Village Vendor, a crafts party plan business. "Now, with records on neat little disks, I just call up what I need instead of fussing through files of papers.''

If computers do not always increase profits, they almost always lead to cost savings while also increasing the professional image of a business. "Thanks to the computer in my husband's dental office,'' says Susan Anderson, "patients know they are dealing with a business that expects payment, instead of 'kindly old Dr. Anderson' who can wait. The computer has enabled us to begin charging a finance charge on late payments, which partially pays for the computer and improves cash flow. In addition, the computers have stopped a number of costly accounting errors and enabled us to bill more accurately.''

"The computer enabled us to make up a small catalog for our customers,'' says Johnnie Kearnery, owner of a crafts business. "The cost is minimal, yet it looks neat and business-like and can be produced quickly. If items or prices change, it is easy to make corrections and print the necessary sheets. Putting our financial information in the computer also makes tax time easier. Records are more accurate, which saves time for the accountant and automatically lessens the size of our bill.''

Bobbie Irwin, the weaver who refuses to love her computer, admits that her professional image has been enhanced by the good-looking copy the printer turns out. "It types a whole lot better than I do,'' she says. "This has been especially important in preparing manuscripts for publication, and for anyone whose business involves a lot of writing. I highly recommend a computer.''

One of the things the computer does best, of course, is speed up a lot of routine jobs, which is automatically beneficial to any business. "In the press of a key I can find out how this month's sales compare with the same month last year,'' says Charlene Anderson-Shea. "It is also a snap to find out what percentage of the budget I have spent on advertising, for example. In short, it has freed up my time to devote to designing or weaving, not paperwork. It did require a substantial investment of both time and money, but I feel it was worth it.''

Eileen MacIntosh enthusiastically agrees. "In retrospect,'' she says, "I should have had a computer from the moment I went into business. I'm certain that the customers I lost, or didn't get in the first place, were far more expensive than what the computer cost me. The work overload is what keeps many homebased businesses small. The computer can handle that, and enable a one-person business to be much larger than before.

"My computer handles all the things I hate (bookkeeping, mailing lists, form letters, general files and paperwork). This leaves me the time (and peace of mind) to focus on the more creative aspects of my business. I hate the busywork but I love the money — and the computer cuts down on the busywork, lets me get more done in my workday, so I can make more money. I like that.''

You've already heard many references to the value of a computer when used to manage a mailing list. Being able to match a segment

(. . . more)

The radiation emitted by VDTs may cause birth defects among pregnant users, according to a study by the Swedish Occupational Health and Safety Administration.

To combat this problem, a shield called "Eye-Guard" has been developed to block the harmful radiation that is believed by some scientists to be released from the computer terminal. The screen is attached to a terminal by using Velcro tabs.

One authority has pointed out that the first true study of the effect on human beings has not yet been completed, and results won't be known for 20 years or more.

Eye-Guard is manufactured by Langley-St. Clair Instrumentation Systems, Inc., New York.

Notes

(more on page 260 . . .)

Tips on Computerizing Your Mail List

The first rule is that you can only get out of your computer what you put into it.

Putting in only address information means you are limited in the ways you can get your names out: by zip code order for bulk mailings, by city or state, last name of individual, and so on. But the addition of special "fields" can reflect a world of additional information that can help you study, analyze, and understand your business. Your database software guide will explain field structures to you, but here are a couple of things that have proven useful to me in managing my own lists totaling more than 25,000 names.

Each address includes an "entry-date" field with a three letter code such as 873, 882, 891, etc., which tells me that names have been entered, respectively, in the third quarter of 1987, the second quarter of 1988, the first quarter of 1989, etc. Even when thousands of names are mixed together, I can easily pull out names from a certain quarter of a certain year for remailing purposes. Keeping track of which segments of a list have been mailed and cleaned is important, and this helps a lot.

I also include a "code" field which tells me the source of all names, whether from specific publications, general publicity, reader referrals, directories, and so on. I then maintain a master list that explains all codes because memory often fails. When I find that names from certain sources are proving worthless for remailing purposes, it's very easy to sort on this code field and "zap" names with a single command.

I also use a "daycode" field, which is particularly useful when adding new names to an existing database. By adding a single letter

of your customer list to a special mailing or sales promotion is a valuable business aid. But having detailed customer information is beneficial in other ways as well. Take Ursula Sarli, for instance. She sells educational toys and books through home parties, and naturally uses the computer to keep tabs on inventory levels. "It's also important for me to know who bought which toy in the event there's a recall on a particular toy. In an instant I can get a list of everyone who has purchased it."

Even if you decide not to computerize your list for rental, it can prove to be useful to other business owners who will exchange lists with you. Says E. S. Matz: "With mailing list capabilities, I am able to exchange valuable mailing lists with other businesses who deal with my target audiences. Not only do I get a good mailing list, but I get them for the cost of a few computer labels."

How Computers Spark New Business Ideas

Clearly the computer has enabled many creative-thinking individuals to expand existing businesses or start new ones. Here are several examples of how this can happen.

Tired of manually preparing family menus each week, Mary J. Reese and her sister-in-law, Georgianne Bender, turned a home computer into a moneymaking machine. The resulting business, Menu Magic, answers the dreaded question: "What's for dinner tonight, honey?" The menu packets they now sell by mail are almost certain to lead to ideas for related products, and I'll bet the computer will play a role in their development.

Johnnie Kearnery was able to expand her craft business, Richlou Crafts, by offering mail list services to local fraternal organizations. "They are pleased with our work because we are accurate and meet our deadlines," she says.

Joyce Jackson, an image consultant, says the computer changed the entire focus of her business, while also giving her more time and a more professional output. "My entire business, Ultimate Image, Inc., is now based on the software I developed for the image industry," she says.

Ed Simpson diversified his periodical publishing business first by writing a book on how to make money with the computer, then by teaching himself to program. "I now have a programming contract," he says, adding that he's always finding new jobs the computer can do.

Linda Gibbs says the computer has enabled her to start a typing service which supplements the family income. "This means I don't have to look for a job outside the home," she says. "I type when I want to, and only advertise when I want business."

Lu Anne Ruttenberg began consulting when she realized how many businesses needed the kind of information she had acquired. "I was also aggravated by the misinformation being given to my clients by too many inexperienced salespeople," she says. "This is now leading me into writing guides on purchasing software and hardware." When a community college asked Lu Anne to present a workshop on making money at home with a computer, this turned her in yet another new direction. "I continue to investigate other possibilities because I don't want my business to get stale," she adds.

Certainly more than one computer novice has traveled a similar route, even people who once shied away from the idea of computers. As Elyse Sommer explains, "Like many former 'machine-phobic' computer users, I've gone completely the other way and become something of an expert. This in turn has brought new business opportunities, such as a computer book assignment and the opportunity to develop training manuals and promotional booklets for several corporate clients."

Like Elyse, E. S. Matz has moved into the area of special services. This year she plans to add a modem to her computer to pick up long-distance typesetting business.

One more example: When the Sarli family bought an Apple computer for their children, Ursula ended up using it for her home party business. Lacking business software, however, she asked husband Jim to write the needed programs. They eventually switched to an IBM PC, and Jim (who had a computer background to begin with) is now building systems for others. "So now we both have homebased businesses," says Ursula.

When Janet Hansen started a homebased mailorder business a few years ago, she had to wade through a bunch of "red tape" like other beginners — from business research to financial matters, to supply sources, and so on.

In time she came to see the humor of all the things that had happened to her, and this gave her the idea for a cartoon book based on her business experiences. At first, she planned to hire a cartoonist to develop her ideas, but when she started to play around with her Apple Macintosh MacPaint program to create some rough sketches for the cartoonist, she was surprised to find how well her drawings turned out. Family and friends encouraged her to illustrate her own book (which she also published), and that hooked her.

"I can hardly walk by the computer without sitting down to add more detail to an already-completed cartoon, or to create a new one," she says.

The computer caused a complete turnaround in Janet's business. She discontinued her t-shirt, apron, and tote bag business and began selling the cartoon book. The book led Janet to establish a product line of over a hundred homebased and small business books and magazines. She then used her Macintosh computer, along with the MacWrite and MacPaint programs to create a 32-page catalog.

↑ Above, a sample page from the 5½ × 8½ in. 12-page catalog created by Sidney Brand, owner of In Stitches, a needlework design company now about five years old.

The catalog features patterns of historic southern houses, among other designs, and promotes the availability of Sidney's custom design services.

"I'm not satisfied with the computer software available," she says, "but I have become enamored with the graphics capability of my Compaq portable computer."

Sidney uses Newsroom to create her original house drawings, and Printmaster to do borders. Both programs have clip art (Newsroom is easier to change, Sidney says), and Printmaster is set up to do calendars, greeting cards, signs, etc. Both programs are IBM compatible and cost about $50.

(. . . more from page 258)

code in this field as I enter new addresses each day, I can easily copy those names to a temporary file for use in printing the day's mailing labels. Then I use a command to remove this temporary letter code from the permanent database, and I'm all set for the next day's input. Or, if I want to go through a database, editing names one by one, and marking certain ones for pull-out later, this daycode field works beautifully.

Finally, if you plan to rent your list, the more information you can offer renters, the better. For example, you may wish to indicate an individual's sex, for promotions targeted to either men or women only. Certainly list buyers will want to know size of average order, which means you'll have to add fields that include order entry information and dollar amounts. Above all, make sure your list is up to date before renting. A list that's only a year old could already be 30% out of date.

Entering a large mailing list on a computer is a time-consuming process, so think things through before you begin. It will take even longer to accomplish the job if you have to go back and make adjustments to data already entered.

Notes

"The computer has saved me lots of money with regard to typesetting and graphic artists," Janet says.

See page 259 for a sample illustration from Janet's book, *So You Want to Start Your Own Business*. (Reprinted by permission.)

How Computers Change the Personal Lives of Users

Since there is often no real separation between "home" and "home business," it's natural to assume that a computer used for business will also affect the personal lives of its users, even if it isn't used for games and other personal activities. But how, I wondered, as I mailed my computer questionnaire. The delightful answers I got only serve to emphasize why you should consider the purchase of a computer for yourself or your homebased business.

There was great evidence of how the computer affected one's feelings of self worth and confidence. Marion Boyer said it especially well: "I have this feeling that I am hedging against the aging process. I think one way to feel like you are not growing old is to keep up with current technology. I have two sons, one in middle school. When he talks ROM and RAM, I at least know they aren't obscure mythical beasts in the *Odyssey* that I have forgotten. In fact, I have conquered my own mythical beast by learning how to use this machine to do me some good, and that is a major confidence-builder for me. It means the brain cells will still accept new concepts and skills, and that's pretty exciting for the entrepreneurial housewife."

Elyse Sommer adds, "The computer has cured me of a lifetime sense of inadequacy vis-a-vis machines and anything too mathematical. You see, it took only the initial leap of faith to make me realize that a computer is only as smart as what I put into it. And it took only a smidgeon longer to realize that you tame your computer with logic and not math skills. Naturally, fine-tuning your logical skills to solve computer problems carries over to everything else you do in life."

Another strong testimonial for the computer comes from Susan Anderson, who says: "I never realized how much I could teach myself and how proficient I could become in a subject all on my own. Two years ago I was just a housewife. Now I converse with university-trained programmers and systems people who are amazed by how much I've been able to do and learn. If anyone had told me I could do all this without going back to college, I would have thought them crazy. I did this because I just *had* to. The computer at my husband's office wasn't working, and someone had to figure out why. I just read, studied, experimented, tried, failed, and eventually succeeded. My newest computer system came to me unassembled, but I wasn't even concerned. I knew I could build it, one way or another."

Comments from several individuals indicate that the computer has a way of unlocking creativity and ideas in people. For example, you've read about Janet Hansen's computer cartoon book on an earlier page, but what you should also know is that Janet had always wanted to be an artist when she was young. Due to her family's financial situation, however, she wasn't able to pursue this. In playing around with her Macintosh computer, she has discovered her creative streak and been able to fulfill a secret desire. But there's even more. As Janet says, "The computer seems to have released my sense of humor.

For years I have suffered through going to movies with other people who always laugh out loud at funny situations while I merely sat and smiled. Now, at movies, I find myself laughing along with the others."

Liz DeCleene's experience adds further evidence of how the computer stimulates the creative instinct. "When I took typing, the grace of God gave me a grade of D," she says. "My mind and fingers just don't seem to function at the same speed. Add terrible spelling to that and you have a real writing problem. I didn't realize, until after I got the computer, that all sorts of ideas were waiting to emerge on paper, but my typing problem was keeping them locked in. The word processor thus was the key to my writing. Now I can design catalogs, write newsletters, and compose columns. My new problem is that I can't find the time to write all the things I want."

Two computer owners told me how their computer purchase had dramatically changed the whole household. Lynn Ocken, for example, agreed to give up her formal living room so the dining room could be moved into that position, thereby freeing up the old dining room space for a new "office, computer, and quiet room." But what I didn't know at the time," says Lynn, "was that our original $3,000 computer would end up costing us almost $10,000 because of all the redecorating and furniture purchases prompted by this rearrangement of our home."

And Jeannie Spears says she can't lay all the blame on the computer's keyboard, "but it set into motion a lot of lifestyle changes, including selling our five-bedroom house and renting a townhouse, freeing us to do more traveling and spend time on things we enjoy." Jeannie also said that her husband, in looking for an activity to replace Barbershop singing, began to play around with the computer. "It is now his best friend, and he delights in teaching it new tricks," Jeannie says. "One of these days he may even accomplish something wonderful with it, like a new program or a definitive book on some subject."

Often, the whole family is affected by the purchase of a computer. Ursula Sarli says her family life has changed in that it has prompted more family fights. "My husband and I fight for its use before the six- and eight-year olds get home from school; then it's their turn to be on it. In the morning before she goes off to preschool, our three-year-old constantly begs to use it. I'm sure we'll soon be buying a second computer — one for us and one for the children."

Others talked about children's involvement with the computer. About her five-year-old granddaughter, E. S. Matz says, "She can zip through simple programs quicker than an adult. By the time she's ten, we figure we'll have another computer operator for our homebased business."

Susan Anderson's children are already on the payroll, helping her with data entry and printing. "My hope is that the children will gain practical business experience and good work habits." "Also," she says, "the business enables us to give income to the children which would otherwise be taxable at a much higher rate."

And now . . . the answer to one of my **BIG** questions: Does a computer save enough time to allow for more housecleaning (especially since computer equipment doesn't take too kindly to dust)? The answers were a unanimous NO!

"I just bought dust covers," said Grace Schmidgall, Linda Gibbs, Ramona Wickstrom, and several others. "Let's just say my computer makes me enough money so I can hire someone else to do my clean-

(continued on page 266)

---

*Basic Computer Terms
You Should Know*

Hardware. *The computer itself.*
Software. *Programs or instructions that tell the computer what to do.*
CPU. *Central Processing Unit — the "heart" of the computer.*
RAM. *Random Access Memory. (Volatile user memory in computer.)*
ROM. *Read Only Memory. (Non-volatile memory containing programs related to computer's operation.)*
Mass Storage. *Where stored data in RAM goes when computer is turned off: either to a (1) floppy disk, or (2) hard disk.*
Floppy Disk. *Thin, flat, mylar disk that stores digital information.*
Disk Drive. *A mechanical device that rotates the floppy disk for accessing information.*
DOS. *Disk Operating System.*
Hard Disk. *Similar to floppy disk, but offers faster access time and greater storage capacity; also rotates inside a sealed enclosure.*
Ports. *What peripherals are connected to.*
Interfaces. *(Serial and Parallel). Connectors between peripheral devices and the computer.*
Peripherals. *Computer hardware devices that include keyboards, hard disk drives, display terminals, printers, etc.*
Modem. *A connector between computer and telephone which enables transmission of data over phone lines.*
Cards *or* **Boards.** *Electronic circuit boards inside the computer which can alter or increase computer's flexibility or capabilities.*

Notes

Desktop Publishing
A Brief Look at an Amazing Phenomenon

The hottest words in today's computer industry are "Desktop Publishing," and it seems everyone wants to get into the act.

Software originally designed for the creation of advertising flyers, brochures, catalogs, and corporate newsletters has opened up exciting new areas of personal expression for many individuals. They are using this business software not only to make greeting cards, signs, and posters, but to publish newsletters, books, and other printed materials.

Seeing this great interest in the computer as a printing/publishing tool, manufacturers of both hardware and software naturally responded by offering special printing and graphic aids programs for desktop computers — thus giving birth to the phrase "desktop publishing."

Now, small business owners everywhere are jumping into the publishing industry with their own newsletters, newspapers, books, directories, special reports, and other publications. (Not surprisingly, many are computer-oriented in one way or another.) The quality of all this printed material ranges from really awful to absolutely dazzling. As one writer puts it, even the best desktop publishing software and laser printer cannot make up for an individual's lack of graphic design skill.

If you can't afford an Apple Macintosh computer and Apple LaserWriter printer (currently considered state-of-the-art equipment), don't be discouraged. Desktop publishing software is now available to PC users as well, and laser printers are becoming more affordable all the time.

In addition, new versions of word processing software such as *WordPerfect* and *WordStar* offer many of the benefits of page makeup software with a lot less hassle and easier learning curve than popular desktop programs such as *PageMaker* and *Ventura*. Depending on your needs, you may find this a more affordable solution to your publishing situation.

Stay informed about computers and software for desktop publishing by reading current computer magazines such as *PC Publishing, Desktop Publishing,* and *Home Office Computing.* This "infant industry" — called a "personal publishing revolution" by some — is coming of age!

Computer Systems Used by Some Homebased Business Owners
(And How They Grew)

Name of User	Business Description	Initial System	How Upgraded	Reason for Change
Janet Attard	Writer of articles & books; copywriter (PR releases, newsletters, etc.)	Sanyo 1000, 64K memory; 1 floppy disk; letter-quality printer & modem	Added Apple IIc with 128k memory. (Will soon add IBM PC-XT clone with 20 Mb hard disk.)	"I plan to keep my original equipment. However, I need more storage space and memory for programs."
Arlene Biales	Manufactures & sells quilting fabric accessories	Radio Shack, 16k memory	Commodore 64; 64k memory	"I needed more flexibility."
Marion Boyer	Markets handcrafted gifts through home parties	Apple IIe, 64k memory, 1 floppy disk drive	Increased RAM to 128k; added another disk drive & Grafstar dot matrix printer	"Needed more memory."
Liz DeCleene	Sells herbal products by mail; writes articles	Apple II, 48k memory; Epson dot matrix printer	Expanded RAM to 120k	"Needed more memory."
Tom Ellison	Book publisher; mail order catalog	Macintosh 128k; 2 floppy drives and Image Writer printer	Increased RAM to 512k and added 20 Mb hard disk	"Equipment quickly becomes obsolete in this game."
Lorice O'Keefe	Networking/marketing service for businesswomen	IBM PC, 64k; Epson dot matrix printer	Increased RAM to 640k plus new printer with paper feed	"Needed more memory and flexibility."
E. S. Matz	Publishes books & newsletters; sells typesetting service	Apple IIe (rented for one year prior to purchase of Apple IIe with 64k; Image Writer printer	Kept Apple equipment; also bought a Macintosh Desktop Publishing package with 512k memory and 20 Mb hard disk; also Laser Writer Plus printer	"I purchased the Mac for its typesetting capabilities; useful for publishing and also to sell as a service."
Lu Anne Rutenberg	Custom programming and consulting	Zenith Z-90, 64k; Two floppy drives; dot matrix printer	Zenith Z-150 (1 floppy drive plus 10 Mb hard disk); and Zenith Z-160 with 2 floppy drives	"Needed IBM-compatible equipment so I could work at my office and bring programs to my customers on disks."
Ursula Sarli	Sells educational toys and books through home parties	Apple IIe, 128k, with Epson letter quality printer	IBM PC/XT-Compatible with 640k and hard disk; plus IBM graphics printer	"Not enough memory or software to support my needs."
Grace Schmidgall	Farming; real estate sales	Tandy 1000, 128k with dot matrix printer	Expanded RAM to 640k	"Added memory because I had one software program that required it."
Ed Simpson	Periodical publisher, author, computer programmer	TRS-80, Model III, 64k	IBM-XT, 640k with 20Mb hard disk; and Tandy 2000, 128k; plus 2 new printers	"First computer became outdated; needed faster, higher capacity."

Author's Note: The above chart shows a pattern that I suspect is typical of many first-time computer buyers. Granted, this is merely a sampling of information from a random selection of computer owners in my network, but you can easily see that the "problem" encountered by most of them was that they failed in the beginning to buy a computer with sufficient memory (RAM storage space) for their business needs. Also, when additional memory was purchased, several users upgraded their system with better printers and extra floppy or hard disk drives.

A Software Sampler
How Some Homebased Business Owners Are Using Certain Programs

Author's Note: Applications reported by these users are not necessarily a true indication of the complete capabilities of any program, merely a guide for computer novices. See the *Whole Earth Software Catalog* (listed in the Resource Chapter) for more detailed information on this topic. The information on software-hardware compatibility is based both on replies given to author's questionnaire, as well as on information in the above book and, again, is included merely as a guide. You should double check the accuracy of this information before making a purchase.

Name of Software And Some of the Hardware It Runs On (If known)	Software Application Mentioned by Readers — Plus Any Special Comments They Made
APPLEWORKS* Runs on Apple Computers	Word processing and spreadsheets; mailing lists; general recordkeeping. "Does everything I need, from writing to mailing lists," says Eileen MacIntosh. "Great for word processing and file keeping," adds Charlene Anderson-Shea.
DATASTAR	Word processing, database management. Says E. S. Matz: "The word processing program is my 'intelligent typewriter,' which I use for manuscript preparation, business letters, etc. The database program allows me to design forms, create customer and general business records, store research material, and more."
DBASE II* Runs on Apple computers, IBM PC/XT compatibles, most CP/M machines	General data management program. Lu Anne Ruttenberg says: "The quick indexing functions and advanced commands enable me to design and write everything from simple maintenance programs to complex accounting systems." Says Bobbie Irwin: "I use it whenever I need to make lists and categorize data, including mailing lists and inventory control." Adds Dr. Julie Allender: "It took me 20 hours to learn the basics of this program, only to discover that it was going to be too complicated for my needs at this point in time."
DOLLARS AND SENSE* Runs on Apple II family computers; IBM PC compatibles	A personal finances package. Says Charlene Anderson-Shea: "I use this program to keep both my personal and business finances in order. It is easy to learn (as compared to HOME ACCOUNTANT, which I found to be slow, not very versatile, and difficult to learn)."
LOTUS 1-2-3* Runs on IBM compatibles	An integrated spreadsheet/database/graphics program. Says Carol Moore: "When we got this program, we discovered efficiency." Adds Susan Anderson: "This is my most versatile and most-often-used program."
NEWSROOM	Sidney Brand uses this program to create scratch drawings of houses (see illustration elsewhere in this chapter). Says Susan Anderson, however: "I have used this program to make newsletters with graphics, but it takes more time than the finished product is worth. Fun to use for hobby purposes, but not for business use."

THE PRINT SHOP	A graphics program useful for making sales flyers, signs, newsletter illustrations, etc. (See illustration elsewhere in this chapter for a sample invitation created by Ursula Sarli with this program and her Apple computer.) Susan Anderson says, "Really fun!" Adds Marion Boyer: "I love using this software package to make flyers and many times they have served our purposes well enough for the situation and haven't cost us the major price of typesetting or the tedium of working with press-on lettering."
PERFECT FILER Runs on Kaypro computers	Says Jeannie Spears: "I used this database system to keep track of the subscriptions for the magazine. It was easy to use and stored a lot of names in a small space, but it also had some major drawbacks, among them not finding duplications automatically and being difficult to learn."
SPELLBINDER Runs on IBM PC compatibles	Word processing/mail list management program. Says Lorice O'Keefe: "I run my entire office/business singlehandedly using this system. I can update, edit, change, and revise any type of document and store to disk. I can use the system to mail merge; that is, personalize letters in any way I want using a prepared mailing list which can also be manipulated according to various parameters, like alphabetizing, pulling info out according to a set parameter, like numbers paid, or only men or only women from the list. A very flexible and easy-to-use program which does not require memorizing a whole lot of Control Keys."
THINKTANK* Runs on Apple II family, IBM PC/ XT compatibles	"Thinktank is great for brainstorming and making difficult decisions," says Tom Ellison. "Also good for simple project management."
PFS:FILE & PFS:REPORT* Runs on Apple II computers & IBM PCjr & PC/XT compatibles	Data management program. Says Charlene Anderson-Shea: "These programs allow you to set up your database any way you want or need." Says Joyce Jackson: "I use this program to organize and pull specific material."
WORDSTAR* Runs on CP/M machines; IBM PC compatibles	The old standard, now-controversial word processing program. Says Jeannie Spears: "I learned this program and found it had some major advantages. The biggest disadvantage was lack of proportional spacing. I finally found PROPSTAR, which works with WORDSTAR, and gave me even better proportional spacing than did PERFECT WRITER." Says Janet Attard: "This program does most word processing chores I require. There are probably better programs on the market now; however, even when I buy another computer I will get WORDSTAR because many of my clients are set up to receive WORDSTAR files over the modem." Dr. Julie Allender says: "I have found this program to have too many complicated and difficult bugs in it. We are now switching over to WORD PERFECT and expect we will not have to waste so much time just trying to get a program to work."

*These programs were among those recommended in the *Whole Earth Software Catalog* mentioned above.

*from computer owners mentioned in this chapter.

Tips on Buying a Computer*

- *Buy for expandability features and range of software choices.*

- *Don't buy short — purchase as much as you can imagine needing.*

- *Talk with a high-school whiz kid about what computers can do. Take a course in computers before you buy. Read computer magazines to become computer literate.*

- *Find out what the end cost will be. Some ads don't include cards needed for printers, modems, monitors, etc. This can greatly inflate price.*

- *Choose software before hardware. Even though IBM is the current "business standard," there may be some programs you need for your business that won't run on IBM.*

- *Programs keep getting better and easier to use, and prices keep dropping, too. Therefore, if you don't need a particular application now, don't buy now. Wait as long as possible; you'll be glad you did.*

- *Be sure the dealer you buy from services your equipment, so you don't have to send it away for repairs.*

- *Never buy a computer unless computer documentation is available at the time of purchase. If a salesman says it's out of stock, or will be available soon — wait 'til it is.*

- *Don't rely on the instruction manuals which come with the computer. Some are virtually impossible to understand. There are good, independently published books which may be more helpful.*

ing," says Lu Anne Ruttenberg. Adds Susan Anderson, "One of my new clients is a housecleaning service. I may end up trading my services for hers." Ramona concludes: "If you didn't dust before, you won't dust now."

Personally, I was partial to this comment by E. S. Matz: "I have a rule: business before housework. I can stand a messy house more than I can stand unfinished business and grouchy customers."

What You Should Know Before You Buy

In the short time left to us, we can't answer all the questions computer novices are likely to have. But let's come back for a little networking session along the lines of "What I know now that I wish I'd known then." Who wants to begin?

Lorice O'Keefe: "I know now that you don't just pop a program disk into the machine and flick a switch. I've learned a lot about evaluating the user-friendliness of programs and insisting on returning if it does not do what is claimed. It's important to remember that the computer is only as good as the person programming it, and that expensive hardware is worthless if the software won't work on it or is not designed to do the job. One reason I bought an IBM PC was because I knew that most of the software would be written compatible for it, rather than some other system."

Lu Anne Ruttenberg: "IBM does set the standards, and I didn't consider the fact that my market was IBM-oriented. There was no market for services built around the Zenith Z-90 computer I originally bought."

Ursula Sarli: "As you may recall, we first bought an Apple II, not realizing that IBM-compatibles run 95% of IBM programs, yet are the same cost of an Apple computer. And, IBM has a lot more business application software than Apple, as well as an 'honesty program.' They encourage you to copy software, and if you use it and like it, then you pay for it."

You're apparently talking about public domain programs — known as "shareware." I understand they're now available for most computers.

Deborah Robinson: "That's right. Public domain software is around at considerably lower prices than commercial programs. You can get these by writing to a computer user's group or by looking through the ad section in some of the computer magazines for cooperatives that offer public domain programs for various computers, often for very reasonable prices, like $5 per program."

Ursula Sarli: "I've generally paid between $25–$50 for the business software I've obtained in this way. Shareware is a wonderful breakthrough for the industry. I can't tell you how many programs I originally bought, only to find they didn't do what I wanted."

User's groups have been mentioned . . . but how do you find these groups? And are they really valuable?

Jeannie Spears: "I think they're the most valuable resource and teaching tool you can find. If a dealer won't or can't give you information on the local groups, be careful. It may mean he doesn't have good relationships with purchasers after they walk away with their machines. Most users' groups maintain public domain libraries and will share programs for the cost of the disks. Many of the utility programs I use every day were obtained in this manner.''

Janet Attard: "I think it should be emphasized that a users' group, technically, is a group of people who use one particular brand of computer hardware. If you can find a local group, try to attend a few meetings before you buy your computer system. There may be a question-and-answer period in which you can describe the kinds of tasks you want the computer to do and ask for suggestions about the best software to meet your needs.''

How about dealer support? Has this been a problem for any of you?

Margaret Boyd: "My dealer went out of business! I lost out on a lot of instruction there.''

Janet Attard: "You should try to buy from a dealer who has been in business a few years, and from a salesperson who is knowledgeable about computers and your line of business. Try to buy everything from one dealer and have the dealer set it all up and test it out to see that the components (parts of the system) work properly before you bring them to your home office. Then find out if there is a hotline number you can call when you need help, and where you'd have to bring the computer system if it should later need repairs.''

Susan Anderson: "Even if dealers stay in business, they do not always have the expertise they promise. The computer sold to me as being sufficient for my needs was never large enough. The prices were inflated and I paid a lot for dealer support that never materialized.''

Tom Ellison: "That's another reason why computer owners should join user's groups.''

Reputable and reliable dealers are well and good, but the best of them may still have poor salespeople, right? My first shopping experience was quite educational in that it served to warn me to salesman-pitfalls. How do most of you feel about computer salespeople?

Lorice O'Keefe: "It is my belief that computer salespeople will tell you anything you want to hear. And once the package is yours, they don't provide much help.''

Susan Anderson: "I found salespeople telling me bold lies. I also recall asking my computer salesman about the cost of supplies and other things I'd need to keep the system running. His reply was, 'Well, a box of paper and ten floppy disks ought to do it.' For that first computer, I now have over 200 floppy disks alone, plus boxes of different kinds of forms, papers, and stationery.''

Some of you have probably heard the popular computer joke about the difference between a computer salesman and a used car salesman. The answer is that the car salesman knows when he is lying to you.

Susan Boykin: "I believe that. Just because a salesperson knows how the computer operates doesn't mean he or she can help you buy what you need. I once taught sewing, and watched salespeople put those machines through their paces. But they couldn't have made a garment if their lives depended on it. When the men made the

---

Don't Trust Your Computer's Memory

All information on both floppy disks and hard disk drives should be backed up regularly. Make copies of everything and put them somewhere for safe keeping. If electrical power should fail during use of your computer, you could lose masses of information in RAM.

Bobbie Irwin says, "A surge protector will guard against power surges, but it won't do a bit of good if the power goes off while the computer is on."

Janet Attard adds: "To prevent the accidental loss of crucial data, all important information on your hard disk should be backed up regularly with some kind of backup system — either tape or cartridge. How often 'regularly' is depends on your individual business. If you make changes to your customer list or accounts receivable files daily, then you should back up your hard disk every day. While you can copy important files onto floppy disks and use the floppies for backup, if your accounting, customer lists or other essential files are long, copying them onto floppies is a tedious and time-consuming process."

Check computer magazines for the latest information on backup systems that may be right for your needs.

Notes

> *"Contrary to the image of computer users as lonely, isolated workers, I've made many new friends (and not a few business connections) through my computer.*
>
> *"Besides, using a computer is fun. Tasks which once were chores are done with ease and style. If you work from a home office, as I do, you are no longer alone. Flick on a button and you're got a friend at your fingertips."*
>
> — *Elsye Sommer*

Notes

buying decision, they tended to feel the fancier the machine, the 'better' it had to be. Many a woman has thus found herself with a sewing machine that intimidates her. I think the same thing is happening with a lot of computer buyers."

At least the readers of this book have been forewarned, Susan. Thanks to you and all the others who have shared good advice and buying tips, a host of new computer buyers will at least know what questions to ask when they walk into a computer store.

1988 Update

As I review this edition of *Homemade Money,* I am using my Leading Edge computer (with 30 meg. hard disk) and NEC Pinwriter P7 printer to make the job easier. I bought my system in the fall of 1986 immediately after writing this chapter, and it was love at first touch.

Now that I've had the computer for a couple of years, I find it hard to believe I was able to survive in business as long as I did without it. Certainly my work was more stressful then than it is now. The computer has not only made routine work easier and more fun, but has given me enormous peace of mind. It's comforting to know that, each week, I am protecting more and more data. (After entry, I routinely prepare backup floppies which are transferred to a safe deposit box as protection against hard disk failure or loss by fire and other hazards.)

I now use *DBASE III Plus* to manage my growing mail list of more than 25,000 prospect and customer names, and soon will be exploring my options as a list renter. Other special databases include my ever-growing PR list and the resources in all my books. I also use *DBASE III Plus* to do all my business bookkeeping, index my newsletter, and maintain a variety of other information databases.

The Leading Edge software that accompanied my computer has been adequate for all my writing needs to date. (I especially like its logical filing system, which is much like dropping folders into a filing cabinet.) I used this software to create a book I self-published in 1986. Although I had to paste up boards for the printer, the writing job was a snap because of the ease with which I could rewrite or move material in the text.

My newsletter is also created with this software at present, but I'm in the process of switching to *WordPerfect,* which will give me a handy two-column format and more flexibility in general.

While I have a need for genuine desktop publishing capabilities — and may obtain it eventually — I have not yet found the time to think about learning it, nor even decided if I ought to be spending my time doing this type of work. At present, I simply use my Leading Edge software to write new copy, then convert it to ASCII, (a universal language most computer systems can understand), put it on a floppy disk, and send it to a friend for "translation." He drops it into his computer, activates his *PageMaker* software and, voila!, in a few days I have laser-printed, camera-ready copy for my printer with none of the work. I recently created a 16-page catalog this way, and it saved me a lot of grief.

By the way, as much as I love my computer, I find my Adler 1020 electronic typewriter an absolute necessity for the kind of work

Notes

I do, which requires countless notes, memos, and letters, as well as occasional invoices and special labels. I have many routine short memos, standard phrases, and addresses stored in the typewriter's memory, which has been a terrific time saver for me.

I hope all this pep talk about computers has convinced you of their importance to small business success. If you do not already have a computer, at least become more informed about computers and software by reading a variety of computer periodicals, available on newsstands everywhere. You won't understand everything you read at first, but the more you read, the more sense all of it will make. Actual experience with a computer makes an enormous difference in understanding. As you can see from this chapter, learning is part of the fun and the rewards of accomplishment are enormous.

This chapter probably gave you several good ideas on how to use a computer to make extra money or streamline your home business operation. Jot down those ideas now . . . before you forget them.

What a Computer Could Do for Me   Money Making Ideas

_____   _____
_____   _____
_____   _____
_____   _____
_____   _____
_____   _____
_____   _____
_____   _____
_____   _____
_____   _____
_____   _____
_____   _____
_____   _____
_____   _____
_____   _____
_____   _____
_____   _____
_____   _____
_____   _____
_____   _____
_____   _____
_____   _____
_____   _____
_____   _____
_____   _____
_____   _____
_____   _____
_____   _____
_____   _____
_____   _____
_____   _____
_____   _____

Maintaining Control

12.

O N THAT MORNING back in 1984 when I began to write this particular chapter, I was under enormous stress. At that time, I had exactly ten days in which to finish the book, and I had to do an out-of-town workshop during that period. In addition, we were then receiving more than 300 letters a day in response to publicity in *Family Circle*. So, what happened? I further complicated the situation by injuring myself.

I had taken a quick run to the shopping center the day before to buy a new pair of shoes for my upcoming workshop. I put them on to break them in and promptly fell down. Hard. The combination of haste, a slick floor, and the slippery soles of my new shoes resulted in an embarrassing, face-forward fall that bruised my ego, banged up both kneecaps, sprained my left ankle, and hurt one of my best typing fingers. I spent the remainder of that day in bed with ice packs on various parts of my body, feeling sorry for myself and upset because I was losing time away from the typewriter and this book. Meanwhile, Harry was trying to cope with 350 pieces of mail, give me sympathy, and get dinner on the table.

The next morning, however, I was back at my desk. It was business as usual. It *had* to be. Deadlines had to be met. Work had to be finished. And the stress of it all had to be dealt with. Such are the realities of a home business, which insists on being run even when you don't feel like running it.

Ironically, little has changed for me over the years. The reasons are different, of course, but I'm still working under stress. Which brings me to my point: after you have been working for yourself for awhile, you either get good at maintaining control and dealing with stress, or you simply cave in. I have become pretty good at it through the years. Harry and I have been married over 25 years now, and our life together has never been ordinary. Although happy, it has been loaded with stress, much of it of our own making. For instance, Harry's work, in conjunction with his restless spirit, has necessitated fourteen changes of residence in our married life. Seven of those moves have occurred during the time we have been operating a home business. It's not easy to meet publishing deadlines and keep a mail-oriented business running smoothly when you're forced to move about this often, but somehow we've always done it. Not without stress and special coping techniques, however.

I recall a letter I received from a friend shortly after Harry and I had relocated to Springfield, Missouri in the spring of 1982. "The

> *"The great advantage of a hotel is that it's a refuge from a home-based business."*
>
> — *Beverly Neuer Feldman,* Homebased Businesses

Notes

trouble with moving," said Sarah, "is that it realigns your priorities whether you want it to or not. Getting your house/life in order takes precedence over a lot of things that you need to be doing to keep your business running. If you should feel an anxiety attack coming on, and you feel guilty and inadequate because you can't do everything fast and efficiently, just remember that you are demanding too much of yourself. Say to yourself, 'I am one person. What needs to be done . . . will get done. Now, what needs to be done *today?*'"

Sarah's letter arrived shortly after the moving van, and as I read it, half of me was concerned about where I had put the frying pan, so I could get a quick meal on the table; the other half was trying to figure out how to set up a temporary office to handle the mail that had piled up since we had packed the office. Sarah's advice brought a smile to my face. "Ask yourself what needs to be done before Friday of this week, then make a list. Go through this process and set reachable goals for the month, three months, and one year. Just making the list will relieve a lot of pressure."

She was right, of course. I had made just such a list before leaving our old residence, and although it took a whole day to plan my last month's work in that area, it was as if a giant weight had been lifted from my shoulders when my day-to-day schedule was completed. I knew then that I only had to worry about what was on each day's list of things to do. Try it. You will be amazed at how much it helps when you feel you can't cope with all the work ahead of you.

Living and Working in the Same Place

One of the first problems facing the typical home business owner is where to set up shop, do the work involved, and store related merchandise, supplies, or files. It's not so bad if you have a four-bedroom home, but it takes real skill and ingenuity to run a business out of a house trailer or a small apartment.

Naturally, when space is at a premium, a complete separation of business from one's private life is an impossibility. Thus, one never has the sense of quitting at five o'clock to go home. After a while, this can have a disturbing psychological effect on anyone. Surprisingly, even those people who have large living spaces have the same problem, as Beverly Neuer Feldman describes in her book, *Homebased Businesses:*

> Our house, until the business moved in, had four bedrooms. To date, the businesses have spread like uncontrollable lava through three bedrooms, the four-car garage, and at times we sense a warm, molten flow around our feet. It is difficult to confine a home business to its designated place, but failure to do so can be irritating to one's spouse or other family members. They may feel "edged out" of their own home.[1]

How does a business manage to take over like this? It's easy. When we moved to our present house, I was delighted because it had two levels, with a huge family room, basement/workshop, and spare bedroom on the lower floor. That bedroom would be my office. "At last," I thought. "I can close the office door at five o'clock, go upstairs to fix dinner, and not have to see all the work waiting

---

[1]© 1983 by Beverly Neuer Feldman, Ed.D. Used by permission from Till Press.

to be done." But it was a short-lived dream. I still need a desk in the dining room, to handle both personal and business bills and bookkeeping jobs, and it is always piled high with papers. And near my rocking chair in the bedroom a stack of business books and periodicals is always waiting to be read because I don't have time for such things during the day. The kitchen catches its share of business, too. Each day's mail is placed by the door leading to the garage, on its way to the mailbox or post office. Thousands of newsletters, catalogs, books, and other printed materials pass through this door regularly on their usual in-and-out journeys.

Harry's office isn't large enough to handle big rushes of mail, such as we now are having, so work naturally overflows to other rooms of the house, where mail packages are being put together for labeling or stamping. The end result is that we always seem to be surrounded by work, even with two separate offices and a mail room. And the sight of it always makes us feel more tired than we are.

This kind of thing is ordinary to most home business owners of my acquaintance. "Ours is the only home in the neighborhood with three toll-free telephones sitting in the living room," says Susi Torre-Bueno, the diversified business owner you met in the last chapter. "Actually, we don't run the business out of our home, we run the home out of our business."

If you, too, find it impossible to make a complete physical separation of business from your home life, at least try to attain some kind of psychological separation from time to time. Although vacations may seem a luxury you don't seem to be able to afford, some time away from the place where all the work is waiting can be essential to your mental and physical well being.

As a business grows and takes more and more space in one's home, it is only natural to think about moving it to outside quarters. As one entrepreneur put it in a newspaper interview, "Now that the business has begun to grow so quickly, I'm feeling overwhelmed about how much space it occupies. There's a delicate line as to when it's ideal to be home and when it's time to move out," she said.

After twelve years of working in offices and spending all those hours getting to and from work, I don't ever want to see another commuter train or bus, nor do I want to eat lunch in a restaurant every day. And, although I like to dress up now and then, I basically am a very casual person who prefers to work in old slacks and one of Harry's hand-me-down shirts, sleeves rolled to the elbow.

Most of us who work at home do so by choice. Although we all want to realize a substantial profit from the time we spend on our businesses, many of us don't want them to grow too much, because that would only create more problems. After all, who really wants full-time employees coming into their home to work every day? That only destroys the privacy one enjoys by working at home. So, the longer one is in business, and the more successful it becomes, the harder it is to stay in control. The real challenge is to constantly increase the business income and profits while keeping the volume of work at a level that can be handled by family members or outside contractors.

And that's precisely why some home business owners set a limit on the amount of money they want to make. When they reach a certain level, they simply quit striving for more. One of my readers put it well when she wrote:

In an article by Leo Rosten in Reader's Digest, *it was suggested that things which are hard to learn give us rewards which "learning made easy" never can. We gain a special sense of pride each time we overcome an obstacle, and with each new problem we confront and solve, our self-respect increases. Through perseverance, we gain strength.*

Notes

I'm just painting away by myself, teaching some and selling about everything I turn out. Frankly, I'm not interested in getting any bigger or more spread out than I can handle myself. Maybe it's because I'm not supporting myself or anyone else, so what I earn is sort of play money. But it is *very* gratifying to feel that people like my things well enough to buy them. It is the sort of ego boost that many women my age need desperately. My four grown kids are quite impressed with the fact that "mom" is paid $200 a day to daub paint on a board. I need this respect.

Reviewing the Situation

After you have been involved in a business for a while, you will have to sit back and carefully rethink your grand plan. You may have to make certain modifications — perhaps even decide if you are on the right track after all. Or, as Fagin sang in the Broadway musical, *Oliver:*

> *I'm reviewing the situation . . .*
> *I think I'd better think it out again.*

The harder you work on your business, the more likely you are to have ambivalent feelings like these, expressed by another of my readers:

I've run into so many problems that I wonder if it is as worthwhile as I once thought. I feel I'm at a crossroads. I can choose to continue to work extremely hard and possibly overcome my problems, or let my fears get the best of me and stop the ball from rolling any farther. One part of me wants to scream and say, "Hang in there, your rewards are coming," while the other part argues back, "You're only deceiving yourself."

As a home business owner, you must expect feelings like these and learn to cope with them. *They come with the territory.* One day you can be on a terrific "high" because of some new achievement, a big order, or some publicity that boosts your business; the next day you may feel totally overwhelmed by the weight of too many responsibilities, too little time, and not enough money. A fight with one's spouse or even a minor family tragedy often can seem like the last straw. At times like these, you may feel like a salmon swimming upstream. Although you feel compelled to keep going, you no longer are sure you can make it. What seemed like a little swim at first has now become a fierce struggle to survive. In retrospect, you may discover, like so many others before you, that beginning was easy. It's *continuing* that is hard.

Although each new upstream swim gets easier, the decisions to be made only get harder. To grow, or not to grow? To take a risk, or not to take a risk? To stay at home, or move the business out? Is this the right business after all? What's all this doing to the family?

I think I'd better think it out again.

After reviewing the situation, some people throw in the towel, others slow down, still others change directions completely, and a certain percentage forge ahead in the original direction, pushing all the harder. Driven by some force even they do not understand, they probably will work until they drop, supremely confident that the success they dream of one day will be theirs.

Like salmon, some home business owners make it, some don't.

There are no sure bets in this game, but one thing is certain: It *is* a game worth playing. Even those who fail as businesspeople will succeed as individuals. It takes gumption and guts to start and operate a business of any kind, and anyone who does it, even for a little while, is a winner in my book.

Stress Coping Techniques

I would be lying if I said I was always in control of my business activities. But I'm not lying when I say that I quickly regain control on those occasions when things get out of hand. That's because I have made it a point to develop certain bounce-back techniques and set up escape mechanisms which I believe are essential to the successful operation of a home business. If you have a business now, I don't need to tell you that stress is the price of both failure and success. If you haven't started a business yet, be forewarned: A business at home will add extra stress to your life. You will need to develop stress coping techniques if you are going to stay in control of the business, and in control of your feelings about what you're doing.

Making lists of the work to be done is one good way to stay in control of things. But, no matter how many lists I make, something unexpected always seems to happen to upset my work schedule. Like the morning I went to the freezer to take out meat for dinner. To my dismay, I discovered that the door which I had last opened the morning before had not closed, because a package had shifted and jammed against it. Now the ice cream was dripping through the shelves, berry juice was streaming down the inside of the door, and all the green beans and peppers I had worked so hard to freeze the month before had thawed, along with about 30 pounds of meat and a lot of specialty foods we had brought from Chicago on our last shopping trip.

At first, I was close to tears. Then I got angry at myself for being so careless. The office work I had planned to do clearly was second on my list of priorities for this day. After I spent another five minutes feeling sorry for myself, the part of me that always welcomes a challenge came to life. An unsympathetic Harry helped me carry everything to the kitchen, where I made a list of the thawed ingredients, got out my recipe box, and went to work. While stewing about the fine mess I'd gotten myself into, I cooked, baked, and boiled my way out of it. Eight hours later, I had more meals in the freezer than I could count. All in all, it wasn't a bad experience. In fact, those prepared meals turned out to be a great time saver in the busy weeks to follow, and the experience was good for at least one laugh. One evening when Harry complimented me on one of the stews resulting from this fiasco and asked me how I made it, I said, "Well, first you let the freezer thaw . . ."

Obviously, one way to deal with stress is to keep your sense of humor. Always try to look on the bright side of things. For instance, when the freezer thawed, I thought how lucky we were that we had not just put in half a beef. And the green peppers were still growing, so I could replace them. The beans? I just refroze them; although they were a little mushy, they tasted fine. And when I fell in the shopping mall that day, my first reaction was to feel sorry for myself because I didn't need that kind of complication then. But on the way home, I realized it could have been worse. I might have broken my wrist or a couple of fingers and been unable to work at all.

Barb's Belief

Nothing is as simple as it seems, everything takes longer than expected . . . and something unexpected will always *force you to change your well-laid plans.*

Notes

How to Stay Motivated to Work

One secret is to read uplifting publications. Another is to associate with inspiring and enthusiastic people, in person and by mail. Don't listen to discouraging talk. Believe in yourself. Feed your own ego if no one else does it for you, because an ego that is continually fed is one that generates enthusiasm for the next project. Keep a diary of your accomplishments and re-read it periodically for encouragement. Consider all setbacks merely a profitable learning experience. Ask for help when you need it.

— *from* Sharing Barbara's Mail

Notes

And you know what? As that next day wore on, I began to tell myself that my ankle didn't feel all that bad, even though it was twice its usual size. By tomorrow, I told myself, it will feel better and so will I. Actually, what I was doing was having a private conversation with myself, during which time I came to the conclusion there was no real problem. Result? The stress I felt was soon relieved.

Throughout my life, I have tried to maintain a positive attitude about everything, and it has never failed to benefit me. Some people look at a partially-filled bottle and say, "It's half gone," but I say, "There's still half a bottle left." I try to apply the same kind of thinking to the daily happenings of my life and business. When things go wrong, or get out of control, I may not be able to do anything about the situation at that particular moment, but I *can* do something for myself immediately, and I do. I find something positive to think about.

In the end, each of us has a choice about how we perceive our experiences in life, and how our bodies will react to them. You have heard about the power of positive thinking and what it can do for you; where stress is concerned, positive thinking can make all the difference in the world. When you think negatively about anything, your body also responds negatively because the power of suggestion definitely affects the nervous system. But if you force yourself to think in positive terms, your body will respond accordingly.

As experts have confirmed, one's subconscious mind has the ability to accept as real any impression that reaches it, whether positive or negative, constructive or destructive, reliable or unreliable. That's why it is vital to your mental and physical well being to protect your mind from undesirable influences and suggestions which can bring you down. Whenever you feel threatened, try one of these coping techniques:

- Get out of the house, away from everything that reminds you of business. If you have no place to go, just take a walk. Commune with nature.
- Pour out your feelings in a letter to a confidant, or write in your private journal. It can be a great emotional release to put your thoughts in writing.
- Call a friend who understands your situation. A few words of encouragement from someone who cares about you can do wonders for your morale.
- Read an inspirational book, one whose message is "Believe in yourself!"
- Go to the mirror and give yourself a pep talk. Don't say, "I just can't do this." Instead say, "I don't know how I'm going to do this, but I *am* going to do it." At that point, you will have planted a seed in your subconscious mind, one that will grow in strength and eventually help you find the answer to the "how" part of your problem.

"People who work at home successfully learn to crack their own whips and to pat their own backs, sometimes all in one day," said one entrepreneur in an interview. She's right. As a self-employed individual, you may be the only person from whom you can draw the strength you need on any given day, and you may also be the only one around who's going to pat you on the back, and say "Well done!" So use that mirror as a psychological tool to help chase away doubts and fears and reinforce your positive thoughts. This may sound silly to some of you, but I know from experience that it can make quite a difference.

Besides thinking positively, what else can you do to relieve stress? It helps to just stop now and then and take a few deep breaths while also smiling inwardly and sending kind thoughts to your mind. Vigorous exercise also is recommended, of course, but I must admit to a lack in this area. It's hard for me to find time for exercise. This is a goal I must pursue more earnestly in the future.

I think the best escape mechanism of all is networking. I urge you to get involved in my home business network, and also to form a local network — people who share your interests and concerns. Homebased workers often feel a sense of isolation which in itself can be depressing and thus stressful. But contact of any kind with others who understand what you are going through — and are there to lend help when needed — can make all the difference in the world.

Also join some organizations related to your field, and don't just read their newsletters, but attend meetings once in a while. As a member of the Society of Craft Designers says, "I regularly attend an annual educational seminar (held in a different city each year). Although this is an expensive trip, it always has been worth the cost because I come away feeling totally refreshed and newly inspired. And this is after four days of around-the-clock meetings and networking. Here I meet old and new business friends, trade ideas with writers, editors, and publishers, and catch up on the latest information relative to a special field of interest. Meetings like this are actually restful for me because they break the daily routine of business and allow me to get away from it all."

Positive Workaholism

Because I'm always coping with one kind of stress or another, I tend to read a lot about this topic. Some people believe you must avoid stress at all cost, but that's ridiculous since stress is essential for life. Its absence is death, says Dr. Hans Selye, one of the world's leading authorities on this topic. While *distress* (negative stress) can play havoc with your mind and body, *eustress* (positive stress) is energizing. For example, if you challenge yourself by setting a worthwhile goal and then work very hard to achieve that goal, this can be healthful stress — especially if you enjoy what you're doing.

In an excellent article in *Reader's Digest*, Dr. Selye said that all the talk about the dangers of overwork and excessive striving is exaggerated, and only arouses unnecessary anxiety. He maintains that each of us gradually develops an instinctive feel that tells us whether we are running above or below the stress level that suits us best. His recipe for the best antidote to the stresses of ordinary life is first to decide if you are a racehorse or a turtle (do you want to run fast or slow?). Then choose your own goals (don't let others impose their goals on you). Finally, Dr. Selye suggests the practice of "altruistic egoism" — which is looking out for yourself by being necessary to others. Nothing in life is as stressful as a feeling of purposelessness, he maintains.

In a survey of 450 entrepreneurs, a Boston university professor learned that most of them believed that total immersion in their work was necessary for success, and that personal and family sacrifice was almost universal. Although most of the entrepreneurs in this particular survey could afford to take vacations, few of them did, preferring instead to work.

A lot of people believe that so-called A-type personalities like

---

No Jam This Year

"I began narrowing down my life in my mid-30's," says Miriam Irwin, owner of Mosaic Press, a publisher of miniature books (Cincinnati). *"I gave up bridge, needlework, and reading current novels to concentrate on writing and researching.*

"In my mid-40's, I planned my publishing company. I gave up even more things I love to do. I have zeroed in on the one thing that has become by now almost a passion: I absolutely LOVE publishing miniature books. It uses all my skills; all my talents, all my maturity, all my PATIENCE!

"This past year, I have given up one more thing in order to buy time to pursue publishing. I have a raspberry patch, and last summer it occurred to me that if I didn't pick and preserve raspberries, I would gain three or four days a year. This is the second year I haven't given in to the raspberry urge; and would you believe I still have jam left over from three years ago? This just shows that whatever I did, I did with great gusto — but it diverted precious time and I have the discipline now to not do everything.

"Of course, by next year I may be out of raspberry jam and feel entirely different about all this,"

— *from* Sharing Barbara's Mail

Notes

Notes

these are prone to heart attacks, high blood pressure, ulcers, and a number of other health problems. Some of them — those who cannot deal with stress — probably are. But a lot of hard-working entrepreneurs, myself included, tend to agree with author Dennis Hensley, who claims that it isn't stress that kills, but boredom. Dennis believes the answer to all problems is hard work that a person enjoys. He urges ambitious entrepreneurs to work as hard as they want, because the satisfaction they realize from productive work probably will do more to combat the ordinary stresses of life than anything else.

There must be something to this theory. I have lived what I believe to be a stressful life for years, yet I am healthy. I don't have ulcers, my blood pressure is normal, and my attitude remains positive. I do suffer from insomnia, but not because of stress. More likely, it's because of an overactive mind and the fact that I would like to accomplish more in one day than hours will allow. I think I try to steal time by not sleeping. Or, as John Steinbeck wrote in *Journal of a Novel,* "Last night I hardly slept at all. It was one of those good thinking nights."

Dennis Hensley coined the term "positive workaholic" in 1976, and he is living testament of his own positive workaholic systems. His philosophy is that success is obtainable to everyone who desires it and is willing to work for it, and he cites four common denominators among positive workaholics:

- a winning attitude
- high levels of energy
- fierce independence
- and a "mystical sense of destiny."

In summary, don't fret if you find you're always having to defend your work habits to others who keep telling you you're going to kill yourself by working so hard. It could be that working hard on your own business is the most healthful thing you could be doing.

Epilog

13.

I HATE TO END A BOOK, perhaps because I see books as natural beginnings to all kinds of wonderful things. It was a book, after all, that led me to start my first small home business. That book, *You Can Whittle and Carve*, released a stream of creativity in me that has yet to cease. I never got rich selling my woodcarvings, but oh, what I learned in the process.

A few years later, another book, *On Writing Well*, by William Zinsser, changed my life because it changed the way I thought about myself. It convinced me that I could be a professional writer if I chose to be. Many other books, in between and since, have taught me additional things and propelled me in exciting new directions, as I hope this book will do for you.

In the process of writing it, I have learned something about dreams and goals that I want to share with you. After I finished my first book in 1977, I told myself that I definitely was going to write another one. *Someday*. When I had more time. I dreamed about that book for five years. For a long time, I used the excuse that I was overwhelmed by work, and couldn't possibly find time to write a book. In time, I came to realize that part of my reluctance to start a new book was that I was afraid I would not be able to write a second book that would measure up to my first. I think a lot of one-book authors must feel this way. You have done it once . . . but can you do it again?

There was only one way to find out. Thanks to a publisher who kept nudging me, I finally stopped dreaming about this book and made plans to write it. Believe me, there is nothing like a written contract with a firm deadline to spur one onward!

Curiously, while the "dream" of a book had been an impossibility for five years, the book — *as a clearly defined goal* — suddenly seemed achievable. There can be no doubt about it. We do not make gains by dreaming about things. *We must set firm goals and then work like the dickens to achieve them, else they will remain dreams forever.*

It was difficult for me to write this book in the time I allotted to it. In fact, I never have worked such long hours in my life. A lot of other work has piled up as I have been writing. My house hasn't had a thorough cleaning in months, and my husband's patience has been stretched to its absolute limit with all the evening and weekend hours I have been putting in. But I have achieved a worthwhile goal, and I feel an enormous sense of accomplishment

> *"The toughest thing about success is that you've got to keep on being a success."*
>
> — *Irving Berlin, 1958*

> *"Life is either a daring adventure, or it is nothing."*
>
> *— Helen Keller*

at this point. I know my hard work will reap its own reward, and, in due time, Harry will forgive me for neglecting him so these past months.

It will be that way for you, too. The hard work you put into your home business, now or in the future, is likely to cause problems in your day-to-day life. It definitely will add to your stress level, and it positively will exhaust you time and again. But, oh, the exhilaration of it all! I don't believe there is anything quite so satisfying as the achievement of a goal that's important to you.

Whew! After so many weeks of writing, it really is hard for me to wind down. I still have many things I'd like to say, but I guess they will have to be said in future issues of my newsletter. Or in my next book. Sure, I'm going to dream about it for awhile. Books need a certain incubation period before they can be hatched. But I know the next one will be easier to start than this one, and I hope it will be better, too. Would you like to be a part of it? If so, see the boxed message at the end of this book.

Well, I really must go now. It's five o'clock, and a hungry husband awaits. I take my leave with these final words of advice: Stop dreaming about the things you want to do, and start making plans to do them before another season passes. Set firm, written goals and then get to work. It's absolutely amazing what you can accomplish when you believe you can do it. This book is proof positive.

Remember the rhyme?

Believable . . .

Conceivable . . .

Achievable.

It really works.

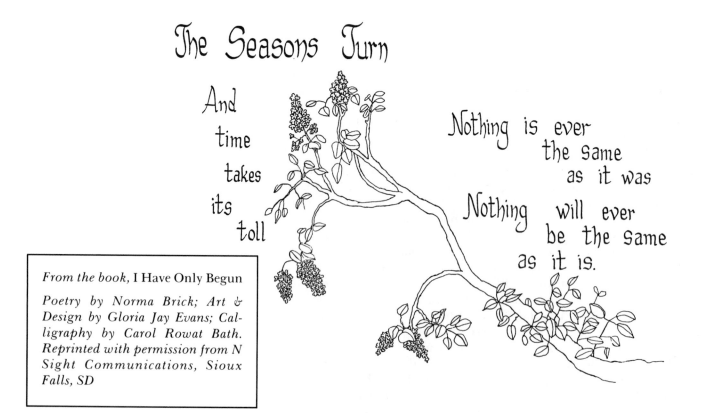

From the book, I Have Only Begun

Poetry by Norma Brick; Art & Design by Gloria Jay Evans; Calligraphy by Carol Rowat Bath. Reprinted with permission from N Sight Communications, Sioux Falls, SD

Resource Directory

14

How to Use This Directory

There are four sections.

Section I describes resources related to individual chapters in the book, while also serving as a convenient mail-order catalog. To avoid needless duplication of addresses, none have been included in Section I, but the code in parentheses after each listing tells you exactly where to find the related address in one of the three other sections of this chapter. It's quite logical:

B-II means "Book Publishers," listed in Section II under that heading.
P-II means "Periodical Publishers," listed in Section II, etc.
G-III means "Government Resources," listed in Section III.
O-III means "Organizations/Associations," listed in Section III.
A-IV means "Authors and Other Information Providers," listed in Section IV.
M-IV means "Marketing Connections," listed in Section IV.
S-IV means "Suppliers," listed in Section IV.

The Table of Contents enables you to locate specific resources when you want them, now or in the future. Or, if you happen to know the name of a publisher, organization, company, etc., you can turn to the appropriate address section and check the alphabetical listing.

Not all book publishers sell books by mail, and when no how-to-order information is given in a descriptive listing, it means you should inquire at local bookstores or the library for that particular title. When you can order by mail, you will find a notation, "Order by mail at . . ." with the *postage-paid price* indicated. Simply send payment with your order to the publisher, mentioning this book as your source of information.

The notation after directory descriptions reads "available in libraries." In most cases, however, this means main or central libraries only — not branches. Only a few basic directories are carried by small, branch libraries.

Although listings in Section I do not always indicate the availability of free brochures or catalogs, additional information is available on request from each resource. Subscription rates have not been indicated for periodicals because they tend to change fairly

> *Information is most meaningful to us when it applies to us at the moment we obtain it. But since nothing stays the same, information that is useless to us one day can often seem priceless a short while later.*

Notes

frequently. Just ask for subscription information and the availability of a sample copy when you write.

When contacting trade periodicals or organizations, as well as other businesses, *inquire on your business letterhead only*. These companies and associations do not serve hobby sellers. Handwritten letters on note paper probably will be ignored.

The many resources in this chapter — approximately 500 of them — are just the tip of the iceberg where information relative to your business is concerned. I am sharing with you my favorite business resources and have added an assortment of new ones which would appear to be useful to many of this book's readers. Visit a library soon and see what else you can turn up. If you would like to share the results of your research with me, I would be pleased to hear from you.

Tips for Doing Your Own Research

A directory of any kind begins to go out of date almost as soon as it is compiled simply because businesses are always moving, books go out of print, periodicals cease publication or change names, and so on. To my knowledge, all the listings herein are correct as the book goes to press. However, if your mail to any resource comes back marked, "Addressee unknown," or "Moved, left no forwarding address," simply visit the library and check the latest edition of a directory related to that resource.

If you live miles from a library, don't forget that you can telephone any library for assistance. Someone in the reference department will be glad to assist you.

If you need an address for an individual or small business or publisher not listed in library directories, you can send me a self-addressed, stamped envelope with a request for the specific address you need. If I have it, I will send it at once; if not, I'll hold your SASE until the new address is known.

To stay abreast of new and forthcoming books in your field, get acquainted with the *Books In Print* directories in the library. Even many branch libraries carry this reference, which is updated annually and supplemented with periodic editions of *Guide to Forthcoming Books*. Look under subject categories of interest to turn up new book titles and pertinent information regarding each book's publisher, publication date, price, and so forth.

If a new book is not available in local bookstores or the library, you can write to the book publisher for information on how to order by mail. Since not all book publishers invite consumer inquiries, you may not always get an answer, but it's worth the effort for a book you really want to obtain. Remember that you can find trade publishers' addresses in library directories such as *Writer's Market* and *Literary Market Place*.

If you would like to telephone a business or organization listed in this resource directory, obtain the telephone number by dialing Information. First dial the area code of the city you want to reach, then 555-1212. Large companies may have a toll-free number. To find out, dial 800-555-1212.

Finally, it would be helpful to me — and might result in a quicker reply for you — if you would mention this book when you contact anyone listed in the resource directory.[1] Thank you!

---

[1]Neither the author nor the publisher will accept responsibility for any action or transaction which may occur as a result of using the information provided herein.

Table of Contents
Resource Directory

SECTION I

SECTION I

Chapter One Resources
Home Business — General

Note: For complete addresses, see Sections II, III, or IV, as indicated by the code in parentheses.

Books/Information

☐ *Climb Your Own Ladder — 101 Home Businesses That Can Make You Wealthy,* by Allen Lieberoff. Simon & Schuster, 1982. Paperback, $7.95. Among the businesses which are discussed in brief detail are local moving, automotive services, the entertainment field, fashion design, catering, tour guide, tutoring, and others. Available in bookstores and libraries.

☐ *Earn Money At Home,* by Peter Davidson. McGraw-Hill, 1982. Paperback, $6.95. Ideas and information on more than 100 businesses that can be started at home, including a band-booking agency, professional grant writing, laundry service, dog raising, used paperback bookstore, games instructor, and others. Available in bookstores and libraries.

☐ *Growing A Business, Raising A Family — Ideas and Inspiration for the Work-at-Home Parent,* by Jan and Charlie Fletcher. This is a collection of essays based on homeworking parents' first-hand experiences in growing a business while raising a family. Free brochure from Next Step Publications details book and companion newsletter, *Home Business Advisor.* (B-II)

☐ *Help For Your Growing Homebased Business,* by Barbara Brabec. A companion to *Homemade Money,* featuring the best home-business articles, marketing information and resources from out-of-print issues of the author's quarterly *National Home Business Report.* $13.45 ppd. from Barbara Brabec Productions. Free catalog. (B-II)

☐ *Homebased Businesses,* by Beverly Neuer Feldman, Ed.D. Till Press, 1983. Paperback, $9.95. A special feature of this book is its two sections which list products and services from A-to-Z, giving brief paragraphs about each of the home businesses that fall under that alphabetical category. Good idea-starting book with sound business advice. Order by mail at $11.45 ppd. from Till Press. (B-II)

☐ *Homemade Money.* Additional copies of the book you are now reading can be ordered by mail at $18.95 ppd. from either Betterway Publications or the author, Barbara Brabec Productions. (B-II)

☐ *How to Start a Family Business and Make It Work,* by Jerome Goldstein, editor of *In Business* magazine. M. Evans & Co., 1984. Hardcover, $9.95. A warmly-written guidebook for the family that has pooled its talents to build a successful business. In bookstores, or order by mail for $11.95 ppd. from *In Business.* (P-II)

☐ *The New Era of Home-Based Work — Directions and Policies,* by Kathleen E. Christensen. $38.50 HC. Examines the real forces influencing the growth of homebased work and takes a hard look at the social/economic status of the homebased workforce, impact of homework on the family, and the potential role of the federal government in regulating home labor. Available in bookstores, or for $41 ppd. from Westview Press. (B-II)

☐ *The New Entrepreneurs — Women Working From Home,* by Terri P. Tepper & Nona Dawe Tepper. Universe Books, 1980. Forty women from different parts of the country tell how they operate home businesses, how they got started, obtained financing, solved problems, etc. Order by mail at $8.75 ppd. from Terri Tepper. (A-IV)

☐ *Office at Home,* by Robert Scott. Scribner's, 1985. Hardcover, $16.95. How to set up and operate an efficient homebased office; covers office machines and equipment, general business advice. In bookstores and libraries.

☐ *Stay Home and Mind Your Own Business,* by Jo Frohbieter-Mueller. A successful homebased business entrepreneur addresses all elements involved in working at home: business, family, household, community obligations. In bookstores or order for $10.95 from Betterway Publications. (B-II)

☐ *Tips on Work-at-Home Schemes,* a pamphlet available for 25¢ and a self-addressed, stamped envelope. Council of Better Business Bureaus. (O-III)

☐ *Turn Talent Into Dollars through Home-Based Business.* This self-study manual by extension specialist Margaret A. Duffy may be the only guide of its kind. It includes a series of lessons with a brief test and suggested activities at the end of each chapter. Should make learning about business fun for the beginning entrepreneur. $5 ppd. from Massachusetts Cooperative Extension. (A-IV)

☐ *The Whole Work Catalog.* Your mail order source for more than a hundred of the best books in the categories of career development, self-employment, and better ways of working. Includes useful business articles. Order a two-issue subscription to this catalog for $1 from New Careers Center. (B-II)

☐ *Women's Handbook — How the SBA Can Help You Go Into Business.* Helpful information on applying for a loan and finding business assistance locally. Free from Consumer Information Center. (G-III)

☐ *Women Working at Home: The Homebased Business Guide & Directory,* 2nd ed. WWH Press, 1983. Paperback, $12.95. Features articles by a number of business experts, plus photographs and a national directory of homebased businesses. Check the library.

☐ *Work is Dangerous To Your Health* — A Handbook of Health Hazards in the Workplace and What You Can Do About Them, by Jeanne M. Stellman, PhD., & Susan M. Daum, M.D. Pantheon, 1973. Paperback, $5.95. Of special interest to those whose work involves chemicals, welding, excessive noise, vibration, heat, or cold. Available in bookstores. (Note: May also be available by mail from the Center for Occupational Hazards.) (O-III)

☐ *The Work-at-Home Sourcebook: How to Find "At-Home" Work That's Right for You* (2nd edition), by Lynie Arden (editor of *The Worksteader News*). Live Oak Pub. Lists over 500 companies that regularly hire home-based workers in a wide range of jobs. Includes geographic cross-index, info on pay scales, tax advantages of working at home, and more. Check the library or write publisher to order by mail. The New Careers Center. (B-II)

☐ *Working At Home: Is It For You?* by William Atkinson. Dow Jones-Irwin, 1985. This book focuses on the most important element of working at home: adjusting personally to the lifestyle of being a self-manager. Includes other topics seldom discussed in home-business guides. Out of print, but available in libraries.

☐ *Worksteads — Living & Working In The Same Place,* by Jeremy Joan Hewes. Doubleday/Dolphin, 1981. Paperbck, $9.95. "Workstead" is a relatively new word, a joining of terms for "livelihood" and "surroundings." This book is a discussion of the alternative to working a 9-to-5 job, the reasons for combining working and living, and how many people are doing it today. Available in libraries.

Periodicals and Organizations

☐ American Home Business Association. A national profesional organization for people who work at home.

Memberships includes excellent medical insurance plan, toll-free hotline service, discounts on office supplies, and newsletter. For info, call toll-free at 1-800-433-6361 or write for membership brochure. (O-III)

☐ The American Woman's Economic Development Corporation. A nonprofit corporation formed to assist women in realizing their business potential. Services include a telephone hotline, in-depth counseling, and a number of low-cost programs. Write for details, or call 1-800-222-AWED. (O-III)

☐ Association of Part-Time Professionals, Inc. This association is trying to open up higher-paid positions requiring advanced training to part-time workers. One reason for exploring membership is the comprehensive health insurance plan offered to members. (O-III)

☐ *Choices.* A quarterly magazine aimed at women who want to start their own businesses, as well as entrepreneurs who want additional guidance and support. On newsstands; or order sample for $3.50. (P-II)

☐ *Extra Income.* Bimonthly magazine for women interested in a small business at home. Articles, profiles, special departments. Write for subscription info. (P-II)

☐ *Home Business Monthly — The Journal for Home Business Success.* Edited by Michael Piston. Includes articles, business briefs, book reviews, computer tips. (P-II)

☐ *Home Business News.* Bimonthly magazine for homebased entrepreneurs. News, ideas, sources, feature articles. (P-II)

☐ *In Business.* A monthly magazine directed to smaller businesses, especially those in the areas of alternative energy, crafts, natural foods, and family businesses. (P-II)

☐ Mothers' Home Business Network. Membership includes a subscription to the quarterly, *Homeworking Mothers,* free classified messages, directory listing, and other publications/services. Request brochure. (P-II)

☐ National Association of Home Based Business. A private business organization offering development and support services for entrepreneurs. Emphasis is on developing local small business networks. Publishes a quarterly ad paper. Free brochure. (O-III)

☐ The National Association For The Self-Employed. Offers numerous services to members, including a newsletter, toll-free line for business advice, discounted legal, accounting, and other services, plus a group health insurance plan. (O-III)

☐ *National Home Business Report* — Quarterly companion to the books, *Homemade Money* and *Creative Cash.* Edited and published by Barbara Brabec.

Marketing help for the business, stimulation for the mind, and a lift for the spirit, with news, information, and guidance for homebased business owners in all fields of endeavor. Sample copy, $4. Free catalog. (P-II)

☐ North American Students of Cooperation (NASCO.) This nonprofit corporation serves as an information clearinghouse for cooperatives of all kinds, and for groups and individuals interested in co-ops. Many publications on co-ops are offered. (O-III)

☐ *Opportunity Connection* — News and sources for the entrepreneur and small business owners everywhere. Emphasis is on mail order and multi-level marketing techniques. Sample, $3. (P-II)

☐ *Sideline Business Newsletter.* An informative, bi-monthly that gives an overall view of what's happening in the home business industry. Sample, $3. (P-II)

☐ Small Business Service Bureau, Inc. This national organization for small business owners disseminates information and management advice, and also provides legislative advocacy for its 35,000 members. Publishes a bulletin. (O-III)

☐ Support Services Alliance. Publishes a newsletter and offers a good group insurance program for self-employed people, including hospitalization and major medical, short-term disability, vision and dental plans, life and accidental death. Free brochure. (O-III)

☐ *Winning Ways News.* This highly motivational newsletter from Barbara J. Winter will be of interest to all business owners. Published 8 times/year; sample $3 from Winning Ways Press. (P-II)

☐ *The Worksteader News.* This monthly newsletter offers information for homebased workers; regularly lists employers who use home workers. Mention this book to receive a sample issue for $1. (P-II)

Self-Help/Motivational Books & Tapes

☐ *Discover What You're Best At: The National Career Aptitude Test,* by Barry Gale & Linda Gale. Simon & Schuster, 1982. Paperback, $9.95. Includes a complete series of aptitude tests to help you measure your clerical, logical, business, mechanical, numerical, and social skills. Especially designed to reveal your strengths and weaknesses. Available in bookstores and libraries.

☐ *How to Develop Self-Confidence & Influence People by Public Speaking,* by Dale Carnegie. Pocket Books. Paperback, $2.75. A classic in its field. Available in bookstores, or by mail at $3.25 ppd. from Pocket Books. (B-II)

☐ *How to Get Whatever You Want,* by M. R. Kopmeyer. The Success Foundation, 1972. Hardcover, $12.95. Just one of four highly-motivational, inspirational books by this author, dubbed "America's Success Counselor, For more information and a free "Yes, You Can," 80-page guidebook, write The Success Foundation. (B-II)

☐ *How to Motivate Yourself and Others,* by Dennis E. Hensley. Paperback. A motivational book for high achievers who desire success and are looking for someone who understands their drive and ambition. Order by mail at $8.45 ppd. from Denehen, Inc. (A-IV)

☐ *The Magic of Believing,* by Claude Bristol. Pocket Books. Paperback, $2.95. A highly inspirational book that would benefit any reader. Out of print, but check the library.

☐ *Playing Hardball With Soft Skills,* by Steven J. Bennett. Bantam. Paperback, $8.95. Subtitled "How to Prosper with Non-Technical Skills in a High-Tech World," this book will help you reshape and repackage your research, communication, and organizational skills into a terrific business package. In bookstores, or contact S. J. Bennett & Co. to order by mail. (A-IV)

☐ *Success In a Homebased Business — What It Takes, What It Costs, and Why It's Worth It.* A highly personal 90-minute audio cassette featuring Barbara Brabec as interviewed by economist Dr. Gary North. $10 ppd. from Barbara Brabec Productions. (B-II)

☐ *You Can Make It Without a College Degree,* by Roberta Roesch. Reward Books, 1986. Paperback, $8.95. Practical strategies for success; where and how to get the alternate education and job training you may need. Includes case histories and advice from those who have made it without a college degree. In bookstores & libraries.

☐ *What To Say When You Talk To Yourself,* by Shad Helmstetter. An especially good book that will explain why "success secrets" work for some people and not for others, and exactly what you must do to get them to work for you. Hardcover; in bookstores and libraries, or order by mail for $18.95 ppd. from Grindle Press. (B-II)

Learning and Information Resources

☐ American Association of Community & Junior Colleges. The Small Business Administration funds credit and noncredit business, management, and accounting courses offered by colleges nationwide. To find out about courses, seminars, and workshops where you live, write for more information. (O-III)

☐ The Displaced Homemakers Network, Inc. If you are a woman who has spent years as a full-time homemaker, and now find that you have to support yourself and your family because you are widowed, divorced, or separated; your spouse is disabled; or you are no longer eligible for public assistance because your children are grown, you are a displaced homemaker and help is available to you. For information on the Displaced Homemaker Project nearest you, send a self-addressed, stamped envelope to this organization. (O-III)

☐ *Information U.S.A. — An Indispensable Tool for Getting Information,* compiled by Matthew Lesko. Penguin Books. Paperback, $19.95. Guide to the most comprehensive source of information on earth; the U.S. Government. Available in bookstores and libraries.

☐ *Learn to Type,* by Barbara Aliaga. TAB Books, paperback. Explains a unique method that lets you type within five hours. Details on request, or order by mail at $6.50 ppd. from TAB Books. (B-II)

☐ Lifetime Career School. Offers proven home study training methods which have helped thousands of women combine an enjoyable hobby and a satisfying career. Request their free booklet, and specify your particular interest in either dolls, dressmaking, or floristry. (A-IV)

☐ National Home Study Council. A nationally recognized accrediting agency. Request a free brochure which describes the many courses offered by accredited home study schools throughout the country. (O-III)

☐ Other learning opportunities available to you. Investigate the courses offered by local YWCA/YMCAs, adult educational centers, vocational-technical schools, universities, and county extension services.

Chapter Two Resources
Home Business — Specific

Business Services

☐ *Establishing an Accounting Practice.* One of a series of booklets in the Small Business Reporter Series. Available at $2 ppd. in California; $3 ppd. outside the state. Order from Bank of America. (A-IV)

☐ *How to Start and Run a Successful Home Typing Business,* by Peggy Glenn. Aames-Allen Publishing. Spiral or paperback. Sensitive and thorough advice on virtually every aspect of a home typing business. Covers five major markets: academic, medical, business, legal, and professional writers. Order by mail for $15.95 ppd. from Aames-Allen Pub. (B-II)

☐ *Keyboard Connection.* A 12-page quarterly newsletter with news, information, and support for independent typing and word processing professionals. Edited by Carla Culp and Nancy Malvin. Sample, $3. (P-II)

☐ *Marketing Accounting Services,* by Robert Listman. Dow Jones-Irwin, 1987. $39.95. Emphasis is on helping large accounting firms increase business, but individual accountants are given tips on building sales through clients, using the telephone effectively, and selling to prospects. Available in bookstores or libraries.

☐ *Starting and Operating a Clipping Service,* by Demaris C. Smith. Pilot Books, paperback. Explains how to find hidden profits in your daily and weekly newspaper. Includes a listing of publications which buy newspaper clippings. Order by mail at $4.95 ppd. from Pilot Books. (B-II)

☐ *Starting Your Own Secretarial Business,* by Betty Lonngreen and Gloria J. Shoff. Contemporary Books, 1982, $6.95. How to get started, research the market, design a work space, select equipment, locate and negotiate with clients, schedule time, manage business income, hire consultants, and be an employer. Includes an appendix listing related sources of information and office suppliers. In bookstores or libraries.

See also Chapter Eleven Resources for computer-related business books.

Commercial and Fine Art

☐ *Advertising Layout: A Step-by-Step Guide for Print & TV,* by Larry Borgman. Hardcover, $24.95. Explains layout tools, gives how-to demonstrations, how to get started in this field, and more. Available by mail in the free catalog from Dynamic Graphics. (S-IV)

☐ *American Art Directory.* A geographically-arranged directory listing museums, art schools, and art organizations in the U.S. & Canada, plus state art councils, directors, and supervisors of art education in the school system. Published biannually; available in libraries.

☐ *American Artist.* A monthly magazine for practicing visual artists. Material relates to paintings, prints, drawings, illustrations, sculpture, and creative visual arts. Single copy, $1.75. (P-II)

☐ American Council For The Arts. This organization addresses significant issues in the arts by providing information and services, technical assistance, etc. Publishes books, manuals, and a magazine, *American Arts.* Free catalog details publications on grants and awards, consignment agreements, slide registries, etc. (O-III)

☐ Artists Equity Association, Inc. Serves the business and professional needs of American visual artists. Offers artist's all-risk insurance which covers work in the studio, or in transit, plus a collection service that charges only 15% of an amount collected. Write for more information. (O-III)

☐ *The Artists Magazine.* New magazine, 9 issues per year, for professionals interested in marketing; offers technical help and informative reading. (P-II)

☐ *Artist's Market.* Writer's Digest. Hardcover, issued annually. Lists 2,500 buyers of all types of commercial artwork, including magazine and book publishers, advertising agencies, greeting card companies, and more. Plus articles on presenting one's work as a professional, business tips, etc. Obtain price of current edition from Writer's Digest. Free catalog. (B-II)

☐ *The Art Marketing Letter.* News about promotional efforts, book reviews, reader questions, interviews, etc. Issued 10 times per year. Free brochure. (P-II)

☐ "Benefits and Profits From Art Prints." This five-piece, color-filled portfolio kit collection explains how to get into the print business using your original art or photographs. Order by mail at $9.95 ppd. from Art Print Publishers. (A-IV)

☐ Dynamic Graphics, Inc. This company has a broad line of clip art and how-to books that will be helpful to graphic artists and editors. (S-IV)

☐ *The Graphic Artists Guild Handbook, Pricing & Ethical Guidelines.* The only annual reference book of its kind. Keeps artists current on laws affecting contract provisions, provides industry business practices and standards; gives competitive price ranges in each of the graphic arts areas covered. Request descriptive flyer and price of current edition from Graphic Artists Guild. (O-III)

☐ *Graphic Arts Literature Abstracts.* Current literature covering the graphic arts and related subject areas. $3 per copy from Technical & Educational Center of the Graphic Arts. (A-IV)

☐ Greeting Card Association. This association brings out a booklet for freelancers, *Artists and Writers Market List,* with the names, addresses, and editorial guidelines of greeting card companies who are interested in buying from freelance writers or designers. Send SASE to receive an informative pamphlet. (O-III)

☐ *Selling Your Graphic Design & Illustration,* by Tad Crawford & Arie Kapelman. St. Martin's Press, 1981. Hardcover, $15.95. A complete marketing and legal guide for beginning or advanced professionals, with information on contracts, pricing, recordkeeping, taxes, copyright. Includes how to sell art in the form of greeting cards, calendars, posters, etc. Order by mail for $17.20 ppd. from St. Martin's Press. (B-II)

☐ *This Business of Art,* by Diane Cochrane. $17.95. A question-and-answer book about the business side of art, covering contracts, copyrights, exhibiting, commissions, publishing agreements, laws, insurance, and more. Available by mail in the catalog from Dynamic Graphics. (S-IV)

Crafts

☐ American Crafts Council. A nonprofit, educational, cultural organization serving a national membership of professional craftsmen, artists, and designers. Publishes *Craft Horizons,* a contemporary magazine, and many other publications. Request free information about all ACC publications and membership benefits, which include special insurance plans. (O-III)

☐ *Career Opportunities in Crafts,* by Elyse Sommer. Crown Publishers, 1977. Paperback, $6.95. An excellent guide for people who are building careers in crafts. Covers marketing, retailing, designing, and selling tools, processes and kits, teaching, publishing, crafts administration, and more. Especially helpful are the sample contracts and agreements related to designing, writing, consignment, commission sales, and consulting. Order by mail at $8 ppd. from Elyse Sommer. (A-IV)

☐ *The Cloth Doll.* This quarterly magazine will be useful to professional doll and pattern designers who are interested in networking with others in their field. Sample, $3.50. (P-II)

☐ *Cooperative Approach to Crafts,* by Gerald E. Ely. Reviews the background of craft development in the country, discusses the applicability of the co-op approach to craft problems, and offers guidelines for developing craft cooperatives. Free; ask for Program Aid #1001 from the U.S. Department of Agriculture. (G-III)

☐ *Cooperative Approach to Crafts for Senior Citizens,* by Gerald E. Ely & William R. Seymour. Discusses the possibilities that exist for a craft organization, factors to be considered before a program is formulated, and initial steps to be taken in establishing a craft cooperative for senior citizens. Free; ask for Program Aid #1156 from the U.S. Department of Agriculture. (G-III)

☐ *Crafts Marketing Success Secrets,* by Barbara Brabec. Revised 1988. Paperback. A profit-oriented collection of the best articles, letters, and how-to-make-money information from Barbara's earlier crafts marketing periodicals, updated for today's sellers. Topics cover selling to shops, at fairs, through cooperative ventures (party plans, boutiques, co-op shops, etc.). Book includes five special resource lists. Free catalog. Order by mail at $11.45 ppd. from Barbara Brabec Productions. (B-II)

☐ *Craft Resources.* Several pages of information listing federal resources for crafts development. Free from the U.S. Department of Agriculture. (G-III)

☐ *The Crafts Business Encyclopedia,* by Michael Scott. Harcourt, Brace, Jovanovich, 1977. Paperback. An A-to-Z guidebook to business terms and techniques for marketing craftwork. Order by mail at $6.95 ppd. from The Crafts Report. (P-II)

☐ *The Crafts Report.* A newsmonthly of marketing, management, and money for crafts professionals — the "Wall Street Journal" in its field. Provides details about selling opportunities, articles on marketing techniques, tax situations, and money management. Excellent classified ad sections for buyers and sellers. Sample, $2.00. (P-II)

☐ *Craftwork the Handicapped Elderly Can Make and Sell,* by Wiletta Russell. Charles C Thomas, Publisher. Paperback, $16.25. (To order by mail, request additional information and postage charges.) (B-II)

☐ *Creative Cash — Making Money with Your Crafts, Needlework, Designs & Know-how,* by Barbara Brabec. Aames-Allen Pub., 1986, paperback. Called a "crafts marketing bible" by its readers, this book includes everything the beginner seller needs to know. Offers guidelines for expansion of existing craft/needlework businesses. Extensive 300-listing resource chapter details craft periodicals, organizations, trade magazines, directories, books, special services, packaging, printing and publicity aids, government agencies, publishers, manufacturers, and others. Order by mail at $13.95 ppd. from Barbara Brabec Productions. Free catalog. (B-II)

☐ *The Creative Woman's Getting-It-All-Together (At Home) Handbook,* by Jean Ray Laury. Hot Fudge Press. Paperback. A warmly-written book for creative women, particularly those who work in the fiber/fabric fields. A collection of ideas and proposals for accomplishing both personal and family goals. Order by mail at $10.45 ppd. from Jean Ray Laury. (A-IV)

☐ *The Front Room News.* Bimonthly, craft-oriented newsletter with a variety of information useful to

women with part-time, homebased craft businesses. Sample, $3. Inquire about other craft marketing publications available from this source. (P-II)

☐ *Goodfellow Catalog of Wonderful Things.* This publisher is issuing special mail-order catalogs in the form of books which are distributed to bookstores and libraries. Individual catalogs feature (1) handmade items for children; (2) gifts under $50; (3) wearable crafts; and (4) handmade items for the home. Entry is open to all craft sellers in the U.S. and Canada, but only 200–250 people can be included in each book. All work is juried, and there is a participation fee (modest). Details and an application form for a large SASE. (B-II)

☐ *Handcrafts.* One of a series of free SBA bibliographies, this 12-page booklet was compiled by Barbara Brabec. It lists 341 how-to books in 26 different craft and needlework categories, plus 25 crafts business books and related periodicals. Request SBB-1 from SBA Management Assistance Publications. (G-III)

☐ *Handmade Accents.* This colorful quarterly is directed to craftspeople and the community of artists at large, including art patrons, collectors, investors, art directors, and photographers. Issues include craft fair listings. Sample, $4. (P-II)

☐ *Legal Primer for Artists and Crafts Persons,* by John Goodwin. Publishing Horizons, 1986; paperback, $17.95. A guide for serious sellers. Covers contract law, sales contracts and purchase of goods, consignment contracts, copyrights and patents, product liability insurance, and much more. To order by mail, contact Publishing Horizons. (B-II)

☐ *A Practical Business and Tax Guide for the Crafts-Person,* 2nd éd., by F. Bair & J. Norris. Publishing Horizons, 1986. Paperback. A book that will help craft hobbyists enter the world of business. Request info about price/availability of latest edition. Publishing Horizons. (B-II)

☐ Model Consignment Agreement. A sample contract that will be useful to everyone who sells on consignment. 50 for $4 ppd. from The Unicorn. (A-IV)

☐ *The Professional Quilter.* A quarterly business, marketing, and educational publication for the home-based businesswoman involved in the quilting field. Free brochure. (P-II)

☐ *Profitable Crafts Marketing,* by Brian T. Jefferson. Madrona Pub., 1985. Hardcover, $10.95. This guide to successful selling will help you create a marketing plan, identify and select profitable sales outlets, and much more. Check bookstores and libraries.

☐ *Selling Products on Consignment.* A free management aid from the SBA. Ask for #4.007. (G-III)

☐ Society of Craft Designers. A professional organization for designers, writers, book and periodical publishers, editors, teachers, and others who wish to sell in the crafts and needlework industries. The annual educational seminar is one of the best ways for newcomers to get information from the experts and make valuable editorial, publishing, and manufacturing contacts. (O-III)

☐ *Teaching Needlecraft*, by Rosemary Cornelius, Peg Doffek, & Sue Hardy. Van Nostrand Reinhold, 1979. A practical guide that makes teaching easy with lesson plans, sample patterns, etc. Available in libraries.

☐ *Yellow Pages of American Crafts*. Published annually, this directory lists the names, addresses, and phone numbers of more than 15,000 professional craft artists, as well as names and addresses of craft suppliers, publications, retailers, shows and show promoters, guilds and associations, and manufacturer's representatives. A Calendar of Events lists most of the top craft shows in the U.S. $10 ppd. from The Rosen Agency. (A-IV)

☐ *You Can Make Money From Your Arts and Crafts*, by Steve and Cindy Long. Practical crafts marketing information based on the authors' experiences in selling at fairs, by mail, and to wholesale outlets. In bookstores, or order for $16.90 ppd. from Mark Publishing. (B-II)

Cooking/Catering/Food Industry

☐ Breadwinners. This is a network of instructors who teach breadbaking in their homes. Claudia Burns, founder, has developed a comprehensive set of materials to simplify breadbaking instruction and create a profitable home business. For complete details, contact Breadwinners. (A-IV)

☐ *Cooking For Profit — The Business of Food Preparation*. A monthly trade magazine oriented to retail food establishments, but helpful to caterers and others who need food equipment or products. Also available from this source are recipe books, catering ideas, and marketing guides. (P-II)

☐ *Freelance Foodcrafting: How to Become Profitably Self-Employed in Your Own Creative Cooking Business*, by Janet Shown. Live Oak Pub., 1983. Paperback. Explores opportunities in the gourmet food field with an emphasis on businesses which can be started with little capital and little risk. Includes profiles of successful food entrepreneurs. In bookstores, or order by mail at $10.95 ppd. from The New Careers Center. (B-II)

☐ *Professional Catering, Cookery, & Kitchen Practice*, by Douglas Sutherland. Trans-Atlantic Publications, 1987. $16.95. Available in bookstores & libraries.

Day Care/Children

☐ *Caring For Kids: A Concise Guide to Establishing a Successful Day-Care Center*, by Tanya Ashworth. 1988, paperback. $11.95 ppd. from Vade Mecum Press. (B-II)

☐ *Day Care and Early Education*. Periodical for day care administrators and caregivers, educators, and parents. Single copy, $3. (P-II)

☐ Day Care Council of America. If you are thinking about starting a day care center, you can get information about regulations and resources in your area by contacting the Council's new network, National Family Day Care Providers Network. (O-III)

☐ *Starting and Operating a Playgroup For Profit*, by Susan Chidakel. Pilot Books, paperback. A "playgroup" is a business that can be started on a limited budget, either full or part time — for people who really enjoy small children. Order by mail for $3.95 ppd. from Pilot Books. (B-II)

Direct Selling/Multi-Level Marketing

☐ Direct Selling Association. A trade association that serves companies that manufacture or distribute goods and services directly to consumers. The DSA publishes a wide range of literature for consumers on the Association's code of ethics, direct selling methods of distribution, and legal and ethical requirements for direct sellers. Three free pamphlets will be of interest: "Pyramid Schemes: Not What They Seem"; "Customers Mean Business — Tips for Direct Marketers"; and "Promises — Check 'em Out!" Direct Selling Education Foundation. (O-III)

☐ *Opportunity*. A monthly magazine originally known as *Salesman's Opportunity*. Of interest to people in direct sales. (P-II)

☐ *Personal Sales Power*. Bimonthly newspaper designed to help one become a better salesperson. (P-II)

☐ Salesman's Workshop. A self-study course in sales techniques. More information on request to Bureau of Business Practice. (A-IV)

☐ *Selling Power of a Woman* (Never Underestimate The), by Dottie Walters, Royal Publishing, Inc. Now in its 13th edition, this book has inspired thousands of women around the world. Considered a classic in its field, it is "must reading" for every woman in sales. The first book ever written by a saleswoman for women in sales. Not in bookstores, but available by mail at $8.50 ppd. from Royal Publishing. (B-II)

☐ *Tips on Multi-Level Marketing.* A pamphlet available for 25¢ and a SASE from the Council of Better Business Bureaus, Inc. (O-III)

Franchised Businesses

☐ *Buying a Franchise.* A booklet in the Small Business Reporter Series. Order by mail at $2 ppd. in California; $3 outside the state, from Bank of America. (A-IV)

☐ *Franchised Businesses.* A free starting-out-series booklet from the SBA. Ask for #SOS-0106. (G-III)

☐ *Franchising in the U.S.,* by Michael M. Coltman. TAB Books, paperback, $5.95. Examines the advantages and pitfalls of buying a franchise; explains unethical pyramid schemes. Order by mail for $5.95 ppd. from TAB Books. (B-II)

☐ *How to Franchise Your Business,* by Mack O. Lewis. Even though relatively small, a proven business can expand through franchising. This guide tells how. $4.50 ppd. from Pilot Books. (B-II)

☐ *The Source Book of Franchise Opportunities,* by Robert Bond. Dow Jones-Irwin, 1988. Paperback, $24.95. Comprehensive directory with summaries of some 1400 companies in 126 business categories; with info on investment requirements and other pertinent info. In bookstores and libraries; or order for $27.95 ppd. from Dow Jones-Irwin. (B-II)

Herbs & Plants

☐ *Growing & Using Herbs Successfully,* by Betty E. M. Jacobs. Garden Way Publishing, 1981. Paperback, $6.95. Includes a chapter on growing herbs for profit, one on markets and marketing, another on herb products that can be created for fun or profit, plus a list of tips for building a successful business. Order by mail at $7.95 ppd. from Garden Way. (B-II)

☐ *Herban Lifestyles.* Information-packed newsletter published 8 times a year by Christine Utterback. Sample, $2. (P-II)

☐ *Herb Business Bulletin.* A bimonthly devoted wholly to the business side of herbs — from hobby businesses to sellers of herbs and herb crafts, to teachers and lecturers. Sample, $2.00. (P-II)

☐ *Plants For Profit — A Complete Guide to Growing and Selling Greenhouse Crops,* by Dr. Francis Jozwik. Andmar Press, 1984. Hardcover, $39.95. A detailed guide for those wishing to enter the four billion dollar plant/flower industry. Covers both technical aspects of growing and business aspects (labor, marketing, etc.). For more information, contact Andmar Press. (B-II)

☐ *Potpourri From Herbal Acres.* Quarterly newsletter in which herb business owners and hobbyists network to share ideas, successes, recipes, and tips. Send business-size SASE for brochure and free herb chart. From same source: *The Pleasure of Herbs: A Month-by-Month Guide,* by Phyllis Shaudys (Garden Way Publishing, 1986). $13.95 ppd. Includes useful directory of herb businesses and sources of wholesale products. For info, or to order, write to Phyllis Shaudys. (A-IV)

Interior Design

☐ American Society of Interior Designers. Publishes a newsletter of interest to everyone in the field. Write for membership/subscription information. (O-III)

☐ *Interior Design Buyers Guide.* Published annually. Lists suppliers of products and services in this industry. Free to subscribers of *Interior Design* magazine or may be purchased separately from Cahners Pub. (A-IV)

Mail Order

☐ *American Drop-Shippers Directory.* A source book for those interested in contacting companies who will stock and ship products or publications on a no-investment, drop-ship basis. The directory itself can be used as a money-making product which can be advertised and sold by mail. $7 ppd. from World Wide Trade Service. For dealer info, send business-size SASE. (M-IV)

☐ *The Direct Response Specialist.* Monthly how-to newsletter for professional mail marketers, with emphasis on effective response/profit techniques. Request brochure from Stilson & Stilson. (P-II)

☐ *How to Start and Operate a Mail Order Business,* by Julian L. Simon, 4th ed., 1987. McGraw-Hill. Hardcover, $34.95. A classic in its field. Sound advice, basic techniques, and up-to-date info on new developments in the industry. Includes a new section on the fast-growing field of catalogs, a list of 500 mail-order products known to sell well, info on buying/building mail lists, creating ads, dealing with printers, and more. An essential handbook for serious mail-order marketers. Available in bookstores and libraries.

☐ *Key Newsletter.* A quarterly whose purpose it is to help you make more money with mail order through classified advertising. The editor of this publication offers a number of publications, including a computer listing of the top 400 consumer publications for mail order advertising, a question-answering service, ad writing and placement service, and more. Free details on all publications. Sample of newsletter, $5. Voice Publications. (M-IV)

☐ *Mail Order Know-How,* by Cecil C. Hoge, Sr. Ten Speed Press, 1982. Large paperback, $16.95. A fantastic guided tour of direct marketing conducted by people who have sold billions of dollars worth of merchandise through mail order — from kitchen table entrepreneurs to the heads of large corporations. 125 stories tell what works, how to do it, what to look for, and what to avoid. Includes a unique "Self-Help Directory" of 900 books, tapes, newsletter, seminars, and articles vital to anyone who plans to sell by mail. Available in bookstores and libraries.

☐ *Mail Order Moonlighting,* by Cecil C. Hoge, Sr. Ten Speed Press, 1987. Paperback, $9.95. An authoritative guide for anyone in the mail-order business, or planning to start one. Covers every useful detail. A classic in its field. Available in bookstores and libraries.

☐ *Memo to Mailers.* Published monthly by the U.S. Postal Service, this memo is free to customers who originate significant quantities of mail. Request subscription on business letterhead. (P-II)

☐ National Mail Order Association. Membership includes subscription to *Mail Order Digest* and *Washington Newsletter.* This organization sells a variety of books and inexpensive reports on sources for services, supplies, and products. Also available, a form for recording response to ad publicity promotions. Free brochure. (O-III)

Photography

☐ *Photographer's Market.* Writer's Digest, 1987. Hardcover. Issued annually. Includes 2,500 listings of photo buyers — periodicals, advertising agencies, book publishers, galleries, and stock photo agencies. With marketing articles, information on market trends, business tips, etc. Obtain price of current edition from Writer's Digest. (B-II)

☐ *The Photoletter.* Published monthly by Rohn Engh, this marketing newsletter pairs picture buyers with the collections of photographers. For professionals who pursue photography as a serious sideline or full-time business. Free sample if you request it on your letterhead. Inquire about other periodicals and

books for professional photographers. Photo Source Int'l. (P-II)

☐ *Professional Photographer's Business Guide,* by Frederic W. Rosen. Watson-Guptill, 1985. Paperback, $12.95. Available in bookstores and libraries.

Sewing/Apparel Industry

☐ Custom Tailors & Designers Association of America. Publishes the only business journal for the custom tailoring industry. Single copy, $5. (O-III)

☐ *Homesewing Trade News.* This quarterly newspaper has become the official publication of the custom dressmaker. Issues a resource directory of mills, manufacturers, suppliers, etc. (P-II)

☐ *Knitting Machine News/Views.* Ask for more information about this periodical and related publications and books for machine knitters. A good national networking connection for people in this industry. (P-II)

☐ *Monogram Business Booklet.* Informative guide on how to start and maintain a successful monogram business. Free from Meistergram, Inc. (A-IV)

☐ *Sewing for Profits,* by Judith and Allan Smith. Paperback. A basic guide for starting and operating a home sewing business. Available by mail for $11 ppd. from Success Publications. Inquire about other sewing and craft books available from this source. (B-II)

☐ *Sew Business.* Trade magazine published monthly for retailers, wholesalers, and manufacturers; useful to designers and others in this field. Includes an art needlework supplement, a quilt quarterly, and a national directory of resources (suppliers) each July. (P-II)

Miscellaneous Businesses

☐ *Beekeeping — An Illustrated Handbook,* by Diane G. Stelley. TAB Books, paperback. Includes advice on how to turn a beekeeping hobby into a profitable sideline business. Order by mail at $12.95 ppd. from TAB Books. (B-II)

☐ *Can You Make Money With Your Idea or Invention?* A free booklet available from the SBA. Ask for #MA 2.013. (G-III)

☐ Cleaning Management Institute. Offers information for people in the contract cleaning business, including a manual, *The Contract Cleaner Companion.* Free brochure. (A-IV)

☐ *How to Make Big Money Mowing Small Lawn,* by Robert Runck. Teenagers looking for summer employment can use this book to turn a patch of green into a pot of gold, the author says. For more information, or to order at $8.95 ppd., write Brick House Pub. Co. (B-II)

☐ *How to Make Extra Profits in Taxidermy,* by John E. Phillips. Winchester Press/New Century Pub., Inc., 1984. Paperback, $12.95. The money-making taxidermy book for the home hobbyist, the professional, the experienced craftsman, and the young enthusiast just getting started. Available in bookstores or libraries.

☐ *How to Set Yourself Up In Business As A Printing Broker,* by Jack Erbe. Paperback. A business start-up manual that explains the printing industry and the money-making opportunities in it. Inquire about other useful business information available from International Marketing Co. (A-IV)

☐ *Inventor's Guide in a Series of Four Parts,* by Chester L. Cook. A guide on how to protect, search, compile facts, and sell your information. Includes sample letters on how to submit ideas to manufacturers. Order by mail at $11.95 ppd. from the author. (A-IV)

☐ *Inventors Guidebook — A Step-By-Step Guide to Success,* by Melvin L. Fuller, founder and president of Inventors Workshop International. How to bring an idea to the market stage — covers patents, trademarks, copyrights, prototypes, market analysis, etc. $7.50 ppd. from Inventors Workshop International. (O-III)

☐ Inventors Workshop International. Organization for professional inventors to keep them abreast of happenings, marketing ideas, patent legislation, tax info, etc. Publishes a periodical, *Invent!* (O-III)

☐ *Making Money Making Music (No Matter Where You Live),* by James Dearing. Writer's Digest. Paperback, $12.95. Make money and the most of your musical talent. How to build a successful career in your own community. Step-by-step advice. Available by mail at $15.45 ppd. from Writer's Digest. (B-II)

☐ Music Teachers National Association. Publishes *American Music Teacher* for its members, as well as for college and professional school music teachers. Single copy, $1. (O-III)

☐ *Songwriter's Market.* Writer's Digest. Issued annually. How to get your songs published and recorded. Gives 2,000 listings of record companies and producers, music publishers with complete submission requirements, pay rates, etc. Includes tips from successful songwriters and others in the industry. Obtain price of current edition from Writer's Digest. (B-II)

☐ *Start and Run a Profitable Beauty Salon: A Complete Step-by-Step Business Plan,* by Paul Pogue. TAB Books, paperback. What you need to know — in addition to the latest hair styles. Order by mail at $14.95 ppd. from TAB Books. (B-II)

☐ *Start Your Own Bed & Breakfast Business,* by Beverly Mathews. Pocket Books, 1985. Paperback, $7.45 ppd. This book has been approved by the Tourist House Association of America. It covers all aspects of this business, and includes a lengthy section which lists reservation service organizations, sources and resources, and more. Also a special chapter for Canadian readers. The author also publishes other related books and a companion newsletter; sample $4. Write Rocky Point Press. (P-II)

☐ *Your Ideas May Be Worth A Fortune,* by Woodie Hall. Paperback. This self-published book is loaded with wit, marketing wisdom, philosophy, and solid how-to guidelines for success in this field. Order for $10 ppd. from Mark Nolan Assoc. (A-IV)

Chapter Three Resources
Business Suppliers

Art and Camera-Copy Preparation Aids

☐ *Better Brochures, Catalogs and Mailing Pieces,* by Jane Haas, St. Martin's Press, 1984. Paperback, $5.95. This book is directed primarily to those associated with travel and tourism, hotels, attractions, schools and colleges, museums, fundraising and membership drives. However, even the smallest homebased business owner will get hundreds of specific rules and guidelines to help create mailing pieces with more "sizzle and sell" to them. Order by mail at $6.45 ppd. from St. Martin's Press. (B-II)

☐ Dot Pasteup Supply Co. Graphic art aids, border tapes, the tools needed to create camera-ready art, and more, including clip-art books and helpful how-to guides for graphic artists. Catalog, $1. (S-IV)

☐ Dover Publications, Inc. Offers a free catalog of books that include copyright-free designs (their "Pictorial Archive Series") plus clip art booklets and many how-to/pattern/design books. (S-IV)

☐ Graphic art aids. A complete line of transfer lettering, symbols, arrows, borders, etc. is available from Zipatone, Inc., and carried by most art supply dealers. If unavailable locally, write to Zipatone for a free catalog and th name of your nearest dealer. (S-IV)

☐ Graphic Products Corporation. Offers a free range of graphic art aid products, including Formatt cut-out acetate sheets, art tapes, clip art books, etc. If this line is unavailable in local shops, write for a catalog and the name of your nearest dealer. (S-IV)

☐ *How to Do Your Own Pasteup For Printing*, by Edmund J. Gross. Basic data on copy, layout, typesetting, artwork, photography, veloxes, offset printing, etc. Available by mail at $8.50 ppd. from National Mail Order Association. (O-III)

☐ *How to Make Newsletters, Brochures & Other Good Stuff Without a Computer System*, by Helen Gregory. Small Business Handbook on promotion planning, writing, pasteup, and postage. $13.50 ppd. from Pinstripe Publishing. (B-II)

☐ *Pasteups & Mechanicals*. $22.50. A step-by-step guide to preparing art for reproduction. Nontechnical; you need no previous experience to learn current pasteup skills from this book, available by mail in the catalog from Dynamic Graphics. (S-IV)

☐ *Sommer & Gibofsky's Do's & Dont's — 30 Proven Rules to Help You Develop Cost Effective Brochures.* $1, plus SASE. Also available, a brochure on *How to Develop a Cost-Effective Newsletter,* also $1 plus SASE. (If ordering both, just double-stamp the envelope.) From Elyse Sommer. (A-IV)

☐ Volk Art. A major supplier of quality clip art for use in ads and periodicals. Send for a free, illustrated brochure. (S-IV)

Office Supplies

☐ Bucher Brothers. Inexpensive business cards and "mini stickers" in gold or silver. Free brochures and samples. (S-IV)

☐ The Datasort System. Dubbed the "cardboard computer," this inexpensive (under $30) data-retrieval system may help those who are not yet ready for a computer. Free brochure. (S-IV)

☐ Deluxe Computer Forms & Supplies. Standard or custom. Free catalog. (S-IV)

☐ The Drawing Board. Offers a wide variety of office supplies, business forms, labels, etc. Free catalog. (S-IV)

☐ Fidelity Products Co. Supplies and equipment for office and industry. Free catalog. (S-IV)

☐ FlexiList. A unique list-management system for small list owners (up to 3,000 names). Used by many direct sellers, such as those in the Mary Kay Company. Involves the use of clear, vinyl sheets with pockets that hold 33 typed insert cards. Cards can be rearranged to add/delete/change names on a list. The vinyl pages/address cards can be photocopied to create self-adhesive mailing labels. A complete package of information and a sample of the vinyl page and address cards is available for $3 from David T. Sullivan at FlexiList. (S-IV)

☐ Grayarc. Office forms and supplies, shipping labels, etc. Free catalog. (S-IV)

☐ Highsmith. Essential office and audiovisual products; shelf files, computer supplies, office supplies, order forms. Free catalog. (S-IV)

☐ INMAC. Computer supplies, accessories, furniture, etc. Free catalog (S-IV)

☐ Mail order sales record sheets. For use in recording mail order response from publicity, ads, or mailings. A full year's history on one page. Available by mail from the National Mail Order Association. (O-III)

☐ NEBS Business Forms and Office Supplies. Offers a standard line of pressure sensitive labels in bright metallic or fluorescent papers and variety of styles. Free catalog. (S-IV)

☐ Quill Corporation. The nation's leading mail order distributor of office supplies and equipment. Speedy service a specialty. Free catalog. (S-IV)

☐ The Stationery House. Standard stationery supplies; computer supplies. Free catalog. (S-IV)

☐ Vermont Business Forms. Specializes in raised-letter business cards and matching letterheads/envelopes. Works with small business owners by mail. Free brochure and samples, $1.00. (S-IV)

Specialty Printers and Bulk Photo Companies

☐ Atlas Pen & Pencil Corporation. Specializes in advertising give-away items with name and address imprinted. Pens, pencils, keyrings, calendars, balloons, ashtrays, emery boards, buttons, wooden nickels, and more. Free catalog. (M-IV)

☐ Champion Printing Co. Specialists in selling printing by mail to mail order sellers who need self-mailers and other direct-response pieces (package inserts, reply envelopes, etc.) or booklets, catalogs, and other printing. Specify needs when requesting catalog. (S-IV)

☐ Color Lab. Color photos in bulk quantities at reasonable prices. Free brochure. (S-IV)

☐ Color Q. This company specializes in affordable art reproductions, business cards incorporating photos, greeting cards, and postcard reproductions of art. Ask for their free booklet, "Gain Wider Recognition for Your Artistry, and Make More Money, Too." (S-IV)

☐ Direct Mail Printing Co. Specialists in the design and printing of self-mailers and package inserts; brochures with attached reply envelopes. Cost effective in quantities of 5,000 or more. Ask Murray Goldberg for a package of samples. (S-IV)

☐ Direct Press/Modern Litho. Specialists in color printing at economical prices — catalog sheets, bound catalogs or booklets, direct mail pieces, brochures. This company works with small business owners (including craft and needlework designers/self-publishers) and will send samples of their work on request. (Note: This company also can provide help in designing camera-ready art, will take product photos for use on flyers, etc.) Contact Dorrie Silverman at Direct Press. (S-IV)

☐ *Directory of Book, Catalog, and Magazine Printers*, by John Kremer. Lists 1,000 printers of annual reports, books, catalogs, magazines, and other bound publications. $17 ppd. from Ad-Lib Publications. (B-II)

☐ GraphiColor. A well-known printer in the West which specializes in affordable color printing for artists and others who need color brochures, prints, or related color work. They keep costs low by holding jobs, then running several at the same time. (S-IV)

☐ LaSalle Photo. A source for new product and other business photos at bulk prices. (S-IV)

☐ Mohawk Valley Printing. They have a kit to help you make up a camera-ready pamphlet or booklet. Useful whether you plan to use this company as your printer or not. $2.50 brings dummy pages, photo labels, paper and type samples. (S-IV)

☐ Morgan Printing & Publishing. Specialists in short-run book printing, including booklets, catalogs (250–2,500 quantities), newsletters, directories, etc. (S-IV)

☐ Penny Pinchin' Press. Offers an excellent get-acquainted booklet that explains services, prices, etc. Good source for reasonably priced color sheets. Send request for info on letterhead to attention of Crickett Deyo at Penny Pinchin' Press. (S-IV)

☐ Quantity Photo Company. An economical by-mail source for photos in quantity, for promotional purposes, from 4×5 to 8×10 to large 30″×40″ promotional prints. Black and white or color. Free brochure. (S-IV)

☐ Roxanne Studios. Color photos in bulk quantities; low prices. Can work from prints or slides. (S-IV)

Chapter Four Resources
Planning Guides

Management/Money/Marketing/Time

☐ *Business Plan for Small Manufacturers.* Free booklet from the SBA. Ask for #MA 2.007. (G-III)

☐ *Business Planning for the Entrepreneur,* by Edward E. Williams & Salvatore E. Manzo. Van Nostrand Reinhold, 1983. Hardcover, $22.95. A full-scale guide to developing plans for starting a small business and expanding an existing one; also, preparing the business plan itself. Available in bookstores and libraries.

☐ *The Business Planning Guide — Creating a Plan for Success in Your Own Business,* by David H. Bangs, Jr. With 150,000 copies in print, this book has achieved status as an "underground best-seller," earning its reputation through its practical, jargon-free (and humorous) approach to a topic that is usually quite boring. Paperback; in bookstores, or order by mail for $18.95 ppd. from Upstart Pub. Co. (B-II)

☐ Business Planning Worksheets. Designed by Dr. William R. Osgood, these useful worksheets and lists of business planning questions will help you get all your plans on paper. Particularly useful if one of your goals is securing a bank loan. Order by mail at $4.75 ppd. from New Hampshire Small Business Development Program. (A-IV)

☐ *Business Week.* A weekly magazine for business managers, with emphasis on large business, but with management and marketing articles to which all businesspeople can relate. (P-II)

☐ *Financial Control for the Small Business,* by Michael M. Coltman. A primer for keeping a tighter rein on your profits and cash flow. 1982, paperback. Order by mail at $7.00 ppd. from Self-Counsel Press. (B-II)

☐ *Get It All Done and Still Be Human,* by Robbie and Tony Fanning. Chilton. A practical and warmly-written book on time management that explains the valuable technique of "patterning." Order by mail at $4.95 ppd. from Open Chain Pub. (A-IV)

☐ Insurance programs available to homebased business owners. The following organizations (all detailed in this resource directory and listed alphabetically in Section O-III) offer insurance programs of one kind or another. Request more information about them if you write for membership information. [ ] American Crafts Council; [ ] American Home Business Assn.; [ ] American Society of Journalists & Authors; [ ] Artist's Equity; [ ] Association of Part-Time Professionals; [ ] National Writers Club; [ ] Support Services Alliance.

☐ *Marketing Research Procedures.* A free bibliography available from the SBA. Ask for #SBB-9. (G-III)

☐ *The Market Planning Guide: Gaining and Maintaining the Competitive Edge,* by David H. Bangs, Jr. A complete guide to finding customers for your products and services, in workbook form. Good sections on analyzing your products/services, pricing, investigating the competition, strategic marketing, and developing a sales plan. Paperback in bookstores, or order by mail for $26.95 ppd. from Upstart Pub. Co. (B-II)

☐ *The Moneypaper* — A monthly publication for women. Covers investments, taxes, insurance, household expenses, and major purchases of all kinds. (P-II)

☐ *More Than a Dream: Raising the Money;* and *More Than a Dream: Running Your Own Business.* Two informative booklets, free from the U.S. Department of Labor. (G-III)

☐ *The New Financial Guide for the Self-Employed,* by John Ellis. Contemporary Books, 1981. Paperback, $9.95. Examines aspects of insurance, borrowing money, time management, accountants, billing, record keeping, taxes, retirement planning. Geared for people already self-employed or in a home business. Available in bookstores and libraries.

☐ *Plan Your Advertising Budget.* Free management aid from the SBA. #4.018. (G-III)

☐ *Planning and Goal Setting for Small Business.* A free management aid from the SBA. #MA2.010. (G-III)

☐ *Sidetracked Home Executives: From Pigpen to Paradise,* by Peggy Jones & Pam Young. Warner Books, paperback. Offers systematic method of scheduling every job necessary for maintaining the home and one's sanity, freeing time for other activities. Ask for information about this book and its related newsletter and other publications/products. Contact S.H.E., Inc. (A-IV)

☐ *Sleep Less, Live More,* by Everett Mattlin. Ballantine Books, paperback. Offers a plan for safely shortening sleep time in order to gain more time for living/working. Published in 1977, this book is out of print. Check the library for a copy.

☐ Small Business Reporter of booklets on marketing and business. A couple of these booklets have been listed in this directory, but a complete, free listing of all publications — including several of interest to retailers — is available from the Bank of America. (A-IV)

☐ *The Secrets of Practical Marketing for Small Business,* by Herman R. Holtz. Prentice Hall, Inc., 1982. Hardcover, $16.95; paperback, $7.95. One of the best marketing guides any homebased business owner could read. Paperback edition available by mail for $9.95 ppd. from the author. (A-IV)

A-to-Z Business Section

Business, Legal, and Financial Resources

☐ *The ABCs of Borrowing.* Free management aid from the SBA. #MA 1.001. (G-III)

☐ *Accounting Services for Small Service-Firms.* Free management aid from the SBA. #MA 1.010. (G-III)

☐ *Basic Accounting for the Small Business,* by Clive G. Cornish. TAB Books, paperback. How to reduce accounting costs, minimize paperwork, and do the preliminary bookkeeping. Order by mail at $5.95 ppd. from TAB Books. (B-II)

☐ *Business Agreements: A Complete Guide to Oral and Written Contracts.* Chilton, hardcover, $27.50.

How to draft, write, read, interpret, and understand contracts. Out of print, but check the library.

☐ *Business Kits for Starting and Existing Businesses,* by Lawless J. Barrientos, CPA. This series of books eventually will include a guide for each state, giving the businessperson all the forms needed to operate legally in each state. Books are now in print for the states of California, Florida, Georgia, Illinois, Massachusetts, New York, Ohio, Pennsylvania, Texas, and Washington. Available in bookstores and libraries.

☐ *Business Life Insurance.* A free management aid from the SBA. #MA 2.009. (G-III)

☐ *Business Loans From the SBA.* A free booklet available from the SBA. Ask for it by title — no special order number is required. (G-III)

☐ The Center for Occupational Hazards. A national clearinghouse for information on hazards in the arts. Send a SASE to receive their publications list and information about hazards in the visual, graphic, and performing arts, crafts, theatre, hobbies, and art instruction. The COH also maintains a listing of 100 physicians all over the U.S. and in Ontario, Canada who are Board Certified in Occupational Medicine or closely-related health problems. Send an additional SASE if you want to receive this list. (O-III)

☐ *Consumer Product Safety.* Free booklet from the U.S. Department of Commerce. (G-III)

☐ Center on National Labor Policy, Inc. Attorneys at this center are working to change outdated labor laws that affect homebased workers. Home business owners who need legal assistance regarding a cottage industry problem may write to the attention of Edward F. Hughes. (O-III)

☐ *Credit and Collections.* A free management aid from the SBA. #MA 1.007. (G-III)

☐ *Design Your Own Logo,* by Mark Haskett. Self-Counsel Press, 1984. Paperback. This book takes the reader step-by-step through the whole process, from conception to final artwork. Includes case histories of logo-design projects. Order by mail at $11.45 ppd. from Self-Counsel Press. (B-II)

☐ Dun & Bradstreet. D&B has a collection service called "DUNS Direct," which serves the small company with a large number of commercial accounts. This collection service is for small amounts from $20 to $200; at least five accounts must be sent in for collection at a time, with a minimum of 25 accounts entered for the year. If you have this kind of collection problem, write for a free brochure. (M-IV)

☐ *Everybody's Guide to Small Claims Court,* by Ralph Warner. How to make collections more effectively. Available by mail at $17.45 ppd. from Nolo Press. (B-II)

☐ *General Information Concerning Patents.* A free booklet available from the Patent & Trademark Office. (G-III)

☐ *General Information Concerning Trademarks.* A free booklet from the Patent & Trademark Office. (G-III)

☐ Julian Block's *Guide to Year-Round Tax Savings.* This book is temporarily out of print; a new 1990 edition is scheduled for publication in late 1989. Meanwhile, you can connect with Julian through his syndicated newspaper column, "The Tax Report." (A-IV)

☐ H.A.L.T. stands for "Help Abolish Legal Tyranny." This nonprofit organization is leading the fight to reform America's legal system. Membership brings a quarterly newspaper and five free Citizens Legal Manuals, including *Shopping for a Lawyer.* (O-III)

☐ *How to Borrow Money From a Bank,* by Don H. Alexander. An excellent, non-technical paperback guide that provides valuable insight into how bankers examine, investigate, analyze, and evaluate loan applications; includes supporting material, written by a banker in commercial lending. Order by mail at $6.95 ppd. from DHA & Associates. (B-II)

☐ *How to Form Your Own Corporation Without a Lawyer for Under $50,* by Ted Nicholas. According to the author, this book has become one of the best-selling business books of all time, helping more than 650,000 people to incorporate at minimum expense. Whether you incorporate with or without the help of a lawyer, this book will explain the benefits of incorporation and answer a lot of questions you may have. Order by mail at $21.95 ppd. from Enterprise Publishing. (B-II)

☐ *Incorporating a Small Business.* Free management aid from the SBA. #MA 6.003. (G-III)

☐ *Insurance Checklist for Small Business.* Free management aid from the SBA. #MA 2.018. (G-III)

☐ *Introduction to Patents.* Free management aid from the SBA. #MA 6.005. (G-III)

☐ *Keeping Records in Small Business.* Free management aid from the SBA. #MA 1.017. (G-III)

☐ *Making It Legal — A Law Primer for the Craftmaker, Visual Artist and Writer,* by Marion Davidson & Martha Blue. McGraw-Hill, paperback, $8.95. The best book of its kind for the creative person who hates to deal with the legal aspects of their work, yet realizes the importance of it. Written with humor and understanding of the creative individual. (Has an excellent chapter on copyrights, patents, and related topics.) Available in bookstores and libraries.

☐ National Economic Development Law Center. If you have a simple legal question, or are just wondering if you need a lawyer in a specific instance, this center will answer such questions free of charge. (O-III)

☐ *New Product Development.* A business bibliography (#90) free from SBA. (G-III)

☐ *Nolo Small Business Start-Up,* by Mike P. Mc-Keever. Nolo Press, 1984. Paperback. Tells how to prepare a sound business plan and plan package needed to convince lenders and investors to back you. In bookstores or order by mail at $20.45 ppd. from Nolo Press. (B-II)

☐ *Outwitting Bad-Check Passers.* Free management aid from the SBA. #MA 3.008. (G-III)

☐ *Patent It Yourself,* by Pressman. Nolo Press. Hardcover, $32.45 ppd. If you can describe your invention in detail in conjunction with drawings, this book will enable you to prepare, file, and obtain your own patent at a cost of only $450, says the author, rather than the $1700–$3000 which most patent attorneys charge. In bookstores or order from Nolo Press. (B-II)

☐ *Selecting the Legal Structure for Your Business.* Free management aid from the SBA. #MA 6.004. (G-III)

☐ *Small-Time Operator — How to Start Your Own Business, Keep Your Books, Pay Your Taxes, and Stay Out of Trouble,* by Bernard Kamoroff, CPA. Revised annually. Includes "nuts-and-bolts" information, special tax and financial advice, ledgers and worksheets. In bookstores, or order by mail. Request price of current edition from Bell Springs Publishing. (B-II)

☐ *Steps in Meeting Your Tax Obligations.* Free management aid from the SBA. #MA 1.013. (G-III)

☐ *That's a Great Idea!* by Husch & Foust. 1986 paperback. This book is a great idea, one that offers real help for anyone who's trying to develop, protect, or sell new product ideas. Of special value are chapters which discuss when to sell an idea or do it yourself, how to protect ideas, and how to present them for sale. In bookstores, or by mail for $11.45 ppd. from Gravity Publishing. (B-II)

☐ *2001 Sources of Financing for Small Business,* by Herman Holtz. Arco Publishing Co., 1983. Paperback. This "crash course in business economics" is out of print, but may be in the library.

☐ Volunteer Lawyers for the Arts. A nonprofit organization with chapters all over the country. In addition to providing legal aid for performing and visual artists and craftspeople who cannot afford a lawyer, the VLA also provides educational services and publications. Has published "Copyright for Visual Artists," a 16-pg. booklet. Write for more information. (O-III)

Government Resources
(All addresses will be found in the Section G-III)

☐ Bureau of the Census. For information on census bureau programs and products, send 40¢ for a copy of *Factfinder for the Nation* newsletter.

☐ Consumer Products Safety Commission — Bureau of Compliance. If you sell any product to the public, you must protect yourself, your employees, and the environment. Various free booklets from this government agency explain laws and regulations you may need to know about. In particular, ask for [ ] *The Federal Hazardous Substances Act,* [ ] *The Consumer Product Safety Act of 1972;* and [ ] *The Flammable Fabrics Act.*

☐ Cooperative Extension Service. Extension services are a part of the U.S. Department of Agriculture and the Land Grant University of each state. A national office in Washington oversees state programs, and each state has an office with subject matter specialists in many different areas. These specialists train and work with county extension home economists, among others, who in turn work with the general public. Home business owners and others who want to start businesses should connect with their county extension office by calling the county seat.

☐ The Copyright Office. Many free publications are available. Ask especially for these: [ ] *The Nuts and Bolts of Copyright,* (Circular R1); [ ] *Publications on Copyright,* (Circular R2); [ ] *Highlights of the New Copyright Law,* (Circular R99); [ ] *How to Investigate the Copyright Status of a Work,* (Circular R22); and [ ] *Trademarks,* (Circular R13). Registration forms may be ordered by mail, or by telephoning (202) 287-9100 and specifying the particular form desired.

☐ Department of Commerce. Offers several free booklets, including *Product Warranties and Servicing, Advertising, Packaging, and Labeling,* and *Consumer Product Safety.*

☐ Department of Labor, local office. For information relating to your status as an employer or an independent contractor, contact your local Labor Department, Wage & Hour Division. (Look in the telephone book under "U.S. Government.") Ask for a copy of *The Fair Labor Standards Act of 1938, as Amended.*

☐ Department of Labor (Washington, DC). Offers two free booklet titled *More Than A Dream,* (subtitled,

Raising the Money and *Running Your Own Business*). Also ask for *Employment Relationship Under the Fair Labor Standards Act* if you plan to hire help for your business; direct inquiry to the Wage & Hour Division. Women may request *The Handbook on Women Workers,* published by The Women's Bureau of The Department of Labor.

☐ Federal Trade Commission. Write for trade practice rules applicable to your particular business or industry. Some of special interest to some of this book's readers would be: [　] *The Jewelry Industry;* [　] *The Hand Knitting Yarn Industry,* and [　] *Catalog Jewelry and Giftware Industry.*

☐ Food and Drug Administration. Write if you need information about federal, state, and local requirements governing packaging and labeling of food-related products.

☐ Internal Revenue Service. Among the many free publications of interest to home business owners are: [　] *Tax Guide for Small Business,* #344; [　] *Business Use of Your Home,* #587; [　] *Index to Tax Publications,* #900; [　] *Depreciation;* #534, and [　] *Tax Withholding & Declaration of Estimated Tax,* #505; [　] *Determining Whether a Worker is an Employee,* #SS-8; [　] *Tax Information for Direct Sellers,* #911.

☐ National Bureau of Standards. If you work with metals (gold or silver), write for information on the special labeling required for products made from them.

☐ Library of Congress, National Referral Center. They have a subject-indexed, computerized file of some 13,000 organizations and individuals who are willing to provide answers to specific, specialized topics. No charge for information from the Center, but you may have to pay to get information from the people to whom they refer you.

☐ Patent & Trademark Office. Offers free information on how to obtain patents and trademarks.

☐ SCORE. (See U.S. Small Business Administration listing below.)

☐ Superintendent of Documents. Ask to receive "Subject Bibliography Index," which describes the various bibliographies of publications on a single subject or field of interest. The government offers thousands of publications, with as many as 3,000 new ones added to the list each year.

☐ U.S. Fish & Wildlife Service. Write for information about laws and regulations applicable to you if your business involves feathers, bones, claws, ivory, or endangered species.

☐ U.S. Small Business Administration (SBA) and SCORE. Simply put, the mission of SBA is to help people get into business and stay in business. Help is available from local district offices of the SBA in the form of free business counseling and training from more than 8,000 SCORE volunteers (Service Corps of Retired Executives) nationwide. To connect with them, see your local telephone directory under SCORE, U.S. Government, Small Business Administration, or inquire at your Chamber of Commerce. SBA publications include the addresses of district offices.

The SBA office in Washington has a special Women's Business Enterprise section which provides free information on loans, tax deductions, and other financial matters. District offices offer special training programs in management, marketing, and accounting. (Helping women is a special major goal of the SBA because women make up half the population, yet own less than a fourth of the country's businesses.)

The SBA office in Ft. Worth, Texas is your source for the many free and low-cost management assistance publications and bibliographies, several of which have been listed in this resource directory. For a complete listing, request these bulletins: [　] SBA 115-A (Free SBA Publications) and [　] SBA 115-B (For-Sale Booklets).

There also is an SBA "Answer Desk," an SBA toll-free number in Washington. Experts from SBA's Office of Advocacy staff the Answer Desk phones from 8:30 a.m. to 6:00 p.m. Monday through Friday. They welcome questions from home business owners concerned with government regulations, and training and counseling services available to them, as well as questions about the availability of SBA loans. Call 800-368-5855.

Chapter Five Resources
Pricing

Bags, Boxes, Tags & Labels

Write for price lists or catalogs from each of these companies, listed in the S-IV address section:

☐ Action Bag Co. Reclosable polyethylene bags in minimum quantities of 1,000 per size; custom printed paper and plastic bags and labels; white gift boxes, various sizes (available by the case of 100).

☐ Alkahn Labels. Custom-designer labels for clothing

and other items. Expensive unless you're ordering a large quantity. (Minimum order, 1,000 labels.)

☐ Associated Bag Co. Offers catalog of wide variety of bags & related items.

☐ The Designery. Offers "Craft Tags" and care labels for garments or crafts. 36 designs.

☐ Gaylord Specialties Corp. Paper and plastic bags; bows, ribbons, giftware; embossed gold and silver name seals and labels; price tags.

☐ Kimmeric Studio. Has large line of hang tags for craft or needlework products. Illustrated with calligraphy and art.

☐ Perfection Supply Co. Price and merchandise tickets, garment tags, gift boxes (white), cotton-filled jewelry boxes, garment racks and displays.

☐ Retail Stores Tag & Supply Co. Supplier of tags (with string) for larger items. Small minimum order.

☐ SaKet Company. Wholesale source for poly bags and related products, small minimum order.

☐ Sterling Name Tape Co. Makes labels that can be sewn to products, and will do custom labels (incorporating your logo, etc.) at reasonable prices.

☐ 20th Century Plastics, Inc. Vinyl products, including zipper bags that can be imprinted, "Bubblepak," sealing tape, Jiffy Bags, and a wide variety of office supplies & equipment.

☐ Unique Ideas. Care labels for handmade items (how to wash, dry, iron, etc.).

☐ United States Box Corp. Stock packaging; set-up boxes, boxes with acetate covers, air cushion bags, padding.

Directories & Guides

☐ *The Directory of Directories.* Gale Research.

Describes over 9,000 directories, rosters, and buyer's guides available. Found in libraries.

☐ *The Gift & Decorative Accessory Buyer's Guide.* Annual directory published by *Gifts & Decorative Accessories* magazine. Lists some 30,000 manufacturers, importers, distributors serving the gift industry, plus sources for manufacturing and assembling materials, show and shop display cases, classifications of trade names, listing of trade shows, industry associations, etc. Can be purchased separately from the magazine. (P-II)

☐ *How to Set Your Fees and Get Them*, by Kate Kelly. Spiral-bound paperback with excellent guidelines on how to price services, learn to negotiate fees, and set dollar amounts on intangible inconveniences, like tight deadlines. Order by mail at $15 ppd. from Visibility Enterprises. (B-II)

☐ *Pricing For Small Manufacturers.* A free management aid from the SBA. #MA 1.005. (G-III)

☐ *Profitable Craft Merchandising.* A monthly trade periodical edited for craft retailers, but valuable to designers, manufacturers, and publishers in both the craft and needlework industries. Publishes an annual directory of manufacturers and wholesalers, with guide to products by trade name and category. (P-II)

☐ *Thomas' Register of American Manufacturers.* A directory found in most libraries. Its several volumes include a listing of products in alphabetical order, with the names and addresses of companies who make them. When a manufacturer won't sell to you, this directory at least will refer you to your nearest distributor or dealer.

☐ *What's The Best Selling Price?* Free management aid from the SBA. #MA 1.002. (G-III)

Chapter Six Resources
Fairs, Festivals,
Flea Markets, & Home Shows

Periodicals, Calendars, Directories, & Reports

☐ *The Antique Trader Weekly.* The most widely-read publication in the antiques and collectibles field; the "bible" of the hobby, with advertising, news, and articles. Published weekly. Single copy, $1. (P-II)

☐ *Art Show News.* Marketing periodical for artists and craft sellers, with articles and national listing of shows and show tours, promoters, etc. (P-II)

☐ *Art & Crafts Catalyst.* (Formerly *National Calendar of Indoor/Outdoor Art Fairs & Festivals.*) Bimonthly with details on where to find and how to enter, shows across the country. Sample, $4. (P-II)

☐ *The Craft Party Plan Report.* A self-published report and step-by-step outline for organizing and conducting craft-selling parties in the home. Order by mail for $5, plus a large SASE with two stamps, from Susan Scharadin. (A-IV)

☐ *Directory of North American Fairs.* Annual compilation of every fair and exposition that runs three or more days in the U.S. and Canada, with data on managers, demographics, etc. Information available from Billboard Directories. (M-IV)

☐ *Flea Market, USA.* A national, annual directory of 2,500 locations of flea markets and swap meets. $7.50 ppd. Inquire about companion periodical of same name from Charles Clark. (A-IV)

☐ *A Guide to Marketing Crafts Through a Home Party System.* Information gained through experimentation and adaptation in this self-published booklet by the authors, Jo Mucha & Marion Boyer. Order for $5 ppd. from Village Vendor, Ltd. (A-IV)

☐ *How to Make Money in the Antiques & Collectibles Business,* by Elyse Sommer. Pocket Books, paperback, $3.50. A complete guide. Available in bookstores.

☐ *The Flea Market Entrepreneur,* by Charlotte Harmon. Pilot Books. What to sell, where to find merchandise, find shows, set prices, and set up displays. Order by mail at $4.95 ppd. from Pilot Books. (B-II)

☐ *The National Flea Market Dealer.* A monthly magazine dubbed the "official landing pad" for the United Flea Marketer's Organization. Published in conjunction with several related flea market publications. Single copy, $7. (P-II)

Chapter Seven Resources
Wholesaling

Trade Periodicals/Organizations/Shows

☐ *Agents and Lines Bulletin.* Ads and articles on manufacturers' representatives and their principals. Also marketing services offered and wanted. (P-II)

☐ American Apparel Manufacturers Association. Publishes a newsletter for members, plus research papers. (O-III)

☐ American Craft Enterprises, Inc. Sponsors four of the country's major craft fairs (retail/wholesale marketplaces) in West Springfield, MA (formerly the Rhinebeck show), Baltimore, Dallas, and San Francisco. Open to craft sellers nationwide, but the standards are high (as explained in the text). (O-III)

☐ Apparel Industry Sourcebook. A national directory of suppliers and contractors to the apparel industry. Write for price of directory and subscription information to *Apparel Industry Magazine.* (P-II)

☐ *Candy Industry Magazine.* A trade magazine that may be helpful to homebased candy makers/sellers. (P-II)

☐ *Chain Store Age.* Merchandise information, industry news, store operating procedures, plus insight on how to sell to mass merchandisers. (P-II)

☐ *Convention World.* Listings of conventions, trade shows, and events/facts relevant to this market. Single copy, $8.50. (M-IV)

☐ *County Agents Directory.* This is a national listing of names/addresses of cooperative extension workers and other specialists, including home economists who have wide-ranging interests in products and publications. They often buy books and subscribe to periodicals because they work with consumers in so many ways, and are deeply involved in the home business movement. The directory can be ordered for $19.95 ppd. from County Agents Directory. (M-IV)

☐ *Creative Products News.* A free subscription is offered if you are a retailer, wholesaler, manufacturer, manufacturer's rep, arts educator, crafts demonstrator, or other professional in the crafts/needlework/art materials field. (P-II)

☐ *Directory of Wholesale Reps* for Artisans and Craft Professionals. This new directory, compiled by Sharon Olson includes sales rep organizations which sell nationwide to shops, galleries, department stores, and other giftware outlets. Each company has been interviewed, given permission to be listed, and specified type of crafts wanted. Reps seeking new lines may contact publisher to be listed in next edition. The directory is $5 ppd. from Northwoods Trading Co. (A-IV)

☐ *Directory Marketplace.* A quarterly advertising newsletter for directory and reference book buyers. Will connect you with such resources as *Mail Order Business Directory* (10,000 of the most active mail order catalog houses); *The National Directory of Postcard Deck Media* (lists 500 decks); and *The National Directory of Product Publicity Sources.* Write for a list of all available directories. (P-II)

☐ *Discount Merchandiser.* Retail distribution covering discount, supermarket, drug, catalog, and other mass merchandising industries, with emphasis on marketing and merchandising. Single copy, $3. (P-II)

☐ *Elephants in Your Mailbox,* by Roger Horchow. Hardcover, $12.50. An entertaining and informative book by the famous mail-order catalog entrepreneur, who tells all — his secrets to success, and his 25 worst mistakes. Check bookstores or write Horchow to order. (A-IV)

☐ *Exhibits Schedule/Successful Meetings.* Magazine offering information on world-wide trade and public shows — dates, sites, attendance, number of exhibits, plus show executives and addresses. (P-II)

☐ *Food Industry News.* Management, marketing, and sales activities and concerns of companies that manufacture food and related products for distribution through retail food channels. Single copy, $5. (P-II)

☐ *Garden Supply Retailer.* Retail merchandising and management, developments in the lawn and garden field, book reviews, new product news, etc. (P-II)

☐ *Gift & Tableware Reporter.* News (products, suppliers, retailers) and events in or affecting the decorative home furnishings industry. Published for retailers. (P-II)

☐ *Gifts & Decorative Accessories Magazine.* Published monthly for retailers, but helpful to anyone desiring to sell to the gift market. Subscription includes the annual directory, *Gift & Decorative Buyers Guide.* (P-II)

☐ *Greetings Magazine Buyers Guide.* Lists all publishers and manufacturers of products and services purchased by greeting card retailers, with cross index of products, associations, resident buying offices; promotional know-how. (M-IV)

☐ Hobby Industry Association of America. Where to write for a complete schedule of all the craft and hobby trade shows nationwide. (O-III)

☐ *Import/Export: A Guide to Growth, Profits & Market Share,* by Howard R. Goldsmith. How and where to find profitable products to import/export, buy at "right price," establish credit in international business deals, duties, tariffs, customs, etc. With appendix of information sources, customs house brokers, and more. Order by mail at $22.70 ppd. from Intercontinental Trade Specialists. (M-IV)

☐ IBIS Information Services, Inc. Offers international mailing lists and cooperative, shared mailings to libraries in Europe and English-speaking areas of the world. (M-IV)

☐ *Incentive Marketing.* Directed to executives who buy and use premiums as part of their sales programs. Single copy, $2. (P-II)

☐ *Is The Independent Sales Agent For You?* A free management aid from the SBA. #MA 4.005. (G-III)

☐ *Lawn & Garden Marketing.* For those marketing products for lawn care, gardening, indoor and patio plantings, and leisure living. Includes industry news, trends, new products info, etc. Single copy, $2. (P-II)

☐ *Mail Order Product.* A catalog circulated to the buyers and other principals at leading mail-order catalog houses. For $50 or less, you can easily introduce a new product to this market. Details from Voice Publications. (M-IV)

☐ Manufacturers' Agents National Association. Publishes a newsletter and an annual directory of 9,000 members of the association, with information about lines and territories handled. (M-IV)

☐ *The Manufacturing Confectioner.* A magazine for professional candy manufacturers. Covers production, materials, handling, storage, packing, shipping, and merchandising. Single copy, $5. (P-II)

☐ Museum Store Association. An organization for museum shop buyers and sellers. Membership is helpful in breaking into the museum shop market. (O-III)

☐ National Association for the Specialty Food Trade, Inc. Publishes a trade magazine, *Showcase,* and sponsors a trade show. (O-III)

☐ The National Needlework Association, Inc. Publishes *National Needlework News* and sponsors a major needlework trade market, called the TNNA Show. (O-III)

☐ National Stationery Show. Through this show, you can tap into the vast licensing industry, as well as the greeting card industry. (M-IV)

☐ *Nationwide Directory of Gift & Housewares Buyers.* Lists merchandise managers and buyers of gifts and housewares for a variety of retail stores. (M-IV)

☐ *The $100 Billion Market: How to do Business with the U.S. Government,* by Herman R. Holtz. Amacom Publishing. Paperback. How to say "Open Sesame" to the government's 15,000 buying activities, by an author with 29 years' experience in winning government contracts for small businesses. This helpful book is out of print; check the library.

☐ *Playthings.* Serves retailers, wholesalers, and manufacturers of toys, hobbies, and crafts. Single issue, $3. Also publishes *Playthings Directory.* (P-II)

☐ *Publishers Weekly.* The trade magazine of the book publishing industry, for book publishers, booksellers, and authors who take an active interest in the marketing of their own books. (P-II)

☐ *Rep World.* Information on selling with independent manufacturer's reps. Single copy, $2. (P-II)

☐ *The Sales Rep's Advisor.* Monthly publication offering legal, financial, and business strategies for independent sales reps. Single copy, $7. (P-II)

☐ *Selling to Catalog Houses,* by Ron Playle. How you, too, can sell thousands of books and other products to large mail order catalog companies. Inside secrets from a writer/publisher who has sold thousands of his books to national mail-order houses. The only publication of its kind. Order by mail at $10 ppd. from Playle Pub. (A-IV)

☐ The Society of American Florists. This trade organization publishes a quarterly, *American Florist*, useful to marketers in this industry, and to those in the crafts field who work with dried flowers and related materials. (O-III)

☐ *Souvenirs & Novelties*. Periodical offering information about new items and news of the trade. Single copy, $1.50. (P-II)

☐ *Toy & Hobby World*. Published for toy buyers, providing toy and hobby/craft merchandising information to the national mass market. New Product news, trends, manufacturers' promotional activities, etc. (P-II)

☐ *The Where-To-Sell-It Directory*, by Margaret A. Boyd and Sue Scott-Martin. Lists dealers and collectors who will buy almost anything. Order by mail at $4.95 ppd. from Pilot Books. (B-II)

☐ *Women's Wear Daily*. Trade magazine for those involved in the garment industry, with new product info, trade show announcements, trends, etc. (P-II)

☐ *World Gift Review Newsletter*. A monthly that publishes paid reviews of mail order products available to dealers. Gives prices, details, shipping info, etc. An inexpensive way to introduce a new product to a particular group of buyers. (M-IV)

Marketing Aids

☐ *The Buckley-Little Book Catalogue*. Offers marketing help for authors whose publishers are allowing their books to go out of print. Lists books available from authors who have elected to purchase existing inventories. This plan is also open to self-publishers who seek bookstore/library distribution. To have your books listed in a future catalog or to obtain a copy of the current edition, contact Buckley-Little. (M-IV)

☐ *Book Marketing Handbook: Tips and Techniques*, by Nat G. Bodian. R. R. Bowker Co., $59.95. This is a goldmine of information, ideas, and contact sources for the mail order marketer of books — the only guide of its kind. Although written for trade book publishers, even the one-book, self-publisher will benefit enormously from it. Also contains the most extensive listing of direct response card deck mailing programs, with addresses to write for additional information. Available in bookstores and libraries.

☐ *Direct Marketing*. Excellent trade magazine for direct marketers, with good articles on how to write better ad copy, get better results from direct response advertising, etc. Includes announcements of new products, mail lists, distribution programs, premium items, and more. (P-II)

☐ The Direct Mail/Marketing Association. A trade organization representing some 3,000 firms in the direct marketing industry. Offers a directory, *The Great Catalog Guide*, which lists more than 630 mail order sources for clothing, collectibles, housewares, home furnishings, food, gifts, gardening, etc. (A good way to find catalog markets for your own products.) The *Guide* can be ordered for $1. (O-III)

☐ *Dun & Bradstreet Directories*. Available in libraries, these books are the who, what, and where of commercial and industrial activity around the world. Several volumes list companies by annual dollar volume to aid marketers. Selected data from the listings are available in the form of mailing labels or 3×5 cards. Companies are listed alphabetically, geographically, and by product classifications.

☐ *Encyclopedia of Associations*. Gale Research. Available in libraries, this directory lists thousands of U.S. associations by name and by subject categories — trade, business, professional, labor, educational, fraternal, and social.

☐ *Guerilla Marketing*, by Jay Conrad Levinson. Houghton Mifflin Co., 1984. Subtitled, "Secrets for Making Big Profits from Your Small Business," this book is recognized as THE book on marketing with a small budget. This book is fun to read, easy to understand, and highly recommended. Apparently out of print, but try the library.

☐ *Marketing Without Advertising — Creative Strategies for Small Business Success*, by Michael Phillips & Salli Rasberry. You may find it hard to believe, but you CAN operate a business successfully without spending money for traditional advertising, and this excellent book tells how. Paperback, $16.50 ppd. from Nolo Press. (B-II)

☐ National Mail Order Classified. This service will place your classified ads in several publications at once, for so much a word, depending on the number of magazines you wish to try at one time. A great time-saver for those who do a lot of classified advertising. (M-IV)

☐ *Parade, The Sunday Magazine*. Offers per-inquiry advertising of interest to serious mail-order marketers, as detailed in the text. Write for information from Parade Publications. (M-IV)

☐ *The Shoestring Marketer*. This bimonthly newsletter shows small budget advertisers how they can promote their business without spending a fortune. Mention this book to receive a sample for $4. (P-II)

☐ *Successful Direct Marketing Methods,* by Bob Stone. Crain Books, 1984. $29.95. The one and only complete

and definitive book on direct marketing, by an outstanding professional in the field. Available in bookstores and libraries, or by mail from Crain Communications. (M-IV)

Chapter Eight Resources
Direct Response Advertising

Advertising Copywriting Aids

☐ *Advertising, Packaging & Labeling.* A free booklet available from the U.S. Department of Commerce. (G-III)

☐ *How to Write a Good Advertisement,* by Victor O. Schwab. A classic text which offers the basics and techniques — a "short course in copywriting." Order by mail for $16 ppd. from the National Mail Order Association. (O-III)

☐ *Persuasive Writing,* by Herman Holtz. McGraw-Hill. Secrets of persuading readers to buy and believe in products — or hire you. How to write letters, proposals, brochures, newsletters, and other publications. Available by mail from Herman Holtz. (A-IV)

☐ *Product Warranties & Servicing.* What you need to know before you make consumer guarantees on your products. A free booklet from the U.S. Department of Commerce. (G-III)

☐ *Writing That Means Business,* by Ellen Roddick. A book to help you improve your ability to communicate clearly, from organizing thoughts to putting them in writing to achieve desired results. $8.95 paperback in bookstores, or contact Collier Books to order by mail. (B-II)

List Houses & Distribution Programs

☐ American Business Lists, Inc. Offers toy and hobby industry lists — craft supplies dealers, hobby shops, gift shops, toy shops, etc. Compiled from Yellow Page listings nationwide. (M-IV)

☐ R. R. Bowker Co. This company's mailing list division rents up-to-date mailing lists of libraries, schools, bookstores, book reviewers, pre-school centers, and more. (Note: The bookstores lists are available by subject category, such as general book outlets, department store book departments, specialty stores which sell books, and so on.) (M-IV)

☐ COSMEP. Rents mailing lists of some 3,500 libraries and 4,000 bookstores which have made purchases from small, independent magazines and presses. (O-III)

☐ *Creative Products News.* This trade publisher offers a loosedeck direct-response postcard mailing to 40,000 crafts retailers and distributors for less than 3¢ each. Quick way to introduce your products to craft and needlework shops and art material retailers. (P-II)

☐ Hugo Dunhill Mailing Lists, Inc. If you need both a source for mail lists and assistance in creating direct mail pieces, use your business letterhead to request the following free items: "Complete Catalog of Mailing Lists"; "How to Prepare an Effective Direct Mail Letter"; and "How to Prepare a Direct Mail Brochure That Sells." (M-IV)

☐ Leon Henry, Inc. Offers a variety of package insert programs and mailing lists. (M-IV)

☐ *National Mailing List House.* A free bibliography from the SBA which gives names and addresses of major list houses throughout the country, only a few of which have been listed here. Ask for #SBB-29. (G-III)

☐ National Mail Order Association. Offers many lists, including 30 foreign trade associations in the U.S. and 20 trade associations worldwide, suppliers in Hong Kong, Taiwan, Europe, etc. Request a free listing of all available information. (O-III)

☐ Needlework shops mailing list. Over 10,000 shop names available on labels at 3 cents each, no minimum. Specific breakdowns available. Free flyer from Counted Thread. (M-IV)

☐ *Standard Rate & Data Service (SRDS) Publications.* These directories, available in libraries, present listings of more than 3,000 business, trade, and technical publications categorized by markets served; also give marketing demographics, information about mailing lists, and special distribution programs for marketers; more.

☐ Larry Tucker, Inc. Offers a variety of mailing lists, insert programs, cooperative mailings, and other unique distribution programs for the serious direct marketer, including tourist and college "take one's," senior citizen co-op mailings, new mothers, new homeowners, and many others. (M-IV)

Chapter Nine Resources
Publicity

PR Guides, Directories, Services

☐ *Ayer Directory of Newspapers & Periodicals.* Names, addresses, and phone numbers of newspapers, magazines, and periodicals published in the U.S. and Canada. With circulation and rate info, maps, and market data. Available in libraries.

☐ Bacon's Publicity Checker. This company offers various categories of names, such as all the daily newspapers in the U.S., all the weeklies, the top 100 radio stations, women's and fashion magazines, consumer magazines, etc. They will furnish mailing labels you can affix and mail. Bacon's also has a distribution service, through which they will print and mail press releases for you. Also a press-clipping service. (M-IV)

☐ *Become Famous, Then Rich,* by Dennis E. Hensley. R & R Newkirk, 1983. Paperback. A stimulating book that stresses the idea of first building one's name and reputation, then promoting the related business. Especially valuable to service-oriented businesses. $7.45 ppd. from Denehen, Inc. (A-IV)

☐ *Broadcasting/Cablecasting Year Book.* This directory lists, by city and state, key personnel at radio and television stations throughout the country. In libraries, or can be ordered by mail ($80). (M-IV)

☐ *Chases' Calendar of Annual Events.* An annual guide for publicity seekers who want to tie their business news into major events, anniversaries, special occasions, etc. Available by mail from Contemporary Books. Request price of current edition. (M-IV)

☐ *Gebbie Press All-In-One Directory.* Includes names and addresses of daily and weekly newspapers, AM/FM radio stations, TV stations, general consumer magazines, business papers, trade press, black press, farm publications, and news syndicates. If not available in libraries, you may want to order this one by mail. Its size and format make it the kind of guide you will want to keep on your desk for handy reference. (M-IV)

☐ *How to Write and Use Simple Press Releases That Work,* by Kate Kelly. Excellent guide — a condensation of the author's larger work, *The Publicity Manual* (see below) — with how-to guidelines, some samples of press releases, and a media resource directory. Order by mail at $7 ppd. from Visibility Enterprises. (B-II)

☐ *Literary Market Place.* R. R. Bowker. Published annually, and available in most libraries, this directory includes up-to-date addresses for trade book publishers, wholesalers, and distributors, plus book reviewers for radio, television, magazines, newspapers, and syndicates; printers, art & design services; direct mail promotion services and specialists, and more.

☐ Newspaper Feature Report. For as little as $395, you can syndicate a feature story about your book, product, or organization to more than 10,000 newspapers. This service does all the work for you. Just ask them for details. (M-IV)

☐ *The Newsletter Yearbook Directory.* Published annually, it lists some 2,000 newsletters by subject category, with an alphabetical index. This directory is a useful marketing tool because it indicates which newsletters buy freelance material and invite press releases. Can be ordered by mail (request price of current edition) from The Newsletter Clearinghouse. (O-III)

☐ *Party Line.* If your business happens to be publicity, you'll want to subscribe to this weekly newsletter. This is the periodical used by the media to inform publicists of their needs. Periodical editors, writers, and others who wish to receive press releases on specific topics may send their needs to the attention of this periodical's research department. (M-IV)

☐ *Publicity for Books and Authors,* by Peggy Glenn. Aames Allen Pub., 1985. Paperback. Here's valuable inside information from an author who did such a good job of promoting her first book that she was able to build a successful book publishing company of her own. Send for her catalog of business books. This one is $13.95 ppd. from Aames Allen. (B-II)

☐ *The Publicity Manual,* by Kate Kelly. A complete course in how to get publicity, with many sample releases, detailed how-to instructions, and a resource chapter that lists the better-known news and consumer interest publications, news services, and broadcast operations that give publicity. Order by mail at $29.95 ppd. or request additional information from Visibility Enterprises. (B-II)

☐ *The Standard Periodical Directory.* The largest authoritative guide to U.S. and Canadian periodicals — consumer magazines, trade journals, newsletters, government publications, house organs, directories, yearbooks, literary and social group publications, etc. Contains information about more than 60,000 publications. (To have a periodical listed, request listing form from Oxbridge Communications.) (M-IV)

☐ *Ulrich's International Periodicals Directory.* R. R. Bowker. Available in libraries, and updated quarterly, this directory lists 65,000 periodicals published from all over the world.

☐ *The Unabashed Self-Promoter's Guide,* by Jeffrey Lant. Subtitled, "What Every Man, Woman, Child, and Organization in America Needs to Know about Getting Ahead by Exploiting the Media," this hefty paperback is loaded with ideas for no-cost/low-cost marketing of anything through the media — the same ideas the author has used to build a successful publishing empire at home. In bookstores & libraries,

or by mail from the author's company, Jeffrey Lant Associates, at $32.50 ppd. (B-II)

☐ *Washington News Service.* For a small fee, this service will hand deliver 400 copies of your press release to the Washington News Media, which in total reaches 100 million Americans. A good way to promote your product, service, or cause nationally. (M-IV)

☐ *Working Press of the Nation.* National Research Bureau. This enormous directory is published annually in five volumes, one each on newspapers, magazines, TV & Radio, feature writers/photographers/syndicates, and internal publications (those issued by companies for their own personnel or the general public). Available in libraries.

Chapter Ten Resources
Expansion/Diversification

Writing

☐ American Society of Journalists & Authors. ASJA's membership requirements are stiff, but for those who qualify, membership offers many advantages. One must be a freelance writer of nonfiction who has demonstrated professional achievement for two years prior to application for membership. Must have published articles or books to his/her credit. Benefits of membership include an insurance program, important connections with editors, publishers, and other professionals, inside marketing information, and more. (O-III)

☐ Associated Writing Programs. Inquire about their newsletter and the catalog which describes creative writing programs in the U.S. (A-IV)

☐ *Contest Newsletter.* Tips on how to cut down the odds and nab some of the money available from contests and sweepstakes. For a free sample, send a #10 envelope (long, business size) with two first-class stamps. (P-II)

☐ *Empire-Building By Writing and Speaking,* by Gordon Burgett. A how-to guide for communicators, entrepreneurs, and other information merchants. Book offers a 15-step process by which you can turn ideas, through writing and speaking, into action. Available by mail for $13.95 ppd. from Communication Unlimited. (B-II)

☐ *Graphic Words.* A newsletter to help the independent business person engage in typing, graphics, and words usage. Helps entrepreneurs increase professionalism and profitability. (P-II)

☐ *International Writer's & Artist's Yearbook.* Writer's Digest. An annual directory that tells how and where to sell stories, artwork, photography, and songs in English-speaking countries worldwide. Listings include thousands of newspapers, magazines, and book publishers by country, with a description of material each wants and how to submit it. Obtain price of current edition from Writer's Digest. (B-II)

☐ The National Writers Club. Members receive several publications and discounts on writer's supplies. Club offers group insurance (life, medical, disability), a cooperative savings plan that pays high interest on a passbook account. Also inquire about the National Writers Press, a special service for self-publishers. (O-III)

☐ *Poetry Marketing — How & Where to Sell Your Poems,* 1986–87 ed., by Lincoln B. Young. This book lists publishers who buy poems, printers who specialize in poetry book printing, publishers who publish poetry on a royalty basis, plus other resources. Order by mail at $9.95 ppd. from Fine Arts Press. (B-II)

☐ TOWERS Club Newsletter. Edited and published monthly by Jerry Buchanan. The best source of information on how to make money selling information and self-published material. TOWERS Club also sells a complete line of books on writing and publishing, including the author's best selling guide, *Writer's Utopia.* (P-II)

☐ *Write Ideas, Inc.* A monthly newsletter for writers who are interested in selling fillers or entering contests which offer cash prizes. Published by Selma Glasser, whose Glasser Guide to Filler Writing is taught at

Brooklyn College and through the mail. Request free brochure detailing this newsletter and other publications offered by Glasser. (P-II)

☐ *Writer's Market.* Writer's Digest. Hardcover. Published annually, this directory lists more than 4,000 book and magazine markets, syndicates, contests and awards, writer's workshops, and agents. Plus articles on how to sell work, keep track of expenses, etc. Obtain price of current edition from Writer's Digest. (B-II)

Self-Publishing

☐ COSMEP (Committee of Small Magazine Editors & Publishers). An organization of men and women from small presses and little magazines, many of whom are self-publishers. Its newsletter enables readers to make connections with others in this industry. (O-III)

☐ *Directory Publishing — A Practical Guide,* by Russell A. Perkins, 2nd ed. Covers all aspects of directory publishing, including research, planning, editorial, production, circulation, renewals. Contains samples of good and bad cover letters, questionnaires, circulation pieces, etc. Available by mail for $27.95 ppd. from Morgan-Rand Pub. (B-II)

☐ *Editing Your Newsletter,* 3rd ed., by Mark Beach. Good guide for beginning newsletter publishers. Will help you design a masthead, figure out how to reduce and enlarge copy, lay it out, paste it up, etc. Also covers advertising, addressing, and mailing. Order this paperback by mail at $20.50 ppd. from Coast to Coast Books. Inquire about other books related to printing and publishing. (B-II)

☐ *Folio: The Magazine for Magazine Management.* The only periodical of its kind; devoted to the management, editing, circulation, production, sales, and art direction of consumer, business, technical, and trade magazines. (P-II)

☐ *How to Get Happily Published — A Complete and Candid Guide,* by Judith Appelbaum & Nancy Evans. NAL, paperback, $7.95. In addition to giving an excellent overview of the whole publishing world, this book contains an informative section titled, "The Self-Publishing Option," with three chapters devoted to the pros/cons of self publishing, requirements for success, and managing sales. The book also contains a resource chapter of vital interest to freelance writers, authors, editors, and self-publishers. Available in bookstores and libraries.

☐ *How to Produce a Small Newspaper,* Rev. Ed., by the editors of the Harvard Post. Paperback, $9.95. How to produce an offset-printed, small format weekly newspaper, set stories in camera-ready type, set head-lines, use photos, and more. Order by mail at $11.95 ppd. from Harvard Common Press. (B-II)

☐ *The Huenefeld Report.* A monthly newsletter for book publishers. Also available, many excellent how-to books and reports on the topics of book publishing and marketing. (P-II)

☐ *International Directory of Little Magazines & Small Presses.* Now in its 18th edition, this directory offers a record of the many new magazines and presses starting each year. For information on how to be listed, or for how to order current or forthcoming editions of this and related directories, write to Dustbooks. (B-II)

☐ *How to Start Your Own Magazine,* by W. P. Williams and Joseph Van Zandt. Contemporary Books, 1978. This book explains how anyone with a reasonable amount of intelligence and time can become a magazine publisher; then proceeds to give a step-by-step guide for success. Out of print; check your library.

☐ *The Newsletter Clearinghouse.* A private service organization for the newsletter industry worldwide, founded in 1964 by Howard Penn Hudson, author of *Publishing Newsletters* (see below). Publications include *The Newsletter Yearbook* (see Chapter 9 Resources) and *The Newsletter on Newsletters,* which brings readers the latest developments in the newsletter world. If you publish a newsletter, send a copy for possible review in the newsletter, and free listing in the annual directory. (O-III)

☐ Newsletter Association of America. A nonprofit organization dedicated to the interests of newsletter publishing. Offers a newsletter, books, special reports, seminars, etc. (O-III)

☐ Omnipress. This economical printer specializes in short-run printing (500–1,000 copies) of standard 8½×11″ trim-size books of 100 pages or more. They offer excellent customer service. Write for a free brochure, attention Steve Harrell, or call this toll-free number for information: 1-800-828-0305. (S-IV)

☐ *Publishing Newsletters,* by Howard Penn Hudson. Charles Scribner's Sons. Rev. 1988. $12.95. A complete guide to markets, editorial content, design, printing, subscriptions, management, and much more. Available in bookstores, or can be ordered by mail from The Newsletter Clearinghouse. (O-III)

☐ Resource books for independent publishers, mail order businesses, consultants, and other business professionals. Request free brochure for how-to-order info on several essential guides to success in this industry including: *Book Marketing Made Easier, Directory of Short-Run Book Printers* (lists 125 printers who specialize in book runs of 5000 or less); and *Formaides for Successful Book Publishing.* These books and others by John Kremer belong on the bookshelf of all self-publishers. Write Ad-Lib Publications for details. Kremer also edits *Book Marketing Update,* a vital PR tool for all publishers. (B-II)

☐ *The Self-Publishing Manual — How to Write, Print and Sell Your Own Book,* by Dan Poynter. Paperback. A concentrated short course in writing, publishing, marketing, promoting, and distributing books. Order by mail for $15.95 ppd. from Para Publishing. Inquire about other titles available including *Publishing Short-Run Books* and *Is There A Book Inside You?* (B-II)

☐ *Small Press.* Each issue of this bimonthly magazine is crammed with how-to articles on all aspects of publishing — design, paper selection, fulfillment, marketing, promotion, etc. In addition, this periodical now covers desktop publishing and the use of computers in publishing. Includes reviews of small press books as well. Request subscription info from Meckler Publishing Corp. (P-II)

☐ *Success in Newsletter Publishing* — A Practical Guide, by Frederick D. Goss. $37.50. The first authoritative guide to success in the growing field of newsletter publishing. Even the smallest newsletter publisher will benefit from the wealth of how-to information on how to get and keep subscribers, determine subscription rates, market through direct mail advertising, and so forth. Available in bookstores or libraries, or can be ordered by mail from the Newsletter Assn. of America. (O-III)

Speaking/Teaching/Consulting

☐ *Advice — A High Profit Business,* by Herman Holtz. Wiley, $24.95. Hardcover, 1986. This book tells the average individual how to profit from specialized knowledge of any kind. Covers opportunities, the market for advice, how to develop packages (printing and publications, research and writing, canned presentations, seminars and workshops), and how to develop ideas and market advice. Check bookstores and libraries, or order from Herman Holtz at $26.95 ppd. (A-IV)

☐ Cassette Production Services. Speakers looking for a way to expand should consider selling cassette tapes, and this company offers a brochure on their cassette-duplicating service. General Cassette Corp. (M-IV)

☐ *Consultants and Consulting Organizations Directory.* Gale Research Co. This is the most extensive directory of its kind. Helps you find consultants in any field. Also your opportunity to be listed, free of charge, as a professional consultant who welcomes inquiries. Available in libraries.

☐ *Consulting Opportunities Journal.* A bimonthly for those who are serious about profiting from their own consulting practice. How to get started, set fees, self-marketing strategies, etc. Free brochure. (P-II)

☐ *How to Establish and Profit from Running Your own Teaching Studio at Home,* by Sylvia Campbell-Landman. A comprehensive correspondence course and consultation service for at-home teachers. For details, send SASE to Self-Employment Consultants. (A-IV)

☐ *How to Organize and Manage a Seminar — What to Do and When to Do It,* by Sheila Murray. Prentice Hall, 1983. Paperback. $7.95. A chronological outline for the make-or-break details of planning and leading the ideal seminar. Available in bookstores, or contact the author for more information. (A-IV)

☐ *How to Succeed as an Independent Consultant,* by Herman Holtz. John Wiley & Sons, hardcover, $21.95. The first book to reveal how to make a success of consulting as an independent professional enterprise, by an author who is a successful consultant. A true how-to book for serious entrepreneurs. Order by mail for $23.95 ppd. from the author. (A-IV)

☐ Kessler Co-operative Speaker's Bulletins. Publicity service for speakers who want exposure on radio, TV, or in-print media. Free brochure. (M-IV)

☐ Learning Resources Network. For part-time instructors at independent learning centers. Offers a variety of publications, including a book, *How to Teach Adults,* $8.95 ppd. (O-III)

☐ *The Quick and Easy Way to Effective Speaking,* by Dale Carnegie. Pocket Books, paperback. This book literally has put millions of people on the highway to greater success. Updated by Dorothy Carnegie in 1962, it will help you get over the fear of speaking in public, gain self confidence, learn to persuade people, to get action, to inform, to impress, and convince. Order by mail for $3.45 ppd. from Pocket Books. (B-II)

☐ *Sharing Ideas.* This bimonthly periodical is for professional speakers and meeting planners who want to make connections in the industry. Offers special opportunities for speakers to be published, plus a speaker's bureau (booking agency). Single copy, $5. Also inquire about GAB, (Int'l. Group of Agents and Bureaus), a new organization. Royal Publishing. (B-II)

☐ *Yes You Can Teach,* by Florence Nelson. This book will be helpful to anyone who wants to teach adults for profit. Available by mail at $6 ppd. Other titles by the same author include *How to Write a Lesson*

Plan for Adult Classes, and *How to Teach a Demonstration-Type Subject*. Write for a descriptive price list from Carma Press. (B-II)

☐ *Tricks of the Trade*, by Jeffrey Lant. This book lives up to its subtitle, "The Complete Guide to Suc-ceeding in the Advice Business," This large paperback tells what advisors of every kind need to know to profit from America's changing economy and way of life. Free brochure, or order by mail at $32.50 ppd. from Jeffrey Lant Associates. (B-II)

Chapter Eleven Resources
Computers

☐ *The Art of Desktop Publishing — Using the Personal Computer to Publish it Yourself*, by Tony Bove and Cheryl Rhodes. Bantam, $18.95. This book is only one of several by Bove and Rhodes, founding editors of *Publish!*, listed below. They have also written definitive guides to using *Pagemaker* software for both the Mac and IBM-compatibles. As two of the country's foremost computer authorities, you should check bookstores and libraries for their work.

☐ *The Business Computer*, by Franklynn Peterson and Judi K-Turkel. This syndicated column now appears in newspapers across the country. The authors offer reprints of their column, along with some special reports. For a listing of all available information, send a self-addressed, stamped envelope to P/K Associates, Inc., mentioning this book. (A-IV)

☐ Computer Insurance. Homeowner policies and riders generally do not cover computers used for business; a specific business policy may be necessary. Consult a local insurance company, or request free advice on insuring your computer from Safeware, The Insurance Agency. (A-IV)

☐ Computer periodicals. There are hundreds of computer-related periodicals available on news stands, in computer stores, bookstores, and libraries. Among titles you might investigate are *Personal Computing*, *Byte*, *Infoworld*, *Home Office Computing*, and *Computerworld*.

☐ *How to Get a Job Working From Home*, by Paul & Sarah Edwards with Gil Gordon, telecommuting consultant and editor of *The Telecommuting Review*. For those who want to know present and future opportunities for telecommuting, two cassette tapes explain the kind of jobs you can get working from home, most-likely companies and industries to hire telecommuters, and more. Use your computer business letterhead to request a sample of the newsletter mentioned above, or request free brochure from Gil Gordon Associates. (A-IV)

☐ *How to Look It Up Online*, by Alfred Glossbrenner. 1987. Explains how to use your personal computer to find any book on any subject, anywhere in the world; how to summon magazine and newspaper articles to your screen, and get the edge on your competition in business. $14.95 in bookstores, or to order by mail, contact St. Martin's Press. (B-II)

☐ *How to Make Money With Your Micro*, by Herman Holtz (Wiley & Sons, 1984. Hardcover, $14.95) and *The Consultant's Edge – Using the Computer as a Marketing Tool* (Wiley, 1985. Hardcover, $24.95). Available in bookstores, or add $2 to above prices to order directly from author. Send self-addressed, stamped envelope for a listing of other books by Herman Holtz. (A-IV)

☐ Preventive Maintenance of computers and electronic typewriters. Free booklet discusses dust removal, static control, print element cleaning, and more. Ask for "Falcon Computer Care Booklet," from Falcon Safety Products, Inc. (A-IV)

☐ Public Brand Software. For a free catalog of IBM-compatible public domain software and Shareware, write to this company. (S-IV)

☐ *Public Domain Software — Untapped Resources for the Business User*, by DeMaria and Fontaine, 1987. This hefty paperback shows you where to locate and how to use the major sources of public-domain software and Shareware, including catalogs and both commercial and private bulletin-board services. The book also leads you to the best programs available and tells how to avoid dangerous and pirated products. $19.95 in bookstores; or to order by mail, write M & T Books. (B-II)

☐ *Publish!* — The magazine of Desktop and Personal Computer Publishing. This magazine, which premiered in July 1986, deals with personal computing technology and better printed communications for businesses and communications professionals. Check magazine stands for an issue, or write for information from PC World Communications, Inc. (P-II)

☐ *Word Processing Profits at Home*, by Peggy Glenn. Aames-Allen, 1986. A definitive guide that covers all aspects of a homebased, word-processing business, from planning, advertising, and pricing to personal considerations, legal aspects, professionalism and more. In bookstores, or by mail at $15.95 ppd. from Aames-Allen Pub. Send self-addressed, stamped envelope for complete details. (B-II)

☐ *Working From Home,* by Paul and Sarah Edwards. Jeremy P. Tarcher, Inc. Rev. 1987 ed., $12.95 in book-stores. An excellent reference guide for thriving in your electronic cottage. The Edwards have also developed companion work-at-home tapes. You can connect with them through the "Working From Home Forum" on CompuServe Information Service, and on the "Home Office Show" on Business Radio Network. More info from Paul Edwards. (A-IV)

SECTION II

Note: The numbers in parentheses are *not* part of the address. They merely relate to the numbered chapter resources in Section I, where descriptive listings will be found. EXAMPLE: Books published by Aames-Allen are described in Section I in chapter two, nine, and eleven resources. The letters "A-Z" refer to the A-to-Z business section.

B-II: Book Publishers

Aames-Allen Publishing Co.
(2, 9, 11)
1106 Main St.
Huntington Beach, CA 92648

Ad-Lib Publications (3, 7, 10)
P.O. Box 1102
Fairfield, IA 52556

Andmar Press (2)
P.O. Box 217
Mills, WY 82644

Barbara Brabec Productions (1,2)
P.O. Box 2137-HMM
Naperville, IL 60566

Bell Springs Publishing (A-Z)
P.O. Box 640
Laytonville, CA 95454

Betterway Publications (1)
P.O. Box 219
Crozet, VA 22932

Brick House Pub. Co. (2)
3 Main St.
Andover, MA 01810

Carma Press (10)
P.O. Box 12633
St. Paul, MN 55112

Coast to Coast Books (10)
2934 Northeast 16th Avenue
Portland, OR 97212

Collier Books (8)
866 3rd Ave.
New York, NY 10022

Communication Unlimited (10)
P.O. Box 1001
Carpinteria, CA 93013

DHA & Associates (A-Z)
P.O. Box 1861
Seattle, WA 98111

Dow Jones-Irwin (2)
1818 Ridge Rd.
Homewood, IL 60430

Dustbooks (10)
P.O. Box 100
Paradise, CA 95969

Enterprise Publishing, Inc. (A-Z)
725 Market Street
Wilmington, DE 19801

Fine Arts Press (10)
P.O. Box 3491
Knoxville, TN 37917

Garden Way Publishing (2)
3599 Ferry Road
Charlotte, VT 05445

Goodfellow Catalog of Wonderful
   Things (2)
P.O. Box 4520
Berkeley, CA 94704

Gravity Publishing (A-Z)
6324 Heather Ridge
Oakland, CA 94611

Grindle Press (1)
8340 E. Raintree Dr.
Scottsdale, AZ 85260

The Harvard Common Press (10)
535 Albany Street
Boston, MA 02118

Jeffrey Lant Assoc., Inc. (9, 10)
50 Follen St., Suite 507
Cambridge, MA 02138

M&T Books (11)
501 Galveston Dr.
Redwood City, CA 94063

Mark Publishing (2)
15 Camp Evers Lane
Scotts Valley, CA 91066

Morgan-Rand Publications
   Inc. (10)
2200 Sansom St.
Philadelphia, PA 19103

New Careers Center (1)
Box 297
Boulder, CO 80306

Next Step Publications (1)
P.O. Box 41108
Fayetteville, NC 28309

Nolo Press (A-Z, 7)
950 Parker St.
Berkeley, CA 94710

Para Publishing (10, 11)
P.O. Box 4232-O
Santa Barbara, CA 93140

Pilot Books (2, 6, 7)
103 Cooper Street
Babylon, NY 11702

Pinstripe Publishing (3)
P.O. Box 711
Sedro-Wooley, WA 98284

Pocket Books (1, 10)
Dept. DCR
1230 Avenue of the Americas
New York, NY 10020

Publishing Horizons, Inc. (2)
5701 North High St., Suite 1
Worthington, OH 43085

Royal Publishing, Inc. (2, 10)
P.O. Box 1120
Glendora, CA 91740

Self-Counsel Press, Inc. (2, A-Z)
1303 N. Northgate Way
Seattle, WA 98133

St. Martin's Press (2, 3, 11)
175 Fifth Avenue
New York, NY 10010

The Success Foundation, Inc. (1)
P.O. Box 6302
Louisville, KY 40206

Success Publications (2)
10258 Riverside Dr., Suite 2
Palm Beach Gardens, FL 33410

TAB Books, Inc. (1, 2, 4, A-Z)
Blue Ridge Summit, PA 17214

Till Press (1)
P.O. Box 27816
Los Angeles, CA 90027

Charles C Thomas, Publisher (2)
2600 South First St.
Springfield, IL 62717

Vade-Mecum Press (2)
1500 W. Alameda Ave.
Denver, CO 80223

Upstart Pub. Co. (4)
P.O. Box 323
Portsmoyth, NH 03801

Visibility Enterprises (5, 9)
11 Rockwood Dr.
Larchmont, NY 10538

Westview Press (1)
5500 Central Ave.
Boulder, CO 80301

Writer's Digest Books (1, 2, 10)
1507 Dana Ave.
Cincinnati, OH 45207

P-II Periodical Publishers

Agents and Lines Bulletin (7)
5030 Otter Lake Road
White Bear, MN 55110

American Artist (2)
1515 Broadway
1 Astor Plaza
New York, NY 10036

The Antique Trader Weekly (6)
Box 1050
Dubuque, IA 52001

Apparel Industry Magazine (7)
Apparel Industry Sourcebook
180 Allen Rd., Suite 300
Atlanta, GA 30328

The Artists Magazine (2)
10 East 40th Street, Suite 1300
New York, NY 10016

The Art Marketing Letter (2)
Amy Mongillo
2539 Post Road
Darien, CT 06820

Art & Crafts Catalyst (6)
P.O. Box 433
So. Whitley, IN 46787

Art Show News (6)
The Art Conspiracy, Inc.
2101 Ford St., #3
Golden, CO 80401

Business-Week (4)
McGraw-Hill, Inc.
1221 Avenue of the Americas
New York, NY 10020

Candy Industry Magazine (7)
Edgell Communications
7500 Old Oak Blvd.
Cleveland, OH 44130

Chain Store Age-General
   Merchandise (7)
Lebhar-Friedman, Inc.
425 Park Avenue
New York, NY 10022

Choices (1)
Entrepreneur Group, Inc.
2392 Morse Ave.
Irvine, CA 92714

The Cloth Doll (2)
P.O. Box 1089
Mt. Shasta, CA 96067

Consulting Opportunities
   Journal (10)
Gapland, MD 21736

Contest Newsletter (10)
P.O. Box 505, Dept. BB
Fernandina Beach, FL 32034

Cooking For Profit (2)
P.O. Box 267
Fond du Lac, WI 54936

The Crafts Report (2)
700 Orange Street
P.O. Box 1992
Wilmington, DE 19899

Creative Products News (7, 8)
P.O. Box 584
Lake Forest, IL 60045

Day Care and Early Education (2)
Human Sciences Press
72 Fifth Avenue
New York, NY 10011

Direct Marketing (7)
Hoke Communications, Inc.
224 Seventh Street
Garden City, NY 11530

Directory Marketplace (7)
Box 301
W. Nyack, NY 10994

Discount Merchandiser (7)
Schwartz Publishing Co.
2 Park Ave., 16th fl.
New York, NY 10016

Exhibits Schedule/Successful
   Meetings (7)
633 Third Ave.
New York, NY 10017

Extra Income (1)
P.O. Box 21957
Santa Barbara, CA 93120

Folio (10)
Folio Magazine Publishing Corp.
125 Elm Street, Box 4006
New Canaan, CT 06840

Food Industry News (7)
P.O. Box 19706
Alexandria, VA 22320

The Front Room News (2)
P.O. Box 1541
Clifton, NJ 07015

Garden Supply Retailer (7)
Miller Publishing Co.
2501 Wayzata Blvd., Box 67
Minneapolis, MN 55440

Gift & Tableware Reporter (7)
Billboard Publications, Inc.
1515 Broadway
New York, NY 10036

Gifts & Decorative Accessories
   (5, 7)
51 Madison Avenue
New York, NY 10010

Graphic Words (10)
P.O. Box 596
Hayward, CA 94543

Handmade Accents (2)
P.O. Box 210
Honaker, VA 24260

Herb Business Bulletin (2)
P.O. Box 32
Berryville, AR 72616

Herban Lifestyles (2)
84 Carpenter Road
New Hartford, CT 06057

Home Business Monthly (1)
38 Briarcliffe Rd.
Rochester, NY 14617

Home Business News (1)
12221 Beaver Pike
Jackson, OH 45640

Homesewing Trade News (2)
P.O. Box 286
300 Sunrise Highway
Rockville Centre, NY 11571

Homeworking Mothers (1)
Mother's Home Business Network
P.O. Box 423
East Meadow, NY 11554

The Huenefeld Report (10)
P.O. Bux U
Bedford, MA 01730

In Business (1)
JG Press
Box 323
Emmaus, PA 18049

Incentive Marketing (7)
Bill Communications
633 Third Avenue
New York, NY 10017

Keyboard Connection (2)
P.O. Box 338
Glen Carbon, IL 62034

Knitting Machine News Views (2)
Alles Knitting Publications
18 Marymont Dr.
Penn Hills, PA 15235

Lawn & Garden Marketing (7)
P.O. Box 12901
Overland Park, KS 66212

The Manufacturing Confectioner
   (7)
MC Publishing Co.
175 Rock Road
Glen Rock, NJ 07452

Meckler Publishing Corp. (10)
Small Press
11 Ferry Lane West
Westport, CT 06880

Memo to Mailers (2)
P.O. Box 1
Linwood, NJ 08221

The Moneypaper (4)
930 Mamaroneck Ave.
Mamaroneck, NY 10543

The National Flea Market
   Dealer (6)
11565 Ridgewood Circle
Seminole, FL 33542

National Home Business
   Report (1, 2)
P.O. Box 2137-HMM
Naperville, IL 60566

Opportunity (2)
6 North Michigan Ave., Suite 1405
Chicago, IL 60602

Opportunity Connection (2)
P.O. Box 57723
Webster, TX 77598

Personal Sales Power (2)
P.O. Box 5467
Fredericksburg, VA 22403

PhotoSource International (2)
Dept. 12A
Pine Lake Farm
Osceola, WI 54020

Playthings (7)
Geyer-McAllister Publications,
   Inc.
51 Madison Avenue
New York, NY 10010

The Professional Quilter (2)
Oliver Press
P.O. Box 4096
St. Paul, MN 55104

Profitable Craft Merchandising (5)
News Plaza
P.O. Box 1790
Peoria, IL 61656

Publish! (11)
PCW Communications, Inc.
501 Second St.
San Francisco, CA 94107

Publishers Weekly (7)
R. R. Bowker Company
249 W. 17th St.
New York, NY 10011

Rep World (7)
Albee-Campbell, Inc.
806 Penn Avenue
Sinking Spring, PA 19608

Rocky Point Press (2)
P.O. Box 4814
North Hollywood, CA 91607

The Sales Rep's Advisor (7)
Alexander Research & Comm.,
   Inc.
1133 Broadway, Suite 1407
New York, NY 10010

Sew Business (2)
1515 Broadway
New York, NY 10036

Shoestring Marketer (7)
Ad Mail Management
P.O. Box 1389
Yuba City, CA 95992

Sideline Business Newsletter (1)
Box 323
18 South 7th Street
Emmaus, PA 18049

Souvenirs & Novelties (7)
Kane Communications, Inc.
401 North Broad Street, Suite 904
Philadelphia, PA 19108

Stilson & Stilson (2)
The Direct Response Specialist
P.O. Box 1075
Tarpon Springs, FL 34688

TOWERS Club Newsletter (10)
P.O. Box 2038
Vancouver, WA 98668

Toy & Hobby World (7)
Charlson Publishing Co.
345 Park Ave. So.
New York, NY 10010

Winning Ways News (1)
P.O. Box 35412
Minneapolis, MN 55435

Women's Wear Daily (7)
Fairchild Publications
7 East 12th St.
New York, NY 10003

Worksteader News (1)
2396 Coolidge Way
Rancho Cordova, CA 95670

Write Ideas, Inc. (10)
25 Penn Boulevard
Scarsdale, NY 10583

SECTION III

Reminder: The letters or numbers in parentheses are not part of the address; they merely refer you to the specific chapter resources in Section I, where descriptive listings will be found (EXAMPLE: Publications offered by The Bureau of the Census are described in the A-to-Z Business Section Resources.)

G-III Government Resources

Bureau of the Census (A-Z)
Customer Service
Washington, DC 20233

Bureau of Consumer Protection
(A-Z)
Division of Special Statutes
6th & Pennsylvania Ave., N.W.
Washington, DC 20580

Consumer Information Center (1)
Dept. 517K
Pueblo, CO 81009

Cooperative Extension Service
(A-Z)
U.S. Department of Agriculture
Washington, DC 20250

The Copyright Office (A-Z)
Register of Copyrights
Library of Congress
Washington, DC 20559

Consumer Products Safety
Commission (A-Z)
Bureau of Compliance
5401 Westbard Avenue
Bethesda, MD 20207

Federal Trade Commission (A-Z)
Division of Legal & Public
Records
Washington, DC 20580

Food and Drug Administration
(A-Z)
5600 Fishers Lane
Rockville, MD 20857

Internal Revenue Service (A-Z)
Washington, DC 20224

Library of Congress (A-Z)
National Referral Center
Washington, DC 20559

National Bureau of Standards
(A-Z)
Technical Building, B167
Standards Development Services
Section
Washington, DC 20234

SBA Management Assistant
Publications (2, 4, A-Z, 5, 7, 8)
P.O. Box 15434
Ft. Worth, TX 76119

SCORE — Service Corps of
Retired Executives (A-Z)
1441 L Street, NW, Room 100
Washington, DC 20416

Superintendent of Documents
(A-Z)
U.S. Government Printing Office
Washington, DC 20402

U.S. Department of Agriculture
(2)
Agricultural Cooperative Service
Washington, DC 20250

U.S. Department of Commerce (8)
Office of Consumer Affairs
Washington, DC 20233

U.S. Department of Commerce
(Intro)
National Technical Information
Services
Springfield, VA 22161

U.S. Department of Labor (4)
200 Constitution Avenue, NW
Washington, DC 20210

U.S. Fish & Wildlife Service (A-Z)
Division of Law Enforcement
Department of the Interior
Washington, DC 20240

Patent & Trademark Office (A-Z)
U.S. Dept. of Commerce
Washington, DC 20231

U.S. Small Business
Administration (A-Z)
1441 L Street, NW
Washington, DC 20416

O-III: Organizations/Associations

American Apparel Manufacturers
Assn. (7)
2500 Wilson Blvd., Ste. 301
Arlington, VA 22201

American Association of
Community & Junior Colleges
(1)
One DuPont Circle, Suite 140
Washington, DC 20036

American Council for the Arts (2)
1285 Ave. of the Americas
3rd Floor, Area M
New York, NY 10019

American Craft Enterprises,
Inc. (7)
P.O. Box 10
New Paltz, NY 12561

American Crafts Council (2)
40 W. 53rd
New York, NY 10019

American Home Business
Association (2)
397 Post Road
Darien, CT 06820

American Society of Journalists &
Authors (10)
1501 Broadway, Suite 1907
New York, NY 10036

American Society of Interior
    Designers (2)
1430 Broadway
New York, NY 10018

The American Woman's
    Economic Development Corp.
    (AWED) (1)
The Lincoln Building
60 East 42nd Street
New York, NY 10165

Artists Equity Association, Inc. (2)
P.O. Box 28068
Washington, DC 20038

Association of Part-Time
    Professionals, Inc. (1)
P.O. Box 3419
Alexandria, VA 22302

The Center for Occupational
    Hazards (1, A-Z)
5 Beekman Street
New York, NY 10038

The Center on National Labor
    Policy, Inc. (A-Z)
5211 Port Royal Rd., Suite 400
North Springfield, VA 22151

COSMEP (8, 10)
(Committee of Small Magazine
    Editors & Publishers)
P.O. Box 703
San Francisco, CA 94101

Council of Better Business
    Bureaus, Inc. (1, 2)
1515 Wilson Boulevard
Arlington, VA 22209

Custom Tailors & Designers
    Associations of America (2)
17 E. 45th St.
New York, NY 10017

Day Care Council of America (2)
National Family Day Care
    Providers Network
1012 14th St., NW
Washington, DC 20005

The Direct Mail/Marketing
    Association (7)
6 East 43rd Street
New York, NY 10017

Direct Selling Education
    Foundation (2)
1776 "K" St., NW, Suite 600
Washington, DC 20006

The Displaced Homemakers
    Network, Inc. (1)
1325 "G" St., NW
Washington, DC 20003

Graphic Artists Guild (2)
11 W. 20 St., 8th fl.
New York, NY 10011

Greeting Card Association (2)
1350 New York Ave., NW
Suite 615
Washington, DC 20005

H.A.L.T. (A-Z)
1319 F St., NW
Suite 300
Washington, DC 20004

Hobby Industry Association of
    America (7)
319 E. 54th St.
Elmwood Park, NJ 07407

Inventors Workshop Int'l. (2)
Education Foundation
3201 Corte Malpaso, Suite 304
Camarillo, CA 91320

Learning Resources Network (10)
P.O. Box 1425
1554 Hayes Dr.
Manhattan, KS 66502

Museum Store Association (7)
1 Cherry Ctr., #460
501 S. Cherry St.
Denver, CO 80222

Music Teachers National Assn.,
    Inc. (2)
Carew Tower
Cincinnati, OH 45202

National Association of Home
    Based Businesses (1)
P.O. Box 30220
Baltimore, MD 21270

National Association for the
    Specialty Food Trade, Inc. (7)
215 Park Ave., So.
New York, NY 10003

The National Association for the
    Self Employed (1)
2324 Gravel Rd.
Ft. Worth, TX 76118

National Economic Development
    Law Center (A-Z)
1950 Addison St., Ste. 200
Berkeley, CA 94704

National Home Study Council (1)
1601 18th Street, NW
Washington, DC 20009

National Mail Order Association
    (2, 8)
5818 Venice Boulevard
Los Angeles, CA 90019

The National Needlework Assn.,
    Inc. (7)
230 5th Avenue
New York, NY 10001

The National Writers Club (10)
1450 South Havana, Suite 620
Aurora, CO 80012

Newsletter Association (10)
1401 Wilson Blvd., Ste. 403
Arlington, VA 22209

The Newsletter Clearinghouse
    (9, 10)
44 West Market Street
P.O. Box 311
Rhinebeck, NY 12572

North American Students of
    Cooperation (NASCO) (1)
P.O. Box 7293
Ann Arbor, MI 48107

The Society of American Florists
    (7)
901 North Washington Street
Alexandria, VA 22314

Society of Craft Designers (2)
6175 Barfield Rd., Ste. 220
Atlanta, GA 30326

Small Business Service Bureau,
    Inc. (1)
544 Main Street
Worcester, MA 01601

Support Services Alliance (1)
P.O. Box 130
Schoharie, NY 12157

Volunteer Lawyers for the Arts
    (A-Z)
1285 Ave. of the Americas
3rd Floor
New York, NY 10019

SECTION IV

Reminder: The letters or numbers after each listing relate to numbered chapter resources in Section I, where descriptive listings will be found. (EXAMPLE: The information available from Art Print Publishers is described in Chapter Two Resources of Section I.)

A-IV: Authors and Other Information Providers

Art Print Publishers, Inc. (2)
P.O. Box 9100
Seattle, WA 98109

Associated Writing Programs (10)
Department of English
Old Dominion University
Norfolk, VA 23508

Bank of America (2, 4)
Dept. 3401
P.O. Box 37000
San Francisco, CA 94137

S. J. Bennett & Co. Inc. (1)
P.O. Box 1090
Cambridge, MA 02238

Julian Block (A-Z)
3 Washington Square
Larchmont, NY 10538

Breadwinners (2)
231 W. Wisconsin Ave., #1002
Milwaukee, WI 53203

Bureau of Business Practice (2
Salesman's Workshop
24 Rope Ferry Road
Waterford, CT 06385

Cahners Publishing Co. (2)
249 West 17th St.
New York, NY 10011

Charles Clark (6)
2156 Cotton Patch Lane
Milton, FL 32570

Chester L. Cook (2)
P.O. Box 1511
Slidell, LA 70458

Cleaning Management Institute
(2)
15550-D Rockfield Blvd.
Irvine, CA 92718

Denehen, Inc. (1, 9)
4316 Marvin Drive
Ft. Wayne, IN 46806

Paul & Sarah Edwards (11)
2607 2nd St., Ste. 3
Santa Monica, CA 90405

Falcon Safety Products, Inc. (11)
1065 Bristol Road
Mountainside, NJ 07092

Gil Gordon Associates (11)
10 Donner Court
Monmouth Junction, NJ 08852

Herman Holtz (4, A-Z, 7, 8, 10, 11)
P.O. Box 1731
Wheaton, MD 20902

Horchow (7)
P.O. Box 34257
Dallas, TX 75234

Int'l. Marketing Co., Inc. (2)
17057 Bellflower Blvd.
Bellflower, CA 90706

Jean Ray Laury (2)
Hot Fudge Press
4974 N. Fresno St., Ste. 444
Fresno, CA 93726

Lifetime Career Schools (1)
2251 Barry Avenue
P.O. Box 64758
Los Angeles, CA 90064

Massachusetts Cooperative Ext. (1)
Bulletin Center, Cottage A
Univ. of Massachusetts
Amherst, MA 01003

Meistergram, Inc. (2)
Attn: S. R. Gluskin
5501 Cass Ave.
Cleveland, OH 44113

Sheila Murray (10)
1390 Market Street, Ste. 908
San Francisco, CA 94102

New Hampshire Small Business
Development Program (4)
110 McConnell Hall
Durham, NH 03824

Mark Nolan Associates (2)
P.O. Box 2069
Citrus Heights, CA 95611

Northwoods Trading Co. (7)
13451 Essex Ct.
Eden Prairie, MN 55347

Open Chain Publishing (4)
P.O. Box 2634
Menlo Park, CA 94026

P/K Associates (11)
4343 West Beltline Highway
Madison, WI 53711

Playle Publications (7)
P.O. Box 644
Des Moines, IA 50303

The Rosen Agency (2)
Ste. 300, Mill Centre
3000 Chestnut Ave.
Baltimore, MD 21211

Safeware (11)
The Insurance Agency, Inc.
2929 North High Street
Columbus, OH 43202

Susan Scharadin (6)
20 Windswept Rd.
Breinigsville, PA 18031

Phyllis V. Shaudys (2)
Pine Row Publications
Box 428
Washington Crossing, PA 18977

Self-Employment Consultants (10)
1090 Cambridge Street
Novato, CA 94947

S.H.E., Inc. (4)
401 N. W. Overlook Dr.
Vancouver, WA 98665

Elyse Sommer (2, 3)
110-34 73rd Rd., #3E
P.O. Box 1133
Forest Hills, NY 11375

Technical & Educational Center of
  The Graphic Arts (2)
Rochester Institute of Technology
1 Lomb Memorial Drive
Rochester, NY 14623

Terri Tepper (1)
261 Kimberly
Barrington, IL 60010

The Unicorn (2)
Box 645
Rockville, MD 20851

Village Vendor, Ltd. (6)
8500 Valleywood lane
Kalamazoo, MI 49002

Other Individuals

Note: The following people have contributed to this book, but do not offer business or marketing information per se, thus are not listed in Chapter One Resources. However, readers may wish to correspond with them for other reasons suggested in the text, so addresses have been included for that purpose.

Rex Allen
301 37th St., N.E.
Cedar Rapids, IA 52402

Glen Baker
Pine Ridge Vineyard & Clock
  Works
7218 W. Dupont Road
Ft. Wayne, IN 46818

Colleen Bergman
The Cloth Doll
P.O. Box 1089
Mt. Shasta, CA 96067

Jean Dubois
P.O. Box 1430
Golden, CO 80402

Cathy Gilleland
The Crafters, Ltd.
134 Boston Road
Chelmsford, MA 01824

Anne Grice/Joye Burkhardt
ANJO
100 Virginia Lane
New Bern, NC 28562

Carolyn Isaak
Home Country Fair
P.O. Box 243
Carlyle, IL 62231

Mary Kaufmann
MSK Insurance Consultants
132 W. Mountain, Ste. 200
Ft. Collins, CO 80524

Barbara and Roger Lehman
Luv-Kins, Inc.
P.O. Box 2095
Duxbury, MA 02332

Carolyn Loughridge and Liz
  DeCleene
Herbal Concoctions
P.O. Box 2052
Littleton, CO 80161

Jack K. Mandel
Island Craft & Business
  Consultants
360 Cameo Drive
Massapequa, NY 11758

Dona Meilach
2018 Saliente Way
Carlsbad, CA 92008

Twyla Menzies
2033 E. Wayland
Springfield, MO 65804

Charlene Miller
571 North Madison
Ogden, UT 84404

Mary Helen Sears
Irons & Sears
1800 "M" St., NW
Washington, DC 20036

M-IV: Marketing Connections

American Business Lists, Inc. (8)
5707 E. 86th Cir.
Omaha, NE 68127

Atlas Pen & Pencil Corp. (3)
P.O. Box 600
Hollywood, FL 33022

Bacon's Publicity Checker (9)
332 So. Michigan Ave.
Chicago, IL 60604

Billboard Directories (6)
Directory of N. Amer. Fairs
1515 Broadway
New York, NY 10036

R. R. Bowker Company (8)
Mailing List Division
245 W. 17th St.
New York, NY 10011

Broadcasting Year Book (9)
1735 De Sales St., NW
Washington, DC 20036

The Buckley-Little Book
  Catalogue Co., Inc. (7)
Kraus Reprints
Rt. 100
Millwood, NY 10546

Contemporary Books (9)
180 N. Michigan
Chicago, IL 60601

Convention World (7)
Bayard Publications
600 Summer St.
Stamford, CT 06901

Counted Thread (8)
1285 S. Jason St.
Denver, CO 80223

County Agents Directory (7)
6201 Howard St.
Niles, IL 60648

Crain Communications (7)
740 Rush Street
Chicago, IL 60611

Hugo Dunhill, Inc. (8)
630 3rd Avenue
New York, NY 10017

Dun & Bradstreet (A-Z)
Commercial Collection Division
1 World Trade Center, #9069
New York, NY 10048

Gebbie Press All-In-One
  Directory (9)
Box 1000
New Paltz, NY 12561

General Cassette Corporation (10)
2311 North 35th Avenue
Phoenix, AZ 85009

Greetings Magazine Buyers
  Guide (7)
Mackay Publishing Corp.
309 Fifth Ave.
New York, NY 10016

Leon Henry, Inc. (8)
455 Central Avenue
Scarsdale, NY 10583

IBIS Information Svcs., Inc.
152 Madison Ave., #803
New York, NY 10016

Intercontinental Trade Specialists
  (7)
17340 Boswell Place
Granada Hills, CA 91344

Kessler Co-Operative Speaker's
  Bulletins (10)
1100 Glenwood Ave.
Los Angeles, CA 90024

Manufacturers' Agents National
  Association (7)
P.O. Box 3467
Laguna Hills, CA 92654

National Mail Order Classified (7)
P.O. Box 5
Sarasota, FL 33578

National Stationery Show (7)
George Little Management, Inc.
2 Park Ave.
New York, NY 10016

Nationwide Directory of Gift &
  Housewares Buyers (7)
The Salesman's Guide, Inc.
1140 Broadway
New York, NY 10001

Newspaper Feature Report (9)
Bradley Communications
101 W. Baltimore Ave.
Lansdowne, PA 19050

Oxbridge Communications (9)
183 Madison Avenue, Ste. 1108
New York, NY 10016

Parade Publications, Inc. (7)
Information Center Program
750 Third Ave.
New York, NY 10017

Party Line (9)
P. R. Aids
35 Sutton Pl.
New York, NY 10022

Larry Tucker, Inc. (8)
607 Palisade Avenue
Englewood Cliffs, NJ 07632

Voice Publications (2, 7)
Key Newsletter
1016 S. Fly Avenue
Goreville, IL 62939

Washington News Service (9)
1265 National Press Building
529 14th St., NW
Washington, DC 20045

World Gift Review Newsletter (7)
616 9th Street
Union City, NJ 07087

World Wide Trade Service (2)
Medina, WA 98039

S-IV: Suppliers — Office Supplies/Equipment, Packaging, Clip Art

Action Bag Company (5)
630 Thorndale Ave.
Bensenville, IL 60106

Alkahn Labels (5)
110 E. 9th, Ste. A-493
Los Angeles, CA 90079

Associated Bag Company (5)
160 2nd Street
Milwaukee, WI 53204

Bucher Brothers (3)
726 Leo Street
Dayton, OH 45404

Champion Printing Company (3)
3250 Spring Grove Ave.
Cincinnati, OH 45225

Color Lab (3)
8 Burnett Ave.
Maplewood, NJ 07040

Color Q (3)
Box 1007
Dayton, OH 45401

The Datasort System (3)
Indecks, Inc.
Arlington, VT 05020

Deluxe Computer Forms (8)
1275 Red Fox Rd.
P.O. Box 64046
St. Paul, MN 55164

The Designery (5)
P.O. Box 2887
Kalamazoo, MI 49003

Direct Mail Printing Co., Inc. (3)
448 West 16th Street
New York, NY 10011

Direct Press/Modern Litho (3)
386 Oakwood Road
Huntington Sta., NY 11746

Dot Pasteup Supply (3)
1612 California Street
P.O. Box 369
Omaha, NE 68101

Dover Publications, Inc. (3)
31 E. 2nd St.
Mineola, NY 11501

The Drawing Board (3)
256 Regal Row
P.O. Box 220505
Dallas, TX 75222

Dynamic Graphics, Inc. (2, 3)
6000 North Forest Park Drive
P.O. Box 1901
Peoria, IL 61656

Fidelity Products Company (3)
5601 International Pkwy.
P.O. Box 155
Minneapolis, MN 55440

FlexiList (3)
2 Westbrook Drive
Nashua, NH 03060

Gaylord Specialties Corp. (5)
225 Fifth Avenue
New York, NY 10010

GraphiColor (3)
3018 Western Avenue
Seattle, WA 98121

Graphic Products Corp. (3)
3601 Edison Place
Rolling Meadows, IL 60008

Grayarc (3)
Greenwoods Industrial Park
P.O. Box 2944
Hartford, CT 06104

Highsmith Co., Inc. (3)
W5527 Highway 106, E.
P.O. Box 800
Ft. Atkinson, WI 53538

INMAC (3)
2465 Augustine Drive
Santa Clara, CA 95054

Kimmeric Studio (5)
P.O. Box 3586
Napa, CA 94558

LaSalle Photo (3)
1700 Diversey Parkway
Chicago, IL 60614

Mohawk Valley Printing Co. (3)
309 Miller Avenue
Herkimer, NY 13350

Morgan Printing & Publishing (3)
900 Old Koenig Lane, Ste. 137
Austin, TX 78756

NEBS Business Forms (3)
500 Main Street
Groton, MA 01471

Omnipress (10)
454 West Johnson Street
Madison, WI 53703

Penny Pinchin' Press (3)
1398 N.E. 125 Street
North Miami, FL 33161

Perfection Supply Co. (5)
6434 N. Central Avenue
Chicago, IL 60646

Public Brand Software (11)
P.O. Box 51315
Indianapolis, IN 46251

Quantity Photo Company (3)
119 West Hubbard Street
Chicago, IL 60610

Quill Corporation (3)
100 S. Schelter Road
Box 464A
Lincolnshire, IL 60069

Retail Stores Tag & Supply Co. (5)
Box 527
West Chester, PA 19380

Roxanne Studios (3)
Box 1012
Long Island City, NY 11101

The SaKet Company (5)
6151 Colbath Avenue
Van Nuys, CA 91401

The Stationery House (3)
1000 Florida Avenue
Hagerstown, MD 21740

The Sterling Name Tape Co. (5)
9 Willow Street
Winsted, CT 06098

20th Century Plastics, Inc. (5)
3628 Crenshaw Boulevard
Los Angeles, CA 90016

Unique Ideas (5)
Box 627-B
No. Bellmore, NY 11710

United States Box Corp. (5)
1296 McCarter Highway
Newark, NJ 07104

Vermont Business Forms Co. (3)
RD 4, Box 1690
Montpelier, VT 05602

Volk Art, Inc. (3)
Box 72
Pleasantville, NJ 08232

Zipatone, Inc. (3)
150 Fencl Lane
Hillside, IL 60162

Index

P.S.

Earlier editions of this book carried a note on this page asking readers to write to me about their businesses. As a result, I now receive interesting and highly informative notes and letters every week, many of them accompanied by sample brochures, catalogs, business cards, or books and periodicals for review.

While it's impossible for me to correspond with my readers (unless I'm working with them in regard to publishing some of their information), I literally devour such mail, and I invite you to write to me, too. Reader mail not only gives me inspiration and encouragement to continue my work, but fuels the fire that blazes in my quarterly *Report*. This mail has also convinced me that I should write other books for homebased business owners, and when I do, I hope you'll be in my readership once again. (If you write to me for any reason, your name will be placed on my mailing list to receive announcements about new books of possible interest to you. Please use the specially-coded address below, which automatically tells me you've read this book.)

You may be interested to know that *Homemade Money* has been recognized as one of the most helpful guides in its field. It is recommended by the SBA, directors of small business development centers, leaders in the Cooperative Extension Service, and business editors and book reviewers across the country. In addition, many colleges, universities and workshop leaders now use this book as a text in their courses on small business and entrepreneurship.

I trust this revised and enlarged edition of *Homemade Money* will prove beneficial to your business and that you'll recommend it to others. Thanks for your interest, and I look forward to hearing from you some day.

Barbara Brabec
HMM Feedback
P.O. Box 2137
Naperville, IL 60565